D1602787

American by Birth

American by Birth
Wong Kim Ark and the
Battle for Citizenship

Carol Nackenoff and Julie Novkov

University Press of Kansas

Published by the University Press of Kansas (Lawrence, Kansas 66045),
which was organized by the Kansas Board of Regents and is operated and
funded by Emporia State University, Fort Hays State University, Kansas State
University, Pittsburg State University, the University of Kansas, and Wichita
State University.

Library of Congress Cataloging-in-Publication Data
Names: Nackenoff, Carol, author. | Novkov, Julie, 1966– author.
Title: American by birth : Wong Kim Ark and the battle for citizenship /
    Carol Nackenoff and Julie Novkov.
Description: Lawrence : University Press of Kansas, [2021] | Includes
    bibliographical references and index.
Identifiers: LCCN 2020040363
    ISBN 9780700631926 (cloth)
    ISBN 9780700631933 (epub)
Subjects: LCSH: Citizenship—United States. | Immigrants—Legal status,
    laws, etc.—United States. | Emigration and immigration law—United
    States. | United States. Constitution. 14th Amendment. | Ark, Wong Kim. |
    Asian Americans—Legal status, laws, etc.
Classification: LCC KF4700 .N33 2021 | DDC 342.7308/3—dc23
LC record available at https://lccn.loc.gov/2020040363.

British Library Cataloguing-in-Publication Data is available.

Printed in the United States of America

10 9 8 7 6 5 4 3 2 1

The paper used in this publication is acid free and meets the minimum
requirements of the American National Standard for Permanence of Paper
for Printed Library Materials Z39.48-1992.

Contents

Acknowledgments

Our journey toward *American by Birth: Wong Kim Ark and the Battle for Citizenship* began with a collaboration we initiated for what became a symposium issue on the Family, the State, and American Political Development for *Polity* (2016), and we thank editor Roger Karapin for suggesting that project. Additional aspects of our research, focusing on the relationship between federal courts and administrative agencies in determining the minimum legal protections the Chinese should be accorded in a tightening exclusion regime, appeared in our coedited volume, *Stating the Family: New Directions in the Study of American Politics* (University Press of Kansas, 2020). Everyone involved in these projects helped us think about how we would come to frame Wong Kim Ark's story.

We thank David Congdon, Acquisitions Editor in Political Science and Law, University Press of Kansas, for suggesting this project to us and encouraging us at every step in the process. Reviewer Sam Erman and one anonymous reviewer made *American by Birth* a much better book.

Eileen McDonagh, Ruth O'Brien, Patricia Strach, and Kathleen Sullivan, participants in a summer writing group, read and provided valuable feedback on parts of the manuscript. Jim Greer, Carol's husband, as always, was available to read and comment on draft material. Robin Dale Jacobson at the University of Puget Sound generously offered comments on chapter 6.

Marit Vike, Swarthmore College class of 2019, was a significant contributor to chapter 7 and helped with chapter 4. Swarthmore College research assistants Abigail Diebold '20, Natasha Markov-Riss '20, and Michael Meyer '22 also provided excellent help.

We presented a portion of this work at the 2019 meeting of the American Political Science Association, at which discussant Anna O. Law was extremely generous, making excellent comments. Both of us also presented part of the project at the University of Maryland Francis King Carey School of Law Schmooze, organized by Mark Graber, in March 2020, and we thank Mark and other participants in this small conference for their contributions. Julie Novkov thanks the Department of

Political Science at Fordham College, particularly Boris Heersink and Zein Murib, for providing the opportunity to discuss this project. Finally, Carol Nackenoff thanks Swarthmore College for research and sabbatical support that made this work possible.

Introduction

In the late nineteenth century, the United States was a difficult, and at times threatening, environment for people of color. After being driven out of tribal lands, Native Americans were encouraged to seek recognition, rights, and landownership in exchange for giving up their tribal identities and community belonging.[1] Whites systematically undercut the rights guaranteed to Mexicans incorporated into the United States through the 1848 Treaty of Guadalupe Hidalgo.[2] African Americans, who had briefly glimpsed a future of political incorporation and civil equality, faced increasingly systematic and violent exclusionary tactics that closed off their avenues to political participation.[3] And Chinese immigrants, invited into the United States in the 1850s and 1860s as laborers and merchants, faced a wave of hostility that played out in organized private violence, discriminatory state laws, and increasing congressional efforts to choke off immigration and remove many long-term residents.[4]

The federal courts, including the Supreme Court, were important agents in this developmental process. Before the Civil War, the Court had ruled that Indian nations were domestic dependent nations rather than independent sovereigns in *Cherokee Nation v. Georgia*.[5] The Supreme Court under Chief Justice Morrison Waite's leadership interpreted the Reconstruction Amendments cautiously, insisting on full cooperation between Congress and the executive branch to address southern resistance. When Melville Fuller replaced Waite as chief justice in 1888, the Court took a substantially harder line, stripping the amendments of any capacity to promote meaningful equality and opening the door for southern creation and implementation of Jim Crow.[6] The Court also interpreted the Fourteenth Amendment as extending no new privileges or immunities of citizens of the United States to women seeking to practice law or other professions, or seeking to vote on the same terms as men.[7] And the federal courts, backed by the Supreme Court, supervised the development of an increasingly restrictive and exclusionary immigration regime that targeted Chinese, and then Asians, for suspicion and removal.

In 1898, two years after deciding the notorious case of *Plessy v. Ferguson*,[8] which established the constitutionality of state-sponsored segregation under the Fourteenth Amendment through the notorious separate but equal formulation, the Supreme Court had another chance to interpret a key clause of the Fourteenth Amendment. The question was whether individuals born within the geographic boundaries of the United States were citizens, regardless of their parentage. The plaintiff, Wong Kim Ark, had been born in San Francisco in the 1870s. Like many members of the Chinese community in the American West, he had ties to China. He traveled there more than once, but when he attempted to return to the United States after a journey in 1894–1895, he was refused entry and detained. Protesting that he was a citizen and therefore entitled to come home, he challenged the administrative decision in court. Remarkably, the Supreme Court granted him victory.

This victory was important for Wong Kim Ark and his talented elite legal team, for the ethnic Chinese community in the United States, and for all immigrant communities then and to this day. The principle that people born in the United States were citizens dated back to well before the American Civil War, but the Court's ruling both inscribed the principle in constitutional terms and clarified that it extended even to the children of immigrants who were legally barred from becoming citizens.

A Biography of a Case

This book provides an extended biography of the 1898 landmark case. It identifies its roots significantly further back in history, beginning with a 1608 dispute over birthplace and sovereignty connected to the troubled aftermath of Elizabeth I's death in England. The link between birthplace and allegiance established in English common law traveled to America, but as we explain, citizenship had a complicated history fractured by race during the antebellum era. We explain how this history influenced the passage of post–Civil War legislation and the Fourteenth Amendment. We also trace the jurisprudential path of the postbellum citizenship question through an aside in the *Slaughter-House Cases* to a full analysis in *Elk v. Wilkins* concerning Native American citizenship and finally to its direct presentation in *Wong Kim Ark*.

The story of the *Wong Kim Ark* case is also the story of nineteenth-century Chinese immigration in particular and policymakers' anxieties about immigration more generally. The history of Chinese migration to the United States between the 1870s and the 1890s and efforts to restrict it tends not to be read alongside the history of Reconstruction and its collapse. In the post–Civil War era, though, states could not be left to manage nationally salient issues on their own, and Chinese migration became such an issue. Initially, nationally prominent Republicans stood together behind an early Reconstruction strategy of empowering and attaching Black voters, but as local resistance grew, their will crumbled. Congressional Democrats supported the interests of westerners from both parties who opposed immigration, playing to increasing anxieties about Chinese as competitors in the labor market but also more fundamentally about the Chinese in cultural and racialized terms.

As the political atmosphere became more challenging, the Chinese and their advocates turned to the courts. Wong Kim Ark himself was a cook born to a Chinese family of fairly modest means in San Francisco, yet the case that bore his name featured prominent legal talents on both sides, from the initial writ of habeas corpus to its final resolution before the Supreme Court. The participants recognized from the beginning that this case had high stakes for the Chinese and Chinese American community and accordingly invested fully in the fight.

The book tells this story from Wong Kim Ark's initial detention aboard a steamship when he tried to reenter through the port of San Francisco in August 1895. It addresses the contestation in the district court over his writ of habeas corpus and analyzes the case's ascent to the US Supreme Court. It provides a close analysis of the hundreds of pages of briefs filed, Justice Grey's majority opinion, and Justice Fuller's dissent. It also recounts the reactions to the ruling, both in the popular press and in the legal academy.

The book turns to literal biography in discussing Wong Kim Ark's life. Like many men in Chinese communities in the United States, Wong Kim Ark lived a transnational life. He worked in San Francisco but traveled several times by steamship to and from his family's ancestral home in Guangdong Province, marrying a woman who would bear and raise his children through their early lives there. His sons, born in China, had derivative American citizenship through birth and would try to find their own ways in the United States, facing suspicion when they tried to enter the country. Wong Kim Ark himself would eventually return to China for good in the early 1930s, although most of his descendants made their homes in the United States. The book also traces forward the implications of the ruling for birthright citizenship in the United States, ending with a discussion of current controversies over limiting its scope.

Previous Scholarship

This book relies on the work of historians, legal scholars, and political scientists to tell the story. Previous scholars have traversed much of this ground, and interested readers can engage a wealth of historical work addressing the development of birthright citizenship and the American state's uneasy relationship with immigrants. Historians have also studied the immigration experiences of Chinese migrants and their descendants. Other scholars have illuminated the litigation dynamics of Chinese litigants seeking writs of habeas corpus, including Wong Kim Ark himself. Finally, the struggle over birthright citizenship reached its peak as the age of American empire dawned, a topic of related historical interest.

We have relied on several scholars' understandings of how citizenship functioned in the antebellum era. The general origins of birthright citizenship and its early applications have garnered attention from legal scholars.[9] Martha Jones's work explains the tenuous hold that free African Americans had on birthright citizenship and shows how free men and women in Baltimore navigated their status in everyday legal proceedings.[10] As noted later, Anna Law's work resists the common narrative that citizenship was largely unregulated in early American history, showing how states exerted significant control over migration and the conditions under which citizens could exercise the right to travel.[11] Mark Graber's analysis of *Dred Scott v. Sandford* helpfully situates the notorious case's account of the relationship between state and national citizenship.[12]

A wealth of research addresses the debate and passage of the Constitution's Fourteenth Amendment and the immediate aftermath. Particularly helpful to us were Garrett Epps's account of the political and legal maneuverings and Rebecca Zietlow's discussion of the debates around the amendment and Congress's early use of it.[13]

Intertwined with these considerations is a great deal of scholarship concerning the history of immigration. While our interest is primarily in Chinese immigration, Paul Spickard's work provides an extensive historical overview of immigration and its relationship to race from the colonial era through the policy transformations and reforms of the late twentieth century.[14] The Chinese experience with immigration to the United States in the middle to late nineteenth century has received significant attention from historians. Several have focused on the economic and political factors that contributed to immigration from China to the United States.[15]

The experiences of Chinese immigrants and their families play an important role in our story. Beth Lew-Williams's work explains the difficulties that Chinese immigrants experienced as Western xenophobia grew, sparking violence.[16] Erika Lee's work explains how exclusion laws marked the lives of Chinese immigrants and their families. Along with Lucy Salyer, Lee shows how restrictions on Chinese immigration influenced the development of immigration policy more generally, contributing to the development of administrative institutions and capacity to manage the exclusionary process.[17] George Peffer and Kitty Calavita focus on the impact of these regulations on Chinese women and families.[18] Kerry Abrams and Peggy Pascoe explain how concerns about prostitution and polygamy shaped immigration policy and the lives of Chinese women living in America.[19]

Many scholars have studied the legal machinery around exclusion and how Chinese litigants sought to thwart it. Lucy Salyer's *Laws Harsh as Tigers* comprehensively explores the Chinese legal struggle to resist the imposition of discriminatory and anti-immigration legislation.[20] Christian Fritz's work describes the "habeas corpus mill" that developed in the 1880s in the Ninth Circuit to process the huge number of challenges to orders of exclusion and deportation.[21] Ellen Katz's work looks specifically at resistance to the 1892 Geary Act, which required most resident Chinese to register and threatened deportation or exclusion for those without the appropriate paperwork.[22] Additional authors provide in-depth considerations of key cases addressing exclusion. Gabriel Chin has written on the role of Chinese exclusion cases in establishing the principle of congressional plenary power.[23] Gerald Neuman has discussed *Wong Wing v. United States* and that case's role in securing minimal legal protections for undocumented migrants.[24] Erika Lee, Lucy Salyer, and Bethany Berger have written about the *Wong Kim Ark* case itself, with Berger providing an extensive analysis of both *Wong Kim Ark* and an earlier case, *Elk v. Wilkins*, which also addressed questions about the Fourteenth Amendment's impact on birthright citizenship.[25]

Our own research has explored the role family status played in the disposition of West Coast federal court habeas corpus cases brought by Chinese litigants in the late nineteenth and early twentieth centuries. Women faced particular barriers to entry and were especially vulnerable to deportation. We have also examined conflict between federal courts and administrative agencies over the minimum procedural safeguards and legal standards that had to be met in handling these cases; this dynamic had an impact on the shaping of the emerging administrative state.[26] Independently, we have investigated social movements and policies (often with interactions) involving the citizenship status of African Americans, Native Americans, immigrants, and women during the late nineteenth and early twentieth centuries.[27]

Finally, the Supreme Court's decision in *Wong Kim Ark* came at a time when the United States was embarking upon imperial adventures. The Court's ruling took place on March 28, 1898, but the day afterward, the front page of the *New York Times* was consumed by the tensions between the United States and Spain over Cuba and the sinking of the *Maine* in February. Bartholomew Sparrow's book on the *Insular Cases* vividly illustrates the new questions that arose about citizenship in relation to empire.[28] Sam Erman recounts the path that led to the determination that, while Puerto Rico would be under US dominion, its residents would, like Filipinos, be neither citizens nor aliens.[29] Paul Kramer has explained how American colonial rule in the Philippines relied on and transformed racial politics both in the Philippines and in the United States.[30]

Wong Kim Ark and the Building of an American Immigration Regime

As the discussion of previous work illustrates, *Wong Kim Ark v. United States* had enduring significance beyond its role in establishing the Fourteenth Amendment's guarantee of birthright citizenship. The ruling stood at the juncture of several significant developments in US law and politics. In telling the story of the case, this book links *Wong Kim Ark* to the history of immigration and citizenship, and the history of how legal struggles over immigration and citizenship contributed to the rise of legally supervised administrative control over immigration.

We read the case in the context of the coordinated litigation brought by advocates for the Chinese to challenge immigration restrictions. As noted earlier and discussed at length in the book, birthright citizenship had a history at common law that dated back to long before the founding of the United States. This history, however, was not universal. The status of citizenship intersected with how individuals came to the colonies, and then the nation, and who these individuals were. While leading political figures from the colonial era through the late nineteenth century were often eager to bring new denizens to American shores, not all new Americans were embraced and incorporated as full participants in the body politic. Indeed, some were not really considered to be Americans at all by those who encouraged, financed, and sometimes coerced their immigration.

In strict terms, the ruling in *Wong Kim Ark* is simple. The case rests on the plain language of the Fourteenth Amendment, which guaranteed citizenship to individuals born in the United States and subject to its jurisdiction, regardless of their parentage. Ambassadors, public ministers, and invading or occupying troops were the kinds of persons not subject to US jurisdiction; Native Americans were not, at the time of the passage of the Fourteenth Amendment, considered subject to the jurisdiction of the United States. But both the Fourteenth Amendment and the common-law rule it enshrined in the Constitution were steeped in the politics of race and the politics of immigration from the founding until the dawn of the age of American empire.

The antebellum development of citizenship was largely a state-driven process, and incorporated significant variation and complexity. While the concept of birthright citizenship made early appearances in American case law, the major cases litigating its meaning addressed the descendants of Europeans. These judicially acknowledged citizens—the descendants of Dutch and English and eventually Scots, German, Irish, and other immigrants—were desired, and the colonies and then states had incentives to incorporate them politically in ways that quelled questions about their allegiance. By the time of the Constitution's drafting, the practice of incorporation appeared to require no specific textual explanation, though the framers did ensure that eligibility for the presidency was tied to citizenship from birth.

However, the idea of heritable status also had a lengthy history in American law. As far back as the late 1600s and early 1700s, several colonies established rules that children of enslaved mothers would themselves be slaves, regardless of their fathers' status or the circumstances of their birth. Race emerged in the late 1600s as a fundamental dividing line, as white indentured servants birthed children who would be eligible for full political incorporation. While colonies and then states agreed that slaves could be freed, the process was regulated at the state level, and the meaning of freedom as a status was ambiguous in the states and territories. Even in territories that never allowed slavery, freedom did not necessarily imply full citizenship, and some free states made it clear that that they wanted no Black denizens, regardless of their status.

Part of the difficulty in understanding *Wong Kim Ark* and its significance today is that, from our twenty-first-century vantage point, we readily imagine immigration policy and the attribution of citizenship as exclusive creations of national authority. These background understandings create the perception that the regulation of immigration and citizenship was sparse during the antebellum era. This perspective sees both immigration and citizenship as national matters resting primarily on Congress's general authorization for naturalization in 1790 and modest changes pursued until the Civil War. Only a few scattered antebellum cases addressed citizenship in light of birthplace, parental allegiance, and subjection to national sovereignty.

Centering the lack of extensive regulation and institutional management at the national level produces a particular understanding of immigration. In the antebellum era, the United States as a nation generally supported and encouraged immigration, never opting to exclude immigrants based on race and not taking other measures, like imposing literacy tests, to identify and restrict a flow of "undesirable" immigrants. Immigration increased in each decade between the 1820s, when 128,502 individuals entered as permanent residents, and the 1850s, which saw 2,814,554 immigrants admitted as lawful permanent residents.[31]

This open stance and rapid growth, however, did not mean that immigrants were free once they entered the nation. Anna Law's work on state and local regulation of freedom of movement illustrates that migration policy, often even restrictive policy, did exist.[32] Moreover, she shows that migration policy exhibited significant regional variation as states sought to manage the kinds of people who entered their sovereign domains and control the kinds of rights and privileges to which both sojourners and denizens would have access.

Many states prevented convicts from entering, and northeastern states discouraged ship owners from landing "sickly, disabled, or poor immigrants." Eastern coastal states passed and enforced measures to extract reimbursements for supporting immigrants who could not support themselves.[33] While state policymakers on the Eastern Seaboard generally encouraged immigration to supplement the labor force, they took measures to prevent the in-migration of individuals who would not serve these purposes. Southern states were concerned with the movement of Black residents and sojourners, particularly after Denmark Vesey's Charleston rebellion, which involved both free Black individuals and slaves, in 1822.[34] Laws regulating slavery had impacts on migration, and southern policymakers particularly restricted both free Black residents and Black sailors, regardless of their national allegiance.[35]

During this period, Native Americans were not fully sovereign, and rarely were they citizens. As members of "domestic dependent nations," they were seen as wards of a guardian nation and were dealt with by treaties and also by force.[36] Native Americans were not considered subject to state law, and the commerce clause (Article I, Section 8 of the Constitution) gave Congress the power to regulate commerce with the Indian tribes. By the time of the Indian Removal Act of 1830 if not before, it became clear that Native Americans were mere occupants, not invested title holders, of the land whose claims could be expunged, and by 1850, their mass expulsion from the East was generally completed.[37] A few groups who gave up claims to tribal lands were granted citizenship.

In addition, while the courts very occasionally had opportunities to determine whether or not people were citizens, citizenship itself did not imply the same set of rights and privileges everywhere. Prior to the Civil War, while states largely accepted the children of white immigrants as citizens, they had fairly broad authority to determine the meaning of state citizenship. At the same time, national citizenship remained inchoate, without any independent significance. Even with regard to naturalization as defined through federal law, while Congress made the broad rules, state and local authorities managed the process. Desired immigrants' children became citizens without any significant debate or concern, and the states developed and exercised their capacity to limit both citizenship and what it entailed with respect to racially marked denizens.

The Civil War, by its end, had transformed citizenship and, less dramatically, had wrought changes to immigration and naturalization as well. The destruction of slavery through war, emancipation, and constitutional amendment established briefly the dream of a new re-public reforged around egalitarian ideals. The great struggle over slav-ery and the meaning of emancipation overshadowed other struggles over identity and membership in the American polity. Nonetheless, questions simmered. In the West, federal officials worried about the spread of polygamy and sought means of controlling the efforts of the Latter-day Saints to establish a theistic state. The federal government warred with the Sioux and other tribes of the Great Plains, pressing for land concessions and subjugation. Fewer people immigrated to the United States in the 1860s than in the 1850s, but Chinese immigration raised concerns as well.

While the Thirteenth, Fourteenth, and Fifteenth Amendments fun-damentally changed the structure of American constitutionalism, they built on the ground that had preceded them. The Fourteenth Amend-ment's language intentionally codified the common-law principle of birthright citizenship. While the new amendments looked forward to prevent any other race from being subjected to slavery and to bar proac-tively its re-creation as a status, they did so in the immediate context of war and Black emancipation. The amendments also served the Republi-can Party's political and partisan imperatives, but some elements of the bitter partisan divide left by the Civil War would be disrupted soon as new political alignments developed that complicated divisions between Republicans and Democrats.

The early congressional and judicial interpretations that defined the meaning of these constitutional changes took place in a nation caught between two long-standing and competing imperatives: that of growth and expansion through generous immigration and integration of new residents, and that of white supremacy. These imperatives had oper-ated alongside each other during the antebellum period, for the most part not coming into conflict. With the addition of the Reconstruction Amendments to the Constitution, they increasingly came into tension with each other. A nation of presumptive equals and citizens could not also be a nation that rested on attributed status distinctions linked to racial identity. The period between the end of the Civil War and the turn of the century was one of racial renegotiation that encompassed Black identity and status but had implications beyond it. Immigration soon became a highly salient location for national concerns about race, status, and belonging, and the national government acted to take more visible and direct command of the policy space previously managed largely by states.

While bitter struggles over the proper scope and limitations of federal authority continued with respect to Black rights and status, Congress soon came to collaborate with western state governments in addressing concerns about immigration. Between 1875 and 1924, the system of broadly permissive entry on the national level coupled with a variety of state regulatory regimes gave way first to national rules implemented unevenly by state and local actors, and then to a vigorous process of building administrative capacity and authority on the national level. States remained partners, but the management of immigration itself became a federal responsibility.

As these developmental processes unfolded, so too did questions about Americans, Americanization, and who was to determine the boundaries of citizenship. The question of who was a citizen was intimately intertwined with contemporary questions about immigration; state and federal authority to regulate entrance into the United States; the rise of administrative authority; the creation of different types of American denizens, including both long-term legal residents ineligible for citizenship and the so-called illegal alien; and the significance of sovereignty in the late nineteenth century, at the dawn of the age of American empire.

While Congress largely drove the process by passing laws and empowering administrative agencies, Chinese migrants and their advocates contested these efforts. The political struggle over Chinese migration and the question of the status of children of Chinese migrants incorporated an institutional debate over how these decisions were to be made and which institutions would have the authority to settle these issues. The early wave of migration involved international negotiations at the elite level: diplomats, railroad magnates, and industrialists established the structure through which a Chinese labor pool built the railroads and contributed to early agricultural development and mining in the West. At the same time, political and economic elites promoted trade, with Americans negotiating for business footholds in China and welcoming Chinese merchants to build networks based in the United States. Over time, however, as opposition to migration grew, the venue for policymaking and policy struggles shifted. Western mobilization drove congressional action, but even though the Chinese community had political connections, their efforts could not stave off regulation. The courts were the final and most effective site for resistance.

Wong Kim Ark confirmed the constitutional baseline for citizenship, and citizenship derived from patrilineal descent remained a stable feature of American law, at least in formal legal terms. As the United States entered the imperial age, however, citizenship for individuals of Chinese ancestry provoked suspicion. The rise of Jim Crow as a system of governance and American acquisition of territorial possessions at the turn of the century laid the groundwork for graduated forms of citizenship and civic membership. While African Americans were citizens, both legally and in practical terms their citizenship was of lesser scope and meaning than white citizenship, with white supremacy serving as the explicit basis for state constitutional governance in the South.

Advocates for American territorial expansion overseas were not eager to incorporate the new imperial denizens as citizens. After an initial debate over how to address the problem of new subjects of American sovereignty, Congress ultimately settled on the solution of declaring residents of some new territories to be US nationals rather than citizens. One element in the debate over how to categorize these new allegiants from the Philippines was the presence of many Chinese immigrants in the islands. The rise of empire likewise transformed the politics around exclusion. The annexation of the Philippines provided a new base for American economic incursion into the Far East, but "Chinese and Japanese protestors and officials drove a wedge down the center of U.S. Pacific politics with claims that there was a fundamental contradiction between empire and exclusion."[38]

As regulations regarding immigration tightened, citizenship became an increasingly salient marker for individuals of Chinese ancestry. Individuals who had emigrated could not naturalize and remained forever aliens, but both birthright citizenship and derivative citizenship were valuable. Like African Americans, individuals of Chinese, Japanese, and Korean ancestry faced discrimination both by private actors and on the part of the state. Citizenship, however, enabled travel and reentry to the United States, important for men who wanted to maintain households in China, and their Chinese sons, who wanted to come to the United States for economic advancement. Citizens could also challenge administrative decisions in court, including deportation threats, although both Congress and the courts worked to limit this access.

Conclusion

While Wong Kim Ark was victorious in court in 1898, the ruling proved to be no bellwether of a change in US policy toward Chinese immigrants—or, indeed, toward many immigrants deemed undesirable by country of origin or deemed nonwhite. The rising tide of xenophobia in the United States peaked legislatively in 1924 with the passage of the Johnson-Reed Act. This act sharply reduced immigration, allowed immigrants to enter only through a quota based on national origins, and completely closed the United States to Asian immigration. The act and future congressional appropriations also provided substantial funding to enforce exclusion and deportations. During World War II, the Chinese Exclusion Act of 1882 was officially repealed, a political gesture spurred by negative Japanese propaganda meant to weaken ties between the United States and the Republic of China, but only a few Chinese immigrating from anywhere in the world were permitted entry. Not until 1952 would substantial reform come, and only in the 1960s did the United States shift to a system that abandoned national origin as a criterion for privileging and denying immigration. By the 1970s, with increased migration into the United States from the Caribbean and from Mexico, a new arena for policing borders emerged.

The story of Wong Kim Ark illustrates both the capacity of the Constitution to protect rights and the limits of these rights on the ground. After the ruling in the case that bore his name, Wong Kim Ark continued his transnational life. Despite his key role in establishing birthright citizenship, he remained an object of suspicion by administrators investigating Asians seeking entrance to the United States. His sons, second-generation citizens, also had trouble entering the United States at times, as did many descendants of Chinese immigrants. For Wong Kim Ark, his family, and other descendants of immigrants, national immigration policy continued to cast a shadow over their lives despite their clear constitutional entitlement to citizenship. Understanding the case in its deeper context illustrates the cultural and political limits behind its ringing endorsement of citizenship for almost all individuals born in the United States, regardless of their parentage.

Suspicion and fear of immigrants again have significant political resonance in the United States. Both the ruling in *Wong Kim Ark v. United States* and its long-term impact are now, more than ever, vitally critical for us to understand.

American by Birth

1 | The Foundations of American Citizenship

What is citizenship in legal terms, and how do people become citizens? In the United States, as in most nations, two major pathways exist. One is to be born a citizen, and the other is to go through the process of naturalization, in which the new citizen pledges allegiance to and accepts the sovereignty of a nation that acknowledges that person as a member of its citizenry. The meanings and significance of citizenship cross the boundaries of law, society, politics, economics, and culture, but determining whether an individual is legally a citizen has mostly fallen to the American courts. In deciding difficult questions about citizenship, the courts have in turn consulted state and federal legislation, earlier American precedents, common-law principles dating back to the nation's English legal roots, and the Constitution.

Naturalization, a power specifically granted to Congress in the Constitution, has largely been a creature of statutory law. Birthright citizenship has been trickier. It encompasses two types, often referred to by their Latin names: *jus sanguinis*, or descent by blood, and *jus soli*, the citizenship gained by birthplace.[1] The United States has always maintained that most legitimate children of American citizens are themselves entitled to citizenship, a premise written into law by the first Congress. And through most of American history, individuals born within the geographic boundaries of the United States have been considered to be citizens, though jus soli has occasionally generated significant debates about what it means to be a citizen and what kind of individuals are eligible for birthright citizenship.

The keystone to modern American understandings of birthright citizenship is *United States v. Wong Kim Ark*. In this 1898 ruling, a Court known for its conservatism and racial regressiveness determined that all individuals born within the geographic boundaries of the United States except for the children of ambassadors and other foreign ministers were citizens of the United States. The justices reached this conclusion by a vote of 6 to 2 in a case involving a claim to citizenship by Wong Kim

Ark, born in San Francisco to Chinese parents. The ruling still resonates in contemporary debates over immigration.

Jus soli survives in America, though as the concluding chapter will discuss, it has recently become controversial in many places globally where it remains. Though American courts largely developed the practice of granting citizenship to children of immigrants from English common law, a pure application of jus soli ended in the United Kingdom with the British National Act of 1981 (it became effective in 1983). This chapter will proceed by briefly explaining the relationship between immigration status and the citizenship status of immigrants' children. It will then delve into the early history of birthright citizenship in the United States. These early developments established the understanding in American law that children born in the United States—at least those who were not enslaved—were, for the most part, citizens. The understanding, however, rested in common law and was not yet rooted in the Constitution. It also prevailed at a time when courts and policymakers disagreed about the proper relationship between national and state citizenship.

Immigration Status and Citizenship

In the immediate aftermath of the Supreme Court's ruling in *Wong Kim Ark*, the legal and constitutional question was settled, although individual Chinese Americans often ran into difficulties entering the United States by asserting their citizenship in an era of increasingly stringent efforts to exclude the Chinese. Still, even as US immigration law began to establish a distinction between legal immigrants and unauthorized or illegal residents, little controversy emerged initially over the citizenship status of children born to unauthorized residents. The United States sharply restricted immigration except for smaller numbers of Europeans and temporary guest workers between 1924 and the civil rights era. This drastic reduction in immigration contributed to the absence of debate over or concern about birthright citizenship among policymakers. Between 1860 and 1920, individuals born abroad reliably constituted nearly 13 percent or more of the American population, but after 1930, this percentage dropped, first to below 9 percent in the 1930s and 1940s, and then declining further to reach a nadir of 4.7 percent in 1970.[2]

In the most recent wave of controversy over birthright citizenship, those advocating against its universal application have primarily singled out the children of undocumented migrants. These children, they argue, should not be entitled to birthright citizenship because the long-standing principle of granting citizenship to individuals born inside territorial boundaries assumes that these children are the offspring of people who have migrated under prevailing legal standards and have proper status as national residents. Yet, in the early history of federal efforts to remove unwanted residents, the problem of how to treat the descendants of individuals who had entered or remained in the country illegally received remarkably little attention. This was true even though Congress, the executive branch, and West Coast opponents of immigration knew about and objected strenuously to the continued presence of Chinese immigrants who had entered the country illegally.

The national government first embraced a formal policy of deporting unwelcome foreign sojourners from American soil in 1882 and expanded this policy in the 1892 Geary Act.[3] An amendment to the 1885 Foran Act, which banned the immigration of contract laborers regardless of national origin, provided the first meaningful basis for deportation. Frustrated customs officials realized quickly that barring entry of laborers did little to help them address workers who had slipped into the country and pressed for more authority; Congress's response was to pass the first national authorization for federally managed deportation in 1888.[4]

Initially, deportation primarily targeted Chinese. The need for more capacity to manage it contributed to the creation of the new federal Bureau of Immigration, which became part of the Department of Commerce and Labor in 1903.[5] But between 1909 and 1917, the separate processes for deporting the Chinese and deporting other undesirable residents were merged, leaving a single, streamlined policy by 1917.[6] The shift to a unified policy recognized increasing public sentiment against immigration and immigrants, and an expansion of the deportation process. This policy made it quite difficult to challenge deportation in court, leaving most final decisions to administrators rather than judges.

In the early twentieth century, most of the individuals claiming citizenship whom the Bureau of Immigration sought to bar from entry or to deport were Chinese who claimed citizenship either by virtue of descent from a legitimately married Chinese father or by virtue of their own births in the United States. A brief legal struggle ensued over what would happen when individuals facing a deportation order claimed citizenship. Most were in this position when administrators tried to bar their entrance to the United States. They had few avenues to secure judicial review of their denials; only procedural errors or gross misinterpretations of the facts presented could convince the courts to intervene and allow detained individuals to enter. Individuals already in the United States, however, gained more protection through rulings issued between 1906 and 1922, when the Supreme Court found that due process required judicial review of deportation orders for people who claimed to be citizens.[7]

Despite these legal limits to the expulsion of citizens by deportation, at different times in American history, officials have targeted immigrants and their families, even those born in the United States, for removal. For example, during the Great Depression, local, state, and federal officials collaborated to drive between several hundred thousand and 1.5 million individuals of Mexican ancestry, including birthright citizens, out of the United States.[8] The so-called Mexican repatriation effort relied on deportation but much more so on formal and informal efforts to persuade Mexicans, whether citizens or not, to leave the country. A recent study estimates that approximately 40 percent of the net emigration to Mexico during this period consisted of American citizens.[9]

While acts of mass deportation proved rare, the development of deportation policy strengthened the concept of the illegal immigrant. Stringent immigration enforcement initiated in the twentieth century and enhanced in the 1920s reflected several key commitments, including investing national resources in enforcement. In 1929, Congress created the first land Border Patrol and criminalized unlawful entry; in 1930, almost thirty-nine thousand people were expelled from the United States.[10] As deportation policies became more stringent and more strictly enforced, reformers in the 1930s began to suggest changes to the system that would recognize and respect family ties in families with mixed immigration statuses.[11] The Immigration and Naturalization Service ultimately developed new policies to allow exemptions for some aliens without legal status, suspending deportations largely for European immigrants with strong ties to their communities and families, in effect unmaking their illegality on the basis of their citizen children.[12]

Chapter 6 will detail the current controversies over birthright citizenship more fully, but these controversies often do not take into account the history of birthright citizenship. Opponents of automatic birthright citizenship argue in pragmatic and moral terms that birth alone is an inadequate basis on which to ground citizenship. They object particularly vigorously to granting citizenship to the children born to people who are not long-term legal residents. Supporters often simply cite the language of the Constitution, asserting that the words of the Fourteenth Amendment settle the matter. Beginning with the first postfounding considerations of what made a citizen and continuing through *Wong Kim Ark v. United States* and the case's aftermath, this question was far more contested and complicated than either side acknowledges. To tell this story, we begin not in the bustling port of San Francisco at the end of the nineteenth century but rather in seventeenth-century Scotland, where a child's representatives sought to fend off a legal challenge to his landownership.

The Legal Development of Jus Soli Citizenship Prior to 1898

Jus soli citizenship did not originate in the United States. Rather, jus soli, "the right to soil," or birthright citizenship, emerged as a theoretical solution to a monarchical dilemma in Britain in the early 1600s. The conceptual source of jus soli in England and by extension the United States is the 1608 ruling in *Calvin's Case*, a controversy arising out of the turmoil over sovereignty and allegiance after Elizabeth I died without a direct descendant.[13]

James VI, son of Mary, Queen of Scots, was the king of Scotland at the time of Elizabeth's death and had himself been born in Scotland. As Elizabeth's closest heir, he was the proper successor to the English throne, provoking debate over the extent to which the nations would be unified. For his part, James pressed for a closer union.[14] How, though, were James's Scottish subjects to be understood once James became the king of England and Scotland? Did they, by virtue of their allegiance to James, thereby become English subjects who could assert the rights enjoyed by other English subjects? Or did they remain aliens under English law?

Early Cases Addressing Birthright Citizenship

- *Calvin's Case,* 7 Coke Report 377 (1608): Established the principle in English common law.
- *Murray v. The Charming Betsey,* 6 U.S. (2 Cranch) 64 (1804): A person born in the United States who had made himself the subject of a foreign power was not a citizen.
- *McIlvaine v. Coxe's Lessee,* 8 U.S. 209 (1808): A New Jersey resident owed allegiance to the United States because he failed to depart once New Jersey had established itself as a sovereign at the time of the Revolution.
- *Blight's Lessee v. Rochester,* 20 U.S. 535 (1822): Treaties between the United States and Great Britain did not change the default citizenship, rights, or disabilities of a born British citizen who resided in Virginia and died in 1794.
- *Inglis v. Trustees of Sailor's Snug Harbor,* 28 U.S. 99 (1830): A person born in what would become the United States who left the country before the Declaration of Independence and never returned was an alien.
- *Lynch v. Clark & Lynch,* 3 N.Y. Leg. Obs. 236 (1844): A child born in New York to noncitizen parents who departed at a very young age and never returned was nonetheless a citizen.

Calvin's Case as the Fountainhead of Birthright Citizenship

Calvin's Case, one of the most cited in British legal history, was technically a case of land tenures. Robert Calvin, a Scottish infant born after the death of Elizabeth, was a freeholder of two estates, but two men, Nicholas and Robert Smith, had forcibly taken his estates.[15] The child, represented by his guardians, filed suit seeking redress. The defendants responded that Calvin's representatives could not sustain the suit because Calvin was an alien who could not possess a freehold in England.[16] For Calvin's part, the claim was that James's kingship over both nations extended the rights of English subjects to all of James's subjects. Even those born in Scotland owed allegiance to James as an English king and therefore should enjoy those protections.

The stakes were clearly higher than the disposition of a child's land claim, and the jurists involved recognized this. Fourteen justices heard the arguments, and twelve agreed that individuals born in Scotland after James became the king of England were entitled to the rights of Englishmen.[17] The most influential report of the case came from renowned English jurist Sir Edward Coke. His report provided "the first comprehensive statement in England of the law of naturalization."[18] Resting largely in natural law, *Calvin's Case* established that "a person's status was vested at birth, and based upon place of birth."[19] According to the report by Coke: "Every one born within the dominions of the King of England, whether here or in his colonies or dependencies, being under the protection of—therefore, according to our common law, owes allegiance to—the King and is subject to all the duties and entitled to enjoy all the rights and liberties of an Englishman."[20] Because Scotland was one of those territories owned by the king, when James VI of Scotland became James I of England, his sovereign authority extended to his subjects born in Scotland under his English reign, establishing their entitlement to these rights.

Jus Soli in Antebellum America: The Meaning of Revolution and the Significance of Common Law

This precedent would travel to the New World, but not without questions. Between 1804 and 1844, American courts considered several cases that addressed citizenship. Some inquired about when to consider a person an alien. Others tried to untangle complicated controversies over how to handle shifts in allegiance and sovereignty arising from the American Revolution. The cases, taken together, illustrate the importance of the courts in determining how citizenship was to work in the new nation. For their part, the courts both considered the meanings of sovereignty and allegiance and looked to English rulings to develop their own reasoning.

The Supreme Court first encountered birthright citizenship in 1804. An individual, Jared Shattuck, had been born in the United States but spent most of his life in St. Thomas. He became a burgher and swore allegiance to Denmark. In the tense period when the United States and France edged close to war and Congress sought to cut off commercial shipping between the nations, Shattuck purchased a vessel, which had been an American merchant vessel, and renamed it *The Charming Betsey*, directing the crew to sail the ship and its valuable cargo to Guadeloupe. En route, French privateers captured the ship, but an American frigate, the *Constellation*, recaptured the ship and took it to Martinique. There, the commander sold the cargo and took the vessel to the United States. The commander claimed that the sale of the vessel to Shattuck had been a ploy to evade the existing congressional law barring commercial intercourse between the United States and France.

Ultimately, the Court held that the ship's recapture was illegal, as Chief Justice Marshall interpreted the congressional statute in question so as to avoid provoking international conflict. A key factor in the ruling, however, was how to understand Shattuck's citizenship. The commander seeking to defend the seizure argued that, since Shattuck had been born in the United States and had never formally renounced his citizenship according to existing law, he remained a citizen and fell within the act's restrictions on American citizens' commercial intercourse with France.[21] Justice Marshall sidestepped this question, explaining that "whether a person born in the United States . . . can divest himself absolutely of that character otherwise than in such manner as may be prescribed by law is a question which it is not necessary at present to decide."[22] American citizens did not give up their citizenship by traveling to another country, even for a lengthy sojourn, but "his situation is completely changed where by his own act he has made himself the subject of a foreign power." *The Charming Betsey*, by this reading, was the property not of an American citizen but rather of a Danish burgher who was not subject to the bar on commerce with France.[23]

Other early encounters with citizenship in the American courts often involved how the Revolution affected allegiance and sovereignty. In 1808, the Court considered the circumstance of Daniel Coxe, who had been born in New Jersey prior to the Declaration of Independence but had joined the British forces seeking to suppress the rebellion in 1777. The Court declared that after New Jersey formally joined the new union, Coxe "became a member of the new society, entitled to the protection of its government and bound to that government by ties of allegiance."[24] By the Court's reading, New Jersey's assumption of sovereignty was complete, and Coxe's failure to depart prior to the state's legislative perfection of sovereignty commanded his allegiance to New Jersey.[25]

In 1822, the Supreme Court grappled with a dispute involving the heirs of a Pennsylvania citizen who claimed to have inherited land from his brother James Dunlap. Dunlap was a British subject who lived in Virginia and died in 1794.[26] After the Revolution, British subjects were not legally permitted to leave American lands to their heirs. While no one was claiming that James Dunlap, who had been born in Great Britain, was an American citizen, John Marshall's opinion clarified that the existing treaties between the United States and Great Britain had not changed the default citizenship, rights, or disabilities that James Dunlap held as a born British citizen. The plaintiffs tried to claim that the jury could have presumed Dunlap to be an American citizen, allowing them to inherit the land as his heirs, but Marshall noted that his alienage was "fully proved," and Virginia would have required him to take the oath of fidelity to the commonwealth, which he never did.[27]

The Court revisited the principle of jus soli in 1830 when grappling with another wills case that turned on determining the citizenship of an individual born in New York prior to the Revolution. John Inglis's situation was complex; his father was a British loyalist who left New York with British troops, taking his infant son with him and never returning. The Court had to determine at what point individuals who had been born as British subjects could be considered Americans if they remained in the country. Justice Thompson, writing for the Court, noted, "It is universally admitted both in the English courts and in those of our own country that all persons born within the colonies of North America whilst subject to the Crown of Great Britain, were natural-born British subjects."[28] As to determining the citizenship of individuals born during the Revolutionary era, England placed the cutoff at the Treaty of Paris in 1783, while the US courts endorsed the Declaration. Regardless, for the United States' part, "a person born here, who left the country before the declaration of independence and never returned here, became thereby an alien." Determining citizenship of individuals who remained was more complicated, but the right to choose one's citizenship clearly applied only to the extraordinary circumstances of the Revolution.[29]

Justice Story, who concurred with the judgment, opted to provide a fuller analysis on the alienage question, referring back to *Calvin's Case* for guidance. His influential discussion began with the proposition that "every person who is born within the ligeance of a sovereign is a subject, and . . . every person born without such allegiance is an alien."[30]

Allegiance by birth he defined simply as "that which arises from being born within the dominions and under the protection of a particular sovereign." Citizenship by birth, in this analysis, required birth within the geographic domain of the sovereign and "birth within the protection and obedience" of the sovereign—in an area under the control and authority of the sovereign. These criteria enabled the resolution of otherwise complicated situations. He carved out three exceptions: children born at sea, those born to ambassadors of a foreign power, and the children of the sovereign's military enemies, all of whom followed the citizenship of their parents.[31] For all others, allegiance followed birthplace and could not be dissolved or changed without formal legal action.[32] (Justice Johnson, also concurring, simply saw Inglis as a citizen due to his birth in New York.)[33]

Story later compiled his views on citizenship in his influential treatise on conflict of laws, published in 1834. There, he specified that "the place of birth of a person is considered as his domicil, if it is at the time of his birth the domicil of his parents."[34] Furthermore, he asserted, "Persons, who are born in a country, are generally deemed citizens and subjects of that country." While he would allow as a "reasonable qualification" the exemption of children whose parents were there for temporary purposes like health or occasional business, he explained that "it would be difficult . . . to assert, that in the present state of public law such a qualification is universally established."[35] Further, in general foreigners who resided in a country became inhabitants (though not necessarily citizens), with the exception of ambassadors and other foreign ministers, who retained their connection to the countries they represented.

An 1844 ruling in New York state court finally addressed the jus soli question directly and extensively. The case presented a controversy over the inheritance of a lucrative spring water business. Thomas Lynch, the senior partner in the Saratoga Springs mineral water dealer Lynch & Clarke, died childless in 1833, leaving behind property in Saratoga Springs "of immense value." Thomas had two brothers, one of whom had died before him but had produced a daughter, Julia, who was born in New York in the spring of 1819 before her family returned with her to Ireland later that year. Thomas's other brother, Bernard, who had naturalized, entered into a dispute with Thomas's business partner, Clarke, over the land and the business. New York had embraced the common-law principle that aliens were barred from inheriting land, but

Clarke claimed that the land in question descended to Julia as a citizen rather than following the business.[36]

No one claimed that Julia's father was attached to the United States or intended to become a citizen himself. He had resided in the country for only three or four years and visited only once after returning to Ireland. When he died, his daughter was fourteen and, aside from her birth in New York, had no attachment or connection to the United States. The ruling nonetheless asserted that "it is an indisputable proposition, that by the rule of the common law of England, if applied to these facts, Julia Lynch was a natural born citizen of the United States," this proposition dating back to before the English first arrived on American shores.[37]

The question, then, was whether this widely accepted common law rule was indeed the accepted rule in New York or in the United States. The ruling acknowledged that individual states had the authority to manage their own affairs and determine the specific disabilities and privileges of aliens. Citizenship, however, could not be merely a state concern—it had a "*national right* and character." While citizens owed particular allegiances to their state sovereigns, they also were bound by general allegiance to federal sovereignty, and only one national rule distinguishing alienage could prevail. The Constitution's comity clause and the attribution of authority over naturalization to Congress "exhibited in the strongest light the absolute need of guarding against different and discordant rules for establishing the right of citizenship in the future."[38]

But if the rule had to be a national one, what was it? In the absence of legislation, common law readily prevailed at the state level but was not controlling at the national level. Bernard Lynch argued that the proper rule at the national level was "that of the public law, by which a child follows the *status* of its parents." The court noted, however, that during the Revolutionary era, the simple practice was that children born in the United States to citizens were presumed citizens. This left the question of the citizenship of aliens' children open but dedicated by the Constitution to Congress to resolve, should that body opt to do so.[39] Congress had not exercised its authority in this manner; to the contrary, prior to the Constitutional Convention and in the early constitutional era, immigration was encouraged and citizenship was dispensed liberally.[40]

The opinion carefully analyzed the question of whether the United States itself had common law that had carried over from British law.

While earlier discussions of the matter had denied that a national common law existed, in *Lynch* the court limited this proposition to state law and regulation, noting that many common-law principles were enshrined in the Constitution. For citizenship, then, common law was an appropriate source for interpretive inspiration. The failure of the Constitution's framers to define and delimit national citizenship implied an embrace of common-law understandings.[41] Ultimately, the judge concluded, "I can entertain no doubt, but that by the law of the United States, every person born within the dominions and allegiance of the United States, whatever were the situation of his parents, is a natural born citizen," providing a long list of statutory and treatise-based acknowledgments of this rule.[42]

Thus, while questions about birthright citizenship occasionally bubbled up, for the most part, policymakers and courts seemed to presume that the states and the nation would follow the familiar principle from common law that individuals born under a sovereign's authority owed that entity their allegiance and received some form of citizenship in return. These rules, however, presumed that the potential citizens in question were white in an era when the United States was eager to recruit suitable new citizens to build the nation. These premises did not hold firm across the entire spectrum of possible new citizens.

Jus Soli in Antebellum America: Grappling with Race and Citizenship

While English common law's influence was a given in the early considerations of citizenship and belonging, race complicated the questions. Racial concerns have shaped policies concerning both immigration and citizenship since the colonial era. From that time through the early 1800s, policymakers aggressively sought to attract some individuals to migrate and settle permanently, more ambivalently invited others with the idea that they would be sojourners, endorsed the forcible migration of many whom they admitted as property rather than persons, and barred others from migration altogether.[43] These policy initiatives dovetailed with the status attributed (or denied) to descendants of the different groups of people who came to America. Once the United States had the capacity to set national immigration policy, race played a significant role in how naturalization was to work.

Scholars debate how the racial category of "white" developed in colonial and antebellum America and disagree about when historically it became a stable, fully formed category, but from the beginning of American colonial history, English, Scots, Irish, and Germans in the Chesapeake region began to identify themselves as white and to unify members of various African tribes and their descendants as Black.[44] While the categories were not fully stable or comprehensive and allowed for significant flexibility at the margins, over time they became increasingly influential and took on not just social but also legal meaning. By the late colonial period, while free Black individuals and Indians lived with whites, the groups were recognized as different, and one of the tasks of the revolutionary state governments was to decide how to understand and legally delimit the status of these denizens. The egalitarian fervor of the Revolution encouraged a few states to read the Declaration's language as an endorsement of civic membership without regard to race, but this sensibility was fleeting.

One of Congress's first achievements after the ratification of the Constitution was to pass legislation governing naturalization. In this 1790 law, Congress established the naturalization process, lodging it administratively in the courts. Naturalization was available to "any alien, being a free white person, who shall have resided within the limits and under the jurisdiction of the United States for the term of two years." The law further clarified that once such individuals naturalized, any children they had under the age of twenty-one who resided in the United States would also be considered citizens. Further, children of any citizens were to be considered "as natural born citizens," with the caveat that citizenship would not be extended to children whose fathers had never resided in the United States. Congress also clarified that persons "heretofore proscribed by any state" were barred from citizenship unless the state proscribing them passed legislation rendering them eligible for citizenship. This rule implied that, while citizenship was managed at the state level, some crucial aspects of it required national uniformity.[45]

The line demarcating whiteness, while not fully clear, initially excluded people of African and Asian descent; even whites who were indentured servants were eligible for naturalization. A few thousand Native Americans gained citizenship (Spickard estimates the total prior to the Civil War at three thousand), but largely because they had abandoned their tribes or had experienced the forcible disbandment of their tribes. Others had assimilated and intermarried with whites sufficiently to be understood as white.[46] Generally, white immigration was encouraged in the early Republic, though nativist sentiment gained strength quickly between 1830 and 1850. Despite the hostility and discrimination directed toward Jewish and Catholic immigrants in some quarters, however, no serious attempts were made to deny naturalization to them or to regulate their children's access to birthright citizenship.[47]

The cases that the Supreme Court decided analyzing allegiance and sovereignty in the early antebellum era all involved plaintiffs and defendants who were understood in the racial categories prevailing at the time as white. As the Supreme Court was sorting out when American citizenship began to attach to white individuals born in territory that was or would become the United States, Congress encountered a thorny racial question about citizenship when it considered admitting Missouri to the union in 1821.

Missouri wished to enter the union as a slave state and submitted a proposed state constitution establishing slavery, but also barring the in-migration of "free negroes and mulattoes" intending to settle there "under any pretext whatsoever."[48] This provision gave pause to some congressional representatives, who saw it as running afoul of the US Constitution's comity clause, which guaranteed to the citizens of each state "all the Privileges and Immunities of Citizens in the several States." The validity of the clause would hinge upon whether Black residents who were not enslaved were citizens, and if so, what kind of citizens they were. Some legislators took the position that jus soli applied on equal terms to Black Americans: if born as free people, they were citizens of the states in which they were born and correspondingly were US citizens entitled to all the rights and privileges connected with that status. State legislatures in New York and Vermont weighed in immediately to support this understanding as well. Southern legislators responded with equal vehemence, objecting to the idea of Black citizenship and the implications for their own restrictions on unenslaved Black denizens and sojourners in their states.[49] Congress crafted an awkward settlement, allowing Missouri to retain the clause in its constitution but warning the state not to "enact any law that would impair the rights of citizens from other states, including citizens of color."[50]

In 1821, New York also grappled with the rights of free Black residents on the state level when a constitutional convention considered removing the state's property qualification for voting. After bruising debate, lawmakers adopted a workable if ideologically incoherent com-

Cases Addressing the Relationship between Race and Citizenship

- *Cherokee Nation v. Georgia*, 30 U.S. 1 (1831): Native American tribes were considered domestic dependent nations.
- *Dred Scott v. Sandford*, 60 U.S. 393 (1857): Justice Taney's opinion claimed that Africans and their descendants could never be citizens.

promise, requiring only free Black men to demonstrate that they held $250 in property to be eligible for the franchise but implicitly ushering them into some form of citizenship.[51]

The chancellor of New York, James Kent, who had been present for these debates, incorporated discussion of the issue in his influential treatise *Commentaries on American Law*.[52] In a lengthy footnote in the second volume, he described the "degraded" status of free African Americans and described the controversy over Black citizenship in litigation and among legal scholars. In this discussion, however, he remarked that New York saw Black state residents as citizens and reasoned, "If, at common law, all human beings born within the ligeance of the kind, and under the king's obedience, were natural born subjects, and not aliens, I do not perceive why this doctrine does not apply to these United States, in all cases in which there is no express constitutional or statute declaration to the contrary."[53] The real question for Kent was not one of sovereignty or allegiance but rather whether African Americans born in the United States should be considered subjects or citizens. His answer to this question was that citizens were free inhabitants, and "if a black man be born within the United States, and born free, he becomes thenceforward a citizen," though Kent allowed for the states' authority to impose disabilities on Black citizens.

The questions of how state citizenship was to work and how it related to national citizenship continued to simmer quietly as sectional divisions grew increasingly threatening. The next significant controversy involving sovereignty, citizenship, and race, however, concerned the Cherokees, who turned to the courts for recourse against the state of Georgia. Frustrated and angered by Georgia's efforts to impose its laws in Cherokee territory and take Cherokee lands, the tribe filed suit in the US Supreme Court. The Cherokees asserted that the Court had original jurisdiction under Article III's language authorizing suits in which a state was a party.[54] The Court rejected the suit, holding that "an Indian tribe or Nation within the United States is not a foreign state in the sense of the Constitution" and therefore that the suit did not fall within its jurisdiction. In his opinion for the majority, Justice Marshall described the tribes as "domestic dependent nations," which established them as peculiar entities not precisely equivalent to foreign nations.[55] Tribes' status as dependent nations left them subject to US sovereignty but granted individual tribal members no access to US citizenship or the rights connected to it.

The most controversial discussion during the antebellum era about the relationship between race and citizenship took place in *Dred Scott v. Sandford*. As sectional tensions worsened, the Supreme Court increasingly represented viewpoints from the South that sought to protect slavery. By the time the famous case, involving an appeal of a Missouri state claim by Dred Scott and his family for their freedom, reached the Supreme Court in 1856, national institutions had proved themselves to be unable to quell the tensions over the expansion of slavery. As constitutional scholar Mark Graber has explained, southerners, emboldened by their strong position in national politics, rejected all efforts by the North to stop the spread of slavery into the nation's territories, viewing these efforts as the first step toward abolition.[56]

Dred Scott had originally filed suit in Missouri's state court system, the appropriate venue for a question of an alleged freedman's status, as such matters were generally understood to be state law questions. He won at trial, but the Missouri Supreme Court reversed his victory. Scott then sued John Sanford, who was handling the case for his sister, the widow of Scott's original owner. Scott claimed that the federal court had jurisdiction in the case because he, Scott, was a citizen of Missouri and Sanford (misspelled Sandford in the Supreme Court case) had moved and was at that time a citizen of New York.[57]

Dred Scott lost his bid for freedom, with only two justices endorsing his side of the case. However, despite the dominance of southern power on the Court, the justices fractured badly over the reasoning supporting the outcome. Chief Justice Taney's opinion became a lightning rod for discussion, both immediately after the ruling was announced and for decades to come. He framed the central question in the case as a jurisdictional one: "Can a negro whose ancestors were imported into this country and sold as slaves become a member of the political community formed and brought into existence by the Constitution of the United States, and as such become entitled to all the rights, and privileges, and immunities, guarantied by that instrument to the citizen?"[58]

Taney's interpretation of the scope of this question was expansive. He questioned citizenship not only for individuals who had been born slaves but also for those descended from slaves, and even those "born of parents who had become free before their birth." For him, the descendants of Africans were unique and distinct from Native Americans, who, though "uncivilized . . . were yet a free and independent people." While he defined Native Americans as "in a state of pupilage," he allowed that they were eligible for naturalization, and individuals who opted to leave their tribes and live "among the white population" should be granted equal rights with any other emigrant.[59]

For Taney, the descendants of Africans were entirely different because of their inferiority and subjugation. While individual states could choose to confer the rights and privileges of citizenship to these people, no state could be forced to recognize such a grant by one of its fellow states. This status would be significant only within the state that recognized it, and it had no bearing on national citizenship. The Constitution, in Taney's view, created a political community to which only the national government, not the individual states, could add.[60] Tracing the history of chattel slavery through the development of the colonies and then the nation, he concluded that in both law and common practice, this "unhappy race" was in a permanently "degraded condition," barring them and their descendants from ever being politically incorporated.[61] He also noted that Chancellor Kent, in the sixth edition of his *Commentaries*, had pointed out that only in Maine did Black denizens have equal political rights with whites.[62] The constitutional choice to lodge the power of naturalization exclusively in Congress further bolstered Taney's argument. In his view, the power to create new citizens belonged only to Congress and did not encompass the authority to "raise to the rank of a citizen anyone born in the United States who, from birth or parentage, by the laws of the country, belongs to an inferior and subordinate class."[63] Acknowledging that states did recognize a variety of conditional forms of citizenship, like that held by children, women, and men in states that imposed property qualifications for voting, he explained that this variation nevertheless did not enable any state to create the kind of citizenship that would demand acknowledgment from another state without national endorsement.[64]

Taney was not the only member of the Court to place citizenship at the center of the inquiry. Justice Daniel, who also sided with Sanford, began with the premise that no slave could coherently be considered a citizen. The question for him, then, was whether emancipation would transform a slave not just into a free person but also into a citizen.[65] Turning to Roman law, he reasoned that the private emancipatory act of a master could not compel the state to recognize a freed slave as a citizen.[66] Bootstrapping from the 1790 bar against naturalization of non-whites, he denied that individuals descended from Africans belonged within the "class of persons to whom alone the character of citizen of the United States appertained at the time of the adoption of the Federal Constitution."[67] Implied in this chain of logic was the idea that some racial groups, regardless of the circumstances of their birth, were unfit for citizenship.

Justice Grier, who dissented in the case, had a different answer to the question of whether persons of African dissent could be citizens. He pointed out that when the Articles of Confederation were ratified, "all free native-born inhabitants of . . . New Hampshire, Massachusetts, New York, New Jersey, and North Carolina, though descended from African slaves, . . . were citizens of those States."[68] He explicitly noted the jus soli citizenship extended to "people of color" born in Massachusetts.[69] From his analysis of the history of the early Republic and the text of the Constitution, he concluded that "every free person born on the soil of a State, who is a citizen of that State by force of its Constitution or laws, is also a citizen of the United States," attributing to the states the authority to confirm birthright citizenship. In grounding this principle, he read the Constitution's language of natural-born citizenship as following the common-law principle of jus soli.

Throughout the case, all parties and judges focused on the contested status of Dred Scott. His wife, Harriet, and their two daughters, Eliza and Lizzie, appear marginally in the recitations of facts; Justice McLean's dissent provides the fullest description of the family whose freedom also hung in the balance.[70] Yet even Justice McLean did not seriously engage with the presence of one person in the case who had a clear claim to birthright citizenship. Dred and Harriet's daughter Eliza, described as fourteen at the time of the Supreme Court case but more likely around twenty, was born on a steamship on the Mississippi River north of Missouri. Had she not been of African and slave ancestry, according to the prevailing legal standards of the day, she would have been a citizen. However, after her birth, she was brought with her parents to Missouri, where she and her parents and eventually her younger sister were held as slaves. Her history as a slave seemed to overwrite her birth so completely as to render it invisible to the jurists considering her status.

The Court's ruling in *Dred Scott*, which the justices in the majority had intended to settle the national questions about slavery in the territories, instead fanned the sectional conflict into conflagration. The new Republican Party's adherents bitterly protested the ruling, with some representatives, including Maine's William Fessenden and Ohio's John Bingham, pressing for national recognition of some citizenship rights for free Black persons prior to the Civil War.[71] During the Civil War, with Southern defenders of *Dred Scott*'s theory of citizenship out of the picture, Congress repudiated it by passing legislation to end slavery in the District of Columbia and the territories. After the Civil War, it remained a target, not only provoking congressional action but also inspiring the Fourteenth Amendment's redefinition of citizenship.

The Civil War, Reconstruction, and New Understandings of National Citizenship

Over the course of the Civil War, American policymakers' ideas about citizenship changed radically. Lincoln and his cabinet, responding to persistent Black advocacy and direct actions, moved from a position of seeking to suppress the Southern rebellion to supporting emancipation and ultimately advocating for Black citizenship. The Republican Party's ultimate embrace of Black citizenship would transform thinking about citizenship, though some of the changes would take more than a century to come to fruition.

The Republicans in Congress from 1858 on bitterly opposed the *Dred Scott* ruling and targeted it for reversal. It, along with the Fugitive Slave Act, became effective dead letters during the Civil War due to both military policies and congressional changes, but fundamental changes to citizenship took place after the war and after it became clear that federal legislative action was needed to address Southern attempts to retrench. These actions would not merely be undertaken to thwart Southern resistance. More fundamentally, Republicans would seek to reunify a nation reeling from both the Confederacy's collapse and Abraham

Lincoln's assassination, in the process confronting and defeating Andrew Johnson's alternative model for national reconciliation.[72]

By 1866, the Republican Party had embraced a more robust national conception of citizenship with a critical role for Congress to play. Both the Civil Rights Act of 1866 and the Thirteenth and Fourteenth Amendments rested on a uniform baseline of rights that the federal government would enforce.[73] The Civil Rights Act of 1866 relied on the Thirteenth Amendment to mandate equal rights for citizens. The act also declared that "all persons born in the United States and not subject to any foreign power, excluding Indians not taxed, are hereby declared to be citizens of the United States."[74] This language notably omitted any mention of race, rejecting the path established in previous national legislation concerning citizenship.

Not all legislators, indeed not even all Republicans, however, believed that Congress had the authority to change citizenship. Further, some doubted Congress's authority to enforce provisions protecting citizenship so fundamentally. Opponents of the legislation argued that the clause would grant citizenship to Indians not living on reservations, Chinese born in the United States, and Roma, as well as freed slaves.[75] Andrew Johnson vetoed the 1866 Civil Rights Act, calling out the shift in citizenship particularly: "This provision comprehends the Chinese of the Pacific States, Indians subject to taxation, the people called Gipsies, as well as the entire race designated as blacks, people of color, negroes, mulattoes, and persons of African blood." Despite his opposition, Congress was able to muster the necessary votes to override the veto.[76]

While Senator Lyman Trumbull of Illinois and Representative Russell Thayer of Pennsylvania believed that the Thirteenth and Fifth Amendments worked together to empower Congress to this extent, Ohio's John Bingham, though a staunch believer in Black rights, expressed concerns about the constitutionality of these transformations. In the wake of the controversy over the 1866 act, Bingham and like-minded legislators in both houses thus pushed for another constitutional amendment that would authorize direct congressional action to define, protect, and defend rights.[77] The amendment had both short-term and long-term goals, but the short-term remaking of the nation the Republicans envisioned was written into the Constitution to prevent its long-run reversal, as these legislators were wise enough to recognize that they would not possess their current majorities in perpetuity.[78] Both proponents and opponents of the amendment in Congress recognized

Early Interpretations of the Citizenship Clause of the Fourteenth Amendment

- *Slaughter-House Cases*, 83 U.S. 36 (1873): In dicta, Justice Miller claimed that the citizenship clause excluded the children of "ministers, consuls, and citizens or subjects of foreign states born within the United States."
- *Elk v. Wilkins*, 112 U.S. 97 (1884): A Native American born as a tribal member who renounced his membership and assimilated was nonetheless not automatically transformed into a citizen.

that it would shift the balance of power from the states to the national government, limiting the states' abilities to control and dole out the privileges and immunities of citizenship on a differential basis.[79]

The full Congress vigorously debated the Fourteenth Amendment's citizenship clause. The clause first appeared as an amendment proposed to Section 1 on May 29, 1866, by Detroit Republican Jacob Howard, who was the full Fourteenth Amendment's shepherd in the Senate.[80] Howard's original language declared, "All persons born in the United States and subject to the jurisdiction thereof are citizens of the United States and of the States wherein they reside." He described this clause as a simple declaration of the law as it already existed and as a measure that would remove any lingering doubts about who was and was not a citizen.[81]

His reassurances did not succeed in masking the amendment's radical effect on state sovereignty. The Democrats did not have the numbers to block the amendment in Congress, but they took pains to make their opposition clear, and did so in racial terms. Democrat Edgar Cowan of Pennsylvania warned that the amendment would make citizens of "a certain number of people who invade her borders; who owe to her no allegiance . . . who . . . settle as trespassers wherever they go, and whose sole merit is a universal swindle . . . I mean the Gypsies." He railed further that the amendment would lay the groundwork for the annexation of California by the Chinese emperor if China were to take advantage of the measure by flooding the state with immigrants.[82] Indiana's Thomas Hendricks complained that the amendment would link white citizens to "the negroes, the coolies, and the Indians" while clothing the federal government with "absolute and despotic power."[83] The Republicans, however, had the votes, and in June 1866, both houses of Congress approved the amendment.[84] Andrew Johnson expressed his displeasure with the process and refused to endorse the amendment, but it nonetheless went forward to the states for approval.[85] In 1868, with many southern states having approved the amendment as the price of readmission to the union, Congress declared its ratification complete, and Secretary of State William Seward certified it.[86]

The Supreme Court's first significant encounter with the Fourteenth Amendment came in 1873, in the *Slaughter-House Cases*. While the ruling is best known for drastically limiting the reach of the privileges and immunities clause by denying that it could be used to protect against substantive denials of rights by the states in matters such as licenses to practice a trade, the majority also touched on the citizenship clause of the amendment. Justice Miller, while declaring the "pervading purpose" of the Reconstruction Amendments to be securing the freedom and rights of the former slaves, now elevated to freemen and citizens, noted the expansive language. The Thirteenth Amendment, he explained, would prevent "Mexican peonage" or "the Chinese coolie labor system" from developing into a new racialized form of slavery. The other amendments would likewise apply to protect individuals "though the party interested may not be of African descent."[87]

Miller's majority opinion went further, however, exploring the history of citizenship and noting that neither the original Constitution nor Congress had defined the term. He asserted that prior to *Dred Scott*, state citizenship was a prerequisite for national citizenship. "Those, therefore who had been born and resided always in the District of Columbia or in the Territories, though within the United States, were not citizens." *Dred Scott* called this understanding into question, and the Fourteenth Amendment settled the debate, overturning *Dred Scott* "by making all persons born within the United States and subject to its jurisdiction citizens of the United States."[88] He then posited a reading of the "subject to its jurisdiction" clause, understanding it as intending "to exclude from its operation children of ministers, consuls, and citizens or subjects of foreign States born within the United States."[89] In this brief aside, he shook the foundation for citizenship of thousands of children born to immigrants over the decades who had never naturalized. He did not, however, elaborate on this statement, moving on to the relationship between state and national citizenship.

The majority opinion did not embrace a definition of the scope of national citizenship that authors of the language of Section 1 probably envisioned. Senator Howard, shepherd of the Fourteenth Amendment in the Senate, had quoted from *Corfield v. Coryell* when introducing the language that would ultimately be adopted in Section 1.[90] In *Corfield v. Coryell*, Justice Bushrod Washington, riding circuit in 1823, reflected on the meaning of privileges and immunities in Article IV, Section 2. He wrote that these privileges and immunities "are, in their nature, fundamental; which belong, of right, to the citizens of all free governments; and which have, at all times, been enjoyed by the citizens of the several states which compose this Union, from the time of their becoming free, independent, and sovereign."[91] He elaborated on at least some of these:

> Protection by the Government; the enjoyment of life and liberty, with the right to acquire and possess property of every kind, and to pursue and obtain happiness and safety; subject nevertheless to such restraints as the government must justly prescribe for the general good of the whole. The right of a citizen of one State to pass through, or to reside in any other State, for the purposes of trade, agriculture, professional pursuits, or otherwise; to claim the benefits of the writ of *habeas corpus*; to institute and maintain actions of any kind in the courts of the State; to take, hold and dispose of property, either real or personal; and an exemption from higher taxes or impositions than are paid by the other citizens of the State.[92]

Even Washington's list may not have been enough for some of the amendment's framers. John Bingham, Republican representative from Ohio, who was a chief architect of the Fourteenth Amendment in the House and to whom Justice Hugo Black referred as "the Madison of the first section of the 14th Amendment,"[93] had also repeatedly promoted a dynamically empowering view of the amendment. He thought that the privileges or immunities clause would "arm the Congress . . . with the power to enforce the bill of rights as it stands in the Constitution today,"[94] granting the federal government extensive powers.

In dissent, Justice Field read the Fourteenth Amendment as recognizing (if not creating) citizens, making their citizenship "dependent upon the place of their birth . . . and not upon the constitution or laws of any State," but he did not address Miller's remark about the children of aliens.[95] Neither Justice Bradley nor Justice Swayne discussed birthright citizenship in their dissents.

These preliminary considerations in *Slaughter-House*, however, did not constitute a full analysis of the citizenship clause and its impact. The first Supreme Court case to grapple directly with its meaning was *Elk v. Wilkins*, decided in 1884. John Elk, born in the United States as a member of a Native American tribe, left his tribe and took up residence in Omaha, Nebraska. Nebraska had universal manhood suffrage for resident citizens and aliens who had declared their intent to naturalize at least thirty days prior to the election. Elk believed this provision entitled him to vote and sought to cast a ballot, but the state rejected him as a voter.[96] He objected, arguing that the Fourteenth Amendment granted him citizenship because he had severed his relation with his originating tribe and had voluntarily put himself under American sovereignty.

Justice Horace Gray, who would go on to write for a majority of the Court in *Wong Kim Ark*, wrote the majority opinion in the case. An intellectual and elite from Boston, Gray had attended a Harvard Law School still strongly under the influence of nationalist Joseph Story. He served for a time as the editor for the *Massachusetts Reports* and established a reputation as a fine trial lawyer in Boston.[97] He was an active member of the Free Soil Party prior to becoming a very early Republican, and was known as an authority on early Massachusetts law.

Gray was no stranger to thorny questions about citizenship. Along with fellow legal expert John Lowell, in 1857 he published a vigorous attack on the *Dred Scott* ruling, focusing particularly on Chief Justice Taney's assertion that no descendent of an African could be or ever was a citizen of the United States. After disproving Taney's claims by reviewing the clear citizenship rights of free Black residents of several states at the time of the Revolution and afterward, they pronounced, "No candid man can read the acts of congress without being convinced that the laws of the United States acknowledge no qualification of color or race, as essential to the citizenship of native-born inhabitants."[98]

In 1864, at the age of thirty-six, he became the youngest man ever appointed to the Massachusetts Supreme Judicial Court, where he quickly gained a reputation as a careful student of common law and equity in historical context.[99] President Arthur nominated him to the Supreme Court in 1881, and he earned confirmation by a vote of 51 to 5, the nays coming from Democrats who had been prominent Confederates. When he joined the Court, it was still heavily populated by Lincoln's justices.[100]

In considering John Elk's suit, Justice Gray identified the central question as "whether an Indian, born a member of one of the Indian tribes within the United States, is, merely by reason of his birth within the United States and of his afterwards voluntarily separating himself from his tribe and taking up his residence among white citizens, a citizen of the United States." While the tribes were not foreign states, they were, in Gray's understanding, "alien nations, distinct political communities," and tribal members owed allegiance to their tribal leaders, not to the United States. He noted, however, their unique circumstances: "They were in a dependent condition, a state of pupilage, resembling that of a ward to his guardian."[101] Individual members of tribes could not change their "alien and dependent condition" without a corresponding action on the part of the United States, a process that had taken place with regard to a number of tribes.[102]

Justice Gray endorsed *Slaughter-House*'s identification of the main purpose of the Fourteenth Amendment as settling permanently that "all persons, white or black, and whether formerly slaves or not, born or naturalized in the United States, and owing no allegiance to any alien power, should be citizens of the United States." Citizenship came through either birth or naturalization. To be subject to the jurisdiction of the United States meant being "completely subject to their political jurisdiction and owing them direct and immediate allegiance," and anyone not experiencing this kind of relationship with the United States at birth would have to go through naturalization to achieve citizenship.[103] In his analysis, he did not mention Justice Miller's side comment about the lack of eligibility of the children of foreign subjects.

John Elk, in Justice Gray's estimation, did not meet the criteria for allegiance at birth. Although he was born geographically within the United States, he was no more subject to its national jurisdiction than "the children of subjects of any foreign government born within the domain of that government, or the children born within the United States of ambassadors or other public ministers of foreign nations."[104] Because the tribes themselves were "alien but dependent powers," Indians were not citizens at birth and could not become citizens of their own volition. Treaties granting citizenship to some tribal members and provisions developed to naturalize others illustrated that "no one can become a citizen of a nation without its consent."[105] Throughout his analysis, Justice Gray made no reference to the question of birthright citizenship for the children of aliens.

Justice Harlan dissented. He believed that the recent legislative history of the Civil Rights Act of 1866 and the Fourteenth Amendment revealed an intent on the part of Congress to admit Indians to citizenship if they had separated from their tribes and lived in the states rather than on reservations. The addition of the clause "excluding Indians not taxed" in his view further bolstered the idea that individual Indians could choose to take on the burdens and benefits of citizenship.[106]

The ruling in *Elk v. Wilkins* combined with earlier legal understandings of Native Americans' status to produce an environment in which some Native Americans had gained citizenship through treaty, but individuals could not wrest citizenship from the United States simply by abandoning their tribes. Only congressional recognition could extend citizenship rights to them.

The ruling served as a catalyst to reformers, who, in securing passage of the General Allotment Act (Dawes Act) of 1887, believed they had established US citizenship for Native Americans who left their tribal affiliations and resided on their allotted lands—at least after the twenty-five-year period of tutelage built into the act. A great deal of confusion persisted on the ground about when, in this process, Native Americans became citizens, especially as the period of tutelage was sometimes extended.[107] The American Indian Citizenship Act of 1924 finally extended citizenship to all Native Americans born within the United States. Even that act, however, left substantial room for state-based discrimination in terms of the civic rights citizenship entailed for Native Americans.

As described in the next chapter, a distinct history of immigration was unfolding as courts and policymakers produced the first readings of the Fourteenth Amendment. The trickle of Chinese immigration begun in the 1850s soon grew into a mighty stream. While the framers of the Fourteenth Amendment were aware of the growing scope of Chinese immigration, they did not address the Chinese in the amendment's final form. Congress showed little reluctance to legislate to manage the entrance of immigrants, particularly the Chinese, during the period following the Civil War. Congress also changed who was eligible for naturalization and created new penalties for fraudulent attempts to gain citizenship. Yet, after passing the Civil Rights Act of 1866, Congress did not legislate further to address birthright citizenship. The question of citizenship for the descendants of Chinese remained vexed and provoked its own line of litigation, a story that chapter 4 will tell in more detail.

2 | Chinese Immigration and the Legal Shift toward Exclusion

Before we can understand Wong Kim Ark's story, we must understand the larger forces that led to his presence in the United States, first as a child born in San Francisco and later on as an adult looking to come back in after a trip to China. His personal history resembled the immigration experiences of the many Chinese who migrated and made homes incorporating their connections to both the United States and China. This chapter provides a brief history of the rise of Chinese immigration to the United States in the middle to late nineteenth century and the increasingly strident backlash against these new residents, which troubled American diplomatic relations with China and convinced Congress to pass legislation sharply restricting immigration for the first time. By the time that Wong Kim Ark's case reached the Supreme Court, a new status existed under American law: that of the illegal alien.

Chinese Migration to the United States

China had been largely closed to Western influence and economic engagement until the mid-nineteenth century. Only a few Chinese men, primarily merchants, came to the United States in the nation's early history. The opium wars of the mid-nineteenth century opened the door to China for Great Britain, and other Western powers soon followed, destabilizing the Qing dynasty.[1] Both in response to political and military disruption and with the generation of new opportunities, impoverished peasants began to enter the global labor market. At first, the number of immigrants coming to the United States was small, but the factors pushing them out of China and attracting them to the United States shifted, creating a drastic change, in the early 1850s.

On the pull side, the first laborers came in response to the California gold rush, solicited to serve as dependable workers.[2] This wave, however, was dwarfed by the influx of laborers brought in at first to build the western railroads and then increasingly to serve in a variety of laboring occupations. The gold rush itself had a lasting impact on California's economy. The population influx and many miners' abandonment of their quests stimulated the rise of manufacturing facilities, agriculture, and animal husbandry, quickly situating California as a significant player in global economic markets both to sell its goods and to seek the laborers to fuel this development.[3] The transaction costs for securing workers born in the United States and for imported European labor were unacceptably high, making Chinese labor attractive, a factor enhanced by the Chinese laborers' reputation for productivity and dependability.[4] Between 1849 and 1870, gold mining (1852–1855) and railroad construction (1868–1870) both accounted for sharp spikes in Chinese laborers' immigration to California.[5]

Most of the Chinese who emigrated to North America in the second half of the nineteenth century came from the Guangdong Province's Pearl River Delta, close to the newly internationalizing seaports of Canton, Hong Kong, and Macao.[6] Historians for years identified four factors as highly important in encouraging a wave of departures from the Pearl River Delta: the struggle between the Hakka and the Natives (a local indigenous population), the Red Turban Rebellion, the Taiping Rebellion, and the Opium War.[7] Between 1851 and 1864, the Taiping Rebellion and the Red Turban Rebellion took more than twenty million lives.[8] Fighting between the Hakka and the Natives over scarce arable land increased the misery for all.[9] These disruptions, however, cannot fully explain the emigration patterns. While the Red Turban Rebellion and the Hakka-Native war did take place within Guangdong, their effects spread beyond the province and thus, despite their destructiveness, cannot fully explain the geographic concentration of emigrants. The Taiping Rebellion "basically took place outside of Guangdong."[10] The Opium War had a broad effect and particularly damaged the textile industry by subjecting it to competition from Western goods in several provinces, not just Guangdong.[11] And while evidence shows that Guangdong was importing grain, this seems to have been a function of affluence and population growth due to an increase in commerce in the region.[12]

With the economic shift away from agriculture and toward craft manufacturing and commerce, some areas within Guangdong began to produce "ready pool[s] of laborers with experience, and willingness to travel and work elsewhere."[13] Beyond this, American connections in the region included those forged by early American traders and missionaries and grew as local residents went to the United States and returned with positive reports from the "Flowery-flag Country."[14] Among the early-wave participants, around a third returned to China permanently, increasing the chances that people in the region might know someone, or have heard about a successful sojourn in California or other parts of the United States.[15] An imperial ban was placed on emigration in the Ming dynasty and reissued multiple times during the Qing dynasty, but neither the provincial government in Guangdong nor the weakened Qing dynasty proved capable of enforcing the prohibition.[16]

While Chinese laborers gained the most attention in the wave of immigration in the 1850s, Chinese merchants were among the earliest arrivals. By late 1849, several hundred Chinese were reported to be in San Francisco, all men with enough resources to pay for their transport and who primarily engaged in "mercantiles and trading pursuits."[17] These early arrivals seem to have come with the intention of using their business skills to reap the economic benefits of the wealth in California generated by the gold rush, setting themselves up as traders and import-export specialists. Many of these individuals hailed from Canton and surrounding areas.[18]

Communities in many Chinese provinces experienced social and political disruption and drastic economic changes for the worse in the mid-nineteenth century.[19] Residents of the Pearl River Delta, to a greater extent, had concrete information about potential alternatives, and some had acquired some valuable cultural capital through interactions with returned emigrants, American missionaries, and other American sojourners.[20] While many individuals had enough knowledge and contacts to navigate the uncertain path to new opportunities, unscrupulous labor marketeers lured others into predatory arrangements, transporting them to Cuba, Peru, Indonesia, and other undesirable and often deadly locations where the primary difference between them and chattel slavery was their possession of labor contracts. Those who had more resources and sought emigration voluntarily tended to go to Hawaii or California.[21] Even these emigrants, however, were "generally poor men of rural background . . . hired hands, sharecroppers, or small landowners."[22]

Chinese immigrants and their descendants retained close connections with their homes. Those who were successful remitted funds home, but many also used their wealth to lend funds to other individuals from their home districts who were hoping to emigrate. Prospective emigrants turned to local kin networks for advice and loans as well.[23] The wave of immigration was "a movement of unmarried men" who sought to build up the funds during their sojourns to support a family in their home villages.[24]

Another factor in migration was the formation of *huiguan*, or associations linking people from the same region who were sojourning together far away, in California. In 1862, six such associations became a federation known unofficially to Americans as the Chinese Six Companies.[25] In San Francisco, the Six Companies built houses and temples and established a mutual aid society that provided everything from short-term financial help to dispute resolution services. Chinese seeking to leave Guangdong Province knew that they could begin to rely on kin assistance from these networks even before they entered the United States if they came in through the port of San Francisco. The Six Companies also kept careful records of Chinese not just in San Francisco but across the entire United States.[26]

The initial influx of Chinese to California in particular had a dramatic effect. Thirty-five thousand Chinese migrated to California between 1848 and 1852, swelling the sparsely settled new state to the point that "they constituted at least 10 percent of the population during the 1850s."[27] By 1860, the Chinese had become the largest foreign-born ethnic group in the state.[28] Some of these early migrants were merchants, eager to establish themselves as traders and importers in San Francisco in the wake of economic recessions in Canton.[29] Many more, however, were laborers. While labeled "coolies" by many Americans, this was not strictly correct: most male emigrants bound for the United States wanted to come and were not kidnapped or coerced.[30] They were not, however, completely free and independent upon arriving in the United States. They tended to borrow the funds needed to secure passage, agreeing to pay back their brokers with interest from the wages earned when they arrived and established themselves.[31] They were strongly and at times illegitimately enticed by the shipping firms enriched by their transit and the economic interests in the United States that would benefit by paying their significantly lower wages. Many men dreamed of coming to the United States and returning to China with enough resources to fund a comfortable life for themselves and their families, but of the more than two hundred thousand who had come by the late 1870s, only about a quarter returned to stay in China.[32]

Mixed American Responses to Chinese Migration

While individuals and entities like railroads hoping to employ cheap labor were happy about the increasing numbers of Chinese immigrants, tension over these new residents rose soon after they began to come in large numbers. The tighter labor market of the 1850s inflamed prejudice that had been simmering since the 1830s.[33] California's legislature took action very soon after statehood, passing a law requiring foreign-born miners to pay $20 monthly to purchase licenses to mine for gold.[34] After experimenting with changing the rates for a few years, the legislature distinguished between foreigners who could become citizens and those who could not, targeting the Chinese with a tax that would ratchet up by $2 per month every year.[35] In 1852 and 1853, additional laws imposed a $500 bond requirement for each foreign passenger on incoming ships, though the bond could be commuted by a lower direct payment, and in 1855, the legislature passed a $50 capitation tax on ships carrying individuals ineligible for citizenship.[36] Lawmakers finally overstepped in 1858 by attempting to ban Chinese immigration entirely; the state supreme court invalidated this measure.[37]

Undaunted, the California legislature continued in this vein, enacting additional taxes on Chinese fishermen and miners and, in 1863, barring Indian, Mongolian, and Chinese immigrants from testifying in a courtroom in favor of or against a white man. In 1864, the legislature limited contract laborers to one-year terms.[38] Hostile policies at times created brief periods of net Chinese migrant loss as measured by the flow through the San Francisco Customs House, but overall the Chinese continued to come.[39]

The crosscutting tensions between western opponents of Chinese immigration and business interests eager to promote and benefit from it contributed in part to international efforts to clarify the reciprocal rights of Chinese and American subjects and citizens sojourning abroad. In 1868, Congress ratified the Burlingame Treaty with China, which granted free immigration and legal protections to Chinese in America and strengthened the United States' trading relationship with China.[40] Advocating for the treaty was a ticklish business in a political environment roiled by President Johnson's impeachment and continued debates over Reconstruction, but Anson Burlingame and William Seward, both holdovers from the Lincoln administration, proved capable of avoiding major public controversy.[41] The treaty, signed on the same day that Secretary of State William Seward declared the Fourteenth Amendment to have been ratified, also targeted California's anti-Chinese legislation, guaranteeing to the Chinese enjoyment of the "same privileges, immunities or exemptions in respect to travel or residence as may there be enjoyed by the citizens or subjects of the most favored nation."[42] While Democrats predictably opposed the treaty, northern and East Coast Republicans were more supportive than Republicans in California.[43] Seward and Burlingame's masterful manipulation of national politics nonetheless secured victory for a short time, even managing to achieve a unanimous vote on the treaty.[44]

While Congress furthermore passed legislation in 1870 barring the states from imposing head taxes on immigrants, national legislators, even Republicans, had some uneasiness with Chinese migration. The Chinese question lurked in the background as Congress debated questions around citizenship arising in the context of Reconstruction legislation and constitutional amendments.

In 1870, Congress passed and President Grant signed an amendment to the 1795 Naturalization Act, declaring that the naturalization laws, which had previously restricted citizenship to "any alien being a free white person" who had resided in the United States for two (later amended to five) years, "are hereby extended to aliens of African nativity and to persons of African descent."[45] With Black citizenship inscribed in both law and constitutional language, the Senate briefly considered further altering the principle, first adopted in 1790 and prevailing since, that only whites should be permitted to naturalize.[46] The proposal was quickly dropped, with one West Coast Republican warning that any attempt to open up naturalization to the Chinese would provoke mass slaughter by West Coast whites.[47] By making no mention of Asians, who were already entering the United States in considerable numbers, the 1870 act, by remaining silent on the subject, effectively excluded them from naturalization; this would soon be made more explicit. The Chinese continued to come. Aided by the bridge funding from the Six Companies, young male laborers from China emigrated in large numbers.[48] While the figures kept by different US institutions did not always match, the overall trend was upward.[49] As the threat of economic competition and racial prejudice increased, particularly in California, resistance to the treaty's terms grew. By 1876, both Democrats and Republicans, eyeing California's role in national electoral terms, included planks in their party platforms addressing

"Mongolian immigration"; the Democrats called for an end and the Republicans pressed for an investigation, implying that legislative action would follow.[50]

The Path toward Stringent Legislative Exclusion

Questions soon arose about the extent to which individual hostile states, particularly California, could act independently to thwart Chinese immigration and encourage the Chinese to depart. Prior to the Civil War, states had regulated the entry of foreigners, sometimes barring the immigration of paupers, those likely to become public charges, and the ill, but Congress had not yet established any nationwide means of addressing these issues. The first significant answer came in 1874 from the pen of Supreme Court Justice Field, sitting as a circuit judge for the district of California. Ah Fong, a Chinese woman, arrived in the port of San Francisco in August 1874, but the commissioner of immigration, himself a Polish immigrant who had arrived in California in 1849, determined that she and twenty-one other Chinese women traveling with her were "lewd and debauched women" and refused to allow them to land without presenting the expensive bonds required under California law.[51] The shipmaster then detained them, and Leander Quint, a prominent San Francisco attorney who had served as district attorney and had been a member of the California Senate, filed a lawsuit in the state district court seeking a writ of habeas corpus on the behalf of Ah Fong and her twenty-one fellow detainees.[52]

The state court granted the writ but, upon hearing the petitioners, determined that they were indeed unfit for entrance into the United States and remanded them to the custody of the steamship master. Leander Quint then sought relief from California's chief justice, but the California Supreme Court upheld the state statute and the finding that the women were properly detained.[53] The case then advanced into the federal system based on the claim that the women's treatment violated the Burlingame Treaty and congressional law. The case came before a three-judge panel that included Supreme Court justice Stephen Field, who was riding circuit.[54] While Justice Field declared himself to be "aware of the very general feeling prevailing in this state against the Chinese," and expressing some sympathy for this feeling, he nonetheless denied that the states could act upon it. "If their further immigration is to be stopped," he explained, "recourse must be had to the federal government, where the whole power over this subject lies."[55]

Congress was not slow to accept the invitation. In May 1875, it passed the first comprehensive restriction on immigration, targeting Chinese women with the Page Act. Spearheaded by California Republican Horace Page, who vehemently opposed Chinese immigration, the act invoked deep anxieties about Chinese women, identifying most immigrants as prostitutes or as, at best, polygamous (and therefore illegitimate) wives.[56] In congressional debates, Page argued furthermore that by sending these women and masses of servile coolie laborers, China had acted in bad faith, violating the Burlingame Treaty by supporting the involuntary migration of debased individuals.[57] The law criminalized the importation of prostitutes and coolies, imposing a requirement that Chinese women seeking to emigrate obtain a certificate verifying that they were neither prostitutes nor intended for a life of prostitution. The act also attempted to solve the contract labor problem by imposing greater restrictions on the importation of involuntary "coolie" laborers.[58] While Congress had extended naturalization to Africans in 1870, the body now also took specific steps to clarify that Asians were ineligible to naturalize.[59]

Enforcement of the Page Act had a significant effect on Chinese women's migration to the United States, largely closing off their entrance. The statute's process, requiring searching inquiries by the consulate in China, thwarted many emigration attempts, with numbers going from the thousands annually to only a handful.[60] Even if they managed to reach the West Coast, some women were further denied entry if they could not convince the customhouse investigators that they were neither prostitutes nor entering the country for "lewd and immoral purposes."[61] While the chief administrators of the law in Hong Kong were accused of corruption, all three appear to have been dedicated to the proposition of the law that Chinese women were to be regarded with heightened suspicion, leading to a 68 percent decline in the immigration rate for women compared with the previous seven-year period.[62] This policy change made it far more difficult for resident Chinese men to marry and start families in the United States. Strict controls on Chinese women's migration limited opportunities for descendants of Chinese immigrants to be born in the United States and encouraged the transnational formation of marriages and families between Chinese men residing in America and women still residing in China, who might then either attempt or not attempt to migrate as wives.[63]

Beyond the gender question, the distinction between classes of Chinese immigrants was important to policymakers and the public in the 1870s, though overall hostility toward and suspicion of the Chinese as a group grew among whites. The same year that the Page Act became law, Yung Wing, "the first Chinese student to graduate from an American university," made history in another way by marrying Mary Louise Kellogg, daughter of a prominent New England family.[64] While southern and some western states were busily adopting statutory bans on interracial marriage, initially the place of Chinese in the rush to recodify long-standing American racial hierarchies was unclear. Indeed, in New York, marriages between Chinese men and Irish women prompted some chatter in a few newspapers, a few of which went as far as to scold the Chinese for their "clannishness" when they sought to import wives from abroad rather than looking to their non-Chinese neighbors.[65] The specter of intermarriage, however, increasingly prompted anxieties in the West that paralleled in some regards white southern concerns about the decline of racial purity in the wake of the extension of fuller rights to Black Americans.[66]

In October, only a few months after the passage of the Page Act, the Supreme Court underlined the states' limits in *Chy Lung v. Freeman*. This case, brought on the behalf of one of the twenty-two women whose detentions were at issue in *In re Ah Fong*, upheld Justice Field's earlier ruling rejecting California's attempt to restrict Chinese women's entrance, itself a less harsh measure than the Page Law.[67] Attorney General Edwards Pierrepont appeared for the United States, arguing that the California law could bring the United States into international conflict and that it violated Congress's exclusive authority to regulate international commerce; the state of California declined even to argue the case.[68] The Court agreed, noting that Congress alone could regulate the admission of "citizens and subjects of foreign nations," though it did reserve some minimal power for states to address problems that immigrants and immigration might create on the ground after arrival.[69] The justices, however, declined to endorse Justice Field's reasoning concerning equal protection.

The 1876 election was the first nationally competitive election in the post–Civil War era, and California's electoral importance underlined the shift in national orientation from the engagement with China characterized by the Burlingame Treaty to more hostility toward mass Chinese immigration. Both parties' platforms included planks supporting more restrictions.[70] In this environment, with the national regulatory path now clearly preferred in institutional terms and possible in political terms, congressional Republicans divided sharply as several new bills seeking to limit immigration came forward. In 1879, unified Democrats and split Republicans in both houses passed a bill allowing ships bound for the United States to transport no more than fifteen Chinese passengers, imposing both a $100-per-passenger head tax and a six-month prison term on captains for violations.[71]

President Hayes was torn over the bill; he characterized Chinese migration as "the present Chinese labor invasion," noting that "women and children do not come" and fretting further that the Chinese threat would bring out the worst in white Americans who opposed it. Nonetheless, he believed that the Burlingame Treaty tied his hands, as the bill directly contradicted its core premise of free and open migration. Rejecting the bill on constitutional grounds and warning Americans of the potential diplomatic consequences of unilaterally abrogating a treaty, President Hayes sought a negotiated solution with China.[72] He placed primary responsibility on the shoulders of James Angell, who was joined by San Francisco exclusionist John Swift and South Carolina moderate William Trescot. Secretary of State Evarts met with the commissioners but gave them only a list of considerations to maintain, including "sentiment on the Pacific coast, United States commercial relations with China, American traditions of liberal admission of foreigners, and the opposition of certain religious groups to exclusion."[73] The commissioners also received both party platforms, underlining the support for enabling more restriction. The commission, after a brief stop in San Francisco by Angell, arrived in Beijing in August 1880 and negotiated a new treaty.[74] This treaty, which modified the Burlingame Treaty of 1868, sought balance on the question, yielding to strong American demands to enable Congress to "regulate, limit, or suspend" the immigration of laborers in exchange for allowing freer immigration by students and merchants and for securing greater legal protections for the Chinese already present.[75]

The Angell Treaty was ratified in 1881, and Congress wasted no time exploring the new regulatory authority it granted.[76] California Republicans in the House and Senate led the effort, despite the opposition of

Massachusetts senator George Hoar, who had started his political career as a Free-Soiler and ended it as an opponent of American imperialism at the turn of the century.[77] Congress sent a bill exercising close to its maximum authority to President Chester Arthur, who vetoed it as too extreme. A revised bill that reduced the bar on the entry of Chinese laborers from twenty years to ten garnered a few more votes and became law under Arthur's signature in May 1882.[78] When news of the legislation reached China, it triggered a wave of migration in advance of implementation, with almost forty thousand individuals entering (some for the first time, and some returning) in 1882.[79]

On paper, the door was firmly and almost entirely closed to the Chinese, allowing only merchants, students, diplomats, and tourists to enter as new (and sometimes temporary) residents. Government statistics supported this narrative. The reality on the ground, however, reflected the lack of concrete resources needed to administer and police exclusion. The new law entrusted responsibility for implementation and enforcement to the Department of the Treasury, with the idea that customhouses would be the primary agents of control. Legislators, however, added only $5,000 to an annual budget that was already in the multimillions.[80] Furthermore, the law barred only new migrants, allowing those already in the United States to leave and return if they procured a return certificate. By August 1885, more than thirty-five thousand return certificates had been issued, creating an atmosphere ripe for fraud.[81] Further, as the next chapter will discuss in detail, those barred from entry had expert legal support and advice, and many filed successful court challenges to their exclusion.

While migration rates were somewhat lower than in the previous decade, the Chinese continued to come. Historian Beth Lew-Williams estimates that between 1883 and 1889, "the mean number of documented migrants admitted in San Francisco per year was 8,746," a drop of only 16 percent from the previous period's annual mean. This number also did not include Chinese who came in through other routes or the uncertain number who entered without creating any formal records.[82] Congress attempted to strengthen the exclusion process in 1884 by "requir[ing] customs collectors to record identifying information on all Chinese leaving the United States and . . . giv[ing] them reentry certificates" along with mandating identity certificates for those in the protected classes, but the influx continued.[83] Frustrated members of Congress passed the Scott Act in 1888, which barred entrance to all

Chinese laborers, even those who were American residents who had left only to visit China.[84]

The Scott Act is often overshadowed by its more famous successor, the Geary Act, passed in 1892. The Scott Act, however, not only targeted individual undesirable Chinese seeking to enter the country but also further thwarted the formation of Chinese families by making it more difficult for laborers in the country to be assured that they would be able to reenter if they departed. Many of the targeted American residents who had been traveling to and from China were doing so, as legal scholar Kerry Abrams explains, "to continue to support their extended families in China with the wages they earned in America, and in many cases so that they could father children with the wives they had left behind."[85] If these individuals could be barred from reentry, their family members in China could be prevented from achieving links to the United States as well, thus shutting down the rapidly growing trend of Chinese establishment of transnational families.

In 1892, Congress confronted the end of the ten-year period set by the first exclusion act and, upon revisiting the question, doubled down. The Geary Act attempted to stop almost all Chinese migration for ten more years, but in addition targeted Chinese already residing in the United States. Chinese noncitizens in the United States were directed to register with the collector of revenue within one year of the act's passage. They were further burdened with demonstrating to administrators' satisfaction that they had the right to remain in the United States. Chinese who could not establish this right were subject to summary deportation, even if they had been in the United States for years.[86] When the question of extending exclusion arose again at the end of the ten-year period initiated in 1892, Congress passed legislation making exclusion permanent. This extension was not repealed until World War II, when it became a diplomatic issue in the United States' alliance with China.[87]

The Mechanics of Exclusion and Resistance

It was one thing to pass laws. It was quite another to ensure their enforcement. As noted earlier, the 1882 Exclusion Act contemplated a much more extensive and vigorous effort to keep unwanted Chinese laborers out of the United States. Congress, however, neither created new institutional capacity to accomplish this mandate nor did it substantially expand the resources of existing institutions to fulfill the legislative will. Congress designated the Treasury Department as the owner of this agenda. Enforcement was to take place through the actions of collectors of customs at ports of entry.[88] Legislators in Congress embraced essentialist understandings of the Chinese as a servile and distinct race, but they further distinguished between the "educated and cultivated" upper classes of Chinese and the degraded and inferior "coolie" laborers.[89]

The restrictive regime initiated in 1882 created a new concept in American law, that of the illegal immigrant. The Chinese who evaded the government's regulatory mechanisms and did not fit into the status categories exempted from restriction were committing criminal offenses.[90] Enforcement faced three distinctive challenges. First, at routine ports of entry, particularly San Francisco, administrators had to distinguish between the Chinese who were entitled to enter and those who were not. Second, the border itself, particularly the southern border with Mexico and the northern border with Canada, had to be defended against unauthorized crossing and settlement. And third, particularly after the passage of the Geary Act in 1892, those residing in the country illegally had to be identified and expelled.[91]

The early laws that sought to limit Chinese immigration drastically were particularly problematic in their implicit understanding of how migration occurred. As noted, the 1882 legislation lodged enforcement authority with collectors of customs. This approach seemed like an efficient and inexpensive way to effect the statutory aim, but it presumed that migrants would dutifully present themselves at the large port cities like San Francisco and Port Townsend for entry.[92] When Congress first excluded contract laborers from the United States, the statute the legislators passed in 1885 was so weak in enforcement mechanisms that Congress had to return to it almost immediately to fill in the gaps.[93]

The changes, however, did not provide much concrete assistance to address border crossings. Prior to the 1900s, the Canadian border proved to be a substantial problem. Many Chinese laborers who had resided in the United States emigrated to Canada to work on building the Canadian Pacific Railroad in the 1870s and then found themselves targeted by law when they wished to return to the United States after the passage of the first exclusion act.[94] Finding an entrance point in Washington or to a lesser extent farther east, however, was not exceptionally difficult. The passage of the 1882 Restriction Act sparked the growth of smugglers despite the act's harsh criminal penalties; customs officials believed that in addition to a network of Chinese labor smugglers, Indians and whites were also playing the game.[95]

As Congress's repeated attempts to regulate suggest, working out ways to exclude Chinese laborers was a highly salient policy question from 1875 through the turn of the century. The concept of illegal immigration took hold in the American press. Newspapers on the West Coast but increasingly in the east as well portrayed the threat in terms of racial stereotypes of the Chinese as "either cunning criminals or 'coolies' whose immigration constituted a harmful invasion of inferior and unassimilable aliens."[96] While Congress maintained the class distinction among Chinese, separating the desired merchants, diplomats, and students from the masses of Mongolian laborers, customs collectors were left to settle these questions on the ground when confronted with individual migrants bearing papers and stories of questionable validity. Indeed, customs collectors, recognizing the large unauthorized and undesirable Chinese presence in the country, viewed all documents and testimony with suspicion, and Congress continued to tinker with the definition of the exempted class of merchants.[97]

Dealing with Chinese women generated even more confusion both for lawmakers and for the bureaucrats responsible for enforcing these policies. The mechanics of exclusion both ideologically and practically demanded the distinction between desirable merchants and undesirable laborers, but by the early 1880s, law and policy increasingly settled on the proposition that women's status followed that of their husbands if they were married. Exclusionary policies toward women had enhanced the already transnational nature of Chinese familial relations. Wives of returning laborers shared their husbands' status as laborers but were required to obtain independent certificates for entry, which was increasingly difficult to do.[98] In contrast, after some struggles, merchants' wives were understood to be subsumed within their husbands' preferred status, which enabled them to be considered part of an indivisible family unit that the United States was bound to protect in order to reap the economic benefits of merchants' investments.

Beyond the legislative and legal wrangling, though, Chinese immigration continued in the shadow of the law. Many Chinese opted to evade the law, entering the country informally or by fraud and, as much as possible, avoiding encounters that might call their entry or continued residence into question. Others, however, used the tools of American law to resist the legal machinery of exclusion. Their efforts, and the federal courts' responses to them, profoundly shaped the development of American administrative and constitutional law in the last quarter of the nineteenth century and laid the groundwork for Wong Kim Ark's effort to establish his entitlement to citizenship.

3 | The Legal Battle over Exclusion

Many Americans think of the famous campaign launched by the Inc. Fund of the National Association for the Advancement of Colored People (NAACP) to destroy segregation as the first use of lawsuits as an organized tool to address perceived injustices. The series of lawsuits that led to *Brown v. Board of Education* in 1954 is justly celebrated as a distinctive accomplishment. The Inc. Fund, however, was not the first group to understand that when minority groups were on the losing end in elections, the courts could provide an alternative place to fight. While some early litigation on behalf of the Chinese was undertaken by the corporate interests seeking to import Chinese labor, the Six Companies soon became involved in the struggles to defend the Chinese in the rapidly changing legislative environment. The Six Companies were not, however, perfectly analogous to modern legal mobilization organizations. While they advocated aggressively for the interests of individual Chinese caught in legal struggles and on behalf of Chinese immigrants generally, they were primarily supportive of the more elite transnational merchants. At the same time, they also held significant influence within the immigrant Chinese community and overwhelmingly shaped the agenda for Chinese strategies of engagement with the American state.

This chapter discusses the legal battles waged by advocates for the Chinese and their opponents in the 1880s and 1890s. The Six Companies and other organizations both defended individual Chinese threatened with deportation and challenged the constitutionality of congressional legislation. The federal government defended its actions in court, supporting administrative decisions and advancing strong theories about the scope of congressional authority to address the problem of Chinese migration. Federal courts, under the guidance of the US Supreme Court, largely supported Congress's efforts to curb migration and ultimately to expel unwanted Chinese sojourners, but maintained some limits on administrative discretion. At the same time, however, a quieter line of federal jurisprudence developed around the question of birthright citizenship and how far it extended.

The Advocacy Network for Opposing
Exclusion and Deportation

The "Chinese had a long history of hiring the best American lawyers to challenge anti-Chinese legislation even before 1882," and many were able to retain counsel to make their case for admission or fight deportation.[1] Even those without robust financial assets participated; historian Erika Lee estimates that as many as 90 percent of Chinese relied on immigration attorneys.[2] According to one estimate, Chinese litigants filed at least seven thousand appeals in the first ten years of the Exclusion Act's operation, and between 1891 and 1905 there were another twenty-six hundred.[3] Not all of the experts who defended the Chinese in court were directly connected to the Chinese community.

A number of the lawyers and law firms that mobilized to defend Chinese litigants did so at the behest of corporate interests. Many highly visible counselors had served as ambassadors or cabinet officials or had held other prominent positions. In the early years of litigation, those defending the Chinese included major law firms representing steamship companies, which bore the financial responsibility to return to China those rejected at the border, and which (prior to the opening of Angel Island in 1910) might have to maintain San Francisco detainees on board ship pending disposition of their cases. Harvey E. Brown, former district attorney in San Francisco and close associate of Leland Stanford, illustrates one route by which elite lawyers became advocates for the Chinese. Brown represented the Oriental and Occidental Steamship Company beginning in 1874, a company owned by Stanford. Stanford brought Chinese workers to the country to build his railroad lines, and Brown served as legal counsel for both businesses, participating in the early challenges to state laws discussed in the previous chapter.[4]

Nonetheless, by the 1880s, the Chinese benevolent associations that aided residents, kept order, and spoke local dialects were providing the underpinning for most legal challenges. These local associations sent representatives to the Chinese Six Companies. Originally formed to resolve disputes among Chinese in America, the Chinese Six Companies expanded to advocate for the Chinese, keeping an attorney on retainer to combat anti-Chinese practices and legislation.[5] The Chinese Six Companies supported many of the lawsuits challenging the constitutionality of legislation establishing exclusion, as this chapter will discuss. With the backing of the Six Companies, the Chinese could turn to "an organized network of immigration lawyers who facilitated Chinese entry and reentry by keeping track of the necessary paperwork and lobbying on behalf of clients."[6] As exclusion laws grew more complex and enforcement became more vigorous, the number of immigration lawyers serving Chinese clients grew. The US Department of the Treasury observed in 1899 that the San Francisco Chinese tended to be represented by the "very best attorneys in the city."[7]

This expertise did not come cheaply. A Treasury Department special agent told Congress in 1885 that "a new and presumably profitable kind of litigation has sprung up and the calendars of the courts are burdened with Chinese cases. The recognized attorney's fee in each case is $100."[8] Given the number of Chinese habeas cases filed in the first five years after the 1882 Exclusion Act, the Chinese likely paid at least $400,000 for legal counsel over those five years.[9]

The lawyers representing the Chinese were driven at least in part by pecuniary motives, and entities beyond the immediate families of detained Chinese had incentives and means to pay. Yet as Daniel Ernst notes, most lawyers of the period identified closely with the judiciary and were supportive of it when it defended civil liberties or, in the latter decades of the 1800s, insisted on the robust enforcement of treaty agreements.[10] This suggests that distinct interests beyond money, and yet separable from sympathies for the Chinese, led some lawyers to provide support. Handling Chinese cases even brought some lawyers and firms into disrepute, since public sentiment was so strongly opposed to the Chinese—a fate that befell a lawyer consulted by Wong Kim Ark, as we will see in chapter 4.

Throughout this period, the specialized immigration bar, particularly in San Francisco, was reinforced by its success. The lucrative nature of the practice, in which "lawyers could earn between seventy-five and one hundred dollars for a case," generated significant competition for this business, though the Six Companies remained an outside player.[11] They retained a group of attorneys who handled cases in San Francisco and paid the fees for indigent immigrants.[12] Detained immigrants could also turn to Chinese brokers and family members for help in securing expert legal assistance. And the wave of litigation initiated in the 1880s was highly successful; "by 1885, one-fifth of all Chinese immigrants to enter the country had done so through such [habeas] petitions."[13]

One of the most notable attorneys to become involved in litigation on behalf of the Chinese was San Francisco's Thomas Riordan. In addition to handling individual cases referred to him by the Six Companies, he was occasionally retained by the Chinese consulate to litigate high-profile cases, including suits launching constitutional challenges against the congressional immigration restrictions passed in the 1880s and 1890s.[14] While he never held political office, he was a powerful figure in the Republican Party, having chaired the San Francisco Republican Committee from 1899 through 1905. Upon his death in 1905, the *San Francisco Call* identified him as having "stood at the top of the legal profession in this city for many years."[15]

Legal management of disputes over Chinese exclusion was also lucrative business for officers of the court. Added to the recognized attorney's fee in cases brought to challenge detentions "must be added clerk's, district attorney's and marshal's fees and a charge of $5 for the interpreter."[16] Federal court clerks "were entitled to $15 for filing a *habeas* petition; the court commissioners were entitled to an additional $2.50 fee." The structuring of these positions generated further opportunities for remuneration: "As one person held both positions they received a minimum fee of $17.50 every time a Chinese sought to get ashore on habeas corpus."[17] By January 1, 1887, with 1,684 challenges filed, the clerks to the district and circuit courts had already received nearly $29,500 in fees. In addition, federal marshals received $2 for serving the writ, and the court stenographer and interpreter each received at least $1 for each case heard. Not included in these totals were fees for appeals. With the structure of these charges and fees, "seven or eight court officials shared $36,206 in fees during the first four years of restriction."[18] By the beginning of 1888, the number of petitions filed to challenge detentions was over four thousand and the clerks to the courts alone had received at least $61,162 for five years.[19]

Perhaps more important, "these [Chinese] cases were a source of profit to the federal district attorney."[20] Even though this official sought to keep the cases out of court, prompted by the urgings of the customhouse, a newspaper source estimated that in the first two and a half years of restriction, the federal district attorney received $4,344 in fees from these cases.[21] Material interests may help explain why the cases kept getting to court in the early years of restriction, and why cooperation of some federal officials, essential to the Chinese campaign in the earliest years, was forthcoming.

While motives for serving an increasingly vilified clientele varied, and business interests were an important part of the push to bring these cases to federal courts, even unskilled Chinese heritage laborers tended to have access to strong legal representation. In this regard, their good fortune cannot simply be explained by the demand of US employers for inexpensive labor. The Chinese Six Companies looked after the interests of Chinese businessmen, and even small-scale merchants and businessmen would have had an interest in retaining a supply of Chinese labor. Access to the court owed a great deal to the strength and financial capabilities of Chinese organizations on the West Coast, especially at the early stages of federal litigation. Some of the most prominent lawyers involved in arguing appellate and Supreme Court cases were surely drawn by the high-stakes issues involved, including who had a right to have rights, the issue of birthright citizenship, and claims about unreviewable, plenary power to make determinations about who could enter or stay within, and who had to depart from, the United States. Wong Kim Ark, a cook, had remarkable legal talent on his side when the federal government decided to challenge his right to return to the United States from China.

The Explosion of Habeas Litigation in San Francisco

The tool that Chinese and their advocates used was the writ of habeas corpus. The history of the writ of habeas corpus stretched back to well before the founding of the United States. The "Great Writ" was in both English and American tradition the ultimate check that the judicial branch could exercise against any state actor's illegitimate detention of a person. Protected from suspension under the original Constitution, the writ of habeas corpus had, by the late nineteenth century, developed into a means of challenging unjust detentions in federal court through the process authorized by Congress. Advocates for Chinese who had been denied entry into the United States or were otherwise being held in preparation for deportation used this powerful tool to challenge deportation orders.

Although advocates for detained Chinese filed petitions frequently prior to 1882, when Congress sharply curtailed laborers' entrance, the practice increased dramatically. The California district courts became the center of the battleground, with two judges, the Northern District's Ogden Hoffman and presiding circuit judge Lorenzo Sawyer, hearing an extraordinary number of cases.[22] While neither Hoffman nor Sawyer

Chinese Exclusion Cases Prior to Wong Kim Ark's Appeal

- *In re Ah Fong*, 1 F. Cas. 213 (D. Cal. 1874): Decided that state police power to exclude a foreigner is limited to self-defense; California statute violated Burlingame Treaty and Fourteenth Amendment.
- *Chy Lung v. Freeman*, 92 U.S. 275 (1876): Decided that immigration is a matter for the federal government, not the states; Congress has power to regulate commerce with foreign nations and conduct foreign relations.
- *Chae Chan Ping v. United States*, 130 U.S. 581 (1889) (the Chinese Exclusion Case): Upheld Scott Act reentry certificate requirement for Chinese laborers, even if traveling abroad when the law was passed; Congress has broad powers over immigration despite international treaties.
- *Fong Yue Ting v. United States*, 149 U.S. 698 (1893): Upheld registration provision of Geary Act and found power to exclude/expel aliens an inherent right of sovereign nation, vested in political departments of government.
- *In re Ny Look*, 56 F. 81 (C.C. S.D.N.Y. 1893): Decided that, absent adequate administrative provision or funding for deportation under Geary Act, an unregistered laborer could not be detained indefinitely pending deportation.
- *Lem Moon Sing v. United States*, 158 U.S. 538 (1895): Upheld General Appropriations Act provision making decision by immigration or customs official to exclude an alien final unless the secretary of the Treasury reversed on appeal.
- *Wong Wing v. United States*, 163 U.S. 228 (1896): Invalidated provision of Geary Act authorizing one-year hard labor before deportation; Chinese entitled to due process.

had any particular fondness for the Chinese, "the local federal judges simply could not justify excluding Chinese from the country in the absence of any opportunity to establish their right to enter."[23] Further, both were committed to dealing with the thousands of Chinese who came before them on an individual basis. Hoffman, who spent most of his career as a judge for the Northern District of California, "expressed his personal delight at being able to avoid separating Chinese children from their parents"; the multitude of hearings forced him "to see and hear them as human beings with distinct explanations and histories that had to be dealt with on a case-by-case basis."[24] This approach was not shared by later judges such as Gilbert, Ross, and Morrow of the circuit court of appeals.[25] Several judges who joined the new Ninth Circuit in the 1890s seemed to harbor more pronounced anti-Chinese sentiments and demonstrated these views before they joined the Ninth Circuit.[26]

After the passage of the 1882 Exclusion Act, implementation fell to the collectors of customs. San Francisco's collector of customs, Eugene Sullivan, publicly declared his intent to enforce the law strictly, demanding that all Chinese attempting to return to the United States, even those who had left before the passage of the legislation, present a return certificate before being permitted to reenter the country. He further insisted on the presentation of a Canton certificate obtained in China.[27] In considering habeas petitions challenging these practices, Justice Field (on circuit court duty), Judge Hoffman, and Judge Deady of Oregon all retorted that some form of due process had to be provided to entrants contesting their detention, and highlighted the need to respect existing treaty obligations.[28]

Justice Field departed from California, leaving the lower federal courts to handle a growing wave of habeas petitions. In San Francisco, the increasing volume reflected both the collector's and his deputies' aggressive denials of entry and the local knowledge that the northern California judges would consider novel legal questions and grant relief when they observed procedural problems or heard evidence of clearly biased fact-finding.[29] In 1883, Judge Hoffman ruled that a Chinese laborer who had left for China prior to the passage of the Exclusion Act could reenter the country without the certificate. Further cases extended this principle to all laborers who had departed prior to June 6, 1882, inviting an influx of returning Chinese.[30]

Judge Hoffman in particular found himself in a difficult position. While unenthusiastic about the continuing influx of Chinese immigrants, he was committed to due process and insisted that, with no other oversight or procedural protections in place to review administrative decisions, habeas petitions had to be considered by courts. Concerned about indefinite detention, he went further, arguing that time limits had to be established on holding individuals denied entrance, and if a decision could not be reached, they should be released. Citing his own overwhelming workload, which included night sessions of court just to handle habeas petitions, he pressed for a congressional solution.[31]

Congress amended the entry process in the second Exclusion Act in 1884, making return certificates the only path for laborers to reenter the United States and clarifying that nonlaborers had to obtain consular visas. Hoffman, Sawyer, and other federal judges, however, continued to grant habeas relief, highlighting the inconsistencies between the exclusion decisions and the terms of treaties between the United States and China. While Hoffman complained about the Chinese and their unscrupulous and deceptive efforts to circumvent the law, he continued to grant petitions in cases in which the commissioner or his deputies had violated procedures or ignored clear evidence that the individual was a legitimate entrant.[32]

When Justice Field returned to California in 1884, his view on hewing strictly to the Burlingame Treaty had changed. He arrived "determined to take a harder line with the Chinese and correct his misguided colleagues."[33] An 1884 case, *Chew Heong v. United States*, took up the question of how to handle resident Chinese who had left for China prior to the passage of the 1882 Exclusion Act and now sought to reenter. Thomas Riordan, serving as the Chinese consul's lead attorney, selected the plaintiff and argued the case along with Chinese vice consul Frederic Bee and three other prominent lawyers.[34] A Ninth Circuit panel consisting of Sawyer, Hoffman, Sabin, and Field considered it. In the oral argument, Thomas Riordan, who by this time was a noted defender of the Chinese, argued that in previous cases, all three of the local judges had held that return certificates were not required for Chinese who had left the country prior to 1882. Justice Field pressed him, asking, "How many Chinamen will try to come in the same way?" When Riordan responded, "about 12,000," Justice Field exploded in frustration. He ranted:

> And what shall the Courts do with them? Can it give each one of them a separate trial? . . . No; it was because the Courts were overcrowded that the second Act was passed. . . . Congress never supposed that Chinamen intended to go back to China and stay several years. If they do not come back at once they should not be allowed to come at all. We can't have them going away and staying as long as they want to.[35]

Riordan, apparently nonplussed, speculated that there was no use in further pressing the case. Justice Field replied curtly, "Not in the least.

My mind is made up on the matter," and advised him to take his complaint to the Chinese minister for resolution with the US secretary of state or to go to the US Supreme Court.[36]

Judges Sawyer, Hoffman, and Sabin believed that simple equity should prevail: the law that had been in effect when they left should apply, not the new requirement that they would have had no opportunity to meet. But Justice Field, sitting in his authoritative capacity on the panel, could and did disagree, ordering Chew Heong (and all others in his situation) to be deported.[37] When the Supreme Court reversed the ruling, Field dissented and accused his colleagues of engaging in "ingenious reasoning" and developing "fanciful notions of a purpose not declared" on the face of congressional legislation.[38] Sawyer, for his part, sent a confidential letter to his colleague in Oregon, Judge Deady, describing the ruling as "consolation" for the "lying, abuse, [and] threatening of impeachment," as well as the "grand glorification of brother Field for coming out here and . . . sitting down on us and setting us right."[39]

Through these struggles, the stance of San Francisco's collector of customs remained consistent. Eugene Sullivan left, but his successor, John Hager, acquired a reputation of virulent opposition to the Chinese.[40] He and his deputies routinely denied entry on any available grounds and refused to change their behavior in response to the courts' efforts to exercise oversight. For their part, both Hoffman and Sawyer continued to be overwhelmed by the volume of habeas petitions, with Hoffman experiencing ill health in part attributed to the unrelenting workload.[41] The stream of petitions and federal judges' willingness to grant many of them throughout the Ninth Circuit contributed to increasing pressure on Congress and the president to do something. In 1888, after a weakened China consented to modifications in its treaty relationship with the United States, Congress responded with new legislation.

The Scott Act and Its Triumph in Court

As discussed in chapter 2, the Scott Act marked a significant ramping up of restrictive policies against Chinese immigration. Legal struggles over the Scott Act laid important groundwork supporting Congress's capacity to restrict immigration, not only determining that the new restrictions were legitimate but also allowing their immediate enforcement against resident Chinese who were outside of the United States when the statute was implemented.

Under the terms of the Scott Act, Chinese laborers seeking reentry after travel abroad had to show that they had a "lawful wife, child or parent in the United States" or that they either possessed one thousand dollars' worth of property or held debts that added up to that amount. Reentry certificates were now the only means for securing reentry and were valid for only one year. So eager was the national government to address the situation that customhouse officials and federal judges in San Francisco received telegrams advising them of the new rules within twenty-four hours of Grover Cleveland's having signed the bill into law.[42]

Chae Chan Ping was by any account a cautious man. A laborer who had arrived legally in San Francisco in 1875, he recognized the dangers in the political climate he inhabited. Before leaving for China in June 1885, he first secured a government certificate that identified him as a legal US resident who was entitled to return.[43] In September 1888, he boarded the steamer *Belgic*, the same vessel on which he had departed, to return to the United States.[44] At this point, the Scott Act had not yet been introduced in Congress, but by the time Chae Chan Ping reached San Francisco a month later, the new restrictions were in effect. When he arrived, customs officers detained him and refused to allow him to disembark.[45]

Chae Chan Ping's case was ideal for testing the law. Representatives filed a habeas corpus petition immediately, and both Sawyer and Hoffman considered it. Chae Chan Ping's attorney was Thomas Riordan, a renowned legal champion of the San Francisco Chinese. The judges, despite their earlier willingness to allow work-arounds, ruled against Chae Chan Ping but granted bail as he immediately filed for appeal.[46]

All involved recognized the importance of the case. The appellate brief arguing for Chae Chan Ping and seeking to limit Congress's power to enforce tighter restrictions with no notice had two authors, George Hoadly and James Carter. Hoadly, a Democrat, had served as Ohio's governor from 1884 through 1886; Carter was a prominent New York lawyer. Riordan was joined by Harvey Brown, a lawyer who had represented both the Oriental and Occidental Steamship company and the Southern Pacific Railroad company to argue Chae Chan Ping's claim before the Court.[47] The US solicitor general filed a brief supporting the law, and the state of California retained John Swift, who had been one of the American commissioners involved in revising the United States' treaty with China, who filed an amicus brief defending the law.[48]

Justice Field wrote the majority opinion for the Court in a case commonly styled *The Chinese Exclusion Case*. He relished the opportunity to return to ground covered in the *Chew Heong* case. This time, his argument for literal and unbending application of the statute prevailed.[49] Justice Field grounded his ruling in favor of the application of the statute in an "innovative" interpretation of Congress's power over immigration. Stepping away from the traditional view that Congress had only the powers specifically attributed to it in Article I, Justice Field endorsed the idea that Congress had broad authority, as an attribute of sovereignty, to exercise reasoned judgment about any legislation that would benefit the common national good.[50]

Justice Field took the opportunity to provide his own history of Chinese immigration to the United States. After detailing (with a decidedly Western and pro-British slant) the early engagements between China and the United States, he described the Burlingame Treaty as "the harbinger of a new era in the history of China," but noted that the golden era of "friendship and good will" and support for "free intercourse" was quickly overtaken by events.[51] In Field's analysis, early migration by Chinese laborers was beneficial, but soon the nation saw an immigration wave composed of "industrious and frugal" Chinese, who were primarily men without families, who lived on a pittance and "were content with the simplest fare, such as would not suffice for our laborers and artisans."[52] These cultural characteristics, as well as their expansion into a variety of labor fields, generated competition with white laborers that sparked bitterness culminating in "open conflicts, to the great disturbance of the public peace."[53]

While this framing might be read to blame American admiration for the Chinese's labor virtues, Justice Field also identified some commonly disparaged Chinese racial characteristics. Despite the Burlingame Treaty's welcome of the Chinese and extension of privileges and immunities to them, they refused to assimilate. In his view, "they remained strangers in the land, residing apart by themselves, and adhering to the customs and usages of their own country."[54] Although Justice Field seemed to recognize that perception did not necessarily reflect reality—"the people of the coast saw, or believed they saw . . . great danger that at no distant day that portion of our country would be overrun by them"— he nonetheless endorsed congressional legislation that sought to curb "an Oriental invasion."[55] Justice Field then described a common uprising among Californians to press for a renegotiation of the Burlingame Treaty, to which China acceded, allowing a differentiation in both treaty and statutory terms between the small and elite class of Chinese merchants, teachers, and students, on the one hand, and the mass of undesired and threatening laborers, on the other.[56]

Justice Field then discussed the Chinese Exclusion Acts, emphasizing fraud and questionable proof on the part of Chinese seeking entrance. He provided a lengthy discussion of congressional authority, culminating in the endorsement of a very strong view of Congress's power to manage immigration and border control. Was it within Congress's power to bar the reentry of laborers who had resided in the United States but had traveled away? Justice Field reasoned, "Those laborers are not citizens of the United States; they are aliens. That the government of the United States, through the action of the legislative department, can exclude aliens from its territory is a proposition which we do not think open to controversy."[57] Congress, by this interpretation, did not need to wait until a war or armed hostility broke out to act if the legislature judged that "the presence of foreigners of a different race in this country, who will not assimilate with us, . . . [is] dangerous to its peace and security."[58] The opinion asserted sweeping power on the part of Congress to exclude foreigners "at any time when, in the judgment of the government, the interests of the country require it."[59]

Chae Chan Ping was ultimately deported in the late summer of 1889. The Court's ruling in his case became part of a growing body of precedent that recognized that both the federal and state governments could use racial categories to distinguish among people and allocate rights and protections.[60] Congress would not be slow to accept this invitation, but advocates for the Chinese were not ready to give up yet.

The Geary Act, Planned Litigation, and Civil Disobedience

The original Chinese Exclusion Act passed in 1882 had a ten-year clock. As it approached expiration, Congress revisited exclusion, extended it, and made the restrictions tougher. As noted in the previous chapter, the Geary Act, passed on May 5, 1892, attempted to halt the entrance of almost all Chinese and oust resident laborers who could not establish their right to remain.[61] Any resident laborer who did not register with the collector of internal revenue was subject to arrest and deportation.[62] By its terms, the statute established a registration period of one year, after which the penalties for noncompliance would be imposed.[63] In addition to reinstating the ban on laborers' entrance and requiring registration, the law decreed that individuals found to be present illegally would also be subject to imprisonment and hard labor. The harsh statute also eliminated the availability of bail for deportation proceedings.[64] Many Chinese, already mobilized by the increasing legal restriction and the wave of extralegal violence targeting them in the previous decade, mobilized for resistance as the Six Companies directed strategies from the background.

The Six Companies immediately and publicly condemned the Geary Act, claiming that it violated both due process and existing US treaties with China.[65] They worked with the Chinese legation to try to solve the problem through international negotiation, but they also fought the Geary Act in and outside of court. When the statute went into effect, they advocated a boycott of the registration provision, and initially less than 15 percent of the resident Chinese who were required to register did so.[66] Through this mass civil disobedience, the Six Companies hoped to convince national institutions to relent—either Congress might soften the law or the courts might refuse to endorse its constitutionality, despite Justice Field's unyielding language in *Chae Chan Ping*.[67]

Going to court was an obvious strategy, given that federal courts in the Ninth Circuit had often granted writs of habeas corpus to individual Chinese who objected to exclusion or deportation orders. The wave of litigation in response to the Chinese Exclusion Acts of the 1880s had relied on and reinforced the specialized immigration bar, and by the time *Chae Chan Ping* began moving up the appellate ladder, the Chinese had achieved victories in 85 percent of their cases.[68] Even after the Supreme Court's ruling, petitions continued to be a highly successful solution to the problem of exclusion.[69]

The Six Companies could not thwart the Geary Act's passage, but the principals believed the act's harshness, elimination of opportunities for due process, and potential conflicts with existing treaties rendered it unconstitutional. Working with other organizations, particularly the Chinese Civil Rights League in New York, the Six Companies organized resistance and publicized their call to individual resident Chinese to ignore the registration requirement.[70] The nonregistration push was wildly successful; as the deadline approached in San Francisco, only 439 individuals of the approximately 26,000 resident laborers had registered. Indeed, in New York, a Chinese laborer's decision to defy the Six Companies and comply with the Geary Act was considered front-page news for the *New York Times*.[71] Representative Thomas Geary was so angered by the Six Companies' campaign that he encouraged San Francisco's US attorney to indict the presidents for interfering with the statute, a tactic rejected by the US attorney general as unlikely to survive judicial review.[72]

The US government itself seemed to be concerned about both constitutionality and implementation. On May 4, the day before the statute's deportation provision became active, the Treasury Department issued an order warning officials not to arrest nonregistered Chinese. The attorney general followed up, "instructing the United States district attorneys to defer proceedings . . . until the necessary arrangements for the arrest, imprisonment, and deportation of the persons accused can be perfected."[73] These decisions provoked outrage on the West Coast, but both proponents and opponents of the legislation recognized that the courts would have to have their say.

The first test cases took place in New York rather than in California. The registration period established by the act ended on May 5, 1893, and on May 6, US marshals ceremonially arrested three men to launch the inquiry. Fong Yue Ting and Wong Quan were laborers who had refused to obtain certificates, and Lee Joe had applied, but his application was denied.[74] The cases moved exceptionally quickly—the Southern District of New York ordered the men deported on the same day they were arrested, and after their habeas petitions were brushed aside by the circuit court of appeals, the Supreme Court heard oral arguments on May 10. It took only five days for five of the eight sitting justices to uphold the act.[75]

This time, Justice Gray, who had also written the majority opinion in *Elk v. Wilkins*, wrote for the Court. Citing another recently decided case involving a Japanese woman who was excluded, he underlined the idea that the ability to forbid the entrance of aliens was a fundamental sovereign power that the Constitution housed both in the president's and Senate's authority to make treaties and in Congress's authority to legislate.[76] He also quoted extensively from Justice Field's opinion in *Chae Chan Ping*, linking it to the history of the British Crown's exercise of prerogative power to deport and exclude aliens. He then presented a highly constrained picture of the federal courts' authority to review the legislation or specific applications of it: "The power to exclude or expel aliens . . . is vested in the political departments of the government, and is to be regulated by treaty or by act of Congress, and to be executed by the executive authority . . . except so far as the judicial department has been authorized by treaty or by statute, or is required by the paramount law of the Constitution, to intervene."[77]

Justice Gray, like Justice Field, provided a history of the Chinese experience and the American government's vexed efforts to curb immigration. He noted that in 1868, Congress had reinforced the Fourteenth Amendment by guaranteeing that naturalized citizens would hold the same civic rights as native-born citizens, but emphasized that these rights accrued only to citizens. He remarked, "Chinese persons not born in this country have never been recognized as citizens of the United States, nor authorized to become such under the naturalization laws."[78] He also described Chinese laborers as "of a distinct race and religion, remaining strangers in the land, residing apart by themselves, tenaciously adhering to the customs and usages of their own country, unfamiliar with our institutions, and apparently incapable of assimilating with our people."[79] All of this, he reasoned, set into motion efforts to negotiate a supplemental treaty with China and for Congress to limit migration.

Ultimately for Justice Gray, the Chinese were in a bind created by the US government's policies. While residing in the United States, regardless of the length of their sojourn, they were entitled to remain at the pleasure of the government and enjoy the basic constitutional safeguards and legal protection "in regard to their rights of person and property." However, there was a catch: "They continue to be aliens, having taken no steps towards becoming citizens, and incapable of becoming such . . . and therefore remain subject to the power of Congress to expel them, or to order them to be removed . . . from the country, whenever, in its judgment their removal is necessary or expedient for the public interest."[80] In fact, had Congress desired, it could have authorized the immediate removal of any Chinese laborer not in possession of a certificate without providing any opportunity to challenge the removal before a judge.[81]

Justices Brewer, Fuller, and, remarkably, Field, who had written the opinion in *Chae Chan Ping*, all dissented. They objected to the breathtaking scope of congressional power expressed by the majority. They also distinguished between individuals seeking to enter the United States and residents facing deportation; while exclusion was, for them, a component of congressional authority and a legitimate exercise of plenary power, deportation had to meet a higher standard. All three, in different ways, saw deportation as a form of punishment that required access to a far more rigorous form of process before it could be imposed.[82]

The Chinese community reacted to the ruling with shock and dismay. San Francisco newspapers reported that confidence in a court victory had been high, and rivals of the Six Companies used the defeat to challenge their leadership. Placards posted in the Chinese residential areas of the city attacked the Six Companies' president and offered $300 for his murder. He was removed from his post as the Six Companies sought to regain suddenly lost footing and trust in the community.[83] Across the country, tens of thousands of Chinese braced for enforcement, though the lawyers had one more gambit to try.

On May 24, another Chinese laborer, Ny Look, was also arrested in New York for being without a certificate. The arrest and his subsequent challenge were the next phase of the coordinated test strategy. Ny Look himself was well selected as a plaintiff. A sixty-five-year-old, white-haired man, he arrived for his court hearing by cab, and by some accounts was carried into court on a cot.[84] The *New York Times* reported that he was a Civil War veteran, having served honorably in the navy as a cook and been wounded in service.

When the judge inquired as to how this unexceptional man had been arrested, his lawyer, Joseph Choate, responded, "Oh, I suppose the Marshal was walking along the street and, finding him without a certificate, arrested him."[85] Choate, noted as a strong orator, had already made at least one appearance before the Supreme Court, would later be appointed ambassador to the Court of St. James, and would argue several additional high-profile cases before the Supreme Court.[86] In addition to Choate, Ny Look was represented by Maxwell Evarts, who like Choate had been involved in representing the plaintiffs in *Fong Yue Ting*. Evarts, whose father had served as secretary of state, attorney general, and a US senator, had attended Yale University and Harvard Law School, had served in the Vermont House of Representatives, and became counsel for the Southern Pacific Railroad.[87] The *Washington Post* speculated that the lawyers had arranged for Ny Look's arrest in New York because they believed that a New York judge, unlike a West Coaster, would decline to have him detained while the government was sorting out how to enforce the Geary Act.[88]

Ny Look's counselors offered to "prove by a credible white witness" that he had been a legal resident when the Geary Act was passed, but they offered no explanation or excuse for his failure to secure a certificate.[89] Their game now was a direct attack on the administrative process—or rather on Congress's and the executive branch's failure to design one. Circuit Judge Lacombe initially ruled in the case without providing a written opinion but produced one after Ny Look's attorneys requested it.[90] He acknowledged in the opinion that the now constitutionally validated statute required judges to order deportations in such factual circumstances, but then identified a problem. The Geary Act authorized Ny Look's arrest and his appearance in court but, beyond instructing judges to order deportation, made no administrative provisions for deportation to occur.[91] What, then, was he to do with his detainee? "I find no provision authorizing the United States judge, in such cases, to order the person found without certificate to be imprisoned for an indefinite time, while awaiting deportation."[92] To the amusement of the New York press, he ordered Ny Look's discharge, mandating that he be deported when proper administrative provisions were established for doing so. Ny Look, who was released and congratulated, departed the courtroom as he had arrived, by cab.[93] Joseph Choate's strategy paid off: copies of Judge Lacombe's opinion were immediately sent to the US attorney general and slated for distribution across the federal bench.[94]

Judge Lacombe's ruling provoked vigorous speculation as to what would happen next. The *Washington Post*, while claiming that his ruling was unquestionably correct, expressed concern that the New York pronouncement would stir up "the good people of Seattle to another mass-meeting and the arraignment of Judge Lacombe in the same anarchistic category to which they have already consigned the President and Attorney General" when the initial announcement was made that they would not seek immediate and vigorous enforcement.[95] The ruling, if extended nationally, would render enforcement of the Geary Act against resident Chinese quite difficult, as it prevented their detention until the government could construct an administrative process to engineer their removal.

This proved to be no small concern, given the massive resistance. Congressional authorities reviewing the situation found that eighty-five thousand unregistered Chinese aliens resided in the United States and estimated that it would cost between $7 and $10 million to remove them all.[96] The original appropriation for enforcement totaled $60,000, aimed primarily at covering the costs of deportation.[97] The pause on enforcement announced on May 4 continued, and Chinese diplomats pressed the United States to extend the deadline for registration and soften plans for enforcement. West Coast xenophobes exploded in rage, and mobs threatened Chinese residents in some cities.[98] Some members of the anti-Chinese Labor League attempted to take enforcement into their own hands by going to court to complain about the presence of unregistered laborers, and a few district judges issued warrants in response to the complaints.[99]

In the fall, Congress finally responded to internal demands for enforcement, pressure by the Six Companies and other US advocates for the Chinese, and diplomatic pressure from China by passing additional legislation. The compromise crafted in the McCreary Amendment extended the registration period for six more months and discontinued prosecutions and deportation orders brought under the original legislation. In exchange, the Six Companies and other advocates for the Chinese dropped their opposition, and resident Chinese rushed to register before time ran out.[100] While the Six Companies would continue to advocate for individual Chinese, the Court had closed the door to constitutional attacks on Congress's broad regulatory authority. Legal challenges in the future would focus more on the line between administrative discretion and judicial oversight, and on what kind of process would be necessary for individuals challenging exclusion or deportation orders.

Administrative Discretion and Its Limits and the Creation of the Illegal Alien

While the courts continued to provide some oversight, Congress used its plenary power to regulate and restrict Chinese immigration further. In 1894, Congress included in the General Appropriation Act a provision that made any decision by an immigration or customs officer to exclude an alien from admission into the United States final unless the secretary of the Treasury reversed it upon appeal.[101] In a high-profile challenge, Maxwell Evarts represented Lem Moon Sing, a merchant and member of a San Francisco wholesale and retail drug firm who was denied reentry after a business trip for a few years to China. Justice Harlan, writing for the Court, rebuffed the challenge despite Lem Moon Sing's claim that he had been improperly excluded and that his exclusion threatened property and liberty interests protected both by the Constitution and by treaties.[102] While the Court's majority explicitly declined to consider whether Sing was "entitled of right under some law or treaty to reenter the United States," the justices agreed that Congress had properly assigned the task of final determination to officers of the executive branch.[103]

The following year, a case involving four Chinese men who had been subjected to the penal provision of the Geary Act reached the Supreme Court. While the registration provision of the Geary Act threatened nonregistrants with deportation a year from its adoption, Section 4 had gone into effect immediately, allowing any Chinese person accused of being in the United States unlawfully to be taken before a judge or commissioner and sentenced to up to a year's imprisonment at hard labor prior to deportation.[104] In the summer of 1892, the deputy director of customs in Detroit charged the men with being "Chinese persons unlawfully within the United States," and the commissioner of the circuit court agreed, sentencing them to sixty days' hard labor followed by immediate deportation. While their legal representative, Frank Henry Canfield, referred to them as poor men, Canfield was likely hired by the Six Companies or another organization to pursue the case. He was a member of the legal elite and an admiralty law specialist, and had assistance from another prominent litigator from Chicago.[105]

The case, *Wong Wing v. United States*, languished on the Court's crowded appellate docket for two years, and in the interim, the cases validating other portions of the Geary Act went forward.[106] Upon finally hearing the case, the Supreme Court readily agreed that deportation could take place on the say-so of administrators, but the justices also agreed unanimously that criminal punishment was different. "When Congress sees fit to . . . subject . . . such aliens to infamous punishment at hard labor, or by confiscating their property, we think such legislation, to be valid, must provide for a judicial trial to establish the guilt of the accused."[107] Anyone in the United States fell under the protection of the Thirteenth and Fourteenth Amendments, which guaranteed that even aliens had the right to formal presentment of criminal charges and full due process before being held accountable for significant crimes.[108]

The sweeping legislative changes of the 1880s and early 1890s had another important effect. Prior to registration, Chinese could and did evade the various restrictions on immigration, entering the United States without authorization or under false pretenses. The registration requirement and the Geary Act's thwarted attempt to impose administratively determined criminal punishments against Chinese without certificates generated for the first time a broadly popular, simple distinction between legal and illegal immigrants who were residing in the United States. While *Wong Wing* confirmed that aliens present in the United States illegally had some basic constitutional rights, the developments of this period both popularized the category of the illegal alien in many white citizens' minds and racialized the category.[109]

Exclusion and its enforcement produced different forms of illegality. Some Chinese were undocumented, having crossed the border in secret, often by land. Others were fraudulently documented, coming into the United States and remaining there with immigration documents that identified them improperly as having an exempt status, "likely that of a merchant or returning resident."[110] Another category encompassed young women brought into the United States to supply "a thriving network of organized prostitution in Chinese immigrant communities."[111] And developments in the law at the end of the nineteenth century introduced a new and growing category: the fraudulent citizen, who falsely claimed citizenship through birth in the United States or descent from a citizen.[112] Some small number of these illegal residents eventually became legal. They were mostly immigrant women who, under the protection and supervision of mission homes, escaped prostitution and became the wives of Chinese men who sought arranged marriages through the missions.[113] Most, however, if they succeeded in entering the United States, lived precariously, at risk of deportation if they were found not to be legal residents.

With significant numbers of Chinese in the United States without authorization and an environment of increasing hostility against all Chinese regardless of class or status, even legal residents had plenty to fear from a state determined to enforce limits. The legislative and administrative developments in the late 1880s and early 1890s maintained and increased the strong atmosphere of suspicion directed at Chinese seeking to enter the United States through the most common ports of entry.

Moreover, they augmented the idea of the illegal resident alien—the person who, merely by living in the United States, was committing an act against the American state.

While these illegal residents could not be punished through summary administrative action, they could be identified and ousted from the country with little recourse to formal judicial review. Congressional action and administrative implementation, responding to heavy political pressure from West Coast xenophobes, created the illegal and deportable alien as a status-based category in law and procedure. These actions, however, neither prevented Chinese from entering the United States without documentation or with fraudulent documentation nor established an enforcement regime that systematically identified and ousted these aliens.

Most important, neither Congress nor the Treasury Department or any other federal agency specifically took action against the children of these aliens born in the United States. By the mid-1890s, even as the Supreme Court considered and largely approved expanding congressional efforts to control Chinese migration and residence, another line of case law regarding the American-born children of these Chinese residents was developing in the lower federal courts.

Early Cases Addressing Chinese American Citizenship

The first reported case to grapple with the question of Chinese eligibility for American citizenship was *In re Ah Yup*, decided in 1878.[114] Ah Yup applied for citizenship, using the standard petition required of prospective citizens, and everyone agreed that, aside from his being a Chinese native, he fulfilled all the other statutory criteria. His attorney, Benjamin S. Brooks, was a lawyer representing the Chinese Six Companies and had previously represented Chinese interests in a congressional commission investigating Chinese immigration.[115] The question framed by circuit judge Sawyer was whether the general statute authorizing naturalization at the national level could be interpreted to permit the naturalization of "a native of China of the Mongolian race."[116] In 1870, Congress had amended the naturalization statute to take the Thirteenth and Fourteenth Amendments into account. The body extended naturalization to "aliens of African nativity, and to persons of African descent" but did not address the long-standing limitation of nat-

Considerations of Chinese Birthright Citizenship Prior to *Wong Kim Ark*

- *In re Ah Yup*, 1 F. Cas. 223 (C.C.D. Cal. 1878): Chinese could be barred from naturalization.
- *State v. Ah Chew*, 16 Nev. 50 (1881): In dicta, the court claimed that the Reconstruction Amendments did not confer citizenship upon "the Mongolian race, except such as are born in the United States."
- *In re Look Tin Sing*, 21 F. 905 (C.C.D. Cal. 1884): Son of a merchant born in the United States found to be a citizen.
- *Ex parte Chin King*, 35 F. 354 (C.C.D. Oregon 1888): Daughters of a merchant held to be citizens.
- *In re Yung Sing Hee*, 38 F. 437 (C.C.D. Oregon 1888): Daughter of a Chinese merchant found to be a citizen.
- *In re Wy Shing*, 36 F. 553 (C.C.N.D. Cal. 1888): Son of a Chinese laborer found to be a citizen.
- *Gee Fook Sing v. United States*, 49 F. 146 (9th Cir. 1892): Man born in San Francisco found to be a citizen despite having lived in China since the age of three.
- Related ruling: *In re MacFarlane*, 11 Haw. 166 (1897): Son of British parents permitted to register his steamer under the Hawaiian flag because he had been born in Hawaii.

uralization to "free white persons," a phrase inadvertently omitted but then reinserted in a correction.[117]

In one of the earliest attempts by a US court to understand race beyond the categories of Black and white, the opinion reviewed dictionary and encyclopedia definitions, ultimately concluding that "neither in popular language, in literature, nor in scientific nomenclature, do we ordinarily, if ever, find the words 'white person' used in a sense so comprehensive as to include . . . the Mongolian race."[118] Based on this, and the legislative reinsertion of the restriction, the court ruled against Ah Yup based on his race.[119] The case had other repercussions as well: Yung Wing, a Chinese man who moved to the United States as a young man, earned a degree from Yale, and married into an elite New England family, had naturalized successfully in 1852. In 1898, his citizenship was revoked while he was abroad. Wong Chin Foo, who had grown up in the

United States, also had his passport recalled and revoked in 1898 pursuant to a new policy from the State Department stating that passports were to be denied to any "Chinese holding naturalization papers that were issued before March 6, 1882, or at any other date."[120]

The first court to address the question of American-born Chinese eligibility for citizenship may have been the Nevada Supreme Court, though its mention was clearly an aside. In 1881, Chinese defendant Ah Chew was convicted of selling opium to Frank Connor in violation of a Nevada law that barred the sale of opium without a valid prescription by a licensed physician. Ah Chew objected on several grounds, including that the empaneled jury was unconstitutional under the Fourteenth Amendment. The Nevada Supreme Court clarified that the Reconstruction Amendments "did not confer the right of citizenship upon the Mongolian race, except such as are born within the United States."[121] This aside, however, was not a definitive point in the case.

The first major reported case involving a Chinese litigant produced a panel ruling from the circuit court, for which Associate Justice Field, serving as a circuit judge, wrote the opinion. Look Tin Sing was born in Mendocino, California, in 1870 to parents who had resided there for at least twenty years. Look Tin Sing was no common laborer—his father was a merchant, though, as the parties agreed, not a diplomat or other official representative of the Chinese government. Look Tin Sing's father sent his son to China in 1879, intending for him to return, which Look Tin Sing did in September 1884. Because Look Tin Sing was not a laborer, he did not apply for a certificate under the 1882 legislation requiring them for laborers; he expected to be admitted as the son of a merchant and as a citizen. He was, however, denied entry because he had no certificate.[122]

The young man's family was apparently determined to achieve a good outcome. The case was handled by Thomas Riordan and William M. Stewart, a prominent railroad attorney, former attorney general of California, and, at the time of the case, a senator from Nevada. In the case, US district attorney Foote apparently raised the question of citizenship "at the insistence of the Department of Justice."[123] He argued that Look Tin Sing owed his allegiance to the emperor of China and was therefore ineligible for citizenship.[124]

Justice Field launched in with an analysis of the Fourteenth Amendment, focusing on the "subject to the jurisdiction" clause. He read the clause as encompassing those "who are within their [the United States'] dominions and under the protection of their laws, and with the consequent obligation to obey them . . . and only those subject by their birth or naturalization are within the terms of the amendment."[125] He then explained his view of the American rule allowing the transfer of allegiance, explaining that individuals could effectively transfer their allegiance from their countries of birth to new national homes. This right, he noted, was specifically protected in the Burlingame Treaty.[126]

With this foundation established, Justice Field examined the situation of the petitioner, noting that "the jurisdiction of the United States over him at the time of his birth was exclusive of that of any other country."[127] He understood the purpose of the Fourteenth Amendment to be not only to establish "an authoritative declaration of the generally recognized rule of the country," but also to overrule *Dred Scott* specifically. The dismantling of *Dred Scott*, in his view, changed the status of Black Americans to citizens. By eliminating the liminal status of the freedman, the amendment established that all native-born persons stood on an equal footing. Furthermore, he reasoned, the elimination of this category of status provided a crucial precedent. Prior to emancipation, or perhaps the Fourteenth Amendment, Black individuals could not become citizens, but their inability to become citizens—and for their children to become citizens—was erased. In other words, birth to a person who was ineligible for citizenship no longer mattered.[128]

For Field, with *Dred Scott*'s birth barrier removed, the case at hand involved a simple continuation of the principles already operating with respect to other children born to alien parents. He reviewed *Lynch v. Clark*, noting the comprehensive analysis of the question there and adopting it. In that case, he noted, the place of birth was the only question, not the status of the parents.[129] Field also rejected the district attorney's attempt to bar reentry on the basis of Look Tin Sing's Chinese ancestry as a trump even over citizenship. Field noted impatiently that as the son of a merchant, Look Tin Sing was exempt from the certificate requirement, but beyond this technicality, Look Tin Sing belonged to the United States, not China. Requiring an American citizen to "look to the government of a foreign country for permission to return to the United States" was outrageous, and excluding a citizen from the country could only happen as part of a criminal proceeding: "Exclusion for any other cause is unknown to our laws, and beyond the power of Congress."[130] Look Tin Sing was a citizen and therefore was entitled to entry.

Justice Field's analysis quickly proved influential. In 1888, a British ship arrived in Portland. A Chinese girl, Chan San Hee, and a young woman, Chin King, were detained aboard and forbidden to land by the collector of customs, who objected because neither had a return certificate. They claimed through their attorney that they were natural-born citizens.[131] The hearing revealed their story. Their father, Chung Yip Gen, was a Chinese merchant who had been doing business in Portland for thirteen years and in San Francisco for more than a decade before. He had married in San Francisco twenty-three years earlier, and Chin King had been born there. Chan San Hee had been born in Portland. In 1881, the daughters traveled to China with their mother, "from whence they were to return when they pleased."[132]

The judge in the case was Oregon's only district court judge, Matthew P. Deady. Judge Deady had begun his career as a politician supporting slavery in the 1850s. His views shifted during the Civil War, but his jurisprudence remained consistent in its approach: he preferred careful, narrow analyses that in constitutional cases hewed closely to the text.[133] Portland, while not as busy an Asian port as San Francisco, had substantial involvement in the import-export business, and some Chinese sought entry there. When Judge Deady encountered cases involving Chinese immigrants, like his colleagues in San Francisco, he sometimes gave significant weight to due process, voiding local ordinances that seemed to have little purpose other than to harass the Chinese. In two cases, he invalidated convictions of Chinese men who had been convicted of smoking or smuggling opium.[134] In 1886, he sternly directed a Portland grand jury to indict individuals who had mobbed and attacked Chinese residents.[135]

When Judge Deady considered the case of Chin King and Chan San Hee, he asserted first that a child born "within the allegiance—the jurisdiction—of the United States, is born a subject or citizen thereof, without reference to the political *status* or condition of its parents."[136] Turning to both the antebellum *Lynch* case and Justice Field's reasoning in *Look Tin Sing*, he reasoned that this case fell squarely within the bounds of accepted precedent. The district attorney had placed weight on the finding that the mother and daughters had not intended to return to the United States after their departure, claiming that this was disqualifying. Judge Deady, though, understood a minor child's birth as establishing that child's status as an American citizen, a status that "can only be lost or changed by the act of the party when arrived at majority, and the consent of the government."[137] Chin King's and Chan San Hee's status as citizens entitled them to the fundamental privileges and immunities protected for all citizens under the Constitution, including the freedom to travel. Judge Deady reached the same conclusion in another case he heard in 1888, ordering Yung Sing Hee to be released from custody.[138]

In 1888, the same question arose regarding Wy Shing, a young man born to a Chinese laborer and his wife in San Francisco. After his mother's death, Wy Shing's father sent his six-year-old son to China in the care of his uncle. Like many transnational Chinese, Wy Shing spent some time in China, returned to the United States, and then returned to China again, arriving in the port of San Francisco in 1888 just after the passage of more restrictive legislation.[139] Despite the fact that Wy Shing's father was still in California and had never left, Wy Shing was detained and denied entry. In a companion case, Wong Gan, a twenty-year-old man, claimed birth in San Francisco but had been living in China since he and his parents had traveled there together in 1881. Returning to the United States alone, he was also refused permission to disembark. Judge Sawyer made short work of the cases, citing Justice Field's opinion in *Look Tin Sing*. In addition to the respect he expressed (in formal public writing at least) for Justice Field, he noted that if *Look Tin Sing* had been decided incorrectly, "then children of Caucasian parentage, born under similar circumstances, are not citizens; and hundreds of thousands have, for years, been, unlawfully, enjoying and exercising all the rights of citizens, civil and political."[140]

Oregon judge Deady was part of a three-judge panel for the Ninth Circuit Court of Appeals in 1892 that considered a writ of habeas corpus filed for Gee Fook Sing. Gee Fook Sing was denied entry at the port of San Francisco and detained, but he petitioned for a writ of habeas corpus, protesting that he had been born in San Francisco and was a citizen. The writ was granted temporarily, but the investigating commissioner found that Gee Fook Sing was a "subject of the emperor of China," and a district court agreed.[141] On appeal, Judge Hanford, writing for a unanimous panel, confirmed that the measures excluding Chinese laborers did not apply to individuals born in the United States, even if such individuals' parents were not citizens and were ineligible to naturalize. Any individual claiming citizenship was entitled to "a hearing and a judicial determination of the facts so alleged," and Congress could not pass legislation closing off access to the courts on such matters.

These broad statements of principle, however, did not resolve the case. While all parties agreed that he was of Chinese parentage, he and his advocates claimed that he had been taken to China before he turned three and remained there until arriving in the United States in 1890. Under these circumstances, the Ninth Circuit ruled, his own evidence about his birthplace was not definitive, and worse yet, "he is corroborated on this vital point only by the testimony of other Chinese persons, who confessedly have seen him but a few times, and can give only hearsay evidence."[142] The appellate panel could not find a reason to reverse the district court's finding of fact that Gee Fook Sing had failed to establish himself as a birthright citizen.

The principle of birthright citizenship and the influential reasoning in *Look Tin Sing* had an impact even beyond the reach of organized litigation by the Chinese. In 1897, Hawaii's supreme court grappled with a question about an island resident's entitlement to register a steamer under the Hawaiian flag.[143] Objections were raised in part because MacFarlane's parents were British, though he had been born in Hawaii in 1847. The Hawaiian Constitution adopted after the American-sponsored Hawaiian revolution mirrored the language of the Fourteenth Amendment, declaring that all persons born or naturalized in the islands and subject to the Hawaiian Republic's jurisdiction were citizens of the republic.[144] Citing *Look Tin Sing*, *Chin King*, and *Gee Fook Sing*, the court claimed that the rule of birthright citizenship was at this point firmly established and not subject to further objection.[145]

Generally, between 1878 and the mid-1890s, district and circuit courts had several opportunities to look directly at the question of whether the general principle of birthright citizenship would extend to the children of a class of immigrants who themselves were not believed to be fit for citizenship. While the rulings clarified that evidence about birth would be closely scrutinized, these judges all agreed that the children of Chinese immigrants fell under the generally prevailing rule that extended citizenship to anyone born inside the United States.

Exclusion, Deportation, and the Problem of Citizenship

By the mid-1890s, Congress had constructed the system of exclusion, which was implemented and empowered through administrative processes. While the Supreme Court had weighed in on and modified some elements of it, it had largely upheld this system as a constitutional exercise of Congress's plenary power to control entrance to the nation by aliens. This system made Chinese exclusion and the deportation of individual Chinese an acceptable legal response to the perceived problem of mass Chinese immigration.

The Six Companies and other advocates for the Chinese vigorously resisted the imposition of exclusion. They fought through diplomatic channels, with efforts to influence important political figures in the executive branch and Congress, and in the court of public opinion. When they could not stave off regulation through these avenues, they went to court, drawing on the some of the best legal talent available to construct compelling test cases and take them all the way through to the US Supreme Court. After the passage of the Geary Act, the Six Companies also encouraged mass resistance with the goal of rendering registration too costly and onerous to enforce on the ground.

Despite the energy and resources poured into fighting exclusion and the new agenda of deporting long-term residents, advocates for the Chinese were largely unable to do more than slow the inexorable march toward the almost complete legal ban on Asian immigration that would come in the early twentieth century. By the mid-1890s, most of the substantive legal questions were settled. Advocates were left to press for more rigorous attention to fair procedure and reasonable weighing of evidence, rather than challenging the constitutionality of Congress's authority to act. Much of the power to decide the fate of individual Chinese was placed firmly in the hands of administrative agents.

The legal regime presented in the statute books and administrative rules, however, did not always reflect reality. The system of exclusion and deportation was porous in its actual workings. It often failed to block either the immigration or the long-term residency of many Chinese who were not in technical legal terms permitted to enter or remain under existing statutory criteria. The Chinese and their most virulent opponents were well aware of the shadows and loopholes, and outside of the elite world of congressional debates and habeas corpus appeals, Chinese immigrants and their descendants lived with uncertain status, whether or not they had legitimate papers. These uncertainties were heightened by the transnational lives that many Chinese men created, maintaining their connections with families in China while finding their economic livelihoods in the United States.

Yet even as all of this was happening, the courts confirmed, with increasing certainty, that the children of these marginal, threatened residents were themselves citizens due to their birth within the geographic boundaries of the United States. As the precedents piled up, Congress and the executive branch maintained their silence on the issue. Soon, the Supreme Court would have occasion to settle the question definitively.

4 | Who Was Wong Kim Ark?

Wong Kim Ark himself did not set out to become the plaintiff in a land-mark Supreme Court case. Nonetheless, as a resident of San Francisco's Chinese community, he lived through and observed the United States' development of a comprehensive and stringent system for regulating and limiting Chinese migration. He clearly understood how this system operated and took steps to minimize his risks under the law. Yet, as a member of the Chinese American community, he, like many other young men, chose to live a transnational life so that he could have a wife and family.

Wong Kim Ark's Transnational Life

There is some disagreement about the facts of Wong Kim Ark's life, beginning with the year of his birth. Most sources claim he was born in 1873; this is the year agreed upon by both sides in the famous 1898 Supreme Court case that bears his name. However, some evidence places his birth at least two years earlier, in part because Wong Kim Ark himself used the Chinese imperial calendar to name his birth date at least once, and the immigration official recorded that date as October 20, 1871.[1] Official birth records were not yet the norm. There seems to be general agreement that Kim Ark—as he would have been called (Wong being the family name)—was born in San Francisco at 751 Sacramento Street, the address of the business maintained by his parents. Wong Si Ping was identified as a merchant, a particularly valuable identity once entry into the United States was restricted to diplomats, students, and merchants by the 1882 Exclusion Act. His status as a merchant helps to explain Kim Ark's San Francisco birth—unlike laborers, merchants were entitled to bring their wives from China to the United States. Although the type of business Wong Si Ping was engaged in was unspecified in various affidavits, the name of the business was identified as Quong Sing,[2] and San Francisco directories from 1879 and 1880 identify that address as the establishment of Quong Song or Quong Son "butcher and provisions."[3] The business was located in Chinatown, not far from the present Embarcadero area and north of Union Square.[4] Wong Si Ping and Wong Kim Ark's mother, Wee Lee, had resided in San Francisco for some time, and the family residence must have been just upstairs from their business establishment.

Apart from his visits to China, Wong Kim Ark spent most of the time from his birth until his final 1931 departure from the United States living within about a two-block radius of his birthplace. The Chinese, facing increasing hostility on the West Coast as they came to the United States to work in mining camps and on the railroads, would have had very little discretion about where to live in San Francisco (or in other West Coast cities). Most Chinese could find accommodations only in the Chinatowns of cities with significant Chinese populations. Even when the Supreme Court heard his case in March 1897, both parties agreed to the facts as to the address of Kim Ark's birth and that "he has had but one residence, to-wit, a residence in said State of California, in the United States of America, and that he has never changed or lost said residence or gained or acquired another residence, and there resided claiming to be a citizen of the United States."[5] Wong Kim Ark probably had longtime friends and acquaintances in his neighborhood. However, when he wanted to leave and reenter the United States, most of them would have been regarded by immigration officials as unreliable witnesses or simply as liars; their race was compounded by their class.

Records identify Kim Ark as a cook from age eleven.[6] We do not know why he was unable to succeed his father in business and become a merchant himself. His father, who helped manage the butcher shop, was probably neither a proprietor nor sole proprietor of a business that bore another's name; perhaps the business was not sufficiently robust to offer work to the son. Kim Ark did have an older brother, and it may be that he took over for the father before he eventually returned to the family's ancestral village.[7] For whatever reason, Wong Si Ping's son became a member of what would be classified as the laboring classes. He had relatively little formal education, as best we know,[8] and although both his 1913 and 1931 affidavits were signed by him in both Mandarin and English, he spoke through a translator when he gave testimony for his sons in 1924, 1925, and 1926.

By the 1870s, it was getting harder for those of Chinese ancestry to work and live on the West Coast. Anti-Chinese violence had culminated in a massacre of a tenth of the Chinese population of Los Angeles in October 1871; ten of the eighteen Chinese victims had been publicly lynched.[9] In 1877 in San Francisco, amid a national economic depression that left many unemployed, the Workingmen's Party of California was formed, led by Denis Kearney, decrying "coolie" (unfree Chinese) labor that was perceived as taking white jobs and deploying the slogan "The Chinese must go!" Meeting ostensibly to call a labor strike on July 23 of that year, a mob formed and destroyed $100,000 in Chinese-owned property, burning laundries and leaving four dead.[10] A Seattle mob sought, over three days in February 1886, to forcibly expel the city's Chinese residents, taking their belongings to the dock, demolishing homes, and sending a number of Chinese off to other US cities.[11] A Denver anti-Chinese riot that began on October 31, 1880, destroyed homes, stores, and temples and resulted in one known death; the riot was linked to supporters of the Democratic Party, whose party newspaper had been writing about the "yellow peril."[12] According to one source, 153 anti-Chinese riots occurred in the West in the 1870s and 1880s.[13] The US Census of 1880 recorded 105,465 Chinese residents, and while at least 85 Chinese died as a result of anti-Chinese violence in the mid-1880s, some of the most violent anti-Chinese incidents occurred earlier and later than this period.[14]

Anti-Chinese sentiment found voice in the law of the West as well. As early as 1859, an Oregon constitutional amendment went into effect to stipulate that "no Chinaman, not a resident of the state at the adoption of this constitution, shall ever hold any real estate, or mining claim, or work any mining claim therein."[15] The California constitution of 1879 prohibited employment of Chinese by any business incorporated in California—or by the state or local governments.[16] The same document declared that "foreigners of the white race or of African descent, eligible to become citizens of the United States under the naturalization laws thereof, while bona fide residents of this State, shall have the same rights in respect to the acquisition, possession, enjoyment, transmission, and inheritance of property as native-born citizens."[17] Under that provision, Wong Kim Ark's parents would not have been able to purchase a business or residence if they did not already own them.

The Challenge of Finding a Wife

Another pair of laws—this time, federal—had material consequences for Kim Ark and must have concerned his parents. To whom could he be married? Few single Chinese women came to the United States. As discussed in chapter 2, the 1875 Page Act barred the importation of Chinese prostitutes, and virtually any young Chinese woman traveling without relatives was suspected of being brought to the country to become a prostitute, if she was not already one, or destined for a polygamous relationship.[18] The 1882 Chinese Exclusion Act reiterated the ban on prostitutes and banned the entry of Chinese laborers for ten years (a ban that would later become permanent); no female Chinese classified as a laborer could enter the United States, and likewise, no bride intended for a laborer such as Kim Ark could do so. The gender imbalance among the Chinese on the West Coast was stark. Estimates indicate that females constituted 7.2 percent of the Chinese population in the United States in 1870 but only 3.6 percent in 1890,[19] around the time Kim Ark might have been expected to search for a bride. California had banned intermarriage between white and Black individuals since 1850, but in practice, interracial marriages between Chinese and whites were not sanctioned even before California passed a 1905 law barring intermarriage between whites and "Mongolians," although Chinese could presumably marry Black persons and possibly Native Americans.[20] Federal district judge Lorenzo Sawyer, from the Northern District of California, who kept granting Chinese access to the courts when they filed habeas petitions, nevertheless stated in an 1886 letter what many surely hoped would happen:

> If they [the Chinese] would never bring their women here and never multiply and we would never have more than we could make useful, their presence would always be an advantage to the State. . . . When the Chinaman comes here and don't [*sic*] bring his wife here, sooner or later he dies like a worn out steam engine; he is simply a machine, and don't leave two or three or half dozen children to fill his place.[21]

In 1889, Wong Kim Ark, who was then aged between seventeen and nineteen, left for China with Wong Si Ping and Wee Lee.[22] His parents had decided to repatriate to China, though they had lived in the United States for at least twenty years and witnesses referred to them as permanent residents.[23] Rising anti-Asian sentiment may have played a role in their decision to move back to China, though their decision to return after a long sojourn in the United States was not highly unusual. Like many Chinese who lived for years in the United States, they may have considered themselves travelers whose home remained in the Pearl

River Delta rather than permanent immigrants.[24] But there was another agenda for taking Kim Ark there: to find a wife.

The voyage may not have been Kim Ark's first trip to China. According to one scholar, archival evidence suggests that he made the crossing as a small child. Traveling with his parents, he had attended school for three years in Ong Sing, the ancestral village in Taishan Province, returning to the United States in 1881, the year formal amendments to the Burlingame Treaty of 1868 went into effect.[25] The Burlingame Treaty had provided for the right of free voluntary travel between the United States and China; while the Angell Treaty's modifications temporarily suspended immigration of skilled and unskilled Chinese laborers, as a merchant, Kim Ark's father was not affected.[26] If, as it appears, the family maintained close ties to their home village in China, they would have been behaving typically.[27]

Wong Kim Ark's family returned to the United States from China just prior to the implementation of significant new federal restrictions on entry of persons of Chinese ancestry. Under the Chinese Exclusion Act of 1882, any new Chinese coming to the United States for the first time would need to be vetted in China. Any such nonlaborer

> shall be identified as so entitled [to enter the United States] by the Chinese Government in each case, such identity to be evidenced by a certificate issued under the authority of said government, which certificate shall be in the English language or . . . accompanied by a translation into English, stating such right to come, and which certificate shall state the name, title, or official rank, if any, the age, height, and all physical peculiarities, former and present occupation or profession, and place of residence in China.[28]

This was known as a Section 6 Certificate, after the section of the 1882 act in which this provision appeared.

For those returning to the United States, interrogation of a man's claim to merchant status would become increasingly searching (Had he ever done manual labor? What was the address of his business?); the interrogation of a merchant's wife and children was often even more so.[29] For a Chinese laborer attempting to return to the United States following passage of the Chinese Exclusion Act of 1882, the process was even more daunting and began even before such laborers left the United States. The collector of customs was to board any vessel carrying Chinese laborers and make a list of them "in which shall be stated the name, age, occupation, last place of residence, physical marks or peculiarities, and all facts necessary for the identification of each of such Chinese laborers, which books shall be safely kept in the custom-house." Laborers were then to be provided with the needed return certificate, which would entitle them to reenter the United States when they came back, "upon producing and delivering the same to the collector of customs."[30]

As discussed previously, Congress tightened and clarified this provision in 1884 by stipulating that for a laborer seeking reentry into the United States, a certificate of residence (known as a return certificate) "shall be the only evidence permissible to establish his right of re-entry," and the collector of customs "shall cause the same to be filed in the custom-house and duly canceled."[31] This modification eliminated the possibility that Chinese laborers could present witnesses to confirm their legal status if they were unable to produce the certificates. The return certificate was a single-trip document. As discussed in chapter 3, the Scott Act of 1888 invalidated return certificates issued to laborers that did not fulfill the new requirements and stranded about twenty thousand laborers with certificates issued prior to the act's passage who were abroad. The Supreme Court upheld the act.[32] Attempting to reenter from China after this time, Kim Ark would have to rely on his claim to have been born in the United States. The form he needed was a natural-born affidavit—also a single-trip form.

For persons who appeared to be natural-born white Americans, immigration officials usually merely asked for a correct statement about place of birth. To establish birthright citizenship at this time, a person of Chinese heritage, however, would have had to establish proof of *identity* and proof of *eligibility*.[33] Kim Ark's dress, education, queue, and demeanor would have raised strong suspicions among customs officials that he was a laborer—a member of a prohibited class of immigrants. Wong Kim Ark had apparently been working as a cook's apprentice in a mining camp in the Sierra Nevada prior to his departure to marry in 1889.[34] He was clearly not a merchant, a diplomat, a clergyman, a student, or a tourist; since he was not a resident laborer, only as someone born in the United States could he enter. One scholar has described the system in place that would have evaluated his request to reenter as "a racialized documents regime complicated by class, status, and gender."[35] This system used photos, notarized affidavits, witnesses, and sometimes lengthy investigative interviews to ferret out whether a person was genuinely entitled to enter. Many Chinese appeared to be well informed about these difficulties, and either Kim Ark or his parents took the necessary steps to secure his return in 1890. "In the year 1890 the said Wong Kim Ark departed for China upon a temporary visit and with the intention of returning to the United States, and did return thereto on July 26, 1890, on the steamship *Gaelic*, and was permitted to enter the United States by the collector of customs upon the sole ground that he was a native-born citizen of the United States."[36] In other words, the collector accepted the validity of his paperwork, though, as discussed later, the process was not entirely unproblematic for him.

The Transnational Family

Returning alone to the United States in 1890, Kim Ark left behind not only his parents but also a wife. He had married a young woman named Yee Shee, from a village near his familial one. It was surely an arranged marriage, and cultural traditions would have dictated that the wife live with her husband's family, becoming part of his family; women were even considered as property of a husband's family. It is probable, then, that Yee Shee lived with the repatriated parents of Wong Kim Ark. We do not know whether Kim Ark was often able to send support to his soon-to-be-growing family apart from his actual visits to see them.

With entry into the United States becoming increasingly difficult for persons, particularly women, of Chinese ancestry, men such as Kim Ark began a rather common pattern of travel to China to see their wives and families. Such trips were expensive for a cook, but the cost of transporting a wife and then supporting her in the United States was not inconsiderable. For Kim Ark, even had he been able to afford the expense, he faced other barriers; only members of the exempt classes could bring wives to the United States after 1882, and a laborer had no such option.[37] However, Kim Ark claimed to be a citizen, and for most American males who married foreign women in the latter half of the nineteenth century, their wives became citizens upon marriage or upon the naturalization of the husband. The 1882 Chinese Exclusion Act had declared Chinese ineligible for naturalization, and since Yee Shee herself could not be lawfully naturalized, she did not become a citizen of the United States by marriage.[38] But could she have accompanied Kim Ark to California? The treatment of Chinese wives of American-born citizens of Chinese ancestry at the border was at best inconsistent, and it became increasingly daunting for them to attempt entry.[39] Whether both came together or a wife came to join her husband, immigration officials separated the two and asked both a barrage of questions designed to identify inconsistencies in their claims, knowledge of the other, and details of their families and marriage. If the marriage was an arranged one and the spouse had never met her partner, which was not uncommon, officials were likely to rely on these inconsistencies to determine that the marriage was fraudulent.[40] They were also on the lookout for polygamous relationships, common in China but illegal in the United States. There is no evidence that Wong Kim Ark ever seriously considered trying to bring his wife to the United States under this harsh regime. In 1926, Kim Ark asserted that his wife was still alive and living in the village of Ong Sing, his ancestral village.[41]

We know more about the area from which the Wong family had migrated, and to which they returned. One of his sons, Yook Jim Wong (Americanized name) or Wong Yook Jim, was born in 1913 in the "Toisan area of Guangdong province in southeastern China."[42] As discussed in chapter 2, Guangdong Province lies immediately north of Hong Kong and includes Shenzhen and the city of Canton, now known as Guangzhou. Toisan is local dialect, known more commonly as Taishan or Toishan, and lies in the Pearl River Delta.[43] Taishan refers to itself as the "First Home of the Overseas Chinese." An estimated half a million Chinese Americans are of Taishanese descent.[44] Such a large percentage of the nineteenth-century migrants to American cities came from this region that the local dialect was dominant in American Chinatowns until the late twentieth century.[45] A very small number of villages and lineages dominated migration to the United States in this period; the limited number of family names is another indication of this pattern.[46] Some Chinese left for the United States without formal permission when gold was discovered in California and when labor was needed for the railroads; additional "push" factors leading to out-migration included rural food scarcity. Foreign migration increased after 1860, when late Qing dynasty restrictions on emigration were lifted. Chinese departing for the United States left from "treaty ports" where foreign merchants were allowed to trade (including Hong Kong).[47] The overseas Chinese in the late nineteenth and early twentieth centuries, or *wah kiu*, provided important financial support to relatives in their home villages in Taishan and were treated as heroes.[48] Wong Kim Ark, like many, clearly sent money to his wife at least once.[49]

Before Kim Ark returned to the United States in 1890, he and his wife conceived their first son, Wong Yook Fun, who was born in Taishan after Wong Kim Ark returned to California. Despite the record's contrary suggestion in his 1898 Supreme Court case, it appears that Kim Ark's reentry in 1890 was not completely smooth. Kim Ark carried his native-born affidavit that he had duly obtained before departing. He also had testimony from two witnesses—a white lawyer and a Chinese merchant gave statements to the Chinese consul to attest to Kim Ark's identity and his birth in the United States. The white lawyer claimed he came to know the family when he was a deputy tax assessor, that the family had lived in the same place for at least six years prior to 1875, and that he was therefore confident that "Wong Kim Ock [*sic*]" had been born in San Francisco. The other witness, a Chinese merchant, swore that he knew Kim Ark's father well, and that the son was born in San Francisco.[50] An unnamed Bureau of Immigration official, perhaps suspicious, attempted to verify the white lawyer's claims. He found the lawyer at the address provided, but others in the building were uncertain what work the witness did; a photo of Wong Kim Ark was not recognized on that first trip, but on the second trip, everyone seemed to recognize him. This official left a note in the file questioning the veracity of Kim Ark's claims.[51]

Wong Kim Ark may not have been aware of the notation in his 1890 file, but he likely knew that taking the proper steps to assure one's reentry was no guarantee of readmission for persons of Chinese ancestry. Kim Ark traveled again to China in 1894 to rejoin his wife in his family's village. He may have planned this trip in a state of some anxiety. An epidemic of bubonic plague erupted in Canton, probably in February, though it was not publicly acknowledged in China until March.[52] In June, the news reached the United States via the steamer *Belgic* that the plague was ravaging both Canton and Hong Kong, with death rates still in the neighborhood of two hundred per day in Canton after reaching rates of five hundred per day in March and April.[53] The case fatality rate among Chinese who contracted the disease was reported as almost 96 percent.[54] Plague cases had begun to emerge near Guangzhou in 1892, but when the disease reached Canton and Hong Kong, it exploded in these heavily populated areas.[55] Both British and Chinese doctors agreed that the disease struck down women and children with particular ferocity.[56] The major epidemic had quieted by August, but cases were still intermittently reported.[57]

Wong Kim Ark's Famous Trip

As with his previous trip, he prepared carefully. Ten days before his departure for China aboard the steamer *Belgic* on November 15, 1894,[58] Kim Ark appeared before the notary public for the City and County of San Francisco with a photograph and produced a typed "Application of Alleged U.S. Citizen for Reentry into the United States" (known as a native-born affidavit). Kim Ark presumably signed a statement, possibly in Chinese and English (applications in 1913 and 1931 were signed by him in both languages). For proof of identity, three witnesses also appeared and signed the affidavit, claiming that "the said Wong Kim Ark is well known to us," with additional details about him and his address. Apparently, Kim Ark would have arrived in Ong Sing "in time for the Dongzhi holiday, at which Chinese traditionally connect with family and make offerings to ancestors."[59] Fortunately, his family had remained healthy, and was soon to grow. On this visit, Kim Ark met his oldest son for the first time, and he and Yee Shee conceived their second son, Wong Yook Thue.[60]

When Kim Ark was detained upon his attempted return to the United States in 1895, District Attorney Henry Foote claimed Kim Ark's "[minimal] education and political affiliation" (as a subject of the emperor of China) overcame his claim to citizenship.[61] Calling all Chinese in America subjects of the emperor of China was not just a stereotypical assumption about their loyalties: at the time, the Chinese government held to a "doctrine of perpetual allegiance" such that a Chinese citizen's bonds were indissoluble and natural.[62] This citizenship regime did not change until 1909, and prior to that, even when a person of Chinese descent was naturalized elsewhere, under Chinese governance, they did not cease to be subjects of the emperor.

Despite the federal courts' consistent rulings in the 1880s and early 1890s, immigration officials and even some judges often viewed Chinese born in the United States as "accidental citizens"—citizens by technicality alone. Many officials thought citizenship by birth for persons of Chinese heritage was not appropriate, since all Chinese were, as of 1882, ineligible for naturalization. They were considered unassimilable, immoral, and even dangerous to the moral fabric of the nation.[63] When Wong Kim Ark attempted to reenter the United States in 1895, District Attorney Henry Foote wrote that his claim to citizenship was based on mere "accident of birth."[64] As the next chapter will describe, Foote was searching for a viable test case of the birthright citizenship matter. Wong Kim Ark was not looking for notoriety, but his attempt to reenter the United States in 1895 became that test case.[65]

Documenting Identity

Wong Kim Ark clearly recognized that Chinese would-be entrants were subject to far more searching investigation at the border than persons presumed to be white. He was well aware of the importance of properly completed forms, witnesses, and photographs in crossing back and forth between the United States and China. Passports—or any type of identification documents—were rarely used to manage entrance at the borders of the United States at the time of Wong Kim Ark's first trips to China, except for the Chinese. After passage of the Chinese Exclusion Act of 1882, Chinese merchants, students, and diplomats had to be distinguished from Chinese laborers; efforts to exclude and remove the latter accelerated; and the 1892 Geary Act required Chinese residents to register, obtain, and carry at all times certificates of residency or face deportation.[66] Deportation became an important element of US immigration control,[67] and the Los Angeles area became a center of deportation raids after the Geary Act, though as described in chapter 3, the Chinese organized, resisted, and fought back in the courts.[68] Government-issued identification documents became essential for those of Chinese ancestry, and by the late 1890s, Chinese seeking to enter the United States knew that these documents would be closely inspected and questioned.

Free movement was more or less available for the white population in the nineteenth century; identification documents were chiefly employed to manage travel through Indian territory, to police the movement of slaves and free Black denizens in slave states, and, during the Civil War, to police military desertion.[69] During the American Revolution, the United States began issuing identifying documents to try to protect American sailors against impressment, and in 1796, mariners could obtain new identity certificates from US customhouses that offered proof of American citizenship.[70] Some nineteenth-century travelers such as diplomats and commercial agents used travel documents to enter and leave the country, and tourists might acquire single-use passports to travel to other countries, though most Americans had no need for these documents.[71]

During and after US entry into the first World War, the use of passports began to spread more generally, although there is no evidence
that Wong Kim Ark acquired one for his trip to China in 1931. In May
1918, the US Congress passed the Travel Control Act, allowing the president to require passports during times of war; this passport requirement
remained until 1921. Some scholars, however, date the emergence of
the modern international "passport regime" to the aftermath of World
War I,[72] when a large number of Europeans became stateless refugees,
partly as a result of changes to national boundaries. In 1920, after con-
ducting the Provisional Committee on Communications and Transit
Conference on Passports, Customs Formalities and Through Tickets,
the League of Nations called on the international community to issue
passports.[73] When Lenin, in 1921, revoked citizenship for some hundreds of thousands of expatriate Russians who fled west during the Revolution, the League began issuing what came to be known as "Nansen
passports."[74] While these were internationally recognized documents for
travel, some nations, including Canada, refused entry or citizenship to
their holders.[75] The United States was not a party to the League and did
not accept these refugees either; the quotas measures of 1921 and 1924
effectively precluded entry for most stateless refugees. In the United
States, at the height of exclusionist fever, the desire to keep out large in-
fluxes of foreigners and potential spies helped drive the domestic intro-
duction of passports.[76] The use of passports by nation-states increasingly
became the standard, and in 1926, the United States passport appeared
in its current form.[77]

Birth certificates were not part of the documentation regime at this
time, and it was extremely unlikely that Wong Kim Ark's parents had
such a document for their son. Prior to the early twentieth century,
birth registration and certification were completely within the domain
of individual states, and documents varied accordingly.[78] Many rural
residents, persons born at home, and children of immigrants did not
have formal documents. The Progressive Era brought new efforts to
count, register, and control populations, including "disciplines of birth
registration and certification."[79] The move toward standardization and
centralization culminated in 1902 with congressional establishment of
the Bureau of the Census as a permanent agency of the federal government, authorizing it to develop "registration areas" for births.[80] These
steps were frequently deemed public health measures; Julia Lathrop,
as chief of the new Children's Bureau, produced a 1912 publication

entitled *Birth Registration: An Aid in Protecting the Lives and Rights of Children.*[81] As immigration from Europe grew quickly, reformers pressed the US Bureau of the Census to register births, and gradually a universal method was developed and adopted by the states.[82] It was not until the Social Security of Act of 1935, when recipients were required to obtain official proof of age, that Americans had a material incentive to acquire birth certificates.[83] A standardized birth certificate could also document a claim to birthright citizenship.

In this context, it is unsurprising that when Wong Kim Ark was detained in San Francisco Harbor in 1895, he had no birth certificate and no passport. He had the official documents he had dutifully obtained prior to departure for China. By obtaining and presenting these documents rather than alternatives that were just beginning to be standardized and institutionalized, he was complying with what would have been expected of an individual of Chinese ancestry hoping to enter the United States legally through a western port.

Wong Kim Ark's Case in the Public Eye

Denied entry and held offshore in San Francisco Harbor on the steamer *Coptic* until it departed, Kim Ark was transferred first to the *Gaelic*, and then the *Peking* from August 1895 to January 1896.[84] During his habeas appeal, Kim Ark was only freed from custody and allowed to land when the federal district court of the Northern District of California held that he was, indeed, a citizen of the United States by birth. He returned to San Francisco in January 1896, but the US government appealed the case, and his legal battle was far from over.

The case attracted considerable interest in 1896. At least 79 newspapers ran a story about the district court decision between January 3 and 6, 1896, and at least 115 more did so—a number of them weeklies—between January 7 and 11, 1896, though most of the newspapers repeated the same short piece.[85] The media and the public recognized that the stakes of Wong Kim Ark's habeas petition were quite significant. A Chinese source told the *San Francisco Call* that at least a thousand native-born citizens such as Wong Kim Ark resided in San Francisco at the time of the district court decision.[86]

Given the importance of the issue, it might seem surprising at first that the Supreme Court decision handed down on March 28, 1898, did not garner more widespread attention in the press. Coverage in the *New York Times* was brief. The thirteen-line paragraph announced in its title, "Chinese Born Here Are Citizens."[87] However, the Wong Kim Ark decision was issued the very day the US Naval Court of Inquiry determined (perhaps erroneously) that a mine blew up the *Maine* in Havana Harbor. The fervor to blame Spain and go to war eclipsed any significant coverage. Attention was directed toward Congress and to the president's report on the sinking of the *Maine*.

Notices of the Supreme Court decision did appear in at least 129 papers,[88] such as the *Springfield Republican, Omaha World Herald, Cleveland Plain Dealer, Kansas City Star, Boston Journal, Jackson Citizen Patriot, Butte Weekly Miner, Trenton State Gazette, Augusta Chronicle, Indiana State Journal,* and *New York American.* The majority of the stories republished one of two articles, though a few editorialized. The *Topeka State Journal* (June 29, 1898) claimed that this decision, "the most important regarding citizenship since the famous Dred Scott case has received very little attention at the hands of the people and press, probably because of the war with Spain." Titled "20,000 New Voters," this article pointed to the twenty thousand–plus Chinese residents of the Hawaiian Islands, a territory on course to become part of the United States, and clearly disapproved of the prospect of these Chinese becoming US citizens with a guaranteed right to vote. The piece, lacking a byline, foresaw a conflict with the Fourteenth Amendment as read by the two-thirds of Supreme Court justices holding for Wong Kim Ark: the Newlands resolution (then in the Senate but soon passed by both houses on July 4, 1898) would not allow these Chinese to enter the United States.[89]

The citizenship status of Chinese residents of the recently annexed territory of Hawaii would, indeed, generate controversy (see also chapter 6). Whatever the Supreme Court had just said about those persons of Chinese ancestry such as Wong Kim Ark who were born within the continental United States, most members of Congress were reluctant to incorporate Hawaiian indigenous people and descendants of Chinese residing in Hawaii into the American nation.[90] A bill advanced by Illinois senator Cullom subsequent to his appointment to the commission created by the Newlands resolution to establish a government for Hawaii provided "that all persons who were citizens of the Republic of Hawaii on August 12, 1898, are to be citizens of the United States," thus leaving out nearly all of the Chinese and Japanese residents.[91] Apparently "the decisions to deny U.S. citizenship to the majority of Hawaii's population and to extend the Chinese Exclusion Act to the Hawaiian Islands provoked little if any controversy."[92] As will be discussed further in chapter 6, the *Insular Cases* of 1901 did not provide closure on the issue of citizenship of residents of recently annexed territories.[93] The racial composition of territories more or less drove the calculus of how to configure citizenship for individuals now living under US sovereignty.

Wong Kim Ark's Experiences with the Documentary Regime

Despite his Supreme Court victory, Wong Kim Ark's problems with immigration officials were hardly over; he could not assume his citizenship would be recognized. His was a problem faced by many other birthright citizens of Chinese ancestry. Unless he carried around the 1898 Supreme Court decision with him, Wong Kim Ark would still have struggled to prove to anyone demanding identification that he was a US birthright citizen. The requirement in the 1892 Geary Act that persons of Asian heritage who resided in America carry with them a certificate of identity at all times or face deportation did not exempt Kim Ark or other citizens from suspicion. To avoid deportation, someone without a certificate of identity required testimony by a "credible white witness" to establish his or her lawful residence. Congress amended the statute in 1893 to require "at least one credible witness other than Chinese."[94] Whether or not the application for a certificate of identity he applied for in San Francisco in 1914 was his first, we know Kim Ark did apply after returning from his 1913–1914 trip to China. Perhaps he needed this document to obtain or keep work.

The intrepid Wong Kim Ark had to meticulously fill out the governmental form, "Application of Alleged American Citizen of the Chinese Race for Preinvestigation of Status," when he made trips to China in 1905, 1913, and 1931, despite the fact that his status as a citizen had long ago been settled by the Supreme Court—a fact never mentioned in any of the Angel Island records.[95] Even as a citizen, he had to go through the same process of acquiring a single- trip-use affidavit for each voyage, and Kim Ark had attorneys check his paperwork for each of these three trips.[96] Preparing to leave for China in 1913, Wong Kim Ark hired the law firm of Stidger and Kennah—perhaps the firm doing the greatest amount of work representing individual Chinese throughout the United States at the time[97]—seeking to make sure he would not encounter problems when returning to the United States. The law firm added to his application for a certificate of return the court documents confirming Wong Kim Ark's status as a native-born citizen of the United States.[98]

Oliver Stidger, a vocal critic of exclusion, had been hired by the Chinese Six Companies in 1908 for $2,400 per year, paid monthly.[99] By 1915, he was also the official attorney for the Chinese Chamber of Commerce, and the firm of Stidger, Stidger, and Kennah was one of the leading firms representing Chinese immigrants landing at Angel Island.[100] Henry C. Kennah, who joined the firm around 1912, had served as an immigrant inspector in San Francisco for several years early in the century, one of several lawyers for the Chinese with administrative experience.[101] Anti-immigration forces targeted the firm for their extensive work on behalf of the Chinese and successfully pursued disbarment of both lawyers; the Department of Labor claimed that they were involved in an international smuggling ring through which hundreds of Chinese entered through the port of San Francisco.[102]

Kim Ark's 1905 trip produced a third son, Wong Yook Sue, and his trip in 1913–1914 led to the birth of his youngest son, Wong Yook Jim.[103] We do not know whether all of the four sons linked to Wong Kim Ark were born to him or whether some were related in a different way, or were simply young men from his ancestral village seeking US entry as his sons (see the discussion of "paper sons" that follows). However, Kim Ark's youngest son reported that he had three older brothers, all of whom had died by the time he was interviewed.[104] There is no mention of daughters. There may be reason to believe that his youngest was actually his grandson, the son of the oldest boy, Wong Yook Fun.[105] Kim Ark's sons, although born in China, could claim derivative US citizenship, especially as long as there was no evidence that Kim Ark had another spouse.

However, Kim Ark's sons would not have an easy time trying to enter the United States given an ever-tightening exclusion regimen—and they all attempted the Pacific crossing. To get around increasingly harsh immigration restrictions, men of Chinese heritage seeking reentry to the United States often attempted to bring in others (often relatives) as their alleged sons. Some of these US residents and citizens sold the privilege to men back in China to generate income; they would report the birth of a son upon reentry to the United States, allowing them to then sell a place to someone without a chance to come to the United

States otherwise. While some of these transactions took place within extended families, merchants sometimes served as middlemen in the sale of positions. Regardless, false documents were created, giving someone a chance to impersonate a nonexistent son.[106] So-called paper sons, individuals who fraudulently claimed Chinese American fathers to circumvent immigration restrictions, attracted suspicion, and officials aggressively demanded proof of those claiming birthright citizenship.[107] By the end of the first decade of the twentieth century, derivative status had become a very common claim to rightful entry into the United States. Federal courts had also become more sensitive to rights claims and were more likely to hear habeas appeals from those claiming to be birthright citizens than from others challenging denial of permission to enter the United States.[108] Paper sons who successfully circumvented immigration restrictions by memorizing details about their alleged parentage and upbringing so that they could navigate the barrage of questions they would face, added to the gender imbalance in Chinese immigration.[109] After the San Francisco earthquake and fire of 1906 destroyed local birth records, the Chinese could assert native-born citizenship more readily. If they had to file habeas petitions upon landing, a favorable decision by the federal district court produced discharge papers that "created documentation of native-birth citizenship where none had previously existed."[110]

Kim Ark's eldest son, Yook Fun, had no luck entering the United States when he made the journey in 1910. Detained at Angel Island, the newly opened immigration facility that replaced the older facility at the Pacific Mail Steamship Company docks, Yook Fun was asked hundreds of questions, directed to diagram the village of Ong Sing, and pressed to describe the village's inhabitants. The Chinese inspector then wrote to Angel Island's chief inspector, suggesting that the father be asked similar questions. Several days later, Wong Kim Ark was interviewed in El Paso, with a witness to corroborate his testimony; we do not know why Kim Ark was in El Paso. The father answered a similar barrage of questions. The investigation produced ten discrepancies in their accounts, the most important of which concerned the age of Yook Fun when his grandmother died, whether the younger man had worked after quitting school, the number of houses in Ong Sing between their own house and an uncle's house, and the denomination of currency Kim Ark had sent to his wife when Yook Fun was six. These discrepancies were considered sufficient to deny landing to Yook Fun, and in January 1911 he was returned to China at the expense of the steamship company that brought him.[111]

After that, however, Kim Ark's sons fared better; even after the Johnson-Reed Act of 1924 established strict quotas and barred immigration from China altogether, sons of citizens continued to enter the United States. Yook Sue,[112] the third son, came in 1924, joined by second son, Yook Thue, and finally Yook Jim. All landed successfully between 1924 and 1926, suggesting that Wong Kim Ark and his family had learned how to navigate the highly restrictive system; Kim Ark's queue was now gone, and he wore Western dress. When Yook Thue arrived, immigration officials asked Kim Ark 56 questions, Yook Sue 91, and the intended immigrant 150; only one discrepancy occurred, and he was landed. Then, the family sent for the youngest, Yook Jim.[113] Giving testimony for Yook Jim, Kim Ark said that Yook Sue lived with him and worked in a San Francisco hotel as a pantry boy, that his second son, Yook Thue, worked in railway camps in Arizona, and that he himself had not had work as a cook for two months.[114]

Yook Jim, probably aged eleven, was detained for two or three weeks at the Immigration Station at Angel Island, but his entry proved reasonably easy. His father produced documentary proof that the son was born in China in 1914 and that he had promised to send the boy to an American school.[115] When Yook Jim was finally allowed to land, he stayed with his father for about six months. This was the first time father and son had been together, although Yook Jim's father may have been in China long enough to have seen his child born.[116] When Yook Jim was detained in 1926, it was at that point that Kim Ark had occasion to make the statement about his wife residing in China. After Yook Jim's release and brief period of residing with his father, he went back to China to finish high school.[117] Yook Jim said that he last saw his father around 1930 or 1931, when the young man returned to the United States. Yook Jim had trouble finding a job because of the Great Depression.

When Kim Ark applied to make a temporary visit to China in 1931, his residential address at 878 Sacramento Street, San Francisco, was a tenth of a mile, or a two-minute walk, from the address on the same street where he was born.[118] His application at that time indicated that he was five feet, seven inches tall and sixty-two years old, and that he had a scar on his right temple.[119] Kim Ark was probably no longer able to work at a physically arduous job. He did not return from this visit, and presumably retired from his trade.

Wong Yook Jim heard about his father's death shortly after World War II, in a letter from village elders. He had lost touch with his father during the wars of the 1930s and 1940s; letters between them were not getting through. He had been with his father less than three years, spread out over several separate periods.[120] Yook Jim served as a waiter in several US cities, was inducted into the US Army, and later joined the Merchant Marines during the Korean War, deciding to stay in for twenty-five years; he had the opportunity to travel the world.[121] He heard about his father's legal case when he was young but understood little about its significance. When some newspapers covered the hundredth anniversary of the court case, Wong Yook Jim saw the coverage and told his granddaughter, Alice, then a college student in California who was from Hong Kong.[122] While a handful of scholars had reviewed Wong Kim Ark's records, Wong Kim Ark's great-granddaughter also finally made the trip to the National Archives and Records Administration in San Bruno to find out more about her ancestor's role in the history of American citizenship.

Wong Kim Ark's parents lived and worked on Sacramento Street in San Francisco's Chinatown. Kim Ark would be born at 751 Sacramento Street five to seven years after this 1866 photograph was taken. Courtesy of the Library of Congress.

A STATUE FOR *OUR* HARBOR.

"A Statue for *Our* Harbor." Before the Statue of Liberty began to be assembled, this cartoon by George Frederick Keller appeared in the *San Francisco Illustrated Wasp* on November 11, 1881. (The Statue of Liberty's right arm with torch was being exhibited on the East Coast, and its head was exhibited in Paris.) Keller, born in Prussia in 1846, worked as sole cartoonist for the *Wasp* for roughly six years. Courtesy of The Ohio State University Billy Ireland Cartoon Library and Museum.

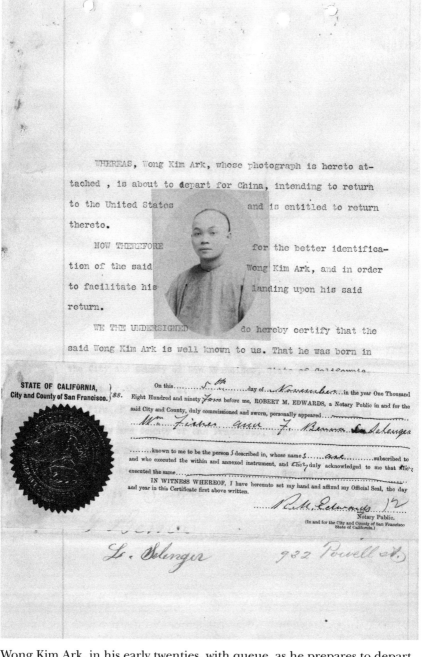

WHEREAS, Wong Kim Ark, whose photograph is hereto attached, is about to depart for China, intending to return to the United States and is entitled to return thereto.

NOW THEREFORE for the better identification of the said Wong Kim Ark, and in order to facilitate his landing upon his said return.

WE THE UNDERSIGNED do hereby certify that the said Wong Kim Ark is well known to us. That he was born in

L. Belanger   932 Powell St.

Wong Kim Ark, in his early twenties, with queue, as he prepares to depart for China in November 1894. He needed two witnesses to his identity. Sworn Statement of Witness Verifying Departure Statement of Wong Kim Ark. National Archives, San Francisco, Records of the Immigration and Naturalization Service. Courtesy of the National Archives.

Identification photograph filed with the Immigration Service in San Francisco in 1904, prior to Wong Kim Ark's May 19 departure on the steamer *China.* The document refers to US District Court, San Francisco Admiralty (Habeas Corpus) Case 11198, May 14, 1904–May 19, 1904. National Archives, San Francisco, Records of the Immigration and Naturalization Service. Courtesy of the National Archives.

Form 430 APPLICATION OF ALLEGED AMERICAN-BORN CHINESE FOR PREINVESTIGATION OF STATUS DUPLICATE 禀號貳

用所之證憑實立返而外由國美離欲生土爲禀專此

Department of Commerce and Labor

IMMIGRATION SERVICE

Office of COMMISSIONER OF IMMIGRATION
Port of PORT OF SAN FRANCISCO

....................................., 19....

To HON. SAMUEL W. BACKUS
COMMISSIONER Chinese and Immigrant Inspector,
PORT OF SAN FRANCISCO

SIR: It being my intention to leave the United States on a temporary visit abroad, departing and returning through the Chinese port of entry of SAN FRANCISCO................., I hereby apply, under the provisions of Rule 16 of the Chinese Regulations, for preinvestigation of my claimed status as an American citizen by birth, submitting herewith such documentary proofs (if any) as I possess, and agreeing to appear at such time and place as you may designate, and to produce then and there witnesses, for oral examination regarding the claim made by me.

This application is submitted in triplicate with my photograph attached to each copy, as required by said rule.

Respectfully,

Signature in Chinese 簽 唐 字 名 德金黃
Signature in English 蓋 番 字 名 Wong Kim Ark
Address 具禀人之住址 766 Clay St. S.F. Calif.

相簽制委亦憑國九而來人遊欲委管
二名間員親據出欺回茲外暫員理外
幅禀口之與呈世之即由埠離知知人
上供照辦人查有在該去之今邦美之入
並附例房到驗之美十埠將國由華出口

船落可方票號壹回換房辦公員委口入外理管到親要先之船落未禀此

SAN FRANCISCO

OCT 17 1913 ...., 19....

The triplicate of this application having been returned to me by the officer in charge at the port of intended departure, with advices that said officer is prepared to approve the original application, this duplicate is delivered to the applicant (with my signature written across the margin of the photograph), who must exchange it at the office of the immigration officer in charge at the port of departure for the original.

THIS DUPLICATE IS OF NO VALUE FURTHER THAN TO IDENTIFY THE HOLDER AS THE PERSON WHOSE STATUS HAS BEEN INVESTIGATED.

(Signed) Samuel W. Backus

11—2947

COMMISSIONER OF IMMIGRATION
PORT OF SAN FRANCISCO

Chinese and Immigrant Inspector.

Application of Alleged American-Born Chinese for Preinvestigation of Status. This was Wong Kim Ark's required travel document, with photo (without queue), that he would present upon return from China. The law firm of Stidger and Kennah attached to the application court documents confirming Wong Kim Ark's status as a native-born citizen of the United States. Issued October 17, 1913, and stamped upon his October 28 departure from San Francisco. Courtesy of the National Archives, San Francisco.

Spl. 5
U. S. DEPARTMENT OF LABOR
IMMIGRATION SERVICE

APPLICATION AND RECEIPT FOR CERTIFICATE OF IDENTITY

Application taken by _Yong Kay_ Date _NOV 9 1914_

NOV 1 - 1914

San Francisco, Cal., _____, 191

RECEIVED FROM COMMISSIONER OF IMMIGRATION, Port of San Francisco—

Certificate of Identity No. _17407_ , issued in the

Name _Wong Kim Ark_ Age _44_

Height : _5_ feet, _6_ inches. Occupation _Cook_

Place _S. F._ Admitted as _nat_

No. _13893_ S. S. _Korea_ Date _Nov 2, 1914_

Physical marks _Scar on right temple_
and right cheek bone.

Give first arrival and all subsequent trips:

First _when woo very small_

" 3 7 —
" 15 — 8 Belgic
" 16 — 6 Gaelic
" 20 — 10 Oceanic
" 21 — 6 ____ic
" 30 — 9 China

Did you register? (If not, give reasons.) _No_

Have you any other papers showing your right to be and remain in the United States? _No_

Address where identification card should be sent _766 Clay St.,_
S. F.

ATTEST: _____ 黄金德 Applicant.

14—546

Immediately upon his return to the United States in November 1914, Wong Kim Ark applied for and received a certificate of identity, required to be kept on his person according to the Geary Act. In response to the question "Have you any other papers showing your right to be and remain in the United States?" the person completing the form responded "No." Courtesy of the National Archives, San Francisco.

Form 430   APPLICATION OF ALLEGED AMERICAN CITIZEN OF THE CHINESE RACE FOR PREINVESTIGATION OF STATUS   **DUPLICATE**

Wong Kim Ark, nat.
(Cer. Iden. lost)

此稟專為土生欲離美國由外返而立實憑證之所用   貳號稟

U. S. DEPARTMENT OF LABOR

IMMIGRATION SERVICE

San Francisco, Calif.

July 14, 1931.   , 192...

To U. S. Commissioner of Immigration

Officer in Charge, Immigration Service,

Angel Island, California

Age 62   Height 5 ft. 7 in.
(In shoes)

Marks Scar right temple

SIR: It being my intention to leave the United States on a temporary visit abroad, departing and returning through the Chinese port of entry of San Francisco , I hereby apply, under the provisions of Rule 16 of the Chinese Regulations, for preinvestigation of my claimed status as an American citizen, submitting herewith such documentary proofs (if any) as I possess, and agreeing to appear at such time and place as you may designate, and to produce then and there witnesses for oral examination regarding the claim made by me.

This application is submitted in triplicate with my photograph attached to each copy, as required by said rule.

Respectfully,

Cook   62

Signature in Chinese   簽名字唐簽   黃金德

Signature in English   簽名字番簽   Wong Kim Ark

Address   其稟人之住址   978 Sacramento St.
San Francisco.

此稟未落船先要到親口入人外理管員公辦房換回壹號稟方可落船

JUL 31 1931

SAN FRANCISCO
JUL 2 2 1931
, 192...

application having been approved, this duplicate is delivered to the applicant (with appropriate ...ment written across the margin of the photograph), who must exchange it at the office of the immigra-...er in charge at the port of departure for the original.

...IS DUPLICATE IS OF NO VALUE FURTHER THAN TO IDENTIFY THE HOLDER AS THE PERSON WHOSE ... HAS BEEN INVESTIGATED.

ACTING Commissioner of Immigration,
Inspector in Charge.

14—72 GOVERNMENT PRINTING OFFICE

42223

Wong Kim Ark's temporary departure document and photo from July 1931, when he was sixty-two years old. He did not return to the United States and died some years later in China. Courtesy of the National Archives, San Francisco.

The Fuller Court in 1899. Justice Gray, the author of the *Wong Kim Ark* decision, sits fourth from the left in the front row. Justice McKenna, appointed in 1898, did not take part in the decision. Courtesy of the Library of Congress.

5 | *Wong Kim Ark v. United States*

The case that would bear Wong Kim Ark's name began in district court, styled *In re Wong Kim Ark*. On the surface, it looked like any one of the thousands of habeas cases filed on the behalf of Chinese seeking to enter the United States but prevented from doing so by administrators acting under the authority of the congressional exclusion regime. The petition filed on his behalf alleged that he had been "unlawfully confined and restrained of his liberty on board of the steamship Coptic," despite being a citizen who was entitled to enter the United States.[1]

As discussed in chapter 4, Kim Ark had arrived in August 1895 after a brief trip to China. He probably did not anticipate trouble upon his return, since his reentry in 1890 was relatively smooth, but before he left, he took precautions to safeguard his reentry. Before his departure in November 1894, Kim Ark secured a notarized affidavit with his photograph attesting to his birth in San Francisco and signed and notarized statements from three white witnesses, Wm. Fisher, F. Benna, and L. Selenger, who confirmed this information.[2]

When Kim Ark attempted to reenter the United States, he ran into trouble. Despite his documentary evidence, his use of the English language, and his claim to have sojourned only briefly in China, the immigration official who interviewed him was skeptical.[3] San Francisco collector of customs John Wise had directed D. D. Stubbs, the general manager of the Occidental & Oriental Steamship Company, to forbid him to leave the steamship and enter the United States.[4] Collector Wise was widely known as a vigorous enforcer of the exclusion laws.[5] Kim Ark remained on the *Coptic* until it departed; officials transferred him to the *Gaelic*, which also left, and then to the *Peking*.[6]

While habeas cases were common and most were not considered noteworthy, Wong Kim Ark's petition attracted immediate public attention. In October, a news item reported Kim Ark's habeas claim, noting that the question of Chinese citizenship status was to be brought forward judicially and characterizing the collector's refusal to allow Kim Ark to land as having been "in accordance with an arrangement made with the Attorney General, who is anxious to test the right of native-born Chinese to land here."[7] This news item, widely distributed across the

---

Wong Kim Ark and the Federal Courts

- *In re Wong Kim Ark,* 71 F. 382 (N.D. Cal 1896): District court consideration of Wong Kim Ark's habeas corpus petition; petition granted.
- *United States v. Wong Kim Ark,* 169 U.S. 649 (1898): Supreme Court rules that children born in the United States are citizens regardless of their parentage.

---

country, alerted interested people on all sides of the Chinese question about both the habeas petition and the expected legal battle to come.

Kim Ark's attorney was Thomas Riordan, the noted advocate for San Francisco's Chinese community. By 1889, he had "gained . . . much fame through his defense in the Courts of the Chinese."[8] Riordan, as discussed in chapter 3, had been a key player in the Six Companies' campaign against the Geary Act, but even after the Court upheld the act, he continued to support individual attempts to escape its application. He maneuvered to get clients without certificates released and to delay the law's full application against San Francisco Chinese through relentless habeas petitions and appeals.[9] After filing appeals in five cases in which writs were denied, he warned that he was ready "to appeal 5000 more cases." Endorsing a purely political understanding of Supreme Court decision-making, he noted that since the Court had upheld the law in *Fong Yue Ting,* Justice Samuel Blatchford, who had voted with the majority, had died, leaving the Court by his count with "four Justices against the Chinese, three against the constitutionality of the law, one member of the bench to hear from on the subject and one member to be appointed."[10]

By the time Riordan appeared in court to argue for Wong Kim Ark, he and collector of customs Wise had a rancorous history. In 1894, one of Riordan's clients accused one of Wise's subordinates, customs inspector Richard Williams, of trying to procure bribes from other Chinese. Inspector Williams was reported to have "spent many years among the Mongolians and knows their language and customs" and to be particularly adept at sniffing out women being imported for "immoral purposes," thereby "earning himself the undying hatred of the slave-dealers and their white assistants."[11] Upon a complaint, Williams was charged with soliciting a bribe of $150 from a Chinese merchant seeking to bring a woman into the country, but in a dramatic reversal, a detective produced evidence that Riordan himself had paid a bribe to suppress evidence in a smuggling case.[12]

The government, too, did not view Kim Ark's petition as simply another attempt by an individual to escape detention. Opposing the petition was Henry S. Foote, whom Grover Cleveland had appointed to serve as district attorney for the Northern District of California in 1895.[13] Foote was not alone in his defense of Kim Ark's detention. George Collins, a member of the San Francisco bar, had been watching matters closely, pressing for the district attorney to seek an appropriate test case and allow him to participate.[14]

Collins had been nominated by the Republicans to serve as state attorney general in 1890 but was unable to run due to health considerations. His writings on citizenship had already garnered attention from the Supreme Court, which cited his reasoning in resolving *Elk v. Wilkins* against extending citizenship to Indians.[15] He entered into a newspaper spat with Justice Field over the Chinese question, attacking Field's ruling in *Look Tin Sing* upholding birthright citizenship as "very poor law" that demanded a definitive rebuke from the Supreme Court. For his part, Field responded that Collins's views were without merit and that his writings primarily served "the vanity of the writer . . . by seeing his crudities in print."[16] Foote accepted Collins's assistance as someone whose "special hobby" was railing against Chinese (and other undesirable groups') birthright citizenship, but despite Collins's urging did not appoint him as special counsel, citing his "bad reputation" with regard to ethics.[17] Instead, Collins was permitted to file an amicus brief based on his "able and interesting articles in the American Law Review" attacking the principle of birthright citizenship for the Chinese.[18]

In re Wong Kim Ark

Even before the celebrated appeal, the case attracted significant attention in the press. Chapter 4 notes the widespread reports on the case after the federal district court ruled, but in San Francisco, reporters closely observed the proceedings themselves. The *San Francisco Call*, which was very invested in the Chinese question, published a story describing the positions taken in oral arguments by both Riordan and District Attorney Foote. Riordan pointed out that a ruling against Wong Kim Ark (or Ak, as the paper spelled his name) would undercut the immigrant foundations of the American nation: "Think of all the people in this country who have been born of parents who owed allegiance to either Great Britain, Germany, Italy, or some other European power. Are all these people to be declared not citizens?"[19] Foote retorted by drawing a racial distinction. The children of these immigrants had descended from "Caucasian parents . . . [who] enjoyed a possibility of becoming citizens which is denied to the Mongolians."[20] Federal authorities also warned that a ruling in favor of Kim Ark would affect the status of Japanese immigrants' descendants, "in fact, all the olive-skinned Orientals." The *Call* ominously reminded readers that California alone already had nearly eight thousand Japanese residents.[21]

Riordan's argument as reported was quite simple; he relied on the congressional enactment of language mirroring the Fourteenth Amendment, which stated that "all persons born in the United States and not subject to any foreign power, excluding Indians not taxed, are . . . declared to be citizens of the United States." His goal for the case was not simply to have Kim Ark admitted. He agreed to waive the fact that Kim Ark had successfully reentered the United States after a trip to China in 1890, explaining that his aim with the petition was "to have the broad principle of citizenship settled for all time."[22]

Both Collins and Foote, on the other hand, argued that the common-law principle of attributing citizenship on the basis of geographic birthplace gave way in the United States to international law. The international principle, they claimed, attributed citizenship on the basis of fatherhood, or motherhood for illegitimate children. Collins read the citizenship clause of the Fourteenth Amendment restrictively, arguing that "subject to the jurisdiction thereof" referred to "political jurisdiction," which followed international law.[23] Collins pointed back to the reasoning adopted in *Elk v. Wilkins* about requiring consent of both a prospective citizen and the state and to Justice Miller's aside in the *Slaughter-House Cases* that the jurisdiction clause excluded "citizens or subjects of foreign states born within the United States."[24]

Both sides agreed to several stipulated facts in order to focus the dispute on the constitutional question. Wong Kim Ark, they agreed, had been born in San Francisco in 1873 to parents who were both Chinese and subjects of the Chinese emperor. His parents had both established permanent domiciled residency in the United States and did not qualify as diplomats.[25] They stipulated as well that Kim Ark had visited China temporarily in 1890 and had reentered "upon the sole ground that he was a native-born citizen of the United States." They also agreed that the only reason Kim Ark had been denied reentry in 1895 was the determination by the collector of customs that he was not a citizen. Both sides stipulated that neither he nor his parents had ever renounced his allegiance to the United States "and that he has never done or committed any act or thing to exclude him therefrom."[26]

The federal district court judge who heard these arguments was no stranger to questions about the Chinese. Prior to becoming a federal judge, William Morrow had represented California in the House between 1885 and 1891, where he had established a reputation for supporting further restrictions on Chinese immigration.[27] Voting on legislation, however, proved to be a different institutional task than deciding a court case covering ground that previous judges had already trod. Judge Morrow reviewed the previous history and noted the rulings in favor of citizenship in *In re Look Tin Sing* and *Gee Fook Sing v. United States,* as well as the pre–Fourteenth Amendment precedents that adopted the common-law principle. He noted further that the case had major practical as well as constitutional implications. If he ruled against Wong Kim Ark, such a ruling imposed nationally

> will inevitably result that thousands of persons of both sexes who have been heretofore considered as citizens of the United States, and have always been treated as such, will be, to all intents and purposes, denationalized and remanded to a state of alienage. Included among these are thousands of voters who are exercising the right of suffrage as American citizens, and whose right as such is not, and never has been, questioned, because birth within the country seems to have been recognized generally as conclusive upon the question of citizenship.[28]

He acknowledged, though, that the question had not been settled definitively by the Supreme Court and was thus open for resolution.

In setting out to resolve it, Morrow noted that the Fourteenth Amendment was "controlling," regardless of the conflict between common-law and international law principles. The key interpretive question for him was in the "subject to the jurisdiction" clause, and like many judges who had preceded him, Morrow noted with approval Justice Field's reasoning in *Look Tin Sing.*[29] He also highlighted the other Ninth Circuit cases from the 1880s that embraced jus soli. In his analysis, since all of these cases—*Look Tin Sing, Gee Fook Sing, Chin King, Lynch,* and

Yung Sing Hee—reached the same result on nearly identical facts, they "are conclusive and controlling upon this court, unless the supreme court of the United States has directly and authoritatively, and not by way of dictum, announced and laid down a doctrine at variance with that expounded."[30]

Judge Morrow then considered the government's claim that the *Slaughter-House Cases* had settled the meaning of the contested clause. Rejecting this claim, he reasoned that the broad meaning of citizenship was not the central question in the case. The discussion was rather over national versus state citizenship, and the implications of this distinction for privileges or immunities.[31] When the majority explained that "'subject to its jurisdiction' was intended to exclude from its operation children of ministers, consuls, and citizens or subjects of foreign states born within the United States," this explanation was "mere dictum" and not binding law.

More significant to Judge Morrow, however, was the language that the Court used afterward, explaining that unlike state citizenship, for a person to acquire national citizenship required only "that he should be born or naturalized in the United States to be a citizen of the Union."[32] He distinguished the Court's ruling in *Elk v. Wilkins* on the ground that the opinion itself likened Indians to individuals born outside of the United States or to children "born within the United States, of ambassadors or other public ministers of foreign nations" because of the special status of Indian tribes, "an alien, though dependent, power."[33]

Judge Morrow offered his view that the international law principle of having citizenship follow parentage "is undoubtedly more logical, reasonable, and satisfactory," but his analysis convinced him that his hands were tied. While he speculated that "the executive departments of the government [may be] at liberty to follow this international rule in dealing with questions of citizenship," he concluded that the courts had no choice "in dealing with persons within our own territory."[34] On January 3, 1896, Judge Morrow declared Kim Ark a citizen and ordered him to be released, but required him to pay a $250 bond.[35] Wong Kim Ark was, at least temporarily, a free man and a citizen.

The Case Advances to the Supreme Court

Everyone involved knew that Judge Morrow's ruling would not be the last word in the case. A statutory reorganization of the federal courts in 1891 had created the circuit courts of appeal, eliminating the need for the justices to ride circuit and allowing for an intermediate level of appeal. Section 5 of the act, however, allowed appeals or writs of error to be directed to the US Supreme Court, bypassing the new intermediate appellate courts, in cases involving "the construction or application of the Constitution of the United States."[36] As in the district court proceeding, the litigants agreed to focus on the question of birthright citizenship, agreeing that the sole ground for Kim Ark's exclusion was the claim that he was not a citizen.

Before the Supreme Court, the lawyers debated the same questions that had prevailed in earlier proceedings: Was there a long-standing and legitimate practice of allowing individuals born in the United States to claim citizenship? And what did the Fourteenth Amendment's qualification "subject to the jurisdiction" mean for the children of noncitizens? The briefs filed for the Supreme Court's consideration investigated these questions exhaustively, with each side claiming support in past precedent and practice.

The Government's Opposition to Citizenship

On the government's side, Solicitor General Holmes Conrad took over the briefing, but George Collins continued to be involved. Conrad, a Virginian, pressed the arguments that Morrow's opinion had rejected, but added a few new twists.[37] Conrad and Collins acknowledged that birthright citizenship was more or less presumed, but they characterized this as "a traditionary dogma" and "a very dangerous error . . . perpetrated by acquiescence and repetition."[38] The argument proceeded to describe birthright citizenship as a "feudal and monarchical" practice inappropriate for the United States' republican government, which, as it traced back to Roman practice, lodged sovereignty in the people and linked citizenship to descent.[39] A domicile, by this reading, was distinct from a *patria* or nationality, and citizenship could not be merely a matter of domicile.

From this point, the argument took a sharper turn. Citing *Dred Scott* approvingly, the brief explained that citizenship was "of the essence" of the sovereignty of the United States. The Constitution's placement of naturalization exclusively with the national government and the preamble's pact with the people established definitively that "no person could be a citizen unless he was of that posterity or naturalized, or the offspring of a citizen."[40] The nation existed primarily for the original inhabitants of the United States (ignoring Native Americans and slaves) and their descendants; naturalization as a conscious and individual mutual choice was to serve all others.

To the argument that the Fourteenth Amendment's plain language extended citizenship to those born in the United States, Conrad and Collins predictably relied on the jurisdiction clause. They claimed that all children of alien parents were "subject to a foreign power" from the moment of birth by virtue of their parentage. Even for Kim Ark, whose parents were legally domiciled in the United States, "when [he] was born in San Francisco of Chinese parents there domiciled he at the moment of birth became a subject of the Emperor of China, and for that reason could not have been born 'subject to the jurisdiction' of the United States."[41] Only Congress, by changing the naturalization process, could grant automatic citizenship to such individuals. The various rulings that had decided otherwise were simply wrong.

But the injury they foresaw from a ruling extending citizenship was worse than a simple misunderstanding of the importance of domicile. Leaving citizenship in the hands of Congress enabled the exercise of wise discretion in selecting the aliens who should be naturalized.[42] In particular, it would enable maintaining the hard line against the children of the Chinese, who were "just as obnoxious" as their parents and "to whom the same reasons for exclusion apply with equal force," enabling the nation to maintain "some honor and dignity in American citizenship that would be sacred from the foul and corrupting taint of a debasing alienage." Repeating a trope sometimes observed in the anti-Chinese press, the brief warned that extending citizenship on this basis would enable the Chinese to be eligible for all civic privileges, including that of serving as president. Such an outcome was, in the authors' views, insupportable and absurd.

Conrad filed a second brief in the case, developing his arguments further. He again rejected Kim Ark's lawyers' claim that birthright citizenship flowed appropriately from the common-law tradition. He argued that, because of the federal nature of government, the United States on the whole had no common law, although individual states could.[43] With regard to citizenship, Conrad strung together lengthy quotes from early postbellum Supreme Court cases to argue that even after the Fourteenth Amendment, the Constitution was not understood

to have any clear definition of natural-born citizenship.[44] He utterly rejected the idea of national citizenship as distinguished from state citizenship as a product of Radical Republicanism, which he described as
"the offspring of that unhappy period of rabid rage and malevolent zeal
when corrupt ignorance and debauched patriotism held high carnival
in the halls of Congress."[45] He also undertook to reject the *Lynch* case
after identifying it as the source of many of the later rulings affirming
birthright citizenship.[46]

Finally, Conrad rejected the claim that the Fourteenth Amendment,
"if ever lawfully adopted at all," changed the nature of citizenship.[47] In
support of his interpretation, he noted the debate over the jurisdiction
clause in Congress, interpreting an exchange over its scope as implying
that the clause "applied to those only who were subject to the complete
jurisdiction of the United States," which did not imagine extension
to Chinese immigrants' children.[48] He read the language of the Civil
Rights Act of 1866 extending birthright citizenship to all persons born
in the United States and not subject to any foreign power as "merely
the negative of 'subject to the jurisdiction of the United States.'" By this
reading, the language did not indicate either that the members of Congress who passed the Fourteenth Amendment envisioned broad birthright citizenship or that the statute itself extended it.[49] And, he argued,
in other legislation, Congress had made its intentions toward the Chinese completely clear: "The citizenship of Chinese infants is inconsistent with the whole policy of the United States."[50] Conrad's "rambling"
(as characterized by Bethany Berger) brief may have also had its roots
in a desire to repudiate the constitutional changes wrought by Reconstruction by limiting and delegitimizing the Fourteenth Amendment.[51]

*Wong Kim Ark's Supreme Court Representatives
and Their Responses*

Thomas Riordan, who had argued Kim Ark's case at the district court
level, was not the primary advocate before the Supreme Court. His brief
for the Supreme Court case was short and straightforward. He argued
that under common law, birth grounded citizenship.[52] The Fourteenth
Amendment, rather than working any significant change, was "only
declaratory of the common law rule; that amendment was adopted to
declare and enforce it uniformly throughout the United States and

the several states."[53] Citing Justice Field's opinion in *Look Tin Sing*, he claimed that Kim Ark was subject to the jurisdiction, and dismissed the claim that Kim Ark's lack of access to the franchise signified any questions about citizenship.[54] *Lynch*, he claimed, was more properly understood if one accepted that only Congress could facilitate naturalization through statute and that common-law practices in the states could not shape outcomes on the federal level.[55]

Maxwell Evarts and J. Hubley Ashton, who had represented the Six Companies in their challenge of the Geary Act in the Supreme Court, each filed more substantial briefs on Kim Ark's behalf.[56] Evarts's brief framed the question as both simple and broad: "Are the children born in this country of alien residents not connected with the diplomatic service citizens of the United States?"[57] He pressed for stripping the question of any racial implications, noting that "the rights of the Chinese race" were "of little importance." Rather, the question addressed all children "born in this country to any alien resident . . . without regard to the country from which their parents came, and irrespective of whether they are of English, Irish, French, German, or any other extraction."[58]

Evarts asserted that the Fourteenth Amendment simply underlined the law as it existed: "Every judicial decision directly upon the question in controversy has been averse to the Government's present position."[59] As for the proposition that the United States had no common law, he noted that this framing misunderstood the function of turning to common-law principles for guidance. In his view, "The question fairly raised here is not whether there is a common law in the United States, but whether it is admissible, in construing and defining words used in the Constitution, to refer to the common law." Reliance on common law and everyday practical interpretations of legal concepts was by his light entirely reasonable and commonplace in a variety of legal settings, including the Supreme Court.[60]

As for the claim that international law should prevail, Evarts argued that this was contrary to established interpretive practice, which directed that individual nations were responsible for managing the citizenship process. He cited a number of cases in support of this proposition, including Justice Taney's opinion in *Dred Scott*, but further noted that ceding the question to the rule of international law would possibly create incoherence in the event of a conflict.[61]

Evarts also addressed the government's argument that *Elk v. Wilkins* settled the question of the subject to the jurisdiction clause against Kim

Ark. He reinforced the claim that *Elk* situated Indians as a special case, "a nation or nations within a nation," and that Elk's decision to abandon his tribe rendered him "a member of the general body of the inhabitants of this country," in the same position as "any other emigrant or alien." Elk, he claimed, was not in the same position as Wong Kim Ark, but rather the position of Wong Kim Ark's father: "They were both alien residents of this country."[62] He also noted language in both *Slaughter-House* and *Minor v. Happersett*, suggesting that the Court had never directly faced the question of birthright citizenship.

In arguing that Wong Kim Ark was "subject to the jurisdiction" of the United States, Evarts noted that even Kim Ark's father was subject to the jurisdiction of the United States "in the sense that he could invoke their protection against the country of his origin and owed obedience to their laws."[63] As for Kim Ark himself, his birth in the United States both entitled him to the protection of the laws and cemented his allegiance. The purpose of the jurisdiction clause was to create an exception for a few categories, most notably the children of foreign ambassadors and "the American Indians who, though born within the boundaries of our country, were deemed independent nations."[64] He also noted the targeting of the Chinese in the case.

Evarts spent some time tracing through the many precedents that supported birthright citizenship involving both Chinese and non-Chinese descendants, and rejected the few policy moves made in the opposite direction. The general rule in American law since the early antebellum period was to extend citizenship, and most children born in the United States had been granted the rights and privileges associated with citizenship with little discussion and no controversy. He read Congress's 1790 specific extension of citizenship to children born to American citizens abroad as further confirmation that in other circumstances, birthright citizenship was presumed.[65] Tracing through an extensive list of precedents, he concluded that, with but one possible exception, birthright citizenship had been the standing norm under American law for decades, and he ridiculed the concern that a "Chinaman" might ever become president.[66]

Ashton's brief was, if anything, even more comprehensive. He presented it in numbered points, filling in some gaps in Evarts's claims. His first argument was that the framers of the Fourteenth Amendment intended to include the "American-born children of Chinese parents" and that no distinctions on the basis of "color or race or alienage or political condition of their parents" were envisioned in the debates.[67] As he noted, the question of the citizenship of the children of Chinese parents had indeed been raised, and no changes were made in response to this possibility. Senator Conness of California had discussed it at some length, concluding that the number of citizens with Chinese ancestry was likely to be fairly insignificant.[68] This reading was consonant with the Civil Rights Act, which proceeded on the theory that Congress's power over naturalization was "merely a power to provide for the removal of the disabilities consequent on alienage by *foreign birth.*"[69]

Like Evarts, Ashton rested his argument on common law, showing that English common law extended birthright citizenship on the basis of the place of birth. He claimed further that this principle prevailed in all of the states at the time of both the Revolution and the Constitution's adoption.[70] The language of the Fourteenth Amendment was crafted, he explained, to incorporate this understanding.[71] The point of the Fourteenth Amendment was not, as the solicitor general had claimed, to prevent generalized jus soli citizenship or to empower Congress to regulate the terms of birthright citizenship, but rather to clarify that the rule of *Dred Scott* barring slaves and the descendants of slaves from resort to the general principle was no longer valid.[72] Citizenship had but two variants: natural-born and acquired. Congress was responsible only for regulating how it could be acquired.

Ashton also construed the jurisdiction clause as asserting in straightforward terms that children born in the United States were subject to its jurisdiction rather than that of their parents' government.[73] Further, the whole concept of national sovereignty implied the authority of the nation "to impress upon the children born of the subjects or citizens of another State . . . the character and quality of citizens of the United States" even if the parents were but temporary sojourners. This power flowed naturally from a nation's "right of empire, its right of exclusive and absolute civil and criminal legislation within its territorial limits, or, in other words, its right of sovereignty within those limits."[74] The jurisdictional limit, he agreed with his colleague, simply clarified that individuals connected to foreign sovereigns, ambassadors and other national public officials, and military forces were not in the same category as ordinary denizens of a nation.[75]

Ashton ridiculed the solicitor general's claims about the "extraordinary theory as that by 'international law' . . . the children born here of foreigners are deemed to be citizens or subjects of their parents' country."[76] Only a nation could determine who were its citizens and subjects, and the consistent application of common-law principles indicated that the United States had chosen to extend jus soli citizenship and had never renounced this principle. Moreover, Ashton argued that the solicitor general's interpretation of international law was itself incorrect, as "the relation of *sovereign and subject or citizen* is the creature of municipal law, and international law does not purport to lay down principles or sanction specific usages in that matter."[77]

Solicitor General Conrad filed a reply to Evarts's brief objecting to the proposition that common law could be a guide in this case. He reiterated his claim that state adoptions of common law did not signal national acceptance of these principles.[78] He further emphasized the particular nature and characteristics of "the Chinaman," noting that protections for Chinese subjects under American law flowed from the treaties between the United States and China, and arguing that obedience to American law did not imply allegiance.[79] Only a citizen owed permanent allegiance, and only those born to citizens were therefore subject to the jurisdiction of the United States. Because Wong Kim Ark was born to a Chinese subject, he "partook of the nationality of his father." Conrad sought to heighten concerns about Kim Ark specifically and the Chinese generally by noting Kim Ark's extensive travels in China, particularly his choice to return to China after reaching the age of majority.[80] (Conrad did not discuss Kim Ark's family in China.) Finally, he launched an additional salvo against *Lynch*, characterizing it as exhibiting "more of knowledge than of wisdom."[81]

With around three hundred pages of written arguments and a spirited oral argument now complete, it was the Supreme Court's turn to weigh in. With its mixed record on Chinese issues and its devastating ruling in *Plessy v. Ferguson* relatively fresh, the Court would now have its chance to determine Kim Ark's fate and thereby the fate of thousands of others born in the United States to a variety of nonwhite, noncitizen parents.

Justice Gray's Majority Opinion

Horace Gray Jr. wrote the majority opinion for the Court. Gray, as discussed earlier, had established his place on the Court as a supporter of national power and a careful analyst of sovereignty. Given these interests, his leadership in determining the fate of litigation concerning the Chinese was not surprising. He had written the Court's opinions in *Nishimura Ekiu v. United States* in 1891 and in *Fong Yue Ting v. United States* in 1893, both of which, as discussed previously, upheld Congress's authority to regulate Chinese immigration.[82] Those debating Wong Kim Ark's fate knew as well that Gray had authored the Court's majority opinion in *Elk v. Wilkins.* He was one of the justices that canny lawyer Thomas Riordan, who kept careful track of the sympathies of the justices, would have counted as being on the side of the Chinese several years earlier.

Justice Gray opened his opinion with the by now familiar and uncontested recitation of the facts, highlighting Kim Ark's alleged birth in San Francisco in 1873, his status as a laborer, his trip to China with his family in 1890, his maturity, and his attempt to return to the United States from a trip to China in 1895 by claiming citizenship.[83] The key interpretive question, Justice Gray agreed, was around the application of the Fourteenth Amendment's first clause.

He began his inquiry by outlining his theory of proper interpretive method. To make sense of any contested provision, he explained, one had to consider three things: "all parts of the act itself . . . any former act of the same lawmaking power of which the act in question is an amendment . . . [and] the condition and . . . the history of the law as previously existing, and in the light of which the new act must be read and interpreted."[84] The Fourteenth Amendment's controversial discussion of citizenship, then, could only be understood properly by starting with the Constitution itself and its provisions for citizenship.

The Constitution, Gray noted, referred to two types of citizenship: citizens and natural-born citizens, setting minimum years of citizenship for congressional representatives and senators and barring any but natural-born citizens from serving as president. The Fourteenth and Fifteenth Amendments both picked up the language of citizenship, but the Fourteenth Amendment distinguished only between born and naturalized citizens. None of this language, by Gray's reading, defined the meanings of these categories "either by way of inclusion or of exclusion, except insofar as this is done by the affirmative declaration that 'all persons born or naturalized in the United States, and subject to the jurisdiction thereof, are citizens of the United States.'"[85]

If the Constitution itself did not answer a question, the proper way to analyze it, in Justice Gray's view, was then to turn to common law, as several previous rulings had endorsed. He noted that "the funda-mental principle of the common law with regard to English nationality was birth within the allegiance . . . of the King."[86] This principle, he observed, could be traced back to *Calvin's Case* in 1608 and had been supported consistently since then. He reviewed cases and commentary from England dating from prior to the Revolution to a digest published just two years earlier and concluded as follows:

> By the law of England for the last three centuries, beginning before the settlement of this country and continuing to the present day, aliens, while residing in the dominions possessed by the Crown of England, were within the allegiance, the obedience, the father or loyalty, the protection, the power, the jurisdiction of the English Sovereign, and therefore every child born in England of alien parents was a natural-born subject unless the child of an ambassador or other diplomatic agent of a foreign State or of an alien enemy in hostile occupation of the place where the child was born.[87]

He thus utterly rejected the solicitor general's reading of English common-law developments in favor of his own analysis, which aligned with Ashton's.

Justice Gray likewise agreed with Ashton and Evart concerning the American tradition. He found that "the same rule was in force in all the English Colonies upon this continent down to the time of the Dec-laration of Independence, and in the United States afterwards, and continued to prevail under the Constitution as originally established."[88] He reviewed the by now familiar cases, beginning with *The Charming Betsy* and recalling Marshall's dictum assuming that persons born in the United States were citizens. In discussing *Inglis v. Sailors' Snug Harbor*, he quoted Justice Thompson's majority opinion recognizing the British practice of recognizing individuals born in the colonies as "natural-born British subjects." He approvingly quoted at greater length Justice Story's analysis of *Calvin's Case*, Blackstone's Commentaries, and *Doe v. Jones* to underline his own understanding of sovereignty.[89]

Justice Gray explained that Story's reading emphasized the two con-ditions required for citizenship: local birth "within the dominions of the sovereign" and birth "within the allegiance of the sovereign." In Story's analysis, the exceptions provided the boundaries of the general rule: a person born at sea "is a subject of the prince to whom his parents then owe allegiance," the children of an ambassador were subjects of the am-bassador's sovereign, and the children of enemy aliens "born in a place within the dominions of another sovereign, then occupied by them by conquest, are still aliens." But for all others born under ordinary conditions, citizenship attached.[90] Justice Gray interpreted the solicitor general's reliance on Story's discussion in a companion case that seemed to incorporate "the more general principles of the law of nations" as a misreading; Story himself, Gray noted, had made his position quite clear both in the *Inglis* case and in his own 1834 Treatise on the Conflict of Laws. There, Justice Gray highlighted, Story had simply explained, "Persons who are born in a country are generally deemed citizens and subjects of that country."[91]

In addition to analyzing Justice Story's discussions, Justice Gray noted that both Justice Curtis in *Dred Scott* and Justice Swayne, writing for the circuit court in *United States v. Rhodes* in 1866, had endorsed the idea that persons born in the United States were natural-born citizens. Drawing from his experience as a state-court jurist, he also noted rulings from Massachusetts, North Carolina, and New York that declared birthright citizenship to be an accepted common-law principle.[92] And he noted the acceptance of this principle in Chancellor Kent's commentaries and the writings of noted jurist Horace Binney.[93]

Justice Gray was equally unpersuaded by Solicitor General Conrad's attempt to lodge his argument in international law. He first asserted that the older principle on the Continent was that of jus soli and then claimed that "later modifications of the rule in Europe rest upon the constitutions, laws or ordinances of the various countries, and have no important bearing on the interpretation and effect of the Constitution of the United States."[94] He depended, as Kim Ark's advocates had, on the concept of national sovereignty and noted that only in certain circumstances were the broad common-law principles specifically modified by statute. These statutes, he claimed, had specific purposes and "applied only to cases coming within their purport, and they have never been considered in either [England or the United States] as affecting the citizenship of persons born within its dominion."[95]

He underlined his comprehensive analysis of English law and practice by noting that the American Congress, in exercising its constitutional authority with regard to naturalization, implied acceptance of citizenship for children born under US territorial authority. Certainly, the national legislature had never seen any necessity to provide specifically for the citizenship of children born in the United States. Specific provisions for citizenship included aliens naturalized by court proceedings, children of naturalized aliens, and children of citizens born outside of US territorial boundaries.[96] An 1802 revision had clarified the limits, but Justice Gray identified no legislation between 1802 and 1855 that embraced a general principle of citizenship solely by blood or descent.[97]

Justice Gray recognized the complications of slavery and race, asserting that prior to the Fourteenth Amendment and the passage of the Civil Rights Act of 1866, "all white persons, at least, born within the sovereignty of the United States, whether children of citizens or of foreigners, excepting only children of ambassadors or public ministers of a foreign government, were native-born citizens of the United States."[98] In 1866, he noted, the Civil Rights Act expanded this scope to "all persons born in the United States, and not subject to any foreign power, excluding Indians not taxed," and granted all such persons equal civil rights to those "enjoyed by white citizens." The Fourteenth Amendment was meant to underline and reinforce these principles.[99]

As for the Fourteenth Amendment, Justice Gray readily conceded that its primary purpose was to establish Black citizenship. The language Congress chose, however, was "general, not to say universal, restricted by place and jurisdiction, and not by color or race."[100] In his reading of the *Slaughter-House Cases*, he found evidence that both Justice Miller's opinion for the Court and dissents by Justices Field, Bradley, and Swayne directly acknowledged or implied that jus soli prevailed. As for Miller's dictum that "subject to the jurisdiction" excluded children born in the United States to foreign subjects, he dismissed it. "It was unsupported by any argument, or by any reference to authorities, and . . . it was not formulated with the same care and exactness as if the case before the court had called for an exact definition of the phrase."[101] He then quoted John Marshall's famous statement about dicta in *Cohens v. Virginia*: "If they go beyond the case they may be respected, but ought not to control the judgment in a subsequent suit when the very point is presented for decision." And only two years later, he noted, Chief Justice Waite's opinion for the Court in *Minor v. Happersett* had raised the possibility of jus soli citizenship.[102]

Justice Gray also addressed *Elk v. Wilkins* directly, as it was the only case that had directly interpreted the jurisdiction clause; he was ideally positioned to do so as the author of the majority opinion in that case. He agreed with Kim Ark's attorneys that the Indian tribes had special status. They were "not, strictly speaking, foreign States, but were alien nations, distinct political communities, the members of which owed immediate allegiance to their several tribes and were not part of the people of the United States." The combination of their alien and dependent status marked them as separate. Justice Gray concluded that his prior opinion "concerned only members of the Indian tribes within the United States, and had no tendency to deny citizenship to children born in the United States of foreign parents of Caucasian, African or Mongolian descent not in the diplomatic service of a foreign country."[103]

Justice Gray also drew from his expertise on sovereignty to develop his analysis of the question. The object of the entire contested text of the citizenship clause was, in his view, to carve out a few narrow exceptions to the general principle extending jus soli citizenship. He detailed the exceptions, explaining their grounding in precedents outlining the sovereignty question with regard to foreign ministers and sovereigns. Chief Justice Marshall himself had made it clear that private individuals, regardless of their reasons for travel, did fall within the sovereignty of the lands in which they sojourned. As Justice Gray emphasized, Justice Marshall explained that "it would be obviously inconvenient and dangerous to society, and would subject the laws to continual infraction and the government to degradation, if such individuals or merchants did not owe temporary and local allegiance, and were not amenable to the jurisdiction of the country."[104] Indeed, one of the requirements that Congress originally established for alien naturalization was residence within the United States for a designated period of time.

Ultimately, by Justice Gray's reading, the Fourteenth Amendment clarified and worked in tandem with Congress's authority over citizenship. The citizenship clause was "declaratory of existing rights and affirmative of existing law as to each of the qualifications therein expressed." It addressed the circumstances of all individuals acquiring citizenship "by facts occurring within the limits of the United States." Congress's responsibility then remained, as it had been since the founding, to establish the process of naturalization and to address questions about the citizenship of children born abroad to American parents.[105]

In Justice Gray's view, Congress's previous exercise of its power with respect to Americans born abroad underlined and distinguished the principle of jus soli citizenship. In 1855, Congress had denied citizenship to individuals born abroad whose fathers had never resided in the United States. By extending citizenship only to selected children of American fathers, Congress "has denied to them what pertains to other American citizens—the right of transmitting citizenship to their children—unless they shall have made themselves residents of the United States." These children born abroad would be subject to the sovereignty of their nations of birth, "entitl[ing] the country within whose jurisdiction they are born to claim them as citizen and to subject them to duties to it."[106] He further endorsed the practical point made at every phase of the litigation by Kim Ark's lawyers that denying citizenship to children born to aliens in the United States would deny citizenship to "thousands" of children born to European immigrants, who had always been recognized as citizens.[107]

Justice Gray recognized, of course, that Kim Ark's being Chinese rather than European was the whole point of the attempt to deny his citizenship. He thus carefully analyzed the legal status of the Chinese under the regime of exclusion, delineating the ways that, despite their ineligibility for citizenship, they nonetheless had some legal status and protection under law. He asserted first that as long as they were permitted to reside in the United States, they were both under its jurisdiction and entitled to its protection "in the same sense as all other aliens residing in the United States." The key precedent here was the Court's 1886 ruling in *Yick Wo v. Hopkins*, which extended the due process and equal protection clauses to resident Chinese. *Yick Wo*, on Gray's reading, likewise underlined Chinese immigrants' subjection to US jurisdiction as residents of both state and nation.[108] He also underlined that no previous ruling considering the Chinese question specifically had denied citizenship to children born to resident Chinese.[109]

Justice Gray followed the reasoning advanced by Ashton and Evarts on Kim Ark's behalf regarding the debates over the Fourteenth Amendment, noting that no proposals had been made in Congress to limit birthright citizenship by excluding the descendants of Chinese. While Congress had indeed acted to exclude the Chinese, these acts were considered and passed fourteen or more years after the Fourteenth Amendment and, in Gray's view, "must be construed and executed in subordination to its provisions." While the Exclusion Acts had gained approval from the Supreme Court, even the power to expel undesirable resident Chinese could not supersede the Constitution's authoritative expression of the boundaries of citizenship.[110]

To the claim that Congress controlled the question, Justice Gray reiterated his belief that of the two sources of citizenship, birth and naturalization, the Constitution attributed control to Congress only for the purpose of regulating and managing naturalization. Citizenship by birth was "established by the mere act of birth under the circumstances defined in the Constitution," requiring no action by Congress and brooking no alterations by Congress.[111] To rule otherwise would attribute to Congress the dangerous and unconstitutional authority to restrict the classes of persons eligible for citizenship at birth.

Justice Gray concluded by explaining his view that Kim Ark's travels had no impact on his claim to citizenship. Kim Ark could have opted to renounce his citizenship, but no evidence suggested that he had done so, and he had not established residency anywhere but in the United States. His two visits to China, Justice Gray noted, had been brief, one lasting for "some months" and the other "for something like a year about the time of his coming of age," and neither suggested or implied any separation from the United States. His intention to return to the United States was consistent and clear, and he did indeed return. There could be no question as to his birthplace, his permanent domicile, or his relationship with the United States. In Justice Gray's view, and in the view of the majority of the Court, Wong Kim Ark was a citizen.[112]

Chief Justice Fuller's Dissent

As noted previously, Chief Justice Fuller had not been particularly supportive of the Chinese in the cases the Supreme Court heard while he was serving as chief justice, although he did file a dissent in the primary Geary Act case, *Fong Yue Ting*. Despite his procedural objections in that case, recent scholarship reconstructing the history of the Supreme Court between the end of the Civil War and the 1920s suggests that under his leadership, the Court took a harder line on racial issues than the Waite Court, which has historically been blamed for the judicial curtailment of Reconstruction.[113] In *United States v. Wong Kim Ark*, Justice Fuller and Justice Harlan disagreed with the majority's resolution of the case. Justice Harlan joined his dissent. (Justice McKenna, who had recently replaced Justice Field, did not cast a vote in the case.)

Justice Fuller turned around the majority's reasoning, which noted the absurdity of denying citizenship to all children born to aliens in the United States. By the majority's logic, he claimed, any child born to a citizen outside of the United States would have to become a citizen through the naturalization process, "and no statutory provision to the contrary is of any force or effect." Worse yet, the children of aliens would be "exempted from the exercise of the power to exclude or to expel aliens, or any class of aliens, so often maintained by this court," a point to which he would return.[114]

Justice Fuller viewed the attribution of citizenship through natal location as a feudal practice that was not smuggled into American practice through the common law. He endorsed Solicitor General Conrad's arguments about turning to international law rather than common law as the proper source for resolving interpretive questions about citizenship and nationality, since these questions involved international relations. The proper rule was thus descent rather than natal location.[115] He rested great importance in the Revolution, which had both asserted independent American sovereignty and broken the links between the former colonies and the sway of English common law. His theory of allegiance rested significantly more in the idea of citizenship by choice, highlighting the consistent presence of options in the United States for consciously embracing or renouncing citizenship.[116]

In further support of this theory of citizenship, Justice Fuller considered the founding and limits placed on national officers based on residence in the United States. He claimed that the residency requirements pushed back against the idea that birth alone could be sufficient to make citizens without either a blood relationship or a deeper connection to US soil. Even if one were to concede that persons born in a country were presumptive citizens, this could be but a presumption that could be answered. Any evidence that their parents were mere sojourners with no deep connections or ties should be sufficient to put to rest the idea that such children were entitled to citizenship.[117]

Justice Fuller cited administrative rulings denying citizenship to two men who had been born in the United States. He placed particular weight on the application of Richard Greisser for a passport, which Secretary of State Thomas Bayard denied in 1885. Greisser, Bayard explained, had been born in the United States but was ineligible "on general principles of international law": his father was a German subject domiciled in Germany, and Greisser himself left the United States before turning two.[118] Fuller's interpretation of jurisdiction distinguished between territorial and political jurisdiction, claiming that uniting the two would lead to problematic double allegiances.[119]

Justice Fuller's reading of the history of the Fourteenth Amendment and associated legislation likewise diverged from the majority's. He read the language of the Civil Rights Act of 1866 as exclusionary—the clause "and not subject to any foreign power" to his mind was meant to deny citizenship to children of aliens who were subject only to the territorial jurisdiction of the United States, retaining permanent allegiance to their home nations. He noted pointedly that some such aliens would not be permitted to shift their allegiance to the United States even if they desired to do so. The Fourteenth Amendment's proposal came just two months after the passage of the Civil Rights Act, and Fuller understood the Fourteenth Amendment's jurisdiction clause to be synonymous with the "subject to any foreign power" clause in the act. In interpreting the same section of the debate on which Justice Gray had relied to illustrate the intent to incorporate birthright citizenship, Justice Fuller cited *Elk v. Wilkins* to claim that aliens and their children were indeed subject to foreign powers and thus did not fall under the United States' political jurisdiction.[120]

While Justice Fuller did not "insist" that *Slaughter-House* and *Minor v. Happersett* settled the question, he believed that these two cases, when read in conjunction with *Elk v. Wilkins*, provided sufficient grounding for his proposition that only complete subjection to the political jurisdiction of the United States would be sufficient to ground citizenship. This point was key in distinguishing the Chinese from other migrants. The Chinese were different on two counts: the laws of China forbade them to renounce their allegiance to China, and the laws of the United States barred them from expressing allegiance to the United States. They could in no way, then, be considered subject to the political jurisdiction of a nation to which they would always and forever be aliens. While Justice Fuller did not indulge in the most vicious stereotypes denying Chinese assimilability, he did invoke the Chinese adherence to tradition and the binding effect of "every conception of duty and . . . every principle of their religion, of which filial piety is the first and greatest commandment."[121]

Justice Fuller also noted the critical role of the Chinese question in establishing Congress's authority to "expel or deport foreigners who have not been naturalized" as an "absolute and unqualified" power as compelling as the authority to prohibit their entrance. Allowing the children of such individuals to become citizens would contribute to the "cruel and unusual punishments" of family separation by "tear[ing] up parental relations by the roots" in the event that the power to expel or deport were properly employed.[122]

Justice Fuller's ultimate argumentative aim was to establish a standard whereby the children of Europeans would continue to enjoy citizenship but the offspring of Chinese would not. The general arguments about international law, English common law, the intentions driving the Fourteenth Amendment, prior precedents, and earlier opinions concerning whether passports should issue to particular individuals could not achieve this distinction. To do so, he had to rest his reasoning on the specific elements and interpretations of US law that addressed the Chinese.

Treaties between nations, he claimed, could not be altered even by constitutional amendment. (He also claimed that no amendment could abridge Congress's power over naturalization, though he clarified that this argument could not apply to "our colored fellow-citizens, who never were aliens.")[123] Looking at the Burlingame Treaty, effective in 1870, he noted that, while the treaty mandated that visitors and immigrants between the two nations be afforded the rights and privileges enjoyed by citizens or subjects of the most favored nation, it also underlined that it did not provide a path toward naturalization for Chinese subjects in the United States. He then noted that the convention thrust upon a weakened Chinese government in 1894 clarified that Chinese residents, whether permanent or temporary, would not have the right to become naturalized citizens, a provision enshrined in US law.[124] Even if the Fourteenth Amendment could be read to grant birthright citizenship to individuals born in the nation, in Justice Fuller's reading it could not override the treaty or the implementing legislation, which forever debarred the parents from citizenship. Because the Chinese as a class could not become citizens, birth in the United States could not Americanize their children.

Beyond the legal analysis, Justice Fuller quoted *Fong Yue Ting*'s description of Chinese laborers as "of a distinct race and religion, remaining strangers in the land, residing apart by themselves, tenaciously adhering to the customs and usages of their own country, unfamiliar with our institutions, and apparently incapable of assimilating with our people." It was impossible for him to imagine "that the children of persons so situated become citizens by the accident of birth."[125]

Justice Fuller closed his argument by claiming that the president and Congress had the authority to "prescribe that all persons of a particular race, or their children, cannot become citizens." Then, to some extent undercutting all of his previous argumentation about the nature of the Fourteenth Amendment, he claimed that the amendment "does not exclude from citizenship by birth children born in the United States of parents permanently located therein, and who might themselves become citizens," but repeated his conclusion that the amendment did not "arbitrarily make" citizens of the children born to those who could not themselves become citizens.[126] Wong Kim Ark, in his estimation, was not a citizen, and the district court's ruling should have been reversed.

It is worth noting that Justice Harlan, the sole and eloquent dissenter in the *Civil Rights Cases* (1883) and *Plessy v. Ferguson* (1896), joined in the dissent. In those cases, he had been the only justice to understand that badges and incidents of slavery extended far beyond the institution of slavery itself; he penned the words that would be so frequently quoted in the twentieth century that "there is no caste here. Our Constitution is color-blind and neither knows nor tolerates classes among citizens."[127] He thought, however, that the matter of the Chinese was quite different from the matter of Black citizens in the aftermath of slavery. Justice Harlan did not believe that immigration law or the law of citizenship had to follow a color-blind principle. The nation had the right to exclude a race of people considered unassimilable.[128] Justice Harlan occasionally upheld procedural protections for Chinese facing deportation or exclusion but was often supportive of harsh and restrictive government policies.[129]

Justice Harlan's stance generally toward Asians was complicated. Analysis of his private correspondence and lecture notes suggests that he shared the common belief that the Chinese were unassimilable.[130] In lecturing to his law students on the question of birthright citizenship for the offspring of Chinese residents prior to the Court's 1898 ruling, he responded that "this is a race utterly foreign to us and will never assimilate with us."[131] His views, however, appeared to change in the wake of America's rapid embrace of imperialism in the early twentieth century. In confronting the constitutional problems of governing new territories inhabited by nonwhite residents now swept within the scope of American sovereignty, Justice Harlan dissented from the Court's rulings that confined the reach of constitutional protections to the continental United States. He reanimated his argument that the Constitution was color-blind and insisted that its protections should ensure access to basic rights by Filipinos.[132]

Public and Scholarly Reactions to the Ruling

The case produced a brief flurry of news coverage when the Court announced its ruling, though, as noted in chapter 4, the news was overshadowed by the announcement that an investigation confirmed that the *Maine* had been sunk by a mine in Havana Harbor. Still, brief news reports appeared concerning the decision in Australia and England as well as in the United States. On March 29, the day after the Court had ruled, the *New York Sun* characterized it as "An Important Decision" on page 9.[133] The *Vermont Sun* noted that the ruling "will have the effect of confirming the citizenship of such persons," totaling "several thousand persons in the United States."[134] While describing the ruling and dissent in fairly neutral terms, the *San Francisco Examiner* ran a story on March 29 under the headline "Chinese Who Are Citizens," subtitling it "Mongols Born in This Country Have All the Privileges of Natives."[135] The *Los Angeles Herald* ran a lengthier story, describing Justice Gray's opinion as "an exceedingly able presentation of the case" but claiming that Chief Justice Fuller's dissent was "hardly less elaborate and even more confident and emphatic in tone." The story noted that the ruling had already generated controversy in legal circles.[136]

Legal commentators exhibited more sustained interest in the case and its ramifications than the mass news media outside of California. A Comment in the *Yale Law Journal* in May noted the ruling, characterizing it as "a ratification of the decisions heretofore reached in the various state and circuit courts." The "exhaustive" majority ruling settled the question in favor of the English common-law principle, but the Comment's author found Chief Justice Fuller's take to be more satisfying. He rested his endorsement on Fuller's analysis of the special status of the Chinese and on his reading of the Fourteenth Amendment as excluding birthright citizenship for the children of resident aliens.[137]

A longer analysis in the *American Law Review* described the case as settling, "once and for all, the question of the citizenship of children born within the United States, whose parents are foreign subjects or citizens."[138] The author, Marshall Woodworth, a US district attorney in San Francisco who would be involved in future Supreme Court litigation addressing the rights of native-born Chinese, conceded that the supporters of the common-law doctrine of birthright citizenship had the superior argument.[139] While he credited the effort on the part of the solicitor general to distinguish between political and geographic jurisdiction, he sided with the majority's rejection of this distinction and simple declaration that the Fourteenth Amendment adopted the long-standing common-law principle. Woodward concluded that the ruling "sets at rest whatever of doubt may have been formerly entertained on the proposition." While the international law principle might be more "logical and satisfactory," the Fourteenth Amendment settled the question, and "it is difficult to see what valid objection can be raised thereto."[140]

Regardless of their evaluations of the Court's reasoning and Chief Justice Fuller's response to it, legal commentators immediately recognized the case's significance for Fourteenth Amendment jurisprudence. In his lectures on the Fourteenth Amendment published in 1898, Supreme Court lawyer and prominent scholar William Guthrie addressed the evolution of judicial thinking about the amendment. He began with Justice Miller's assertion in the *Slaughter-House Cases* that the amendment would be limited to addressing racial wrongs perpetrated against Black Americans and traced it through to the more expansive understandings embraced by the Court in *Yick Wo* and *Holden v. Hardy*.[141] He had little patience for Justice Miller's restrictive interpretation of the amendment, characterizing it as "clearly in conflict with the intentions of the framers," and criticized the chilling effect it exerted, which "for many years dwarfed and dulled the protective power of the amendment."[142]

Wong Kim Ark, Guthrie noted, further underlined the general applicability of the amendment.[143] He looked more specifically at how the amendment had applied in cases involving the Chinese, noting that the Court had frowned upon policies that clearly targeted them. For instance, while the Court had upheld general laws regulating laundries as "a reasonable exercise of the police power of the State, applying equally to all persons of whatever race in the same class," discriminatory legislation constituted "an arbitrary and unreasonable interference with individual liberty."[144]

The primary importance of the case, however, was its holding on birthright citizenship. Guthrie relied on *Elk v. Wilkins* and *Wong Kim Ark* to explain the meaning of the "subject to the jurisdiction" clause. The *Elk* case, he reasoned, had created uncertainty about the legal status of others born to noncitizen parents.[145] In his view, *Wong Kim Ark* resolved that uncertainty, though he framed the rule more narrowly than the Supreme Court had. He explained that the decision rendered almost all children born in the United States "of alien parents permanently domiciled and residing here."[146] He was struck by the breathtaking

implications of this outcome: "A male child born here of Chinese subjects is now eligible to the office of President, although his parents could
not be naturalized under our laws."[147]

Influential commentator and treatise author Thomas Cooley from
the University of Michigan also immediately incorporated his reading
of the case into his treatise on constitutional law in the section concerning citizenship. Cooley's treatises were widely disseminated and
considered by most legal practitioners to be authoritative. He traced
the current status of citizenship questions back to *Dred Scott*, characterizing the case as initiating "earnest and violent controversy" over Black
citizenship.[148] This controversy was not to be resolved until the passage of the Fourteenth Amendment. Cooley described the Fourteenth
Amendment's rule on birthright citizenship as requiring both birth in
the United States and subjection to US jurisdiction: "By this is meant
that full and complete jurisdiction to which citizens generally are subject, and not any qualified and partial jurisdiction, such as may consist
with allegiance to some other government."[149] The *Wong Kim Ark* ruling
settled that "children born within the United States of all persons, of
whatever race or color," were citizens, but it did not Americanize children of foreign ministers, those born on foreign public ships, or those
considered to be enemies.

Cooley noted Indians as being "in an anomalous condition." Embracing the *Wong Kim Ark* majority's analysis of *Elk v. Wilkins*, he highlighted the "semi-independent character" of tribes and the obligation
of individual Indians to acknowledge tribal leaders' sovereignty. This
both debarred their full vesting with the rights of citizens and prevented
them from acquiring all of citizens' obligations.[150] His placement of Indians in a separate category supported the Court's refusal to interpret
the Fourteenth Amendment to allow congressional control over birthright citizenship for the children of aliens. Unlike Guthrie, Cooley did
not claim that the Court's decision applied only to the children of permanent residents.

After this brief flurry of interest, however, new constitutional questions arose that overshadowed the debate over whether Gray or Fuller
had the better of the analysis. The abstract legal principle, once established, was left undisturbed for decades in the pages of the US reports,
though it both generated a path that many Chinese exploited to secure
unauthorized entry and greatly heightened official scrutiny and suspicion of individuals of Chinese descent who sought entry on this basis.[151]

Citizenship in the Balance

The exceptionally detailed analysis provided by both Justice Gray and Chief Justice Fuller signaled the significance of and the deep disagreement over *United States v. Wong Kim Ark* at the critical moment of the decision. Arguments for and against Wong Kim Ark's citizenship could have been made much more concisely, without the painstaking efforts to present the deep common-law history of the question, analyze the Fourteenth Amendment's jurisdiction clause and the intentions behind it, and trace the intricate paths of prior precedents addressing birthright citizenship and the scope of the Fourteenth Amendment. All participants in the litigation, however, understood the significance of the stakes and the need for a definitive resolution.

Citizenship hung in the balance for many groups. The native-born children of Chinese immigrants, of course, were affected. But unless the distinctions that Chief Justice Fuller expressed near the end of his dissent were adopted, so too was the citizenship of any child born in the continental United States to any alien, regardless of race or national origin. While some contributors to the conversation would not have been concerned with ceding the power to manage nationalization of all children of immigrants to Congress, the *Wong Kim Ark* dissenters wanted to distinguish the Chinese (and ultimately other nonwhite groups) from the descendants of European immigrants who did not need legislative or administrative hurdles in the way of access to citizenship.

Looming in the background as well was the United States' new role as an imperial power. While the ruling in the case embraced an expansive view of birthright citizenship, this view did not automatically extend beyond the boundaries of the continental United States. The Court issued its ruling in the critical period between the explosion of the *Maine* in February and Congress's declaration of war against Spain in May 1898. American acquisition of substantial new and far-flung territories at the conclusion of the war raised questions about how to navigate the allegiance and citizenship of territorial residents. While territorial residents' allegiances changed in response to the war, many in both imperial and anti-imperial camps in the continental United States were adamantly opposed to extending citizenship either to these residents or to their children born in the territories (a departure from earlier dealings with continental territorial residents). While part of the concern here was about Filipinos, a substantial Chinese minority residing in the

Philippines had to be addressed. Individuals who, like Wong Kim Ark, were born to Chinese parents but in Manila rather than San Francisco would not be granted the prize of citizenship, and in 1902, exclusion laws were extended to Hawaii and the Philippines.[152]

As described in chapter 4, the ruling in the case did not even definitively settle the status of Wong Kim Ark himself. He faced institutionalized suspicion upon each of his subsequent trips to China, and his own son was detained at Angel Island for two weeks before being permitted to enter in 1926. [153]

6 | Citizenship and Immigration
The Next Battles

Wong Kim Ark presented a substantial obstacle to those who continued to push back against birthright citizenship in the United States for those they considered undesirable citizens. While they did not give up on the matter in the aftermath of the decision, restrictionists found other avenues in which to work to bar US entry to undesirables on the basis of race, ethnicity, or country of origin. If the sons and daughters of those who arrived were citizens if born on American soil, then keeping undesirable migrants out in the first place became even more important to the efforts to shape membership in the polity.

Restrictionists believed the Fourteenth Amendment's citizenship clause, as read by the Court, was at odds with the goals of immigration policies enacted to regulate the entry of persons and ethnic groups deemed undesirable for membership in the body politic—or, indeed, the very ability to define the political community. As Rachel Rosenbloom has pointed out, "There are tensions between the closed borders of immigration law and the open borders of birthright citizenship."[1] This was especially true in the late nineteenth century and roughly the first half of the twentieth century. The tension has come to the fore again in recent years, as we will see in chapter 7.

These additional efforts to police membership in the polity worked to maintain the whiteness of US citizenship. Law and policy critically shaped the characteristics of American citizenship in the early to middle decades of the twentieth century by dealing with newly acquired territories at the time of the Spanish-American War, restricting immigration by imposition of new barriers aimed not only at Asians but at southern and eastern Europeans in particular, creating new policies directed at Caribbean and Mexican migrants, and transforming the treatment of America's first peoples.

Citizenship did not create equal status—not even birthright citizenship. As women soon discovered after passage of the Fourteenth Amendment and African Americans soon discovered after passage of the Fifteenth Amendment, citizenship did not entail the right to vote. It did not preclude racial segregation, discrimination, and restrictions on marriage through antimiscegenation laws. It did not entail the right to serve on juries or in the military. It did not necessarily entail the right to make contracts, especially for women. As Chinese Americans found out and Mexican Americans would soon learn, birthright citizenship did not offer protection in fact against deportation or eviction from one's country of origin. Many female birthright citizens lost their US citizenship upon marrying foreign men. In some states, Native Americans were barred from voting, even in the years immediately following World War II, either on the ground that they did not pay taxes or on the ground that they were under guardianship of the federal government and were not actually subject to the jurisdiction of the state.[2] Many policies and practices reveal the liminality of some US citizens and the existence of forms of what Elizabeth Cohen has called "semi-citizenship," revealing that citizenship is differentiated and not binary.[3] This chapter sketches the complicated nature of restrictive immigration policies, their relationship to citizenship, and the overall impact of these practices in shaping the citizenry of the United States over the course of the twentieth century.

Through much of the twentieth century, the immigration and naturalization system operated to influence the nation's racial composition. The national origins quota system in the 1924 act rolled back the 1921 baseline from the 1910 to the 1890 census and reduced the quotas from 3 percent to 2 percent of foreign-born persons of each nationality who resided in the United States in the baseline year. Moving back the census baseline drastically and deliberately reduced the number of people who could immigrate from southern or eastern Europe. Few Africans would enter under the quota system for many years, since few foreign-born persons from African nations resided in the United States at that time. From 1925 to 1927, the entire continent of Africa was accorded a quota of 1,100 per year, with Egypt adding 100 persons to that total. The entire continental quota was less than the quota for the Netherlands; Ireland's quota was 28,567. Asians, of course, were closed out almost completely, since the quotas were based on the prior legal ability to immigrate.[4] This legislation provided the broad framework under which policies regarding immigrants developed from the end of World War I through the mid-twentieth century.

Exclusionist Work

In the aftermath of World War I, birthright citizenship was again on the agenda, with a special focus on restricting Japanese immigration. While Congress had restricted Chinese immigration through legislation, Japanese immigration fell under the 1907 Gentlemen's Agreement negotiated between Theodore Roosevelt and the Japanese government, in which Japan agreed not to permit the emigration of Japanese workers seeking to enter the United States. The California Oriental Exclusion League found the Gentlemen's Agreement completely insufficient and wanted a comprehensive law to bar entry of all Japanese immigrants, including "picture brides" and the elimination of any opportunity for naturalization.[5] The organization also sought an amendment to the Constitution declaring that "no child born in the United States shall be given the rights of an American citizen unless both parents are of a race eligible to citizenship."[6] At the time, this provision would have limited these rights to whites or those of African heritage, as the latter fell within the 1870 amendments to the 1790 Naturalization Act designed to make citizens of formerly enslaved Blacks. Other groups advanced similar positions, and the American Legion, founded in Minneapolis in 1919, advocated an amendment to the first section of the Fourteenth Amendment with language almost identical to that proposed by the California Oriental Exclusion League.[7] A number of representatives and senators from western states complained of high birth rates among Japanese, their possession of some of the richest irrigated farmland, and their unfitness for citizenship.[8] Several states responded to this threat on the state level by passing laws that restricted aliens' legal ability to hold land, at first directly targeting Japanese residents and then broadening the restriction to address efforts by family members to hold land for Japanese residents who could not naturalize.[9] In 1919, 1921, and 1923, resolutions were introduced in Congress to amend the Constitution with language such as this from 1919 and 1921: no child "hereafter born in the United States of foreign parentage shall be eligible to citizenship in the United States unless both parents are eligible to become citizens of the United States."[10]

With the imposition of quotas in 1921 and 1924 and the nearly universal bar on Asian immigration, these efforts subsided until after Pearl Harbor. After the attack, anti-Japanese sentiment increased sharply, provoking more attention to birthright citizenship. Responding in part to economic concerns among white citizens, the governor of New Mexico reached out to other western governors to collaborate to bring a test case before the Supreme Court to reconsider *Wong Kim Ark*.[11] The Native Sons of the Golden West and the American Legion filed a suit to overturn *Wong Kim Ark*. The immediate trigger was an effort to remove Nisei from the voting rolls at least for the duration of the war, but the suit also claimed that they were not properly US citizens. Represented by former California attorney general Ulysses S. Webb, the organizations argued that *Wong Kim Ark* was "one of the most injurious and unfortunate decisions ever handed down by the Court," and that the intent of the Fourteenth Amendment was simply to benefit African Americans.[12] Attorney General Earl Warren, running for governor, apparently lent his support to their cause.[13] In *Regan v. King*, Webb argued that the Declaration of Independence and the Constitution were made entirely "by and for white people." Support for birthright citizenship and for the Japanese had come from the American Civil Liberties Union (called the League in the district court records), the Japanese-American Citizens League, and the NAACP.[14]

At the trial court level, the federal district court for the Northern District of California rather summarily ruled against the challenge to birthright citizenship. The decision noted that the Supreme Court had twice cited *Wong Kim Ark* approvingly. In 1934, an opinion for the Court authored by Justice Cardozo in *Morrison v. California* had held that "a

---

Major Court Reaffirmations of *Wong Kim Ark*

- *Morrison v. California*, 291 U.S. 82 (1934): A person of the Japanese race is a citizen of the United States if born within the United States.
- *Perkins v. Elg*, 307 U.S. 325 (1939): A child born in the United States of alien parentage becomes a citizen.
- *Regan v. King*, 49 F. Supp. 222 (N.D. Cal. 1942): Ruled summarily against challenge to birthright citizenship for US Nisei in a case involving access to the ballot. Appealed to Ninth Circuit.
- *Regan v. King*, F.2d 413 (9th Circuit, 1943): In a per curiam decision, affirmed ruling in *Regan v. King*. Supreme Court refused to hear the case.

person of the Japanese race is a citizen of the United States if he was born within the United States."[15] In *Perkins v. Elg* (1939), Chief Justice Hughes, writing for the Court, held that "a child born here of alien parentage becomes a citizen of the United States."[16] The plaintiffs' appeal to the Ninth Circuit in February 1943—occurring the same day the Japanese internment cases of *Korematsu* and *Hirabayashi* were heard—was unsuccessful, with the court determining that oral argument by the other side was not even necessary to reach a conclusion.[17] The Supreme Court refused to accept the case.

Direct assaults on birthright citizenship subsequently receded, and the issue faded from national attention from roughly this time until the 1980s.[18] But the status of persons in US territories and immigration continued to be sites for citizenship work and contestation.

Empire and Citizenship

Just as *Wong Kim Ark* was decided in the Supreme Court, the United States and Spain went to war in a confrontation that would soon yield new US territories, including Puerto Rico, the Philippines, and Guam. Cuba gained its independence after the Spanish-American War but fell under the sway of its powerful northern neighbor, and the United States soon acquired a one-hundred-year renewable lease on a naval base at Guantánamo Bay. The war was a significant factor in the annexation of Hawaii in 1898 as well, and its formalized territorial status in 1900. The "Bayonet Constitution" of 1887 restricted suffrage to property owners and reduced the power of the monarchy. Sugar planters led by Dole subsequently overthrew Queen Liliuokalani in 1893, when she tried to recoup some of the monarchy's lost power and reverse many of the constitutional changes imposed in 1887.[19] The American government's interest in Pearl Harbor, obtained as a US naval base in the reciprocity treaty of 1875 and reiterated in the constitution of 1887, was a significant factor in tipping the scales for President McKinley in the face of changing US interests in the Pacific. Pearl Harbor conferred commercial advantages in the Far East, though Admiral Dewey's victory in Manila in the Spanish-American War occurred shortly before approval of annexation, and military interests were also invoked.[20] The rights to the base at Pearl Harbor could have been canceled with one year's notice by either side according to the reciprocity treaty.[21]

The legal status of most of these territories and their inhabitants was initially unclear. With the Republic of Hawaii controlled by American-friendly interests, many of which had resided in the islands for decades, Hawaiians were quickly accorded US citizenship. According to 8 U.S. Code §1405:

> A person born in Hawaii on or after August 12, 1898, and before April 30, 1900, is declared to be a citizen of the United States as of April 30, 1900. A person born in Hawaii on or after April 30, 1900, is a citizen of the United States at birth. A person who was a citizen of the Republic of Hawaii on August 12, 1898, is declared to be a citizen of the United States as of April 30, 1900.[22]

A number of public officials believed that, even with the grant of US citizenship, the political influence of native Hawaiians could be curbed through restrictions on the right to vote, preserving the political dominance of white propertied interests on the island.[23] Left unsettled by this formulation was the status of persons of Japanese, Chinese, Korean, or Indian ancestry who were born in Hawaii on or after August, 12, 1898, if their parents were not citizens of the Republic of Hawaii. Were they also citizens of the United States by virtue of being born in Hawaii? The logic of the newly decided *Wong Kim Ark* case would seem to say yes, but this issue would be contested in US courts.

The Pacific Islanders in what was known as American Samoa were not granted American citizenship when their leaders signed treaties in 1900 and 1904 giving the United States full power and authority to govern them. The State Department, by policy, designated them "non-citizen nationals"; to this day, their US-issued passports state: "This bearer is a United States national and not a United States citizen." Efforts to grant them US citizenship in the 1930s failed to pass the House of Representatives, though measures passed the Senate. They could live and work in the United States, but they could neither hold a government job that requires citizenship nor vote in state or federal elections. In 2019, a federal district court in Utah ruled that American Samoans were entitled to citizenship but shortly after issued a stay while his ruling remains under appeal.[24]

The postannexation Treaty of Paris (1898) did not promise American citizenship to residents of Puerto Rico or the Philippines. Article IX of the treaty stipulated that "the civil rights and political status of the native inhabitants of the territories hereby ceded to the United States shall

Access to US Citizenship by Birth and Naturalization following *Wong Kim Ark* (1898)

- 1900—By statute, citizens of Republic of Hawaii become US citizens, and those born there after April 30, 1900, are citizens by birth.
- 1905—*Matter of Heff:* Native Americans who accepted individual land allotments automatically became US citizens and federal protection must cease for citizens.
- 1907—American-born women who marry foreign men are denationalized (foreign women who marry male American citizens become US citizens).
- 1916—*United States v. Nice:* Citizenship for Native Americans not incompatible with tribal existence or continued guardianship.
- 1917—By statute, collective US naturalization of citizens of Puerto Rico; 1940 Nationality Act later affirms birthright citizenship for those born in Puerto Rico.
- 1922—Cable Act restores American citizenship to women who marry foreign men unless male is ineligible for naturalization, or the woman resides abroad for a period of time.
- 1922—*Ozawa v. United States* finds Japanese not included under "free white person" stipulation in 1870 Naturalization Act; they are not Caucasian.
- 1923—*United States v. Bhagat Singh Thind* holds a high-caste Hindu, even if deemed Caucasian, cannot naturalize because he is not white.
- 1924—Indian Citizenship Act declares Native Americans US citizens.
- 1925—*Toyota v. United States*: Those of Japanese ancestry who served US military in the First World War cannot naturalize; Congress deemed to have authorized naturalization by Filipino veterans only.
- 1935—Alien Veteran Naturalization Act authorizes the naturalization of resident alien veterans of World War I previously forbidden to naturalize.
- 1943—Repeal of Chinese Exclusion Act of 1882.
- 1952—McCarran-Walter Act allows Chinese and Japanese to become naturalized citizens.
- 2019—*Fitisemanu v. United States*: In Utah federal district court, American Samoans deemed birthright citizens; decision stayed pending review by the Tenth Circuit Court of Appeals. Argued September 23, 2020 (20-4017).

be determined by the Congress."[25] President McKinley saw the people of annexed Spanish-speaking territories as less civilized and less advanced than Americans.[26] Filipinos, according to Vice President Taft's report to the McKinley administration, were "ignorant, superstitious, and credulous in remarkable degree."[27] In neither case did the McKinley and Taft administrations foresee immediate self-government or American citizenship. Catholic Filipinos were considered civilized, but non-Christian Filipinos were viewed as savage, and, as Paul Kramer argues, the Philippine-American War (also known as the Tagalog Insurgency) following Spanish cession of the Philippines developed into a race war.[28] Filipinos, seen as neither loyal nor docile by comparison with Puerto Ricans, were never granted US citizenship, and the citizenship status of inhabitants of these two territories would quickly diverge. Filipinos, like American Samoans, were to be designated noncitizen nationals, but the Philippines became independent in 1946, after World War II.

Acquisition of these territories raised questions in academic and political circles about what was the "United States" and what constitutional provisions should apply to inhabitants of these island territories.[29] From 1900 to 1904, the US Supreme Court was "unwilling either to adopt or reject the view that the United States could hold colonies populated by nonindigenous noncitizen subjects."[30] The Court grappled with the constitutional status of these new territories in the *Insular Cases* of 1901 and subsequently. In a fractured opinion in *Downes v. Bidwell* (1901), Justice Brown wrote for the Court that administration of government and justice according to Anglo-Saxon principles in territories "inhabited by alien races, differing from us," might be impossible for the foreseeable future.[31] In Justice Brown's reading, "the power to acquire territory by treaty implies not only the power to govern such territory, but to prescribe upon what terms the United States will receive its inhabitants, and what their *status* shall be in what Chief Justice Marshall termed the 'American Empire.'"[32] Nevertheless, citing several early decisions in the history of Chinese exclusion cases, Justice Brown rejected the view that "the people are in the matter of personal rights unprotected by the provisions of our Constitution, and subject to the merely arbitrary control of Congress. Even if regarded as aliens, they are entitled under the principles of the Constitution to be protected in life, liberty and property."[33]

Justice White's concurrence in *Downes* became the foundation of a view that would gain ascendance: that new territories could be either incorporated or unincorporated, and each stood in a different rela-

tionship to the Constitution.[34] Rather than having their governing controlled by constitutional standards, Congress would have the authority
to establish and change the operation of American sovereignty in the
territories at will. As Justice White explained, "Whilst in an international
sense Puerto Rico was not a foreign country, since it was subject to the
sovereignty of and was owned by the United States, it was foreign to the
United States in a domestic sense, because the island had not been incorporated into the United States was but merely appurtenant thereto,
as a possession."[35] Incorporated territories, such as Alaska, were held to
have the full protection of the US Constitution, while unincorporated
territories had some unspecified "fundamental" constitutional protections. Congress had "power to dispose of and make all needful Rules
and Regulations respecting the Territory or other Property belonging
to the United States" as stipulated in Article IV, Section 3, of the Constitution.[36] Christina Burnett Ponsa argues that the *Insular Cases* should
be read as establishing the possibility of future territorial *deannexation* so
long as US territory remained unincorporated.[37] Yet as Sparrow points
out, the *Insular Cases*—especially *Downes*—"established the political and
constitutional subordination of the United States' island territories."[38]
Full acceptance of the incorporation doctrine crystallized in the unanimous 1922 Supreme Court decision in *Balzac v. People of Porto Rico*, with
Taft, a chief architect of US territorial policies and the first American
governor-general of the Philippines, now serving as chief justice.[39]

The unclear status of the territories extended to the people born
and living in them. In the case of Puerto Rico, the issue came to a head
in the person of Isabel Gonzalez, a twenty-year-old pregnant widow
who sought to move from Puerto Rico to New York in 1902, possibly to
marry another Puerto Rican who had already arrived and settled there.
Between the signing of the Treaty of Paris and the summer of 1902,
while Puerto Ricans were not treated as citizens, they were also not
treated as aliens when they sought to enter the continental states. With
the passage of the Philippine Organic Act of 1902 and the legislative
establishment of the status of "citizens of the Philippine Islands" for Filipinos, the Treasury Department put into place a policy requiring Puerto
Ricans to go through the same examination process as aliens upon entering.[40] Ellis Island's inspectors, using this process, determined that
Gonzalez was ineligible for entry as a potential public charge. Her case
(in part due to her insistence) became the test case concerning whether
Puerto Ricans were citizens.[41]

Before the Supreme Court, the solicitor general argued that Puerto Ricans were nationals rather than citizens, noting the racial differentiations embedded in immigration law and citing Congress's clear intent to protect the mainland from undesirable entrants. Elite New York lawyer Frederic Coudert, arguing on Gonzalez's behalf, pressed for citizenship, albeit in a constrained form that did not carry implications of equality. His framing presented imperialism as posing a new problem for the United States: that of ruling a people who could not be assimilated, exterminated, or driven away.[42] Cosmopolitan Puerto Rican lawyer Federico Degetau, on the other hand, filed an amicus brief arguing for full citizenship for himself and other Puerto Rican men, situating them atop the racial hierarchy of the United States' new colonial possessions.[43] The Court ruled unanimously that Puerto Ricans were not aliens and extended to them the right to migrate freely. The justices pointedly refused, however, to confirm Puerto Rican citizenship.[44]

Bills to grant Puerto Ricans citizenship were introduced in every Congress after 1900, and members of Congress viewed citizenship as a reward for the islanders' loyalty; they also considered Puerto Ricans more white and therefore more assimilable than Filipinos.[45] Without US citizenship, Puerto Ricans did not hold US passports, making it difficult even for merchants to travel. In the 1906 Bureau of Immigration and Naturalization Act, Congress resolved the ambiguity by affording persons born in Puerto Rico a route to US citizenship; they would have to travel to the mainland and go through the then-prevailing naturalization process that applied to other racially eligible immigrants.[46]

Collective US naturalization for Puerto Ricans was ordained by the Jones Act of 1917, signed into law a month before US entry into World War I, and there was, in addition, a bill of rights.[47] Congress declined to naturalize Filipinos at the same time.[48] President Wilson had been pressing for reform of Puerto Rican status, in part to improve America's reputation in Latin America and the Caribbean.[49]

Supporters of the Jones Act in both parties and in the Bureau of Insular Affairs anticipated that citizenship would maintain dependence and would pave no road toward statehood; political and administrative officials on the island would still be appointed in Washington.[50] The Jones Act "reaffirmed the indefinite colonial status of the island by conferring a type of citizenship on its inhabitants that strengthened Puerto Rico's ties to the United States but gave its people few of the civil and political rights normally associated with American citizenship."[51] In the words of Senator Foraker, the grant of citizenship was never intended to confer on the island's inhabitants "any rights that the American people [did] not want them to have."[52] Citizenship meant that Puerto Rico belonged to the United States, and that Congress could, under the Constitution, do with its territories what it wished.[53]

In *Balzac* (1922), the Taft Court held that citizenship for Puerto Ricans was completely consistent with nonincorporation; Puerto Ricans who moved to the United States had full rights as American citizens, but it was locality that determined the application of the Constitution.[54] Puerto Ricans might be US citizens, but only some constitutional protections applied to them as residents of an unincorporated territory, and the United States, acting through Congress, "could exercise sovereignty more or less indefinitely over people and areas outside the boundaries of the states."[55]

Racial hierarchy complicated debates over Puerto Rican naturalization. White supremacy had gained ascendance in national politics, and with dark-skinned peoples structurally disenfranchised throughout the former Confederacy, national actors agreed to extend these principles to address the many African-heritage residents of Puerto Rico. Newly created voters would be expected to meet some mix of property ownership, taxpayer status, and literacy requirements.[56]

The Jones Act did not provide for birthright citizenship to those born subsequent to the act. It also "created thousands of stateless residents of the island," such as children of aliens and children of certain mixed marriages. The Cable Act of 1922, which restored US citizenship to American women who married foreigners eligible for naturalization, was not extended to the island until a 1934 amendment to the Jones Act.[57] In that same amendment, retroactive naturalization was extended to all those who were born in Puerto Rico between 1899 and the enactment of the amendment and who were not citizens or nationals of another country.[58] Finally, the Nationality Act of 1940 replaced the Jones Act, granting jus soli citizenship to Puerto Ricans based on the Fourteenth Amendment's citizenship clause: birth in Puerto Rico now meant, in effect, birth in the United States.[59] The Nationality Act also reaffirmed that those born in the United States and subject to the jurisdiction thereof were birthright citizens, and excluded those whom Congress had deemed US nationals from birthright citizenship.[60] Since then, "Congress has enacted several laws that affirm the Nationality Act's citizenship provisions for Puerto Rico and grant all persons born in the island U.S. native-born citizenship status."[61] Yet Congress still retains power to revoke US citizenship for Puerto Ricans.[62] Under the territorial clause (Article IV, Section 3, clause 2), "the Congress shall have Power to dispose of and make all needful Rules and Regulations respecting the Territory or other Property belonging to the United States." President Trump's 2019 idea of sweetening the deal proposed to Denmark to sell Greenland to the United States by throwing Puerto Rico into the trade was treated as a joke but was hypothetically possible.

Fast-forward several generations. In early 2018, a group of American Samoan plaintiffs asked a federal judge to decide whether they were covered by the Fourteenth Amendment's provision that they were born "within" the United States, and therefore citizens. Alone among the remaining unincorporated territories of the United States, residents of American Samoa do not have US citizenship.[63] The court had to evaluate the precedent of *Wong Kim Ark* in light of the precedent of *Downes v. Bidwell,* one of the *Insular Cases.* Because *Wong Kim Ark*'s establishment of birthright citizenship took place before the *Insular Cases,* the government invited the court to read *Downes* as a modification of *Wong Kim Ark*'s broad principle. In the December 2019 decision, Judge Clark Waddoups of the District Court for Utah looked to the reasoning and history displayed in the *Wong Kim Ark* ruling and held that American Samoans were indeed birthright citizens.[64] The opinion explained that *Wong Kim Ark* governed the question rather than allowing the island's territorial status to determine the status of its residents. Yet the same judge quickly issued a stay until a federal appeals court could review the question. If the District Court ruling is upheld, it would be a striking rejection of more than one hundred years of US policy and of congressional refusal to grant American Samoans citizenship.

Southern Neighbors from the Western Hemisphere

Under the 1848 Treaty of Guadalupe Hidalgo, Mexicans who remained in the annexed territories were declared eligible for citizenship. This established a somewhat ambiguous umbrella presumption that Mexicans seeking to naturalize were eligible for US citizenship. In 1897, a West Texas district court held that Mexicans could naturalize, articulating this principle in the case of a man, Ricardo Rodriguez, who declared himself to be a "pure-blooded Mexican," but "if the strict scientific classification of the anthropologist should be adopted, he would not be classified as white."[65] Despite this, the court relied on the extension of citizenship by the Treaty of Guadalupe Hidalgo to imply Mexican eligibility. It noted in passing that the Fourteenth Amendment "confers the right of citizenship upon persons of all other races, white, yellow, or red, born or naturalized in the United States," citing *Wong Kim Ark* and related cases and distinguishing *Elk v. Wilkins* as applying only to "tribal Indians born and residing within . . . the United States."[66] Nonetheless, some bureaucrats balked on the grounds that US citizenship, under the Naturalization Act of 1870, was restricted to whites and Blacks.[67] Mexican immigration increased during the 1910s, with some fleeing the Mexican Revolution and some drawn by programs encouraging their immigration in the face of World War I labor shortages that extended beyond the Southwest.[68] During this decade, however, Mexican attempts to naturalize did not markedly increase.[69]

Employers in agriculture and some industries continued to seek Mexican and Latin American workers in the 1920s as European immigration dropped with the imposition of national origin quotas, first in the 1921 Immigration Act and more dramatically in 1924. Notably, both acts exempted immigrants from the Western Hemisphere.[70] Concerns about Asian immigration had largely focused on ports, despite a long and largely silent history of Asian immigrants' land border crossings from both Canada and Mexico.[71] The Immigration Service had not been closely policing the southern land border until late in the second decade of the century; only after 1919 were Mexicans entering the United States required to apply at designated ports of entry.[72] Furthermore, Mexican agricultural workers, followed shortly by Mexicans coming to work on railroads, on construction, or in mining, were exempted from the literacy test and head tax requirements in the 1917 Immigration Act during the war and until March 1921.[73] While white interest in securing docile labor was significant in this dynamic, politicians were also reluctant to alter the "special relationship" between Latin America and the United States, justifying preferential treatment in immigration alongside opportunities for intervention in affairs of their southern neighbors.[74] While restrictionists continued to press for limitations by adding Mexicans to the quota system in the National Origins Act (Johnson-Reed Act), they were unable to overcome the political will of business and diplomatic interests.

The promise of open Latin American migration was complicated by Black-white racial tensions as Caribbean migration to the United States increased starting in the latter decades of the nineteenth century. Many Caribbean immigrants came from the British Caribbean and were classified as Black or nonwhite. The number of Black persons coming to the United States from the Caribbean increased dramatically from 1900 until passage of the Johnson-Reed Act of 1924, establishing tight quotas based on nationality.[75] While the Johnson-Reed Act did not establish any quotas for those coming from the Western Hemisphere, immigrants from the British West Indies, largely Black individuals, were required to seek US entry under the quota established for Great Britain, a racially charged caveat to the Western Hemisphere's exemption from the quota system.[76] The British quota in 1925 was approximately thirty-four thousand. Yet even when quotas in one part of the world were not filled, the open positions did not shift to oversubscribed areas: "Remarkably, although Britain consistently underused its quota by several thousands, the Caribbean migration was kept low, never rising in the late 1920s and 1930s to the levels reached before the 1924 legislation."[77]

Even before the depths of the Depression, the number of Mexicans deported across the border between 1925 and 1929 increased nearly ninefold (although the numbers through 1929 included voluntary departures).[78] In many cases, the reason for deportation was entry without a proper visa. Subjected to head taxes, visa fees, delousing, medical inspection, and interrogation, many Mexicans avoided formal admission requirements and ports of entry, thus increasing what became classified as illegal entry.[79] Nativist organizations, including the California Joint Immigration Committee, an umbrella organization that included the Native Sons of the Golden West, state branches of the American Legion, and the Federation of Labor, ramped up efforts to have Mexicans—representatives of "brown" or "red" races—barred from naturalization following two key Supreme Court decisions involving Japanese Americans and Indians from the subcontinent.[80] In the face of restrictionist pressure in 1924, the Coolidge administration curbed Mexican immigration through administrative measures, applying literacy tests more vigorously and barring those considered likely to become public charges.[81] After the Johnson-Reed Act of 1924, prospective immigrants also had to present a medical certificate when applying for a visa before the US consul before traveling to the United States.[82] In the 1920s, Mexicans became the single largest group of undocumented migrants.[83]

At the outset of 1929, preceding the October stock market crash by several months, the State Department instructed American consuls in

Mexico to apply the legal requirements for Mexican would-be entrants more stringently (including implementing literacy tests and enforcing the public charge stipulation) to reduce the numbers of migrants. When the Depression hit, Mexicans were seen as a drain on jobs and resources, and the US Senate passed a bill to apply quotas to Mexican immigration, only to have it die in the House of Representatives after active opposition by the State Department.[84] By 1932, more Mexicans were leaving than entering the United States.[85]

Birthright citizenship offered ethnic Mexicans little protection in the face of pervasive hostility to what Mae Ngai has termed alien citizenship, or the stubborn insistence that one's legal status was based on the ethnicity of one's ancestors. She points out that the tradition of birthright citizenship has been a strategy for immigrant incorporation for those of European background, with national origin receding rapidly, while Asian and Latino birthright citizens have been continually mischaracterized as foreign, alien.[86] These dynamics have frequently resulted in what she terms "citizenship nullification."[87]

National, state, and local governments undertook coordinated efforts to remove Mexicans and individuals of Mexican ancestry through state power, both by deportation and by increasing pressure to encourage them to leave.[88] President Hoover believed that aliens were holding jobs that should be filled by citizens during the Depression—even though many of the aliens were jobless—and "endorsed a strenuous effort to curtail both legal and illegal entries and to expel undesirable aliens."[89] The federal government's deportation campaign aimed to repatriate destitute aliens on the relief rolls. Simultaneously, through either private charitable agencies or local welfare bureaus, US cities and counties sought to repatriate aliens receiving governmental assistance.[90] Some ethnic Mexicans left of their own accord rather than encounter deportation raids. The "persuasive" efforts had a major impact, with somewhere between several hundred thousand and more than a million Mexicans and Mexican Americans leaving the United States.[91] Approximately half of were US citizens, often children born in the United States.[92]

Beyond the efforts targeting Mexicans and Mexican Americans during the Depression, deportation had a broader historical legacy. Even in times when the nation was not experiencing economic upheaval, aliens could be deported for violating any number of US laws.[93] At the beginning of the twentieth century, political concerns became part of administrative policy, and Congress authorized the deportation of anarchists in the wake of William McKinley's assassination. In 1903, British labor activist and anarchist John Turner challenged his deportation in a case that reached the US Supreme Court, which found that Congress was rightfully empowered to determine and defend against threats to the United States in the person of dangerous immigrants.[94] In the 1910s, authorities targeted Russian Jewish immigrant girls who "went wrong," sometimes deporting them to a country they barely remembered and where they could be subject to anti-Semitic violence.[95]

Labor concerns, both economic and ideological, affected immigration policy in the World War I era and afterward. In the Southwest, as noted earlier, the need for labor generated some willingness to accept temporary workers from Mexico, though their status and fitness for long-term residency were controversial. Southwesterners took somewhat different tacks, with many New Mexico political elites doubling down on anti-German sentiments while Arizona saw vigilante violence in defense of patriotism.[96] Throughout the nation, the interest in protecting the United States against radical thought and action intensified during the antisocialist and anticommunist panics that followed World War I and the Bolshevik Revolution. The 1918 Alien Act authorized deportation of "any alien who, at any time after entering the United States, is found to have been at the time of entry, or to have become thereafter," a member of a class of aliens who were considered anarchists or who believed in violent overthrow of American government. During the Red Scare period, and especially in late 1919 and early 1920, Attorney General A. Mitchell Palmer identified myriad "parlor Reds" considered dangerous and sought to round up and deport labor radicals, targeting especially Communists and Communist Labor Party members.[97] He placed J. Edgar Hoover at the head of the Anti-Radical (soon transformed into the General Intelligence) Division of the Justice Department's Bureau of Investigation and coordinated with the Department of Labor, which had jurisdiction over deportations. The object was not to charge labor radicals with crimes, which would require full-dress trials with due process, but simply to deport them as subject to the Alien Act, left to administrative implementation with less judicial oversight.[98] Anyone arrested who claimed to be an American citizen had to produce documentary evidence to that effect.[99] A well-placed public official or two and enough citizens were concerned about civil liberties violations that the federal roundups of suspected radicals did not result in anywhere near as many deportations as Palmer had hoped.[100] As the furor subsided, policy changes facilitated greater access to counsel and fairer bail procedures for immigrants facing deportation, and in 1922, the Department of Labor established a Secretary's Board of Review to prevent abuses.[101] Still, the American-born children of such deportees were often collateral damage.

Deportation of individuals claiming citizenship nonetheless bore its risks for exclusionists. In the early twentieth century, the US courts settled that Chinese individuals seeking to enter the United States on the basis of citizenship could only pursue routine appeals of adverse decisions within the Bureau of Immigration. In 1906, however, the Seventh Circuit ruled in *Moy Suey v. United States* that individuals claiming citizenship as a defense to deportation proceedings could demand that the federal courts resolve the dispute.[102] A deportation order could, if reversed by a court, then lead to a formal finding that the target was a citizen. The Bureau of Immigration's officials complained about the ruling both because it limited their discretion and because individuals appealing deportation orders in court could use the time between the administrative process and the judicial process to develop targeted defenses against the factual picture presented on the administrative side.[103] Some courts sided with the Bureau of Immigration on this issue, but in 1922, the Supreme Court resolved the matter in favor of individuals present in the United States and claiming citizenship. They would be able to turn to the courts for determination of the "essential jurisdictional fact" of citizenship.[104]

The Second World War would again lead to active recruitment of agricultural and industrial labor from Mexico and the Caribbean. In August 1942, the United States and Mexico agreed to allow the recruitment of Mexican temporary workers to fill the wartime gap in American industrial and agricultural capacity. The Bracero program's workers, to both the American government and their employers, "were literally arms for temporary hire, not human beings to whom American society owed anything." To encourage their return to Mexico, the US government withheld 10 percent of their wages and remitted it to the Mexican government, but many workers never received these funds. Despite the poor working conditions and lack of any meaningful legal protections, between 1942 and 1964, more than 5.2 million people participated in the program; additional individuals simply crossed the border without documentation and worked without any engagement with the program.[105] With the exception already noted, formal immigration from

Latin America remained outside the quota system until 1952, when the McCarran-Walter Act provided an annual quota of one hundred persons for each colony in the Caribbean; Congress overrode Truman's veto of the bill.[106] While the Hart-Celler Act of 1965 is best known for eliminating the national origins quota system, it represented the first time that the United States opted to restrict Western Hemisphere immigration in roughly the same way as immigration from Europe and Asia. The act, which went into effect in 1968, allowed for 170,000 immigrants per year from the Eastern Hemisphere, with no more than 20,000 from any one country; 120,000 immigrants were allowed entry from the Western Hemisphere, with no country limitations. In both cases, family ties and skills would confer advantages in the queue.[107] Congress would equalize immigration levels between hemispheres in 1976.[108] Soon after implementation of Hart-Celler, immigration from Latin America and the Caribbean would constitute the largest source of immigration to the United States, and waiting times to get immigrant visas for those in the Western Hemisphere grew.[109] By 1971, congressional concern for illegal immigration, especially from Mexico, would become pronounced.[110]

Gendered and Racialized Gates

American women faced a different form of birthright citizenship nullification and could be actually stripped of birthright citizenship. The laws of coverture, still pervasive in the nineteenth century, dictated that a woman's legal existence followed her husband's. The Naturalization Act of 1855 declared that foreign wives of (male) US citizens were henceforth US citizens, without having to go through the naturalization process, although by 1917, the law made exceptions for alien women of "sexually immoral classes."[111] And yet, female US birthright citizens who married foreign males lost their citizenship upon marriage as of 1907, even if they resided in the United States.[112] As Nancy Cott observes about the asymmetrical situation, "The American man's wife and children were welcomed into political belonging unless the racial limitation was overstepped, but the American woman and her foreign husband were ejected from the national community."[113] Dependent on the laws of the nation where their husbands held citizenship, many women were rendered stateless by US citizenship termination.[114] Elite women—including prominent agitators for woman suffrage such as

Harriot Stanton Blatch—may have been in part the target of such de-nationalization efforts, even when they were marrying men from England or Western Europe. However, the law and its subsequent fixes had racialized consequences.

Female activists worked tirelessly to rectify the injustices they perceived in the 1907 act, and the Cable Act (Married Women's Independent Citizenship Act) of 1922 resolved some of the issues. An American woman who married a foreign man no longer automatically lost her US citizenship, though if she resided in her husband's country for two years or elsewhere outside the United States for five, she would forfeit her citizenship, just as if she had been a naturalized citizen.[115] Instead of automatically conferring US citizenship on the foreign-born wife of an American male, the act established an expedited path to naturalization. However, if an American-born woman had previously married a male racially or otherwise ineligible for naturalization, she did not regain American citizenship even after the Cable Act. Even when a married woman regained citizenship, it was citizenship by naturalization, and government retained prerogatives it would not have had over birthright citizens.[116] A married woman who applied to become a naturalized citizen had to promise to reside permanently in the country, and failure to do so could result in denaturalization. The Cable Act did not fix the problem that an American-born woman who was neither Caucasian nor of African descent would be permanently denationalized upon marriage to a noncitizen; even if she were divorced or widowed, she would not regain her citizenship. With the onset of quotas, if such a woman left the country, she might not be allowed to return.[117]

The citizenship of children born of marriages between American women and foreign men was also at issue prior to the Equal Nationality Act of 1934. These children, like the children of American men who married foreign women, would now be citizens of the United States by birth.[118] An effect of the Cable Act of 1922 was that, since an American woman no longer lost her citizenship when she married a foreigner, the children of such a union were foreigners, who would have to be separately naturalized if their mother returned to the United States after being widowed or divorced.[119] However, the 1934 act required the child of such couples (whether the father or the mother was foreign) to come to the United States and live there for at least five years continuously leading up to the eighteenth birthday and, shortly after turning twenty-one, to take an oath of allegiance to the United States.[120]

We have noted earlier how the immigration and naturalization system influenced the racial composition of the United States. The national origins quota system implemented in 1921 and 1924 purposefully kept out many Jews from southern and eastern Europe. These quotas would also limit the entry of Jews fleeing the Holocaust. There was no separate refugee policy.[121] The quota system operated inflexibly as refugees from Germany and Austria streamed to US consular offices seeking visas.[122] While the German quota was relatively sizable at nearly 26,000 per year (27,370 after the German and Austrian quotas were merged following the Anschluss), only about 30 percent of the allowable visas were given out in Germany from 1933 to 1938.[123] More than nine hundred passengers of the German ocean liner *St. Louis*, almost all Jews, were barred from landing in Miami in an infamous June 1939 incident; forced to return to Europe, more than a quarter of its passengers died in the Holocaust. President Franklin D. Roosevelt and the State Department claimed that Jews fleeing Europe in the late 1930s and into the early 1940s could be Nazi spies and thus posed a national security threat. This became the rationale for refusing visas to many Jews seeking to enter the United States, and the concern seems to have been based on one case from 1942.

After the end of the war, Jewish and other refugees found little sympathy in American public attitudes toward increased immigration from Europe.[124] Congress seemed intransigent, though President Truman issued a directive on December 22, 1945, stating that displaced persons would, at any rate, be given priority for US visas under the existing quota system. Truman's action did permit the entry of thirty-five to forty thousand displaced persons, many of them Jews, between then and mid-1948.[125]

During the Second World War, internment of Japanese, all of whom were presumed to be of dubious loyalty to the United States, revealed another form of what Ngai calls citizenship nullification. About two-thirds of the 120,000 persons of Japanese ancestry who were interned and whose rights were denied were US citizens, many of them birthright citizens.[126] While the US Supreme Court did acknowledge that due process had to be available to individual loyal citizens to challenge their detentions in *Ex Parte Endo* in 1944, *Korematsu v. United States* overshadowed this principle by justifying internment in constitutional terms as an emergency measure.[127]

In 1934, Filipino migration to the US was limited to only fifty persons per year, but in 1946 the Luce-Celler Act extended immigration and naturalization opportunities to Filipinos and Indians from the subcontinent in anticipation of their independence from the United States and Great Britain, respectively. With support for the United States during World War II coming from the Chinese, Indians from the subcontinent, and Filipinos, restrictions were gradually eased. In 1943, the Magnuson Act repealed the Chinese Exclusion Act of 1882 and made persons of Chinese descent eligible for US citizenship through naturalization. Nevertheless, as of 1952, the quota allocated to most Asian nations was a paltry 100 per year; the Chinese had 105, but an ethnic Chinese person born in Europe, Latin America, or somewhere else would be counted toward the Chinese quota, indicating a clear racial basis for considering these would-be entrants.[128] The 1952 McCarran-Walter Act, passed over President Truman's veto, was best known for its strong anticommunist measures, but it did mark the formal end to Asian exclusion as US policy and began the shift toward preferential treatment for skills and family reunification that would mark the 1965 Hart-Celler Act. McCarran-Walter did make it easier for the government to denaturalize individuals for national security reasons and to exclude, detain, or deport aliens seen as politically subversive.

The national origins or quota system would formally end with the 1965 act. Even then, one recent analysis argues that the family reunification aspect of the 1965 act was designed to satisfy those who were anxious to keep America white.[129] It also imposed a global ceiling on immigration and capped immigration from the Western Hemisphere.[130] While the energy behind immigration reform stemmed from Congress's efforts to address the civil rights movement, restrictionists were able to partner with conservative southern Democrats to incorporate provisions that they hoped would prevent an anticipated wave of undesirable immigration.[131]

The Asiatic Barred Zone and the Whiteness of Citizenship

Even as the federal government developed and expanded the scope of racial and ethnic limits on immigration, it continued to focus legislative and administrative energy on restricting Asian migration specifically. The Asiatic Barred Zone Act, also known as the Immigration Act of 1917,[132] eliminated the option of US immigration from much of Asia not already subject to restrictions based on nationality. It did so in terms of meridians of longitude and parallels of latitude and included most of Asia, India, the Middle East, parts of the Arabian Peninsula, and islands adjacent to Asia, excluding the Philippines, whose citizens were now US nationals. The act included a literacy test for immigrants and was actively supported by the Immigration Restriction League, founded in 1894 by several Harvard graduates, whose constitution committed it to "further exclusion of elements undesirable for citizenship or injurious to our national character."[133] Congress overrode President Wilson's veto (which was unrelated to the act's aim to restrict Asian immigration) to enact the legislation.

The Supreme Court weighed in on defining whiteness for purposes of naturalization and citizenship in a trio of cases as anti-immigration sentiment spread in the early 1920s. The Naturalization Act of 1870 opened up a path to citizenship extending beyond "free white person[s] . . . of a good moral character"[134] to those of African descent.[135] As noted earlier, Asians were not encompassed by the 1870 act, and this was surely intentional. Unlike the Chinese, Japanese immigrants were not formally barred by American law, and an 1894 treaty assured free immigration—though not citizenship—for Japanese migrating to the United States, largely for commercial and foreign policy reasons. Even though Japanese residents on the West Coast were more likely to westernize and Christianize than were the Chinese, anti-Japanese sentiment rose in the final years of the nineteenth century as Japanese laborers came to the United States. Despite an agreement in 1900 by the Japanese government to deny passports to laborers seeking to enter the United States, a number still entered by migrating first to Canada, Mexico, or Hawaii. The 1907 Gentlemen's Agreement between the two nations entailed a Japanese agreement to deny passports to laborers who intended to enter the United States and acknowledgment that the United States had the right to exclude Japanese immigrants whose passports were originally issued for other countries.[136]

From 1903, when Korean workers began emigrating to Hawaii to work on sugar and pineapple plantations, until 1905, when Japan converted Korea to a protectorate and stopped emigration to Hawaii, about seventy-four hundred Koreans had made that journey, and about two thousand of these had entered the United States by the time of the 1910 census.[137] The status of East Asians in Hawaii, once Hawaii had been annexed in 1898 and made a territory in 1900, became a matter of contention.

Takao Ozawa, who was born in Japan, came to San Francisco when he was in his late teens, graduated from Berkeley High School, and studied for three years at the University of California before moving to Hawaii in 1906, where he worked for an American company. There, he married a Japanese woman educated in the United States. A Christian, he was fluent in English, and his family spoke English at home, and by all evidence he had assimilated. He had maintained continuous residence in the United States for twenty years. According to Justice Sutherland, "That he was well qualified by character and education for citizenship is conceded."[138] In 1902, Ozawa had filed his declaration of intent to naturalize, attesting that he neither believed nor practiced anarchism or polygamy; legislation passed in 1906 mandated a waiting period of at least two years after a declaration of intent.[139] He petitioned to naturalize in 1914, but his petition was rejected. The Pacific Coast Japanese Association Deliberation Council selected his petition as the test case for whether Japanese could naturalize, since but for race, Ozawa would have been viewed as a desirable, hardworking, educated, and loyal citizen.[140] They hired George Wickersham, former US attorney general during the Taft administration as his chief counsel.[141] The world war and deteriorating relations with Japan delayed Supreme Court action on the case, and the decision was not issued until 1922.

The petition for naturalization (at least the 1906 version) required applicants to identify their color and complexion; Ozawa's Supreme Court brief indicated that the Japanese, "or at least the dominant strains, are 'white persons,' speaking an Aryan tongue and having Caucasian root stocks; a superior class, fit for citizenship."[142] Wickersham and his cocounsel maintained there was no language in the 1870 act or the 1875 amendment containing language about "free white persons," and the 1870 act was designed to enlarge—not restrict—naturalization.[143] Moreover, "white person" as construed by the Court as well as the state courts has meant persons without Negro blood.[144] "The words 'free white persons' had in 1875 acquired a signification in American statute law as expressing a superior class as against a lower class," Ozawa's lawyers claimed.[145] The solicitor general countered that by the time of the 1906 act establishing the Bureau of Immigration and Naturalization, "it had become settled that Japanese and all other people not of the white or Caucasian race were not eligible for naturalization as 'white persons.'"[146]

Justice Sutherland, writing for a unanimous Court in *Ozawa v. United States*, insisted that the words "free white person" "import a racial and not an individual test. . . . Manifestly the test afforded by the mere color of the skin of each individual is impracticable, as that differs greatly among persons of the same race, even among Anglo-Saxons."[147] He noted that, from Judge Sawyer's circuit decision of 1878, *In re Ah Yup*, forward, federal and state courts had limited the racial category of whiteness to "only a person of what is popularly known as the Caucasian race."[148] He reasoned that Ozawa and other individuals of Japanese ancestry were "clearly of a race which is not Caucasian and therefore belongs entirely outside the zone on the negative side," claiming that this classification was supported by "numerous scientific authorities, which we do not deem it necessary to review."[149]

The Court considered what Congress must have intended in 1790 when it legislated about naturalization. Were the framers of the first naturalization act in 1790 intending merely to exclude "the black or African race and the Indians then inhabiting this country"? Faithful adherence to the intent of Congress, the Court reasoned, means excluding all those not specifically included, and those the framers did not consider: "The intention was to confer the privilege of citizenship upon that class of persons whom the fathers knew as white, and to deny it to all who could not be so classified."[150] The Court saw no evidence that subsequent congressional legislation intended to change this understanding beyond the inclusion of "those of African nativity and descent."[151] It would be unreasonable, Sutherland wrote, to conclude that Congress, in passing the 1906 act, made a fundamental change in this constant understanding without consideration, recommendation, or debate.[152] Section 2169 of the 1875 version of the act (Title XXX of the Revised Statutes) was compatible with the 1906 act.[153] While Congress was free to alter the rule if it had so chosen, that was not what it had done, the Court concluded.[154]

The categories of Caucasian and Aryan were not, however, a solid foundation for the racial project the Court wanted to endorse. The very next year, in *United States v. Bhagat Singh Thind* (1923), the Court would revisit the equation of white with Caucasian in *Ozawa*, this time opting for whiteness. Sutherland wrote for a unanimous Court that a high-caste Hindu from Punjab, even if deemed of the Aryan or Caucasian race, was not white under the meaning of naturalization statutes, and thus was ineligible for naturalization. Drawing heavily on *Ozawa*, Justice Sutherland again reasoned that Section 2169 Revised Statutes made provision "not that any particular class of persons shall be excluded, but . . . in effect, that only white persons shall be included within the privilege of the statute."[155] He reiterated that "the intention was to confer the privilege of citizenship upon that class of persons whom the fathers knew as white, and to deny it to all who could not be so classified."[156] When the framers of the 1790 act thought about immigrants, these were almost exclusively from northwestern Europe and the British Isles, "bone of their bone and flesh of their flesh."[157]

In *Thind*, the Court did not rely on scientific evidence about who does, or does not, belong to the Aryan or Caucasian race, since some authorities considered not only Hindus but also Maori, Tahitians, Samoans, Hawaiians, and "the Hamites of Africa" to be Caucasian.[158] In Justice Sutherland's view, "The various authorities are in irreconcilable disagreement as to what constitutes a proper racial division"—there may be four or twenty-nine races.[159] "The Aryan theory as a racial basis seems to be discredited," Sutherland noted. Walking back the Court's reliance on the term "Caucasian" in *Ozawa*, the *Thind* opinion emphasized that the statute used the term "white persons" and again stressed that "these are words of common speech and not of scientific origin."[160] The word "Caucasian" was probably unfamiliar to the original framers of the 1790 naturalization statute. The statutory language must be "interpreted in accordance with the understanding of the common man from whose vocabulary they were taken."[161]

For the Court, the average person knew who resembled whom, and resemblance trumped ancestral history or what we would now call DNA when talking about race: "It may be true that the blond Scandinavian and the brown Hindu have a common ancestor in the dim reaches of antiquity, but the average man knows perfectly well that there are unmistakable and profound differences between them today."[162] Recent congressional intention provided additional evidence for the Court. In the Immigration Act of 1917, India was included by latitude and longitude among those now excluded from this country, and "it is not likely that Congress would be willing to accept as citizens a class of persons whom it rejects as immigrants."[163] Here, Sutherland and his colleagues aligned citizenship and immigration law, reading Congress's limits on immigration as a further gloss on racialized limits to naturalization.

In *Thind*, the Court did maintain the theme of racial inassimilability: "It is very far from our thought to suggest the slightest question of racial superiority or inferiority. What we suggest is merely racial difference, and it is of such character and extent that the great body of our people instinctively recognize it and reject the thought of assimilation."[164] The

Court gave voice to a kind of popular constitutionalism rooted in the wishes, values, and tastes of the American people; noticed the "social fact" of how race is perceived by the common person; and took into account public opposition to assimilation with new immigrant stock as it crafted its understanding of constitutional meaning.

In 1925, the Court closed the discussion on the status of Asians in *Toyota v. United States.* Hidemitsu Toyota had been born in Japan but emigrated to the United States in 1913 and entered the Coast Guard. He served until 1923, routinely reenlisting without issue. After World War I, he petitioned for naturalization as a veteran.[165] While Congress had authorized an expedited process for military veterans to naturalize during the Civil War era, the demand for manpower during World War I had led to that program's statutory expansion. In the wake of passing a comprehensive draft that demanded service even from aliens, Congress followed up by allowing individuals who had served to naturalize without any residence period. The statutory language specifically authorized naturalization for Filipino veterans, "any Porto Rican not a citizen of the United States," or indeed "any alien" who served in the military.[166] In considering the legislative history, the Court traced through the developments that had led to a formal naturalization process for Filipinos, who were not aliens, but underlined their nonwhite status.[167] Justice Butler, writing for an eight-person majority, found that the statutes authorizing the naturalization of veterans passed in 1918 and 1919 did not disturb the racial limitations expressed in the more general legislation of 1906.[168] Race would supersede service to the nation with respect to Toyota and all other racially barred nonwhite veterans unless and until Congress specifically welcomed them in as suitable citizens. Chief Justice Taft, who had served both as the first governor-general in the Philippines and as secretary of war under Theodore Roosevelt, dissented without filing an opinion.

"Indians Not Taxed"

If America's first peoples enjoyed the fruits of the land long before European settlers arrived, when the United States was formed, they were deliberately excluded from "We the People." The commerce clause of the Constitution (Article I, Section 8) gave Congress power to regulate commerce with foreign nations, among the states, and with the Indian tribes. They had not been subdued, removed from ancestral lands, or subject to ordinary statute law and, in general, related to the United States by treaty until Congress ended treaty making with individual tribes in 1871. In Chief Justice John Marshall's famous formulation, tribes were "domestic dependent nations," neither completely inside nor outside the jurisdiction of the United States.[169] In a "state of pupilage," "their relation to the United States resembles that of a ward to his guardian."[170] Their identities and governance being tribal, few were seeking citizenship. They were neither birthright citizens nor foreigners; they were not encompassed in the 1790 Naturalization Act that offered citizenship to "any Alien being a free white person, who shall have resided within the limits and under the jurisdiction of the United States for the term of two years."[171] A different argument against naturalization was that they were ineligible because they were not born outside the United States. However, as early as the 1830 treaty with the Choctaws, Congress held out the possibility of US citizenship for certain Indians who abandoned their tribes. In the antebellum era, citizenship was often conditioned on ceding tribal lands.

In the 1857 *Dred Scott* decision, Chief Justice Taney distinguished between Native Americans and African Americans. Indians, he said, "may, without doubt, like the subjects of any other foreign Government, be naturalized by the authority of Congress, and become citizens of a State, and of the United States, and if an individual should leave his nation or tribe and take up his abode among the white population, he would be entitled to all the rights and privileges which would belong to an emigrant from any other foreign people."[172] Post–Civil War developments did not clarify matters. The "subject to the jurisdiction of the United States" clause in Section 1 of the Fourteenth Amendment suggested the possible exclusion of tribal members, and Section 2 apportioned representatives among the states by counting "the whole number of persons in each state, excluding Indians not taxed," and "individual Native Americans who severed their tribal connections, acculturated themselves into mainstream white society and willfully paid taxes often lacked a distinct legal status."[173]

Confusion about citizenship continued. In 1870, the Senate Judiciary Committee, attempting to clarify the matter, said it thought it clear that "'the 14th amendment to the Constitution has no effect whatever upon the status of the Indian tribes within the limits of the United States,' but that 'straggling Indians' were subject to the jurisdiction of the United States."[174] We have seen, in chapter 3, that the Supreme Court held in *Elk v. Wilkins* that no one could be made a citizen of the nation without its consent, and that included individual assimilated Native Americans.[175] The Dawes Act of 1887 was designed in part to create a path to citizenship for those Native Americans who took up their land allotments and resided on them. But decades later, confusion continued over when and whether Native Americans over whom the federal government still exercised protection, prohibiting them from alienating their allotments, were citizens.[176]

The Supreme Court continued to weigh in on tensions between citizenship and federal government protection of Native Americans against alcohol abuse and against loss of their lands to unscrupulous would-be buyers. In *Matter of Heff* in 1905,[177] the Court contended that Native Americans who accepted individual land allotments immediately became American citizens; they could no longer be protected by federal guardians. As a result, federal efforts sought to slow the rush to citizenship for those considered unable to protect themselves and their small remaining property holdings. That position was reversed, however, in *United States v. Nice* (1916); "Citizenship is not incompatible with tribal existence or continued guardianship,"[178] removing most objections to granting citizenship to those American Indians who had not yet been made citizens. In 1921, the Court reiterated that it was up to Congress to determine when guardianship ceased, "the mere grant of rights of citizenship not being sufficient to terminate it."[179]

Native Americans, who had served in significant numbers in the military in World War I, could apply for US citizenship if honorably discharged, and in 1924 the Indian Citizenship Act granted citizenship unilaterally to all those who had not yet been made US citizens, whether or not they desired it—and not all did.[180] By the time of the 1924 act, roughly two-thirds of Native Americans had become citizens through treaties or congressional legislation.[181] The Indian Citizenship Act created a kind of dual citizenship for many Native Americans, since it did not end the rights and privileges of tribal citizenship, including the right to participate in tribal life and the "right of any Indian to tribal or other property."[182] These two forms of citizenship sometimes come into conflict, including in cases involving reviewability of some tribal actions against their citizens.[183]

As a consequence of the declaration that "all non-citizen Indians born within the territorial limits of the United States are henceforth

U.S. citizens," Native American children born subsequent to the enactment of the 1924 legislation became birthright citizens. Although some Native Americans had demanded citizenship because of military sacrifice and service (some had even served in the Civil War), the 1924 declaration was chiefly about absorption and assimilation.[184] For tribes that crossed either the Mexican or the Canadian border, separating them by national citizenship created new difficulties, instituting settler state boundaries on Native Americans just as the Johnson-Reed Act imposed strict quotas and border patrol policing was enhanced.[185] Some immigration officials, viewing indigenous peoples attempting entry from Mexico or Canada as aliens ineligible for naturalization, impeded entry.

Conclusion

This intermediate history is important for understanding current political debates over both immigration and birthright citizenship. While the orientation of the immigration system changed in fundamental ways through congressional legislation in the 1960s, racially based concerns about immigration subsided but did not disappear. Immigration from Mexico and Central America began to garner more attention in the 1970s, as noted earlier. In 1986, during the Reagan administration, Congress passed the Immigration Reform and Control Act, "generally viewed as a turning point in American immigration policy, marking the advent of a new era in which federal immigration policies have increasingly focused on enforcement."[186] Funds for border control and interior enforcement began to rise, and the law provided sanctions for employers hiring unauthorized, undocumented workers. The 1986 law also provided a chance of legal status and even citizenship for perhaps three million undocumented immigrants—"marking the first large-scale legalization program in U.S. immigration history."[187] In the mid-1980s as well, Peter Schuck and Rogers Smith published *Citizenship without Consent*, discussed further in chapter 7, claiming that democracy is best served by allowing the members of the polity to make determinations about its membership.[188] We now turn to a discussion of current tensions over birthright citizenship and its relationship to immigration in a period when exclusionary logics have reemerged in culture and politics.

7 | Revisiting Jus Soli
Contemporary Developments

Julie Novkov and Carol Nackenoff, with Marit Vike

In 2011, following the passing of her father, Sandra Wong uncovered a series of old photographs that led her to discover that her great-grandfather was Wong Kim Ark, the man whose story and case inspired this book.[1] Her research sparked a bit of new publicity for her great-grandfather; however, even when his name is not invoked, the ramifications of his case command public attention. The automatic grant of citizenship to children born in the United States to noncitizen parents (unless the parent is an official diplomat)[2] has attracted renewed interest in the face of resistance to the arrival and residence in the United States of undocumented immigrants from Mexico and Central America, and concerns in some quarters that the United States will likely, later in this century, become a majority-minority nation. The ruling in *Wong Kim Ark* has never been revisited or questioned by the US Supreme Court, but attacks on liberal citizenship policies in the United States and elsewhere have introduced new precarities into the bedrock foundation of birthright citizenship.

Discussing the possibility of ending birthright citizenship by executive order in a 2018 interview, President Trump said that "we're the only country in the world where a person comes in and has a baby, and the baby is essentially a citizen of the United States for 85 years . . . with all of those benefits. It's ridiculous. And it has to end."[3] In June 2019, President Trump elevated Ken Cuccinelli II to the position of acting director of the US Citizenship and Immigration Services (USCIS). Cuccinelli, an immigration hard-liner, previously served as Virginia's attorney general, a role in which he "once advocated an end to birthright citizenship and policies that would require employees to speak English."[4] In October 2019, he followed up on further comments that Trump had made in August 2019. Cuccinelli announced at a breakfast hosted by the *Christian Science Monitor* that the only question was whether the executive branch required collaboration by Congress or alternatively had the independent power to end birthright citizenship.[5]

Contrary to the president's 2018 assertions, the United States is not alone in granting birthright citizenship; variants of jus soli exist in more than thirty nations throughout the world, although the United States retains one of the most expansive interpretations of birthright citizenship. Jus soli "is always only one part of a citizenship regime, whose character as a whole is determined by the ensemble of citizenship policies with respect also to [jus] sanguinis, naturalisation and dual citizenship."[6] Yet in many national contexts where it exists, birthright citizenship has recently become controversial. The structure of the US controversy depends particularly on its constitutional status, but understanding the scope of birthright citizenship and attacks on it in other nations helps to place the US debates in context. Debates over who has citizenship, and how that citizenship is to be obtained, seem likely to intensify. Climate change and conflict increasingly generate desperate populations seeking safe havens outside their home nations, and political actors around the world have advanced their fortunes by promoting hard-line positions against immigration and immigrants.

Contemporary birthright citizenship policies should be understood as falling along a continuum. Unconditional birthright citizenship rules in national constitutions or laws are now relatively rare, and nations generally impose a range of conditions or stipulations before someone born in a nation is considered a citizen by birth (jus soli) rather than by blood connection to a "people" (jus sanguinis) in nations that have some form of birthright citizenship.

More inclusive birthright citizenship policies are often referred to as more liberal.[7] Nativist, nationalistic, and xenophobic arguments are frequently used to restrict citizenship and privilege jus sanguinis policies for the descendants of desired citizens. Many observers link a shift in sentiment away from generous birthright citizenship policies to a worldwide trend "toward more nationalistic and ethnically-defined identities" as global migration increases.[8] Trends in the past twenty years in a number of nations have tended toward retrenchment of citizenship recognition in response to changing patterns and volume of immigration. Some countries are also revoking or seeking to revoke citizenship for disloyalty, service in a foreign army, extended residence abroad, acquisition of other citizenship, or other reasons.[9]

"Different legal traditions, colonial experience, local social and political circumstance, levels of immigration pressure, and international
conventions" all play a role in the evolution of immigration and citizenship laws nation by nation.[10] However, immigration tends to provoke
two common responses: a backlash and wish to close borders, or an
increased acceptance of immigrants as permanent members of a political community. Both of these standpoints interact in complicated ways
with policies and attitudes toward immigrants who do low-wage labor,
either in an officially sanctioned guest worker program or the like, or
as participants in the informal economy. But in considering immigrants
and immigration perceived as likely to lead to permanent residence,
those who wish to end extensive immigration inflows often seek to reduce access to citizenship, become more aggressive in finding methods
of stripping citizenship from those to whom it has been granted, or
both. Those accepting the permanence of immigration strive to do the
opposite by expanding paths to naturalization, though conditions may
have to be met.

Grants of citizenship based on place of birth vary. Iseult Honohan
has identified five versions of existing rules. The first three of these establish the conditions for automatic grants of citizenship at birth, and
the last two provide for retrospective granting of citizenship to those
born in a country:

1. Mere fact of birth in a country, the purest form of jus soli (e.g.,
   United States).
2. Birth in a country, conditional upon some period of prior
   parental residence.
3. Automatic citizenship at birth for those whose parents were born
   in that country.
4. Citizenship acquired automatically or, more commonly, by
   option or declaration—often at majority—for those born in a
   country. This is sometimes seen as offering a route somewhere
   between automatic citizenship and naturalization.
5. Something more akin to naturalization, requiring application,
   where the conditions for naturalization are less demanding for
   those born within the country than they would be for other
   candidates. Citizenship might be either an entitlement once
   the specified conditions are met, or be subject to official
   discretion.[11]

Many further variations are possible: a nation might grant automatic citizenship, for instance, to one who has one parent born in that country. Honohan adds variables such as immediacy or delay in the grant of citizenship, entitlement versus governmental discretion, and whether citizenship is prospectively (from birth) or retrospectively granted (some fact about the parent is relevant).[12] These different forms of birthright citizenship vary in their impact and inclusivity.

Debates over birthright citizenship are themselves inevitably embedded in wider debates about immigration and access to citizenship; debates over the relationship between race, ethnicity, and national identity; national welfare state obligations and burdens; policing borders; conditions under which residents can be deported or denaturalized; the relationship between state and national governments in federal systems; and more. The politics of birthright citizenship take place within this wider network of issues, intersecting them and at times influencing them. In the case of the United States, America's identity as a nation of immigrants is also in play, with a Statue of Liberty beckoning:

> Give me your tired, your poor,
> Your huddled masses yearning to breathe free,
> The wretched refuse of your teeming shore.
> Send these, the homeless, tempest-tost to me,
> I lift my lamp beside the golden door![13]

But as recent debates have illustrated, the meaning of this aspect of American identity is contested. In August 2019, Ken Cuccinelli, acting director of the US Citizenship and Immigration Services, asserted that the poem invited only immigrants who can "stand on their own two feet" and further, that it referred to Europeans.[14] Demographic changes in the United States, with projections that the nation will become majority minority during this century, generate anxieties in some quarters. Some Americans fear that whiteness no longer conveys privileges—or, if it does, it will soon cease to do so without dramatic changes to immigration. In the United States, the birther movement's claims that Barack Obama was not a natural-born American citizen and therefore not a legitimate president incorporated views about race and the questionable status of someone with a Kenyan father. These claims captured and further activated strongly anti-immigrant forces in American politics and helped to link these forces to Donald Trump, a prominent supporter prior to his presidential election.

Patterns in Conferral of Birthright Citizenship
in Other Nations

Legal debates in the United States have unique features due to constitutional rules and norms. Nevertheless, the current claims made across the aisle and to the public regarding efforts to deny citizenship to children born in the United States to undocumented immigrants are comparable to the nativist, nationalistic, and xenophobic arguments made around the world. While US jus soli policy may look generous to European eyes, the practice of granting birthright citizenship to all persons born within national boundaries is common practice in the Western Hemisphere. In some experts' view, this has contributed to a significantly lower rate of statelessness in that region.[15] However, in many areas of the global north, we observe political movements pressing for legal change to restrict both immigration by and the extension of citizenship to migrants from the global south. Further, even the long-standing liberality of policies in the Western Hemisphere has come under attack as several countries have grappled with refugees from civil conflicts, natural disasters, and dysfunctional states.[16]

The geographic distribution of birthright citizenship is striking: "In general, birthright citizenship is common among Western Hemisphere countries and uncommon in other parts of the world."[17] As one report classifying birthright citizenship rules notes, "Today . . . a country's jurisprudential tradition seems less determinative of its approach to birthright citizenship than geographic location."[18] At least thirty countries still afford relatively generous birthright citizenship provisions, and almost all are in the Western Hemisphere.[19] The count depends on how refined the criteria are (counts tend to range from thirty to thirty-nine). Table 7.1 summarizes some of the salient patterns and recent changes.

While the situation in the Dominican Republic is unstable, and lack of documentation of birth can be problematic, as of 2018, many independent Caribbean island nations as well as Argentina, Bolivia, Chile, Ecuador, Guatemala, Guyana, Honduras, Nicaragua, Panama, Paraguay, Peru, Uruguay, and Venezuela retain generous birthright provisions, joining the United States, Mexico, and Canada. A November 2018 report by the Law Library of Congress excluded Chile and Colombia because they have provisions for parental status or length of residency in the country but added in non-Western nations, including Angola, Pakistan, and Tanzania.[20] Canada secures the right of birthright citizenship

Table 7.1. Birthright Citizenship and Recent Changes

Description	Nations
Western Hemisphere nations with generous birthright citizenship provisions	Antigua and Barbuda, Argentina, Barbados, Belize, Bolivia, Brazil, Canada,* Chile,† Cuba, Dominica, Ecuador, Grenada, Guatemala, Guyana, Honduras, Jamaica, Mexico, Nicaragua, Panama, Paraguay, Peru, Saint Lucia, Saint Kitts and Nevis, Saint Vincent and the Grenadines, Trinidad and Tobago, United States, Uruguay, Venezuela
Non-Western nations with broad birthright citizenship provisions	Angola, Lesotho, Mauritius, Pakistan, Tuvalu
Nations that specifically *include* those born to noncitizen parents	Brazil, Mexico
Nations that formerly granted unconditional birthright citizenship that have recently restricted it to those born to one citizen parent	Portugal (1981), United Kingdom (1983), India (1987), Malta (1989), France (1993), Ireland (2005), New Zealand (2005), Australia (2007)

*Provision is by statute.

†Western Hemisphere nations with birthright citizenship making parental status or length of residency stipulations.

Sources: World Population Review, "Countries with Birthright Citizenship 2020," accessed November 29, 2020, http://worldpopulationreview.com/countries /countries-with-birthright-citizenship/; The Law Library of Congress, "Birthright Citizenship around the World," November 2018, https://www.loc.gov/law/help /birthright-citizenship/birthright-citizenship-around-the-world.pdf; US Central Intelligence Agency, The World Factbook 2020 (Washington, DC: Central Intelligence Agency, 2020), https://www.cia.gov/library/publications/the-world -factbook/fields/310.html.1.

Note: Since sources read stipulations differently for purposes of classification, a nation was generally included as having unconditional or generous birthright citizenship provisions if two of the three sources concurred. We also reviewed disputed nations' provisions.

by statute; the constitution of Mexico stipulates that citizens are "those born in the territory of the Republic, regardless of the nationality of their parents"; and Brazil also includes persons born of foreign parents unless the parents are in the service of their country.[21]

The European context looks quite different. A 2012 survey of a number of Western European nations compiled by the Law Library of Congress found that, in general, these nations granted birthright citizenship only to those children born in that nation when at least one parent was a citizen of the nation.[22] Nations with stringent citizenship laws, such as Germany, may have multiple generations of residents who are consigned to second-class status, though Germany has relaxed some of its rules, permitting children born in the country to become citizens if one parent had lived legally within the country for eight years, and, in 2014, lifting a ban on dual citizenship for those from non–European Union nations who had resided in Germany for eight years.[23.]

One way to make sense of these divergent policies is to situate them in national histories. Settler nations sought to populate newly established territories that were relatively sparsely populated by native peoples, a mindset enhanced by their willingness to shift the indigenous residents to less desirable land and kill them when they resisted. They were especially welcoming of immigrants—particularly those they considered ethnically assimilable. Thus Canada, the United States, Australia, and New Zealand, all former crown colonies, tended to grant citizenship liberally to such newcomers. Scholars of settler colonialism point out that the objective of settler colonial nations was to acquire land for permanent settlements, creating a new home—not simply to extract resources or labor from the colony, as is considered typical of more conventional colonialism.[24] To establish new communities for settlers, indigenous peoples had to make way, by forced displacement, confinement on reservations, genocide, assimilation, or some combination of these. The original inhabitants, born in what would become—or was—the United States, were not citizens unless made so by treaty, subsequent to the Dawes Act if they left their tribes and weathered a period of tutelage,[25] and/or by the Indian Citizenship Act of 1924. Even then, many states denied Native Americans the right to vote, a few until court challenges ended the constitutionality of such restrictions in the 1950s.[26] The liminal status of Native Americans had parallels in the treatment of Aboriginal and Torres Strait Islander people in Australia[27] and the First Nation and Inuit peoples in Canada.[28]

Yet the ground is shifting. The 2018 report *Birthright Citizenship around the World* by the Law Library of Congress notes an international trend to reconsider birthright citizenship. It states: "While most of the countries that provide for unrestricted birthright citizenship are located in the Western Hemisphere, many nations around the world make birthright citizenship conditional on the legal status of the parents, or the age and length of residency in the country of the person applying for citizenship based on the fact of his or her birth in the country's territory."[29] A number of nations in the global community have placed greater restrictions on citizenship in the past few decades, including elimination of jus soli by the United Kingdom, Australia, New Zealand, Ireland, the Dominican Republic, and France. Other nations have introduced more restrictive rules, including Portugal (1981), India (1987), Malta (1989), and France (1993).

The end to birthright citizenship in Ireland in 2004[30] and the Dominican Republic in 2018 had striking similarities to the American situation. In both Ireland and the Dominican Republic, backlash contributed to rapid policy shifts in contexts that bear some similarities to recent discussions in the United States. While these two nations are hardly the only countries to change constitutional provisions regarding immigration and citizenship in recent years, these cases serve as a reminder that constitutional change can come quickly, even to the point of denationalizing longtime citizens. The debate in Ireland even cited the United States' arguments against birthright citizenship.

The impetus for eliminating jus soli in Ireland, while not as highly racially charged as in the Dominican Republic, was nevertheless racialized. Proponents of the change in Ireland were resisting parental efforts to gain citizenship through their children, who became citizens upon birth. They targeted immigrants who were motivated by a desire for Irish and European Union citizenship and rights, rather than by the desire to live and work in Ireland.[31] A referendum was called in 2004, and Irish voters decided by an 80 percent majority that the government should remove the constitutional provision granting territorial birth citizenship to children of noncitizens.[32] A court case catalyzed the movement that led to the constitutional change. The European Court of Justice (the judicial branch of the European Union) issued a preliminary opinion granting the right of residency in Great Britain to a Chinese woman who had traveled to Belfast in order to have an Irish-born child.[33] Beyond this specific controversy, however, immigration had become a hot-button issue, fueling voter discontent. Racist and xe-nophobic tropes were used to blame immigrants for overwhelming the welfare state, specifically the struggling health care system.[34] Leading up to the referendum, proponents of change used racialized images; for instance, newspaper articles would feature pregnant Nigerian women coming to Ireland just to have their children there.[35] The campaign thus bore similarities to the emphasis on undocumented Latina moth-ers and other "chain migration" tropes in the anti–birthright citizenship movement in the United States.[36]

An interesting explanation for the rising Irish sentiment against birthright citizenship is that, when *courts* began to acknowledge the im-portance of family and a child's right to be cared for by a parent—as seems to have been the case in Ireland—noncitizen immigrant parents observed this judicial policy as an opportunity and applied in large num-bers for Irish citizenship. The public backlash to this perceived abuse of both the immigration and citizenship systems led Ireland to abolish jus soli.[37] The change in Ireland functioned as a kind of jurisdiction-strip-ping move to curb court discretion.

While public opinion in Ireland has shifted more favorably, the gov-ernment remains opposed to restoring birthright citizenship. In 2018, about 70 percent of Irish citizens supported a measure that would af-ford birthright citizenship to those born in Ireland who subsequently lived in the country for at least three years, regardless of the citizenship or residency status of the child's parents. The government contends that persons residing illegally in the United Kingdom are likely to move to Northern Ireland, have children there, and then use their children's citizenship to obtain residency in Ireland or even other EU countries following the implementation of Brexit. Those born in Northern Ire-land are entitled to both UK and Irish citizenship.[38]

In contrast to the relatively sharp Irish trajectory toward abandon-ment of birthright citizenship, in the Dominican Republic, the start-ing point should be taken as the long history of anti-Haitian racism. Haitians had long provided cheap immigrant labor in the Dominican Republic. In the early twentieth century, they became the preferred source of labor for the growing sugar industry.[39] As the sugar industry declined, Haitians moved to the cities, sparking a backlash. Many Hai-tians could trace their residence back several generations in the Domin-ican Republic. Generally darker skinned than their neighbors, Haitians were viewed as poor, Black, and valueless immigrants by nationalists who saw themselves as civilized individuals from a European history and culture.[40] While the constitution in the Dominican Republic provided very generous birthright citizenship provisions, a 1929 amendment excluded those "in transit" from birthright citizenship.

As anti-Haitian sentiments increased in the 1990s and the first decade of the twenty-first century, nationalists claimed that everyone with Haitian roots was "in transit." Officials often refused to issue birth certificates to children of Haitian residents or even deliberately destroyed birth certificates; many rural residents (including many of Haitian descent) also lacked official birth certificates.[41] The devastating January 2010 earthquake that sent many more Haitian refugees to the Dominican Republic hardened anti-Haitian sentiment further. A 2010 constitutional change excluded from birthright citizenship children of those "residing illegally in Dominican territory," and a new constitutional tribunal set up in 2010 with "definitive and irrevocable" power to interpret the constitution ruled in 2013 that anyone who could not *prove* that their parents had been legal residents of the Dominican Republic when they were born was "in transit"—and therefore, was not a citizen.[42] Individuals so situated were required to register as foreigners. The constitutional tribunal further held that this policy would apply retroactively to all those born after 1929. Only those who had at least one parent of Dominican blood would be recognized as citizens; most of those affected had come from Haiti. Multiple generations were stripped of citizenship, creating a whole subclass of stateless individuals.[43]

This shift did not go unnoticed internationally. Both the Inter-American Commission on Human Rights and the Inter-American Court of Human Rights objected formally.[44] While the government, under international pressure, backed away from planned mass deportations in 2015, the consequence was the denationalization of tens of thousands, only about nineteen thousand of whom were offered a path back to citizenship.[45] Intense public and private scrutiny created "a state of institutionalized terror, enforced by police, the military, and vigilante mobs" for hundreds of thousands. Over a three-year period, Dominican authorities "deported an estimated 70,000 to 80,000 people of Haitian descent—more than a quarter of the Dominico-Haitian population" according to Human Rights Watch. Tens of thousands fled across the border.[46]

Neither the Dominican Republic nor the United States was a signatory to the 1954 UN Convention relating to the Status of Stateless Persons, nor to the 1961 Convention on the Reduction of Statelessness.

The Dominican government has continued to maintain that even the children of Haitian legal permanent residents are not eligible to register as Dominican nationals, and "thousands of Dominican-born persons of Haitian descent lack citizenship or identity documents," which rendered them "effectively stateless" in the eyes of the US Department of State under President Obama.[47] In other Latin American nations, policies demanding that births be registered in order for individuals to obtain citizenship have operated differentially to limit access to citizenship by the children of migrants, isolated populations, and agricultural workers.[48]

To the north, Canada, like the United States, long embraced a strong birthright citizenship regime. Whereas American laws were influenced by English common law, Canada actually followed it until roughly the 1900s, when Canada decided to assert greater independence. By implementing the Immigration Act of 1910, Canada officially declared sovereign control of its citizenship, determining that Canadian citizens would include those born in Canada, British subjects living in Canada, and persons naturalized in Canada.[49] Citizenship rules established in Canada in 1910 and 1914, however, did impose a number of restrictions, including for those deemed to have poor morals or considered unassimilable.[50] This birthright citizenship configuration has remained in place to this day, although it has faced recent conservative efforts at reform, as in the United States.

Canada began a period of debate beginning around 1994 that anticipated, in considerable part, the tenor of the debate that has arisen in the United States.[51] Concerns in Canada and the United States seem to center on the fear "that illegal immigrants in Canada are abusing the birthright citizenship law by having children on Canadian soil, and then 'using' these children to increase their chances of staying in the country."[52] This relates to both the "anchor baby" and "birth tourism" arguments in the United States.

Attacks on Birthright Citizenship in the Context of Recent Anti-immigrant Activism in the United States

While direct assaults on birthright citizenship by the Trump administration have not proved successful, the executive branch has some room for maneuver in interpreting, administering, and implementing the laws that govern citizenship. In practice, this makes access to US citizenship—including birthright citizenship—more precarious than is often assumed. Still, the authority of the executive branch is limited. Congress, with the power to legislate regarding immigration and naturalization, has played an important role in determining who will be US citizens, as we have seen in earlier chapters. We begin here with the nature of the attacks on birthright citizenship in the contemporary era and then examine efforts by—and claims of authority by—both the president and Congress to circumvent *Wong Kim Ark* or to challenge birthright citizenship in the federal judiciary.

Recent direct assaults on birthright citizenship have identified several targets and have drawn on racially charged imagery. The term "anchor babies" refers to the young children of undocumented immigrants and is a racially charged way of criticizing the implications of the intersection between two aspects of current American immigration law: birthright citizenship and family reunification. The 1965 Immigration and Nationality Act, which established the modern immigration system, mandated that 74 percent of all permanent visas be given to those with family already in the United States.[53] This stipulation was originally designed to preserve racial bias in the immigration system by benefiting the families of a predominantly white and European American population that had been admitted under the highly restrictive Johnson-Reed Act of 1924, which established strict quotas and prohibited the entry of those from the "Asiatic Barred Zone" identified in the Immigration Act of 1917.[54]

Anti-immigration forces in the United States seized on the threat of "anchor babies," with the term spreading from "extreme right-wing and anti-immigrant sites" in the first years of the twenty-first century to use by the mainstream media by 2010.[55] It began to gain wide currency in 2007 when conservative media outlets Fox News and Newsmax amplified it. In 2007, "anchor babies" were mentioned 50,000 times on Google; by 2010, that number was 450,000. *Time Magazine* listed "anchor babies" as one of the most influential buzzwords of 2010.[56] As a presidential candidate, Trump used the term in a 2015 speech.[57]

Critics—including President Trump—assert that pregnant women intentionally enter the United States illegally to birth children in order to gain permanent access to the benefits that come with the infant's residence and/or citizenship, including citizenship for the parents, thus using the baby as an "anchor" to the United States. This phrase, others maintain, debases persons of color, perpetuating the idea that

Mexican and Latina mothers are "infiltrating and undermining America—one baby at a time."[58] While the metaphor warns that the child's status serves as an anchor for the parents and other family members, under long-standing US law, American citizens may not petition for their parents until they reach adulthood.[59] Children's interests are further disfavored in immigration law in multiple ways, including significant limits on considering the hardships caused by parental deportation for a citizen-child.[60] In the United States, a child's citizenship status confers no legal rights on the parents and cannot prevent the deportation of their nondocumented parents.[61]

President Trump has also employed the term "chain migration" to express disapproval of the pattern by which US citizens or legal residents can, he claims, bring in "virtually unlimited numbers of distant relatives."[62] Calling this a broken system, he proposed instead "moving toward a merit-based immigration system—one that admits people who are skilled, who want to work, who will contribute to our society, and who will love and respect our country."[63] He would limit any family-based immigration to spouses and minor children.

Under current immigration policy, however, only US citizens can access Immediate Relative Immigrant Visas, with no quotas or limits, for a spouse, unmarried children under twenty-one years of age, and parents. Any other relative of a US citizen falls under the Family Preference Immigrant Visa system and is subject to annual quotas.[64] Permanent residents can seek visas under the Family Preference Immigrant Visa system, with a limited number offered each year depending on category, for spouses, minor children, and unmarried children older than twenty one. Same-sex spouses of both citizens and lawful permanent residents, along with their minor children, are now eligible for the same immigration benefits as opposite-sex spouses.[65] However, the Family Preference Immigrant Visa program has an extensive backlog, often of more than ten years' duration.[66]

In February 2020, the Trump administration implemented a new rule restricting immigration by expanding the inadmissibility and restricting the upgrading of status of aliens deemed "likely at any time to become a public charge."[67] Any family member who is likely to become a "public charge" is likely to be rejected under this program; both citizens and legal permanent resident sponsors have to legally assume financial responsibility for the immigrant(s) at 125 percent of the poverty line for the new size of the household. The rule permits that anyone using public assistance programs that would now include Medicaid, the Supplemental Nutrition Assistance Program (SNAP), Medicare Part D's Low-Income Subsidy Program, and several housing programs may be excluded from the Family Preference Immigrant Visa program.[68] This policy is being challenged in court due to its differential impact on immigrants of color and statements made by Trump and members of his administration suggesting a racist intent behind it.[69]

In seeking to eliminate the family reunification basis of current immigration policy, the president endorsed the Reforming American Immigration for Strong Employment Act (RAISE), introduced by conservative Republican senator Tom Cotton of Arkansas in 2017. This act would have capped annual refugee intake, cut the number of permanent visas issued annually by half, introduced a points system for the selection of immigrants coming via employer sponsorship, and eliminated all family sponsorship other than spouses and minor children of US citizens and legal permanent residents (reducing the maximum age of minors from twenty-one to eighteen).[70] However, this bill had only one cosponsor and never received a committee hearing.

The term "birth tourism" describes the practice in which travel agencies arrange all aspects of trips for pregnant women to come to the United States (frequently from China but also from Russia) to give birth.[71] It is an expensive practice for families seeking to get US passports for these babies, and lucrative for the companies that engage in it. While there are no official estimates, some say that thirty to forty thousand babies are born in the United States to birth tourist parents each year, while agencies in China estimate that at least fifty thousand babies per year are attributable to Chinese birth parents alone.[72] In March 2015, around two hundred federal agents from the Department of Homeland Security (DHS) raided a number of locations in Los Angeles, Orange County, and San Bernardino County, California, in search of evidence that pregnant women had come "as part of organized tours sold to them by Chinese companies," with amenities including "vacation-style tours of the region, visits to Disneyland, shopping excursions and fine dining"; the women were not arrested but were retained as material witnesses in an effort to prosecute "handlers."[73] In January 2019, federal prosecutors uncovered three multimillion-dollar birth tourism businesses which provided pregnant women with nannies, housing, and advice on how to lie in order to acquire a visa, in exchange for $40,000 to $100,000.[74] In January 2020, the State Department began implementing new rules making it more difficult for pregnant foreign women to enter the United States to give birth.[75]

Birth tourism is not necessarily driven by a desire for the children to take direct advantage of US citizenship in the United States. One major advantage for aspiring Chinese parents of ensuring American citizenship is that a child holding a US passport can move far more easily to metropolitan areas or to other provinces in China than can other Chinese citizens, given the household registration system linking a person to their familial hometown. Moving a household registration is very difficult in China. Educational and housing subsidies are available in cities such as Shanghai, but only for those whose household registration identifies a child as being from Shanghai (the family's household registration, not place of birth, is determinative). Another important advantage of the practice for Chinese is that students with foreign passports can circumvent the national college entrance exam, which is extremely important in determining which universities will admit Chinese students, and even what they study. Those with foreign passports instead simply demonstrate proficiency in Mandarin and go through an admissions interview.[76]

The *Conservative Review* has argued that birth tourism "undermines the fabric of America and attenuates the value of our citizenship."[77] However, many babies born to these enterprising parents do not live in the United States, and it is hard to maintain that they constitute a drain on US resources. Most of these children and their families probably establish little or no connection to the United States. The absence of sustained residence in, or connection to, this nation was one argument officials attempted to use when excluding returning Chinese heritage birthright citizens during the early twentieth century, although federal courts barred this rationale for denial of reentry. This strategically motivated practice of conferring birthright citizenship on babies is among the least popular aspects of the current birthright citizenship regime.

Current Arguments for Reconsidering the Constitutional Guarantee of Birthright Citizenship

More than a century after the *Wong Kim Ark* decision, limiting birthright citizenship has garnered renewed interest in the United States. While the recent challenge did not arise with the candidacy of Donald Trump, he amplified the issue in public discourse, using it as a catalyst to bind like-minded voters not only to the Republican Party but specifically to his campaign. A few other Republican candidates followed his lead, at least stating that birthright citizenship should be reexamined. Since becoming president, Trump has continued to discuss his desire to end birthright citizenship, and his appointment of Ken Cuccinelli II as acting director of US Citizenship and Immigration Services indicates that he may have more than just talk in mind.[78]

During the 2016 presidential campaign, opposition to birthright citizenship became a key position for then candidate Donald Trump. As president, he continued to vow to end birthright citizenship, eventually claiming he could accomplish this by executive order, though he has not attempted to do so—possibly because so many legal scholars and members of Congress say he cannot. In a tweet, he said: "So-called Birthright Citizenship, which costs our Country billions of dollars and is very unfair to our citizens, will be ended one way or the other. It is not covered by the 14th Amendment because of the words 'subject to the jurisdiction thereof.' Many legal scholars agree."[79] He commented again in August 2019 that birthright citizenship was "frankly ridiculous," informing reporters that he and his advisers were "looking at that very seriously."[80] The presumption is that these people, who are, in the view of opponents, erroneous or fraudulent citizens, drain resources rather than contribute to the wealth and prosperity of the nation—they are resource takers rather than contributors. In terms of economic contribution, this may or may not be true.[81] However, opponents also argue that the expanded welfare state, with entitlements that include health care, food stamps, student loans, social security benefits, disability insurance, and the earned income tax credit, provides taxpayer-supported benefits to millions of people "whose presence and membership come in violation of the polity's laws."[82]

The president's claims against birthright citizenship and his assertion that he can eliminate it by executive order have been controversial. In response to his 2018 assault, then Speaker of the House Paul Ryan (R-WI) reacted quickly and negatively: "Well, you obviously cannot do that. . . . You cannot end birthright citizenship with an executive order."[83] He also thought the plain text of the Fourteenth Amendment was clear. Few legal scholars believe such a move would be constitutionally permissible. The president, acting alone, cannot change the law of citizenship, though as we explain later, the executive branch has the capacity to alter many aspects of how citizenship laws are administered. However, a few officials and pundits have supported Trump's position. A former national security official in the Trump administration, Michael Anton, contended in the *Washington Post* that "under the jurisdiction thereof" meant to the framers of Section 1 of the Fourteenth Amendment "not owing allegiance to anybody else," a distinction with some import (remember how it was used to argue that the Chinese in America were subjects of the emperor).[84] Anton also contended that *Wong Kim Ark* only settled the matter of children of legal residents of the United States—and said nothing about children of persons living here illegally.[85] Since Anton believes Congress will not act, he suggests executive action:

> An executive order could specify to federal agencies that the children of noncitizens are not citizens. Such an order would, of course, immediately be challenged in the courts. But officers in all three branches of government—the president no less than judges—take similar oaths to defend the Constitution. Why shouldn't the president act to defend the clear meaning of the 14th Amendment?[86]

His proposed departmentalist reading of the Constitution would authorize chief executives to read the Constitution themselves and direct executive branch agencies accordingly.

Hans A. von Spakovsky, a senior legal fellow at the Heritage Foundation, also argues that an executive order is appropriate. He claims that presidents can use their executive power to enforce their interpretations of the proper allocation of citizenship by "direct[ing] federal agencies to act in accordance with the original meaning and intent of the citizenship clause, and . . . direct[ing] those agencies to issue passports, Social Security numbers, etc., only to those individuals whose status as citizens meet [*sic*] the requirements of the law."[87] His theory relies on the exercise of administrative authority to enforce nonrecognition of some individuals born in the United States, in some ways following the lead of officials in the Dominican Republic with regard to the descendants of Haitians.

While President Trump has not been as bold as to attempt the Dominican Republic's assault on birthright citizenship, the openly anti–birthright citizenship officials he has appointed for positions connected with matters of immigration and border protection have implemented significant unilateral changes of direction. While partly symbolic, under

President Trump, USCIS changed its mission statement. From 2009, the statement read: "USCIS secures America's promise as a nation of immigrants by providing accurate and useful information to our customers, granting immigration and citizenship benefits, promoting an awareness and understanding of citizenship, and ensuring the integrity of our immigration system." When Lee Cissna—who previously served as director of immigration policy at the Department of Housing and Urban Development and who worked to reduce the number of permanent visas issued—moved to head USCIS in 2017–2019, the mission was changed to de-emphasize the nation's promise: "U.S. Citizenship and Immigration Services administers the nation's lawful immigration system, safeguarding its integrity and promise by efficiently and fairly adjudicating requests for immigration benefits while protecting Americans, securing the homeland, and honoring our values."[88]

President Trump's first head of Customs and Border Protection, Kevin McAleenan (who subsequently moved to become secretary of DHS), wrote a memo to then secretary Kirstjen Nielsen recommending that family separation was the best way to increase consequences for illegal crossings.[89] Nielsen herself had been an extremely aggressive DHS secretary, prosecuting first-time border crossers who had done so illegally ("zero tolerance"), cracking down on asylum seekers, increasing detentions at the border by roughly 25 percent, and pursuing family separation as a deterrent, yet she resigned in early 2019 when the president became dissatisfied with her failure to more successfully cut off crossings from Central America.[90]

In its waning days, the Trump administration signaled that it may yet issue an executive order ending birthright citizenship.[91] The idea that the executive branch could unilaterally transform more than a century of law and policy on core questions of citizenship may seem far-fetched, but the executive branch has considerable latitude within which it can alter rules, regulations, and enforcement of policies. While not all of these changes are headline-grabbing executive orders heralding major policy transformations, a number of moves demonstrate the impact that administrative rule changes and practices can have on birthright citizenship. The administration's targeted restrictions on immigration will prevent some births of children with citizenship claims that administration officials would prefer not to recognize. For example, barring immigration from certain majority Muslim nations during the Trump presidency will prevent some future Muslim children from becoming birthright citizens who might otherwise have made such a claim. Likewise, barring asylum seekers coming across the southern border during the COVID-19 crisis will reduce the creation of future Latinx birthright citizens.

Another example illustrates a quieter exercise of executive branch power over matters of birthright citizenship. Some married same-sex couples have found themselves facing administrative hurdles when attempting to bring their young children, born with assistive reproductive technologies, into the United States after residence abroad. In early 2019, advocacy organizations publicized two instances of the State Department's refusal to grant US passports to small children of gay couples. In one case, both parents were US citizens living abroad at the time their daughter was born to a gestational surrogate with help from an egg donor; in the other case, twins were treated differently, each born from a donor egg and sperm from one of the two male parents. In this case, one parent was a US citizen and one an Israeli citizen, but the American citizen parent was not genetically linked to the twin denied US citizenship. The State Department refused to grant the children birthright citizenship, in at least one case deeming the marriage illegitimate. The State Department policy on children born abroad with the assistance of reproductive technology predated the Trump presidency, having been announced in 2014, but it was not enforced in this manner when the same couple sought citizenship for their son in 2016.[92]

The Trump administration has quietly undertaken initiatives to tighten the discretionary application of long-standing rules allowing the stripping of citizenship from naturalized citizens (denaturalization).[93] The Obama administration's DHS initiated the first phase of this process, Operation Janus, which identified more than three hundred thousand naturalized individuals with incomplete digital fingerprint data. The Trump administration dedicated a team to review all such cases and initiate prosecutions against anyone believed to have obtained citizenship on a fraudulent basis.[94] And in February 2020, the Department of Justice announced it was establishing a new denaturalization section in the immigration office. Since 2008 until February, 2020, there have been 228 denaturalization cases filed, with 100 occurring since the Trump administration took office.[95] The State Department has in recent years become more skeptical about attributing citizenship to Hispanics born near the southern border who present birth certificates signed by midwives, denying passports to thousands.[96]

But some commentators would extend this aggressive reinterpretation of federal law further. While the president may well not be able to "unilaterally change an understanding of the law that has been in effect for decades under a duly enacted federal law,"[97] von Spakovsky argues this "assumes the 'understanding' is the correct one. If that understanding actually violates the plain text and intent of the law, the president as the chief law-enforcement officer can, and indeed has an obligation, to direct the federal government to begin applying and enforcing it correctly." For him, the key issue is that both Section 301 of the Immigration and Naturalization Act and the Fourteenth Amendment's citizenship clause have been incorrectly enforced: "There is no question that if President Trump issues an executive order directing federal agencies to apply federal law according to . . . the correct interpretation, that the government will be sued. This issue, whether the U.S.-born children of aliens who are only here temporarily as tourists or students or who are in this country illegally are citizens, has never been directly addressed by the U.S. Supreme Court."[98] His arguments for overturning lengthy and established practices not questioned for years echo the arguments that the solicitor general made against Wong Kim Ark before the Supreme Court.

Legal scholar Garrett Epps insists that "[this] idea contradicts the Fourteenth Amendment's citizenship clause, it flies in the face of more than a century of practice, and it would create a shadow population of American-born people who have no state, no legal protection, and no real rights that the government is bound to respect."[99] In this view, creating a noncitizenship status for children born in the United States risks "creating a modern analogue of the post-slavery subordination that was occurring during the months before the framing of the Fourteenth Amendment, and that the Framers of the Amendment had present in their minds as they constructed its provisions."[100]

How Far Can Congress Go?

A somewhat more plausible initiative to end birthright citizenship focuses on legislation.

The originalist version of this claim is that the phrase "subject to the jurisdiction thereof" in Section 1 of the Fourteenth Amendment does not include citizens of foreign nations, even if they reside in the United

States and have children here. In this analysis, while birthright citizenship for all individuals born in the United States is a default position, Congress may have the power to alter the baseline. The focus on this rereading of the jurisdiction clause is partly due to the revival of this argument (presented comprehensively by the *Wong Kim Ark* dissenters) by law professor Peter Schuck and political science professor Rogers M. Smith in 1985, as elaborated later, but it has gone beyond strictly academic circles.

As we see from other chapters of this book, Congress took steps to extend citizenship to Blacks in 1870; Native Americans not already considered citizens in 1924; and Hawaiians and Puerto Ricans in the aftermath of territorial acquisition. The main law governing aliens and nationality, 8 U.S.C. §1401, also extends US citizenship, with some "physical presence" stipulations, to children born abroad to US parents or one US parent, with considerations of marital status of the parent(s).[101] Congress has exercised—and can exercise—its power to admit former outsiders to citizenship or to refuse this consent. These congressional acts often explicitly create birthright citizens or decline to extend it (see chapter 6). Yet Congress has also embraced an understanding of birthright citizenship for those born within the United States that is consistent with *Wong Kim Ark*'s reading: in almost all cases, those born within the United States are considered US citizens, and Congress has never undertaken any legislative project to undermine this settled understanding.

Judge Richard Posner of the Seventh Circuit, concurring in a 2003 immigration case, claimed that "one rule that Congress should rethink . . . is awarding citizenship to everyone born in the United States (with a few very minor exceptions . . .) including the children of illegal immigrants whose sole motive in immigrating was to confer U.S. citizenship on their as yet unborn children."[102] Posner notes that Congress formally codified the broadly accepted interpretation of the Fourteenth Amendment as Section 301 of the Immigration and Nationality Act of 1952. He argues that this legislation can simply be legislatively undone and replaced by a narrower mandate: "Congress would not be flouting the Constitution if it amended the Immigration and Nationality Act to put an end to the nonsense."[103] Citing arguments and evidence from the Federation for American Immigration Reform (FAIR) and the Friends of Immigration Law Enforcement, both organizations promoting stronger restrictions on illegal immigration, his concurrence encourages congressional reform. Judge Posner asserts, "We should not be encouraging foreigners to come to the United States solely to enable them to confer U.S. citizenship on their future children. But the way to stop that abuse of hospitality is to remove the incentive by changing the rule on citizenship." He endorsed legislation introduced that year that would have denied citizenship to children born in the United States unless they were born to citizens or permanent residents.[104]

In his analysis, Posner cited *Citizenship without Consent* by Peter Schuck and Rogers Smith (1985) and a 1996 law review article by Dan Stein and John Bauer, both of which argue that Congress has the power to eliminate birthright citizenship. These arguments interpret the Fourteenth Amendment not as an absolute grant of birthright citizenship to which all branches of the federal government must defer, but rather only as an insistence that Congress, not the states, has the ultimate authority to establish rules.

Schuck and Smith's book presented itself as a new challenge to what the authors characterized as a long-standing uncritical acceptance of liberal birthright citizenship. The book sparked a sharp debate over the history and meaning of the citizenship clause.[105] Schuck and Smith contend in *Citizenship without Consent* that "the framers of the Citizenship Clause [of the Fourteenth Amendment] had no intention of establishing a universal rule of birthright citizenship"; they emphasize that illegal aliens were not a recognizable category at the time the Fourteenth Amendment was drafted.[106] During the Trump era, they have published new pieces arguing that, since we cannot completely recover the intention either of the founders or of the framers of the Fourteenth Amendment, the matter should be left to Congress and the American people, taking as the default position that commitments to popular self-governance and civil solidarity argue for deference to congressional authority.[107] The argument privileges a default toward representative democracy over rights when the Constitution is unclear: "Broadly speaking, when the Constitution itself does not answer important questions with clarity, decision-making should usually be left to the people's elected representatives in Congress, so long as they do not violate fundamental rights."[108] Schuck and Smith ground their analysis in a claim that the Fourteenth Amendment's framers clearly did not intend to include tribal American Indians. They underline the principle articulated in the Supreme Court's ruling in *Elk v. Wilkins* that "no one can become a citizen of a nation without its consent."[109] Their view then generalizes this principle; they argue that the Fourteenth Amendment did not take this consent power for Native Americans or immigrants out of the hands of the representatives of the people. They read the history as establishing that mutual consent—of the US government and the noncitizen—was necessary to create citizenship.[110] More broadly, they reason that "subject to the jurisdiction" "was meant to leave Congress with the power to regulate access to birthright citizenship for groups to whose presence or membership it did not consent."[111]

Dan Stein, executive director of the Federation for American Immigration Reform, copublished a short article with law student John Bauer in 1996 arguing that the framers of the Fourteenth Amendment could not possibly have anticipated modern dilemmas concerning illegal immigration.[112] The Court, they note, has never specifically considered whether the rule in *Wong Kim Ark* applies to the children of individuals in the United States without any legal standing. In their analysis, the phrase "subject to the jurisdiction" excludes from the direct grant of citizenship the children of individuals who have not gained the nation's consent to reside lawfully within its borders. Citing the Court's notorious ruling in *United States v. Cruikshank*, the case in which the Court overturned convictions of several whites who had perpetrated a political massacre of Blacks in Louisiana, they further argued that citizens were only those individuals who had permanently and completely submitted to the dominion of a government with the expectation that the government would promote their welfare and protect their rights. Aliens, by their reading, did not qualify because their "temporary submission . . . lacks the permanence and promise of allegiance inherent in a complete surrender to jurisdiction."[113] Like Schuck and Smith, they relied on *Elk* to establish the necessity of mutual consent. By their reading, *Wong Kim Ark* was strictly limited both conceptually and by its factual background to the descendants of legal resident aliens. Wong Kim Ark's parents had submitted themselves to the jurisdiction of the United States, presented themselves for admission to the country, and ran a business in San Francisco. The country had, therefore, consented to their presence, and they were lawful resident aliens.[114] Stein and Bauer further claim that the Supreme Court "has never expressly affirmed" the policy that children born in the United States to parents in the country illegally are birthright citizens.[115]

Stein and Bauer are not alone in denying that *Wong Kim Ark* is controlling. Those who seek to distinguish the case emphasize the legal status of Wong Kim Ark's parents and argue that the children of individuals without any legal status are in a different relationship to the American state. Lino A. Graglia makes this argument and explains that, because the 1898 case involved a child born to Chinese parents legally domiciled in the United States, it should not be read to extend to embrace children born to illegal immigrants.[116] While Justice Brennan wrote for a 5–4 majority in *Plyler v. Doe*—a case holding that children of nondocumented residents cannot be barred from free education in Texas public schools—that "no plausible distinction . . . can be drawn between resident aliens whose entry into the United States was lawful, and resident aliens whose entry was unlawful," Graglia claims that this proposition is merely nonbinding dicta.[117] By this logic, the assumption by the Immigration and Naturalization Service that *Wong Kim Ark* extends birthright citizenship to children born to those here without legal status can be (and should be) challenged.[118]

Some critics of the dominant reading of *Wong Kim Ark* focus on the claim that Congress clearly has this power because it has already exercised its power to determine who is subject to the jurisdiction of the United States in the past. According to Edward J. Erler, a senior fellow at the Claremont Institute, Congress's choice to extend citizenship to Native Americans, first on a piecemeal basis and then in the Indian Citizenship Act of 1924, "provide[s] ample proof that Congress has constitutional power to define who is within the 'jurisdiction of the United States' and therefore eligible for citizenship." Lyman Trumbull, chair of the Senate Judiciary Committee, said during debate over the Fourteenth Amendment that the language about jurisdiction meant "not owing allegiance to anybody else and being subject to the complete jurisdiction of the United States," and Erler argues that the Fourteenth Amendment did not speak about those illegally within the United States: "Simple legislation passed by Congress and signed by the president would be constitutional under the 14th Amendment."[119] Erler problematizes birthright citizenship by defining the controversy this way: "Birthright citizenship is the policy whereby the children of illegal aliens born within the geographical limits of the United States are entitled to American citizenship."[120]

From different perspectives, these legal critics argue that we should look neither to *Wong Kim Ark* nor to the Fourteenth Amendment for authoritative statements about the status of children of "illegal immigrants" or "undocumented persons" born in the United States. In their view, the slate is clear for congressional regulation to limit or deny birthright citizenship at a minimum to the children of undocumented migrants, but possibly to other classes of immigrants' descendants as well. Reliance on the requirement of mutual consent, with the identification of Congress as a necessary party, could substantially transform birthright citizenship in the United States. While attempts to exercise this possible authority have not yet gotten far, they have occurred.

Congressional and Interest Group Action

Congressional efforts to end birthright citizenship have aligned with growing problematization of illegal immigration and an overall push for immigration reform. Beginning in the early 1990s, members of Congress began introducing a number of bills to curb birthright citizenship, to amend laws, and to redefine the meaning of citizenship. While occasionally presented as constitutional amendments, these efforts were primarily pursued as congressional statutes. While members of Congress sometimes introduce legislation on lively controversies even if they know it is likely to be found unconstitutional (for instance, congressional action to ban flag burning following the Court's decision in *Texas v. Johnson*),[121] as noted earlier, members had some scholarly support for their belief that at least some congressional action fell within the boundaries of their authority.

Somewhat surprisingly, the author of the first bill in the recent era was Senator Harry Reid (D-NV). This bill (S. 1351), the Immigration Stabilization Act of 1993, would have limited birthright citizenship to the children of US citizens and permanent legal residents. Unlike some of the subsequent bills dealing with this matter, Reid proposed a comprehensive immigration plan, only a few pages of which were dedicated to the matter of birthright citizenship. That section offered the following language:

> The Congress has determined and hereby declares that any person born after the date of enactment of this title to a mother who is neither a citizen of the United State nor admitted to the United States as a lawful permanent resident, and which person is a national or citizen of another country of which either of his or her natural parents is a national or citizen, or is entitled upon application to become a national or citizen of such country, shall

be considered as born subject to the jurisdiction of the United States within the meaning of [Section 1 of the 14th Amendment] and shall therefore not be a citizen of the United States or of any State solely by reason of physical presence within the United States at the moment of birth. [S. 1351, Sec. 1001][122]

Other provisions of that bill would have drastically reduced the number of immigrants admitted in any given year, tightened provisions for admission of relatives other than spouses and minor children, expanded the list of felonies that would have been considered aggravated (and thus requiring deportation or exclusion of additional immigrants), tightened rules for asylum claims, and increased penalties for failing to depart—or for reentering the United States—following a final deportation order.[123]

At the time, Reid said he was concerned about "3.3 million illegal aliens in America . . . [who placed] tremendous burdens . . . [on America's] criminal justice system, schools and social programs."[124] On the Senate floor, he declared that "no sane country" would grant birthright citizenship as liberally as the United States does.[125] President Trump used this remark in a tweet in support of his own position.[126] Reid has openly acknowledged the change to his position. He said in a 2006 speech that this "travesty that [he] called legislation" in 1993 was the "low point" in his legislative career.[127] A newspaper report in 1999 claimed Reid called this "way up high" on his "list of mistakes" and that it was "short-sighted."[128]

Nonetheless, others were quick to follow Reid's lead. Bills to reform the Immigration and Nationality Act have been introduced every session since then, as can be seen in table 7.2. Members who introduced these bills have been Republicans, and with very few exceptions, all cosponsors of these bills have been Republicans. Sponsors have tended to reintroduce their own bills each session. Members of the 104th Congress made two efforts to limit birthright citizenship in the United States. The Citizenship Reform Act of 1995 (H.R. 1363), introduced by Congressman Brian Bilbray (R-CA), would have limited birthright citizenship to children of citizens or immigrants with legal status. Bilbray argued that congressional authority included "defining who is subject to the jurisdiction of the United States." Concurrently, Congressman Mark Foley (R-FL) proposed a *constitutional amendment* (H.J. Res. 93) to limit birthright citizenship in the same manner. Both bills received

Table 7.2. Bills Introduced in Congress to Alter Birthright Citizenship 1993–2019

Bill	Sponsor	Key Provisions	Disposition
S. 1351 (Immigration Stabilization Act of 1993)	Sen. Harry Reid (D-NV), 3 cosponsors	Limits birthright citizenship to the children of US citizens and permanent legal residents (unlike future bills, this was a comprehensive immigration plan with only a small section on birthright citizenship)	Introduced, floor remarks by the sponsor
H.R. 1363: Citizenship Reform Act of 1995	Rep. Brian Bilbray (R-CA), 51 cosponsors	Limits birthright citizenship to those born in wedlock to one citizen or lawful permanent resident parent or born out of wedlock to a US citizen or national or lawful permanent resident *mother*	Joint hearings by the House Judiciary Subcommittee on Immigration and Claims and the Subcommittee on the Constitution
H.R. 7: Citizenship Reform Act of 1997	Rep. Brian Bilbray (R-CA), 70 cosponsors	Denies citizenship at birth to children born in the United States to parents who are not US citizens or permanent resident aliens	Hearing in the House Judiciary Subcommittee on Immigration and Claims, floor remarks by the sponsor
H.R. 73: Citizenship Reform Act of 1999	Rep. Brian Bilbray (R-CA), 47 cosponsors	Same as previous version of Bilbray's proposed act	Introduced, no hearing
H.R. 190: To Clarify the Effect on the Citizenship of an Individual's Birth in the United States	Rep. Bob Stump (R-AZ), 20 cosponsors	A person born henceforth in the United States to a *mother* who is not a US citizen, national, or permanent legal resident, and is eligible to become or is a citizen or national of a country of which either of his or her natural parents is a citizen or national, is not a US citizen solely by reason of US birth	Introduced, no hearing

H.R. 1567: Citizenship Reform Act of 2003	Rep. Nathan Deal (R-GA), 30 cosponsors	Redefines "subject to the jurisdiction thereof" to include only those born to parents who are either (1) US citizens, (2) lawful permanent residents of the United States, or (3) performing active service in the US Armed Forces	Introduced, no hearing
H.R. 698: Citizenship Reform Act of 2005	Rep. Nathan Deal (R-GA), 87 cosponsors	Limits automatic citizenship at birth to a child born in the United States who: (1) was born in wedlock to a parent either of whom is a US citizen or national, or is an alien lawfully admitted for permanent residence who maintains such residence; or (2) was born out of wedlock to a mother who is a US citizen or national, or is an alien lawfully admitted for permanent residence who maintains such residence.	Introduced, no hearing
H.R. 3700: Reducing Immigration to a Genuinely Healthy Total (RIGHT) Act of 2005	Rep. Thomas Tancredo (R-CO), 1 cosponsor	Primarily about immigration quotas, limited birthright citizenship to those with one US citizen, national, or lawful alien (at the time of birth) parent	Introduced, no hearing
H.R. 1940: Birthright Citizenship Act of 2007	Rep. Nathan Deal (R-GA), 104 cosponsors	Considers a person born in the United States "subject to the jurisdiction" of the United States for citizenship at birth purposes if the person is born in the United States of parents, one of whom is: (1) a US citizen or national; (2) a lawful permanent resident alien whose residence is in the United States; or (3) an alien performing active service in the armed forces.	Introduced, no hearing

Table 7.2. Bills Introduced in Congress to Alter Birthright Citizenship 1993–2019 (*continued*)

Bill	Sponsor	Key Provisions	Disposition
H.R. 4192: OVERDUE (Optimizing Visa Entry Rules and Demanding Uniform Enforcement) Immigration Reform Act of 2007	Rep. Thomas Tancredo (R-CO), no cosponsors	Primarily about limiting visas, included a birthright citizenship provision	Introduced, no hearing
H.R. 1868: Birthright Citizenship Act of 2009	Rep. Nathan Deal (R-GA), 95 cosponsors	Same as Deal's proposed 2007 act	Introduced, no hearing
H.R. 5002: No Sanctuary for Illegals Act (2010)	Rep. Dan Burton (R-IN), no cosponsors	Increased funding for border security and penalties for crossing the border, included a provision to limit birthright citizenship to those with one citizen, US national, lawful permanent resident, or active service parent	Introduced, no hearing
H.R. 140: Birthright Citizenship Act of 2011	Rep. Steve King (R-IA), 90 cosponsors	Same as Deal's proposed 2007 act	Introduced, no hearing
S. 723: Birthright Citizenship Act of 2011	Sen. David Vitter (R-LA), 4 cosponsors	The Senate equivalent of King's House bill	Introduced, no hearing
H.R. 140: Birthright Citizenship Act of 2013	Rep. Steve King (R-IA), 39 cosponsors	Same as Deal's proposed 2007 act	Introduced, no hearing

Bill	Sponsor	Description	Status
S. 301: Birthright Citizenship Act of 2013	Sen. David Vitter (R-LA), 2 cosponsors	The Senate equivalent of King's House bill	Introduced, no hearing
H.R. 140: Birthright Citizenship Act of 2015	Rep. Steve King (R-IA), 53 cosponsors	Same as Deal's proposed 2007 act	Introduced, no hearing
S. 45: Birthright Citizenship Act of 2015	Sen. David Vitter (R-LA), no cosponsors	The Senate equivalent of King's House bill	Introduced, no hearing
H.R. 140: Birthright Citizenship Act of 2017	Rep. Steve King (R-IA), 48 cosponsors	Same as Deal's proposed 2007 act	Introduced, no hearing
H.Res. 1143: Calling on the president to resume the interpretation of Section 1 of the Fourteenth Amendment to the Constitution as originally intended and applied as law for a century	Rep. Brian Babin (R-TX), no cosponsors	Expresses disapproval of birthright citizenship	Introduced, no hearing
H.R. 140: Birthright Citizenship Act of 2019	Rep. Steve King (R-IA), 28 cosponsors	Same as Deal's proposed 2007 act	Introduced, no hearing

Table 7.2. Bills Introduced in Congress to Alter Birthright Citizenship 1993–2019 (*continued*)

Bill	Sponsor	Key Provisions	Disposition
H.Res. 140: Calling on the president to resume the interpretation of Section 1 of the Fourteenth Amendment to the Constitution as originally intended and applied as law for a century	Rep. Brian Babin (R-TX), no cosponsors	Expresses disapproval of birthright citizenship	Introduced, no hearing

Chief source: congress.gov.

joint hearings between the Subcommittee on Immigration and Claims and the Subcommittee on the Constitution, but neither made it to the House floor. Neither proposal was incorporated into the Illegal Immigration Reform and Immigrant Responsibility Act of 1996.[129]

In most years, these bills were relegated to the House Judiciary Committee, directed to a subcommittee, and left to die there; occasionally, one of the bills garnered sufficient attention to warrant a hearing. Republican representatives Elton Gallegly (CA), Dan Burton (IN), Nathan Deal (GA), Bob Stump (AZ), Tom Tancredo (CO), and Brian Babin (TX) have actively introduced bills and resolutions in the House to limit or denounce birthright citizenship.[130] For the most part, however, these bills have not moved forward. In only five instances have hearings on these bills been held in subcommittees—none between 2005 and 2014. The most recent took place on April 29, 2015, when Representative King's bill triggered a hearing by the Subcommittee on Immigration and Border Security (House Judiciary Committee) entitled "Birthright Citizenship: Is It the Right Policy for America?"[131]

Notably, despite some denunciation of birthright citizenship by individual senators (recently by South Carolina Republican Lindsey Graham), very little legislation has been introduced in the Senate in the last quarter century. In 2011, Senator David Vitter (R-LA) proposed an amendment to the Immigration and Nationality Act (S. 723) that would deem a person born in the United States "subject to the jurisdiction thereof" only if that "person is born in the United States of parents, one of whom is: (1) a U.S. citizen or national, (2) a lawful permanent resident alien whose residence is in the United States, or (3) an alien performing active service in the U.S. Armed Forces."[132] Senator Vitter reintroduced the Birthright Citizenship Act in 2013 and 2015, with few or no cosponsors; the bills were referred to the Judiciary Committee, and no further action ensued.

Most recently, H.R. 140, introduced by Representative Steve King in January 2019, entitled the Birthright Citizenship Act of 2019, garnered twenty-eight Republican cosponsors. The proposed legislation would amend Section 301 of the Immigration and Nationality Act "to clarify those classes of individuals born in the United States who are nationals and citizens of the United States at birth." A person born in the United States would be considered "subject to the jurisdiction" of the United States under Section 1 of the Fourteenth Amendment if the person is born in the United States to parents, one of whom is a citizen or national of the United States, an alien lawfully admitted for permanent residence in the United States whose residence is in the United States, or an alien performing active services in the armed forces of the United States.[133] King, who has introduced a measure to reform birthright citizenship every year since 2011, explains his reasons for introducing the bill in this way:

> In addition to border security and workplace enforcement, our nation must eliminate needless incentives that encourage illegal immigration and cost taxpayers significant amounts of money each year. I do not believe it is in the best interest of our nation to continue tolerating the practice of illegal aliens giving birth to children in the U.S. in order to obtain citizenship for the child, then moving back to their country of origin with the hopes of achieving uninhibited access to our country for as many family members as possible.[134]

Any such proposals would be stymied in a Democratic House, but determined Republicans seem committed to continuing to press the issue.

Public Reception of Efforts to Curtail Birthright Citizenship

While the bills introduced are critical to understanding the modern debate, they should not be taken as evidence for a groundswell of American opinion rejecting birthright citizenship. While a great deal depends on question wording, public opinion polls tend to support the continuation of current policy when respondents are told that birthright citizenship is that policy; when no information about current policy is offered, opinion is about evenly split.[135] A set of 2018 polls by HarrisX indicated that Republicans are more likely to care about the legal status of the parents than are Democrats, and are less supportive of citizenship even for mothers present on temporary visas. Independents tend to support birthright citizenship whether or not the child is born to those legally within the United States, and Democrats are even more supportive than Independents, including for children of undocumented immigrants.[136]

Attacks on birthright citizenship do not appear to be widely supported, with even many elite Republicans rejecting them. As 2016 presidential candidates, Senator Marco Rubio and former Florida governor Jeb Bush did not support a move to end birthright citizenship (though Rubio later said the president's call to end birthright citizenship for people illegally or temporarily in the country has not been decided by the Court and should be).[137] John Yoo, a chief architect of President George W. Bush's detainee treatment policies violating the Geneva Accord and defender of unilateral executive decision-making, has spoken out against President Trump's efforts to end birthright citizenship: "Conservatives should reject Trump's nativist siren song and reaffirm the law and policy of one of the Republican Party's greatest achievements: The 14th Amendment. According to the best reading of its text, structure, and history, anyone born on American territory, no matter their national origin, ethnicity or station in life, is an American citizen."[138] He is joined by a number of other conservatives. James C. Ho, appointed to the Fifth Circuit Court of Appeals based in New Orleans in 2018, wrote in 2006 that "birthright citizenship is guaranteed by the Fourteenth Amendment. That birthright is protected no less for children of undocumented persons than for descendants of Mayflower passengers." Ho also insisted that "subject to the jurisdiction" of the United States means simply to be subject to the authority of the US government—that is, that one is required to obey US law; those who are not so obliged include foreign diplomats and enemy soldiers.[139] Linda Chavez, staff director of the US Commission on Civil Rights under President Reagan and current chair of the Center for Equal Opportunity, a conservative think tank focused on issues of race and ethnicity, has also defended a generous reading of the birthright citizenship provision of the Fourteenth Amendment.[140]

Looking to the Future

In the unlikely event that a bill altering the meaning of birthright citizenship were to pass Congress and become law, the Court may not defer to the elective branches. For one reason, the Court has, twice since *Wong Kim Ark*, reaffirmed its holding (see chapter 6). For another, the Supreme Court, in recent decades, has shown less deference to Congress when Congress speaks to the meaning of the Constitution than it had in the past. This has been especially pronounced with regard to Congress's enforcement power under Section 5 of the Fourteenth Amendment.[141] A recent case demonstrates that the Supreme Court is likely to insist on weighing the constitutionality of new legislative changes to the Immigration and Naturalization Act. In 2017, the Court stepped in

More Recent Cases Bearing on Birthright Citizenship

- *Plyler v. Doe*, 457 U.S. 202 (1982): Held that public elementary and secondary education cannot be denied to undocumented immigrant children.
- *Sessions v. Morales-Santana*, 582 U.S.__ (2017): Established constitutional limits on what Congress can do when altering citizenship requirements for children born abroad to unmarried US citizen fathers versus mothers.

to invalidate a provision of the Immigration and Naturalization Act in the name of gender equality, establishing constitutional limits on what Congress can do when altering citizenship requirements for children born abroad to one American parent.[142] The law made it easier for a child born abroad to an unmarried, US citizen mother to become a US citizen than if that child had been born to an unmarried US citizen father. The government claimed that it had an interest in ensuring that a child born abroad had a strong enough connection to the United States to be declared a citizen. Yet an unmarried citizen mother only had to spend one year in the United States before the birth of the child, and there was no requirement that she and the child return; an unmarried citizen father, however, was required to have lived in the United States for at least ten years before the child was born, and five of those years had to be after he was fourteen years of age. A second argument offered by the government was that the policy attempted to prevent statelessness—that is, a child of one US citizen having no nationality. In this case, the US citizen was a father who did not meet the higher residency requirements of the statute.

Writing for the Court, Justice Ruth Bader Ginsburg stipulated that when government passes laws that differentiate in their treatment of men and women, the intermediate scrutiny test applies. The government must demonstrate that the distinction serves an important governmental purpose and that the provisions of the law are substantially related and tailored to achieve that purpose. The inequity in treatment of mothers and fathers was, Ginsburg wrote, "stunningly anachronistic"; the stereotype of the unmarried mother as a child's natural and sole guardian and primary family caregiver tends to reinforce that role, at the same time penalizing men who "exercise responsibility for raising their children."[143] The Court rejected the statelessness rationale as well: "there is little reason to believe" Congress was worried about this when it enacted the law in question; furthermore, there was no evidence offered that the "risk of statelessness disproportionately endangered the children of unwed mothers."

While it was up to Congress and not the Court to design laws that do not violate the Fifth Amendment's requirement that government accord all persons the equal protection of the laws, the Court determined that the reading of the law that best comported with what Congress intended (or expected) was to apply the harsher, *longer* residency requirement designed for unmarried citizen fathers to unmarried citizen mothers, since Congress expected the more lenient rule to apply to fewer cases. The result of the Court decision means that fewer children born to unmarried US citizens abroad will be able to claim US citizenship.[144] Morales-Santana himself, a legal resident of the United States since 1975, faced deportation to the Dominican Republic because of criminal convictions, though he had not lived there since he was a child.

It is, of course, possible that, were Congress to pass legislation limiting birthright citizenship, or if some other administrative action were to prompt a legal challenge, the Supreme Court would revisit *Wong Kim Ark*. We think it unlikely that the decision—which has been treated by the Court as clearly settled law—would be overturned. But could the Court then perhaps distinguish *Wong Kim Ark* from a case involving the US-born children of undocumented residents, accepting the argument that *Wong Kim Ark* did not settle the matter of children whose parents were here without permission? While not impossible in the current political climate, we think that textualists, reviewing the history of the Fourteenth Amendment and the understanding of birthright citizenship that we have laid out in this book, are likely to uphold the broader reading of *Wong Kim Ark*. The only likely path to eliminate birthright citizenship for those within the jurisdiction of the United States is an amendment to the US Constitution. An amendment of this nature is not likely to be forthcoming in the foreseeable future. Yet the use of attacks on birthright citizenship as a potent organizing tool for the right troubles many political observers and contributes to a threatening climate for immigrants and their children.

Chronology

1608   *Calvin's Case*, after James I becomes king of England, establishes that a person's status is vested at birth, based on place of birth.

1790   US Naturalization Law limits naturalization "to any alien, being a free white person, who shall have resided within the limits and under the jurisdiction of the United States for the term of two years"; later amendments change duration.

1830   *Inglis v. Trustees of Sailor's Snug Harbor* (28 U.S. 120) acknowledges that both British and American courts recognize all persons born within the North American colonies while subject to the British Crown as natural-born British subjects. Justice Story, concurring (at 155) elaborates that allegiance by birth is "that which arises from being born within the dominions and under the protection of a particular sovereign."

1834   Joseph Story, *Commentaries on the Conflict of Laws,* 44: "Persons, who are born in a country, are generally deemed citizens and subjects of that country."

1844   *Lynch v. Clarke & Lynch* (3 N.Y. Leg. Obs. 237–238, 250) embraces common-law understanding that "every person born within the dominions and allegiance of the United States, whatever were the situation of his parents, is a natural born citizen."

1840s   Opium War forces China to open coastal treaty ports to trade and cede Hong Kong; Chinese begin emigrating from these international ports.

1848   Gold discovered in California; some Chinese begin to arrive, finding work in the camps.

1850s   California passes various laws and city ordinances aimed at restricting Chinese businesses and employment.

1857   *Dred Scott v. Sandford* (60 U.S. 393) holds that US citizenship excludes black persons.

1851–1864 Taiping Rebellion and Red Turban Rebellion claim twenty million lives in and around Guangdong Province, from which the vast majority of Chinese migrants to the United States came.

1861–1865 US Civil War.

1860s   Chinese workers brought to America to work on railroads.

1862   Chinese Six Companies formed in San Francisco.

1866   Civil Rights Act of 1866 states that "all persons born in the United States and not subject to any foreign power, excluding Indians not taxed are hereby declared to be citizens of the United States."

1868   Fourteenth Amendment ratified. Section 1 begins: "All persons born or naturalized in the United States, and subject to the jurisdiction thereof, are citizens of the United States and of the state wherein they reside."

1868   Burlingame Treaty authorizes free migration and permanent residency of Chinese in America. Entered into force November 23, 1869.

1870   US naturalization law extends availability of naturalization to "aliens of African nativity and to persons of African descent," implicitly excluding Asians.

1870   Congress bars states from imposing head taxes on immigrants.

1873   *Slaughter-House Cases* (83 U.S. 36): Fourteenth Amendment made all persons born within the United States and subject to its jurisdiction US citizens; leaves in doubt status of US-born children of immigrants who had not naturalized.

1873   Wong Kim Ark born in San Francisco to merchant parents (may have been as early as 1871).

1874   *In re Ah Fong* (1 F. Cas. 213 (Cir. Ct. D. Cal. 1874)) holds that states lack the power to exclude foreigners from their limits and to prevent their landing based on the immorality of their past lives, inviting congressional intervention.

1875   Page Act, first federal immigration act aimed at Chinese, bars entrance by "coolie" laborers and those suspected of being prostitutes.

1875   *Chy Lung v. Freeman* (92 U.S. 275) holds that in attempting to restrict Chinese women's entrance, California violated Congress's exclusive authority to regulate commerce with foreign nations.

1877   Anti-Chinese violence in San Francisco leads to deaths and destruction of property; other acts of mob violence against Chinese on West Coast in 1870s and 1880s.

1880   Angell Treaty signed, amending Burlingame Treaty, allowing for regulation and limitation of Chinese immigration but confirming US obligation to protect rights of Chinese immigrants then present in the United States. Enters into force July 19, 1881.

1882 Chinese Exclusion Act bars entry of Chinese laborers for ten years.

1884 Amendment to Exclusion Act requires return certificates for laborers seeking to reenter United States from China; nonlaborers seeking to enter require consular visas.

1884 *Chew Heong v. United States* (112 U.S. 536) holds that Chinese citizens were entitled to rights promised in treaties with China unless Congress explicitly repealed treaties; laborer who left without a return certificate prior to 1882 was entitled to reentry without one.

1884 *In re Look Tin Sing* (21 F. 905, Cir. Cal.) finds in the case of a Chinese merchant's son, born in California, "the jurisdiction of the United States over him at the time of his birth was exclusive of that of any other country." The native-born are on equal footing.

1884 *Elk v. Wilkins* (112 U.S. 94) holds that individual members of Native American tribes cannot change their "alien and dependent condition" without a corresponding action on the part of the United States.

1886 *Yick Wo v. Hopkins* (118 U.S. 356) holds that legislation discriminating on the basis of race and ordinance administered in a racially discriminatory manner violates the Fourteenth Amendment.

1887 General Allotment Act provides route for citizenship for Native Americans receiving and living on land allotments.

1888 Scott Act abolishes "returning laborer" status, invalidating certificates of return for around twenty thousand laborers.

1889 *Chae Chan Ping v. United States*, known as "the Chinese Exclusion Case" (130 U.S. 581), holds Congress can exclude aliens "at any time when, in the judgment of the government, the interests of the country require it."

1889–1890 Wong Kim Ark travels to China with his parents, Wong Si Ping and Wee Lee. His parents remain in China. Wong Kim Ark marries Yee Shee there, but she remains. He returns to the United States without incident. He would father four children who traveled back and forth between China and the United States.

c. 1891 Wong Kim Ark's oldest son, Wong Yook Fun, born in Taishan, Guangdong Province (near Hong Kong and Canton).

1892 Geary Act extends ban on entry of labor for ten years and requires those of Chinese origin to carry identification certificates at all times or face deportation; Congress allocates little money for enforcement; Chinese given one year to secure certificates.

1892 *Gee Fook Sing v. United States* (49 F. 146) holds that measures excluding Chinese laborers did not apply to individuals born in the United States; such individuals must still demonstrate birth in the United States.

1893 Amid massive Chinese resistance to registration requirement in Geary Act, *Fong Yue Ting* (148 U.S. 698) states that political departments of the government have the power to exclude or expel aliens, with federal courts playing little role and upholds registration requirement,

1893 McCreary Act provides six-month grace period for registration; enforcement mechanisms enhanced, and advocates for Chinese drop opposition to registration.

1894 General Appropriations Act provides that any decision by an immigration or customs officer to exclude an alien from admission into the United States was final unless the secretary of the Treasury reversed it upon appeal.

May 1894 Bubonic plague outbreak in Hong Kong

November 1894–1895 Wong Kim Ark visits China.

May 1895 In *Lem Moon Sing v. United States* (158 U.S. 538), involving a merchant excluded from reentry, Court points to 1894 General Appropriations Act limiting role for judicial intervention.

August 1895 Wong Kim Ark denied entry and held offshore. Appealed his exclusion on grounds he was a citizen of the United States.

c. 1895 Wong Kim Ark's second son, Wong Yook Thue, born in Guangdong Province.

January 1896 District court finds Wong Kim Ark is a citizen (*In re Wong Kim Ark*, 71 F. 382 (N.D. Cal.)); he is released pending government appeal of the case. Appealed directly to Supreme Court on writ of error.

May 1896 *Wong Wing v. United States* (163 U.S. 228) holds that noncitizens are entitled to jury trial if they are to be sentenced to hard labor; Geary Act provision authorizing up to a year's hard labor prior to deportation for violation of Geary Act invalidated.

February 1898 Explosion of the *Maine* in Havana Harbor.

March 1898 US Court of Naval Inquiry declares a mine blew up the *Maine* the same day the Supreme Court hands down *Wong Kim Ark* decision. Attention turns to war.

March 1898 US Supreme Court declares Wong Kim Ark a citizen and holds that the Fourteenth Amendment establishes the principle of jus soli: anyone born on US soil (with very few exceptions such as foreign ministers) is a citizen.

1902 Exclusion of Chinese laborers made permanent.

1904–1905 Wong Kim Ark visits China.

c. 1905 Wong Kim Ark's third son, Wong Yook Sue, born in Guangdong Province.

1907 In Gentlemen's Agreement, Japan informally agrees to bar immigration to United States for workers and most other categories of migrants, and schools in California will not segregate Japanese.

1910 Wong Kim Ark's oldest son, Yook Fun, attempts to enter United States and is denied entry and sent back to China in January 1911.

1913–1914 Wong Kim Ark makes another visit to China.

c. 1913 Wong Kim Ark's fourth son, Wong Yook Jim, born in Guangdong Province.

1914 Upon return from China, Wong Kim Ark applies for a certificate of identity in San Francisco.

1917 Immigration Act of 1917 imposes literacy tests on immigrants, expands categories of inadmissible immigrants, and bars immigration by individuals within a geographic region encompassing much of Asia and the Pacific Islands.

1922 *Ozawa v. United States* holds that "free white persons" referred to in US naturalization laws does not include Japanese; law means Caucasians.

1923 *United States v. Thind* holds that a Hindu (even if Caucasian) is not a white person for purposes of US naturalization.

1924 Johnson-Reed Act sets tighter quotas for immigrants from various nations than 1921 quotas, and bases quotas on 1890 census; bars Chinese.

1924–1926 Wong Kim Ark's other three sons arrive in the United States and gain entry, although one of these, Wong Yook Jim, is detained for several weeks. Father and brother testify, and he is admitted. Wong Yook Jim serves in US Army, Marines, and subsequently Merchant Marine for a quarter century.

1925   In *Toyota v. United States*, a US military veteran of Japanese ancestry is not permitted to naturalize (Congress permitted some veterans to naturalize).

1931   Wong Kim Ark returns to China and remains there. Date of death unknown; son learned of father's death after World War II.

1934   Supreme Court reaffirms *Wong Kim Ark* in case of Japanese persons born in the United States (*Morrison v. California*).

1939   Supreme Court again reaffirms *Wong Kim Ark* in *Perkins v. Elg*: a child born in the United States of alien parentage is a birthright citizen.

1943   In *Regan v. King*, the Ninth Circuit ruled summarily against those challenging Japanese birthright citizenship (and their right to vote); Supreme Court declines to hear case.

1943   Repeal of Chinese Exclusion Act during World War II; small annual quota established for ethnic Chinese immigrating from any part of the world.

1952   McCarran-Walter Act eliminates Asiatic Barred Zone, allots small number of visas for Asian nations, and allows Asians to become naturalized American citizens.

1965   Immigration and Nationalization Act (Hart-Celler) ends national origins system and creates preference system for relatives of US citizens and legal permanent residents, and for professionals and those with specialized skills.

1980s Some nations reconsider, and sometimes tighten, birthright citizenship eligibility, including nations having some of the most generous provisions.

Notes

Introduction

1. Carol Nackenoff, "Constitutionalizing Terms of Inclusion: Friends of the Indian and Citizenship for Native Americans 1880s–1930s," in *The Supreme Court and American Political Development*, ed. Ronald Kahn and Ken I. Kersch (Lawrence: University Press of Kansas, 2006), 366–413.

2. Paul Spickard, *Almost All Aliens: Immigration, Race, and Colonialism in American History and Identity* (New York: Taylor and Francis, 2007), 149–153.

3. Garrett Epps, *Democracy Reborn: The Fourteenth Amendment and the Fight for Equal Rights in Post–Civil War America* (New York: Henry Holt, 2006).

4. Beth Lew-Williams, *The Chinese Must Go: Violence, Exclusion, and the Making of the Alien in America* (Cambridge, MA: Harvard University Press, 2018).

5. *Cherokee Nation v. Georgia*, 30 U.S. 1 (1831).

6. See generally Pamela Brandwein, *Rethinking the Judicial Settlement of Reconstruction* (New York: Cambridge University Press, 2011).

7. *Bradwell v. Illinois*, 83 U.S. 130 (1873); *Minor v. Happersett*, 88 U.S. 162 (1875).

8. *Plessy v. Ferguson*, 163 U.S. 537 (1896).

9. See, e.g., Polly Price, "Natural Law and Birthright Citizenship in Calvin's Case (1608)," *Yale Journal of Law and the Humanities* 9 (1997): 73–145.

10. Martha S. Jones, *Birthright Citizens: A History of Race and Rights in Antebellum America* (New York: Cambridge University Press, 2018).

11. Anna O. Law, "Lunatics, Idiots, Paupers, and Negro Seamen—Immigration Federalism and the Early American State," *Studies in American Political Development* 28 (2014): 107–128.

12. Mark Graber, *Dred Scott and the Problem of Constitutional Evil* (New York: Cambridge University Press, 2006).

13. Epps, *Democracy Reborn*; Rebecca Zietlow, "Exploring the History, Evolution, and Future of the Fourteenth Amendment: Juriscentrism and the Original Meaning of Section Five," *Temple Political and Civil Rights Law Review* 13 (2004): 485–513.

14. Spickard, *Almost All Aliens*.

15. Scott Alan Carson, "Chinese Sojourn Labor and the American Transcontinental Railroad," *Journal of Institutional and Theoretical Economics* 161, no. 1 (2005): 80–102; Gerald Nash, "A Veritable Revolution: The Global Economic Significance of the California Gold Rush," *California History* 77, no. 4 (1999/1998): 276–292; June Mei, "Socioeconomic Origins of Emigration: Guangdong to California, 1850–1882," *Modern China* 5, no. 4 (1979): 463–501; Spickard, *Almost All Aliens*.

16. Lew-Williams, *Chinese Must Go.*

17. Lucy Salyer, *Laws Harsh as Tigers: Chinese Immigrants and the Shaping of Modern Immigration Law* (Chapel Hill: University of North Carolina Press, 1995); Erika Lee, *At America's Gates: Chinese Immigration during the Exclusion Era, 1882–1943* (Chapel Hill: University of North Carolina Press, 2003).

18. George Anthony Peffer, "Forbidden Families: Emigration Experiences of Chinese Women under the Page Law, 1875–1882," *Journal of American Ethnic History* 6, no. 1 (1986): 28–46; Kitty Calavita, "The Paradoxes of Race, Class, Identity, and 'Passing': Enforcing the Chinese Exclusion Acts, 1882–1910," *Law and Social Inquiry* 25, no. 1 (2000): 1–40; Kitty Calavita, "Collisions at the Intersection of Gender, Race, and Class: Enforcing the Chinese Exclusion Laws," *Law and Society Review* 40, no. 2 (2006): 249–282.

19. Kerry Abrams, "Polygamy, Prostitution, and the Federalization of Immigration Law," *Columbia Law Review* 105, no. 3 (2005): 641–716; Peggy Pascoe, "Gender Systems in Conflict: The Marriages of Mission-Educated Chinese American Women, 1874–1939," *Journal of Social History* 22, no. 4 (1989): 631–652.

20. Salyer, *Laws Harsh as Tigers.*

21. Christian Fritz, "A Nineteenth Century 'Habeas Corpus Mill': The Chinese before the Federal Courts of California," *Journal of American History* 32, no. 4 (1988): 347–372.

22. Ellen Katz, "The Six Companies and the Geary Act: A Case Study in Nineteenth-Century Civil Disobedience and Civil Rights Litigation," *Western Legal History* 8, no. 2 (1995): 227–272.

23. Gabriel J. Chin, "*Chae Chan Ping* and *Fong Yue Ting*: The Origins of Plenary Power," in *Immigration Stories*, ed. David Martin and Peter Schuck (New York: Foundation Press, 2005), 7–30.

24. Gerald L. Neuman, "*Wong Wing v. United States*: The Bill of Rights Protects Illegal Aliens," in *Immigration Stories*, ed. David A. Martin and Peter H. Schuck (New York: Foundation Press, 2005), 31–50.

25. Erika Lee, "Birthright Citizenship, Immigration, and the U.S. Constitution: The Story of *United States v. Wong Kim Ark*," in *Race Law Stories*, ed. Rachel Moran and Devon Carbado (New York: Foundation Press, 2008), 89–109; Lucy Salyer, "*Wong Kim Ark*: The Contest over Birthright Citizenship," in *Immigration Stories*, ed. David A. Martin and Peter H. Schuck (New York: Foundation Press, 2005), 51–85; Bethany Berger, "Birthright Citizenship on Trial: *Elk v. Wilkins* and *United States v. Wong Kim Ark*," *Cardozo Law Review* 37 (2016): 1185–1258.

26. Julie Novkov and Carol Nackenoff, "Civic Membership, Family Status, and the Chinese in America, 1870s–1920s," *Polity* 48, no. 2 (2016): 165–185; Carol Nackenoff and Julie Novkov, "Building the Administrative State: Courts and the Admission of Chinese Persons to the United States, 1870s–1920s," in *Stating the Family: New Directions in the Study of American Politics*, ed. Julie Novkov and Carol Nackenoff (Lawrence: University Press of Kansas, 2020), 197–239.

27. See, e.g., Julie Novkov, *Racial Union: Law, Intimacy, and the White State in Alabama, 1865–1964* (Ann Arbor: University of Michigan Press, 2008); Carol Nackenoff with Allison Hrabar, "Quaker Roles in Making and Implementing Federal Indian Policy: From Grant's Peace Policy through the Early Dawes Act

Era (1869–1900)," in *Quakers and Native Americans*, ed. Geoffrey Plank and Ignacio Gallup-Diaz (Leiden: Koninklijke Brill, 2019), 171–292; Carol Nackenoff, "The Private Roots of American Political Development: The Immigrants' Protective League's 'Friendly and Sympathetic Touch,' 1908–1924," *Studies in American Political Development* 28, no. 2 (2014): 129–160.

28. Bartholomew H. Sparrow, *The* Insular Cases *and the Emergence of American Empire* (Lawrence: University Press of Kansas, 2006).

29. Sam Erman, *Almost Citizens: Puerto Rico, the U.S. Constitution, and Empire* (Cambridge: Cambridge University Press, 2019).

30. Paul Kramer, *The Blood of Government: Race, Empire, the United States, and the Philippines* (Chapel Hill: University of North Carolina Press, 2006).

31. Law, "Lunatics, Idiots, Paupers, and Negro Seamen," 115.

32. Law, 108.

33. Law, 112.

34. Law, 122.

35. Law, 113.

36. The language is from John Marshall's opinion in *Cherokee Nation v. Georgia*.

37. Kunal M. Parker, *Making Foreigners: Immigration and Citizenship Law in America, 1600–2000* (Cambridge: Cambridge University Press, 2015), 89–92.

38. Kramer, *Blood of Government*, 350.

Chapter 1. The Foundations of American Citizenship

1. Only when explicitly referring to the Latin origin of these names will jus soli and jus sanguinis be italicized.

2. Paul Spickard, *Almost All Aliens: Immigration, Race, and Colonialism in American History and Identity* (New York: Taylor and Francis, 2007), 510.

3. Torrie Hester, *Deportation: The Origins of U.S. Policy* (Philadelphia: University of Pennsylvania Press, 2017), 8–9.

4. Hester, 25–26.

5. Hester, 21.

6. Hester, 19–34.

7. Hester, 72–79; see also Julie Novkov and Carol Nackenoff, "Civic Membership, Family Status, and the Chinese in America, 1870s–1920s," *Polity* 48, no. 2 (2016): 165–185.

8. Hester, *Deportation*, 172; Brian Gratton and Emily Merchant, "Immigration, Repatriation, and Deportation: The Mexican-Origin Population in the United States, 1920–1950," *International Migration Review* 47, no. 4 (2013): 944–975.

9. Gratton and Merchant, "Immigration, Repatriation, and Deportation," 959–960.

10. Mae M. Ngai, "The Strange Career of the Illegal Alien: Immigration Restriction and Deportation Policy in the United States, 1921–1965," *Law and History Review* 21, no. 1 (2003): 76–77.

11. Ngai, 94–96.

12. Ngai, 102.

13. Polly Price, "Natural Law and Birthright Citizenship in Calvin's Case (1608)," *Yale Journal of Law and the Humanities* 9, no. 1 (1997): 73–75.

14. Price, 80.

15. Harvey Wheeler, "Calvin's Case (1608) and the McIlwain-Schuyler Debate," *American Historical Review* 61, no. 3 (1956): 588.

16. Price, "Natural Law and Birthright Citizenship in Calvin's Case," 81–82.

17. Price, 82.

18. Price, 83.

19. Price, 74.

20. Sir Edward Coke report in Calvin's Case, quoted in Hester Lessard, Rebecca Johnson, and Jeremy Webber, eds., *Storied Communities: Narratives of Contact and Arrival in Constituting Political Community* (Vancouver: University of British Columbia Press, 2011), 47.

21. *Murray v. The Charming Betsey*, 6 U.S. (2 Cranch) 64 (1804), at 119–120.

22. *Murray v. The Charming Betsey*, 6 U.S. (2 Cranch), at 120.

23. *Murray v. The Charming Betsey*, 6 U.S. (2 Cranch), at 120–121.

24. *McIlvaine v. Coxe's Lessee*, 8 U.S. 209 (1808), at 212.

25. *McIlvaine v. Coxe's Lessee*, 8 U.S. at 213.

26. *Blight's Lessee v. Rochester*, 20 U.S. 535 (1822).

27. *Blight's Lessee v. Rochester*, 20 U.S. at 545–546.

28. *Inglis v. Trustees of Sailor's Snug Harbor*, 28 U.S. 99 (1830), at 120.

29. *Inglis v. Trustees of Sailor's Snug Harbor*, 28 U.S. at 122–123.

30. *Inglis v. Trustees of Sailor's Snug Harbor*, 28 U.S. at 155.

31. *Inglis v. Trustees of Sailor's Snug Harbor*, 28 U.S. at 155–156.

32. *Inglis v. Trustees of Sailor's Snug Harbor*, 28 U.S. at 156.

33. *Inglis v. Trustees of Sailor's Snug Harbor*, 28 U.S. at 136.

34. Joseph Story, *Commentaries on the Conflict of Laws* (Boston: Hilliard, Gray, and Company, 1834), 44.

35. Story, 48.

36. *Lynch v. Clarke & Lynch*, 3 N.Y. Leg. Obs. 236 (1844), at 237.

37. *Lynch v. Clarke & Lynch*, 3 N.Y. Leg. Obs. at 238.

38. *Lynch v. Clarke & Lynch*, 3 N.Y. Leg. Obs. at 239 (italics in original).

39. *Lynch v. Clarke & Lynch*, 3 N.Y. Leg. Obs. at 241.

40. *Lynch v. Clarke & Lynch*, 3 N.Y. Leg. Obs. at 243–244.

41. *Lynch v. Clarke & Lynch*, 3 N.Y. Leg. Obs. at 246–247.

42. *Lynch v. Clarke & Lynch*, 3 N.Y. Leg. Obs. at 250.

43. We discuss this further in chapter 6.

44. Spickard, *Almost All Aliens*, 77.

45. Spickard, 89.

46. Spickard, 90.

47. Spickard, 120–128.

48. Martha S. Jones, *Birthright Citizens: A History of Race and Rights in Antebellum America* (New York: Cambridge University Press, 2018), 26.

49. Jones, 27.

50. Jones, 28.

51. Jones, 29.

52. Jones, 29.

53. Chancellor James Kent, *Commentaries on American Law* (New York: Chancellor James Kent, 1836), 2:258.

54. *Cherokee Nation v. Georgia*, 30 U.S. 1 (1831).

55. *Cherokee Nation v. Georgia*, 30 U.S. at 17.

56. Mark Graber, *Dred Scott and the Problem of Constitutional Evil* (New York: Cambridge University Press, 2006).

57. *Dred Scott v. Sandford*, 60 U.S. 393 (1857).

58. *Dred Scott v. Sandford*, 60 U.S. at 403.

59. *Dred Scott v. Sandford*, 60 U.S. at 403–404.

60. *Dred Scott v. Sandford*, 60 U.S. at 406.

61. *Dred Scott v. Sandford*, 60 U.S. at 411–412.

62. *Dred Scott v. Sandford*, 60 U.S. at 416.

63. *Dred Scott v. Sandford*, 60 U.S. at 417.

64. *Dred Scott v. Sandford*, 60 U.S. at 423.

65. *Dred Scott v. Sandford*, 60 U.S. at 477.

66. *Dred Scott v. Sandford*, 60 U.S. at 479–480.

67. *Dred Scott v. Sandford*, 60 U.S. at 482.

68. *Dred Scott v. Sandford*, 60 U.S. at 572–573.

69. *Dred Scott v. Sandford*, 60 U.S. at 574.

70. *Dred Scott v. Sandford*, 60 U.S. at 530.

71. Rebecca Zietlow, "Exploring the History, Evolution, and Future of the Fourteenth Amendment: Juriscentrism and the Original Meaning of Section Five," *Temple Political and Civil Rights Law Review* 13 (2004) 495–496.

72. Garrett Epps, "Interpreting the Fourteenth Amendment: Two Don'ts and Three Dos," *William and Mary Bill of Rights Journal* 16, no. 2 (2007): 439–440.

73. Epps, 445.

74. Civil Rights Act of 1866, 14 Stat. 27, 39th Cong., 1st Sess., Ch. 31, April 9, 1866, 27.

75. Garrett Epps, *Democracy Reborn: The Fourteenth Amendment and the Fight for Equal Rights in Post–Civil War America* (New York: Henry Holt, 2006), 174.

76. Epps, 182.

77. Epps, "Interpreting the Fourteenth Amendment," 447–448.

78. Epps, *Democracy Reborn*, 226.

79. Epps, 227.

80. Epps, 234.

81. Epps, 234.

82. Epps, 235.

83. Epps, 236–237.

84. Epps, 237–238.

85. Andrew Johnson, "Message to the Senate," *Journal of the Senate of the United States of America, 1789–1873*, June 22, 1866, online by Gerhard Peters and John T. Woolley, The American Presidency Project, https://www.presidency.ucsb.edu/node/202310.

86. Epps, *Democracy Reborn*, 253.

87. *Slaughter-House Cases*, 83 U.S. 36 (1873), at 72.

88. *Slaughter-House Cases*, 83 U.S. at 72–73.

89. *Slaughter-House Cases*, 83 U.S. at 73.

90. Randy E. Barnett and Evan D. Bernick, "The Privileges or Immunities Clause Abridged: A Critique of Kurt Lash on the Fourteenth Amendment," *Notre Dame Law Review* 95, no. 2 (2020): 499–589. For Barnett (see also his *Restoring the Lost Constitution*, updated edition [Princeton, NJ: Princeton University Press, 2013]), there are also unenumerated rights; the list in *Corfield* is considered illustrative and not conclusive.

91. *Corfield v. Coryell*, 6 Fed. Cas. 546 (C.C. E.D. Pa. 1823), at 551.

92. *Corfield v. Coryell*, 6 Fed. Cas. at 552.

93. *Adamson v. California*, 332 U.S. 46 (1947), at 74.

94. Cited in Epps, *Democracy Reborn*, 170.

95. *Slaughter-House Cases*, 83 U.S. at 95.

96. *Elk v. Wilkins*, 112 U.S. 94 (1884), at 98–99.

97. Elbridge Davis and Harold Davis, "Mr. Justice Horace Gray: Some Aspects of His Judicial Career," *American Bar Association Journal* 41 (1955): 421–424, 468–471.

98. Horace Gray and John Lowell, *A Legal Review of the Case of Dred Scott: As Decided the Supreme Court of the United States* (Boston: Crosby, Nichols, and Co., 1857), 20.

99. Davis and Davis, "Mr. Justice Horace Gray," 422.

100. Davis and Davis, 423.

101. *Elk v. Wilkins*, 112 U.S. at 99.

102. *Elk v. Wilkins*, 112 U.S. at 99–100.

103. *Elk v. Wilkins*, 112 U.S. at 101–102.

104. *Elk v. Wilkins*, 112 U.S. at 102.

105. *Elk v. Wilkins*, 112 U.S. at 103.

106. *Elk v. Wilkins*, 112 U.S. at 117.

107. Carol Nackenoff, "Constitutionalizing Terms of Inclusion: Friends of the Indian and Citizenship for Native Americans, 1880s–1930s," in *The Supreme Court and American Political Development*, ed. Ronald Kahn and Ken I. Kersch (Lawrence: University Press of Kansas, 2006), 366–413.

Chapter 2. Chinese Immigration and the Legal Shift toward Exclusion

1. Paul Spickard, *Almost All Aliens: Immigration, Race, and Colonialism in American History and Identity* (New York: Taylor and Francis, 2007), 157–158.

2. Scott Alan Carson, "Chinese Sojourn Labor and the American Transcontinental Railroad," *Journal of Institutional and Theoretical Economics* 161, no. 1 (2005): 82.

3. Gerald Nash, "A Veritable Revolution: The Global Economic Significance of the California Gold Rush," *California History* 77, no. 4 (1998/1999): 278–281.

4. Carson, "Chinese Sojourn Labor," 83–84.

5. June Mei, "Socioeconomic Origins of Emigration: Guangdong to California, 1850–1882," *Modern China* 5, no. 4 (1979): 464.

6. Mei, 465–466. See chapter 4 for more details about the region from which Wong Kim Ark's family migrated.

7. Yong Chen, "The Internal Origins of Chinese Emigration to California Reconsidered," *Western Historical Quarterly* 28 (1997): 525.

8. Spickard, *Almost All Aliens*, 158.

9. Mei, "Socioeconomic Origins of Emigration," 473.

10. Chen, "Internal Origins of Chinese Emigration," 526.

11. Chen, 527.

12. Chen, 534.

13. Chen, 537.

14. Chen, 539.

15. Chen, 544.

16. Elizabeth Sinn, "Beyond 'Tianxia': The 'Zhongwai Xinwen Qiribao' (Hong Kong 1871–1872) and the Construction of a Transnational Chinese Community," *China Review* 4 (Spring 2004): 100.

17. Mei, "Socioeconomic Origins of Emigration," 475.

18. Mei, 475.

19. Mei, 473–475.

20. Chen, "Internal Origins of Chinese Emigration," 540–541.

21. Mei, "Socioeconomic Origins of Emigration," 478.

22. Mei, 481.

23. Mei, 482–484.

24. Michael Williams, *Returning Home with Glory: Chinese Villages around the Pacific, 1849 to 1949* (Hong Kong: Hong Kong University Press, 2018), 42.

25. Yucheng Qin, "A Century-Old 'Puzzle': The Six Companies' Role in Chinese Labor Importation in the Nineteenth Century," *Journal of American–East Asian Relations* 12, no. 3/4 (Fall–Winter 2003): 227–228.

26. Qin, 229.

27. Nash, "Veritable Revolution," 287.

28. Mark Kanazawa, "Immigration, Exclusion, and Taxation: Anti-Chinese Legislation in Gold Rush California," *Journal of Economic History* 65, no. 3 (2005): 781.

29. Mei, "Socioeconomic Origins of Emigration," 474–475.

30. Mei, 478–483.

31. Kerry Abrams, "Polygamy, Prostitution, and the Federalization of Immigration Law," *Columbia Law Review* 105, no. 3 (2005): 651.

32. Mei, "Socioeconomic Origins of Emigration," 486.

33. Lucy Salyer, *Laws Harsh as Tigers: Chinese Immigrants and the Shaping of Modern Immigration Law* (Raleigh: University of North Carolina Press, 1995), 10.

34. Kanazawa, "Immigration, Exclusion, and Taxation," 784.

35. Kanazawa, 785.

36. Kanazawa, 786–787.

37. Kanazawa, 787.

38. Carson, "Chinese Sojourn Labor," 82–83.

39. Carson, 83.

40. David Anderson, "The Diplomacy of Discrimination: Chinese Exclusion, 1876–1882," *California History* 57, no. 1 (1978): 32.

41. John Schrecker, "'For the Equality of Men—For the Equality of Nations': Anson Burlingame and China's First Embassy to the United States, 1868," *Journal of American–East Asian Relations* 17 (2010): 20.

42. Schrecker, 26–30.

43. Anderson, "Diplomacy of Discrimination," 34.

44. Beth Lew-Williams, *The Chinese Must Go: Violence, Exclusion, and the Making of the Alien in America* (Cambridge, MA: Harvard University Press, 2018), 28.

45. Naturalization Act of 1870, Sec. 2169 U.S. Revised Statutes, 16 Stat. 254, 41st Cong., 2d Sess., Ch. 254 (July 14, 1870); preceded by 1 Stat. 103 (March 26, 1790), which was replaced by 1 Stat. 414 (January 29, 1795) changing two years' residency to five. 1 Stat. 566 (1798) extended the period of residency to fourteen years, but that requirement was repealed by 2 Stat. 153 (1802), reverting to five years.

46. Lew-Williams, *Chinese Must Go*, 44.

47. Lew-Williams, 44.

48. Carson, "Chinese Sojourn Labor," 87.

49. Mei, "Socioeconomic Origins of Emigration," 465.

50. Anderson, "Diplomacy of Discrimination," 34.

51. *In re Ah Fong*, 1 F. Cas. 213 (D. Cal. 1874); Abrams, "Polygamy, Prostitution, and the Federalization of Immigration Law," 678.

52. Abrams, "Polygamy, Prostitution, and the Federalization of Immigration Law," 679.

53. *In re Ah Fong*, 1 F. Cas. at 214.

54. Abrams, "Polygamy, Prostitution, and the Federalization of Immigration Law," 687.

55. *In re Ah Fong*, 1 F. Cas. at 217. Field, as it would become clear, was no great friend to the Chinese and viewed them as unassimilable. Abrams, "Polygamy, Prostitution, and the Federalization of Immigration Law," 689–690.

56. Abrams, "Polygamy, Prostitution, and the Federalization of Immigration Law," 691–692.

57. Abrams, 694.

58. Abrams, 695–696.

59. Abrams, 694.

60. Abrams, 699–700.

61. Abrams, 700–701.

62. George Anthony Peffer, "Forbidden Families: Emigration Experiences of Chinese Women under the Page Law, 1875–1882," *Journal of American Ethnic History* 6, no. 1 (1986): 29.

63. Abrams, "Polygamy, Prostitution, and the Federalization of Immigration Law"; Peggy Pascoe, "Gender Systems in Conflict: The Marriages of Mission-Educated Chinese American Women, 1874–1939," *Journal of Social History* 22,

no. 4 (1989): 631–652. See chapter 4 for more on how this impacted Wong Kim Ark's life.

64. Emma Jinhua Teng, *Eurasian: Mixed Identities in the United States, China, and Hong Kong, 1842–1943* (Berkeley: University of California Press, 2013), 28–30.

65. Teng, 37–38.

66. See generally Peggy Pascoe, *What Comes Naturally: Miscegenation Law and the Making of Race in America* (New York: Oxford University Press, 2009).

67. Abrams, "Polygamy, Prostitution, and the Federalization of Immigration Law," 703.

68. *Chy Lung v. Freeman*, 92 U.S. 275 (1876).

69. *Chy Lung v. Freeman*, 92 U.S. at 280.

70. Lew-Williams, *Chinese Must Go*, 45.

71. Lew-Williams, 46.

72. Lew-Williams, 46–47; Anderson, "Diplomacy of Discrimination," 36.

73. Anderson, "Diplomacy of Discrimination," 40.

74. Anderson, 40–41.

75. Anderson, 40–43.

76. Lew-Williams, *Chinese Must Go*, 49–52.

77. Jungkun Seo, "Wedge-Issue Dynamics and Party Position Shifts: Chinese Exclusion Debates in the Post-Reconstruction US Congress, 1879–1882," *Party Politics* 17, no. 6 (2010): 831.

78. Seo, 831.

79. Lew-Williams, *Chinese Must Go*, 59.

80. Lew-Williams, 54–56.

81. Lew-Williams, 57.

82. Lew-Williams, 61.

83. Kitty Calavita, "Collisions at the Intersection of Gender, Race, and Class: Enforcing the Chinese Exclusion Laws," *Law and Society Review* 40, no. 2 (2006): 255.

84. Abrams, "Polygamy, Prostitution, and the Federalization of Immigration Law," 710.

85. Abrams, 710.

86. Richard Cole and Gabriel Chin, "Emerging from the Margins of Historical Consciousness: Chinese Immigrants and the History of American Law," *Law and History Review* 17, no. 2 (1999): 329.

87. Calavita, "Collisions at the Intersection of Gender, Race, and Class," 255.

88. Kitty Calavita, "The Paradoxes of Race, Class, Identity, and 'Passing': Enforcing the Chinese Exclusion Acts, 1882–1910," *Law and Social Inquiry* 25, no. 1 (2000): 5.

89. Calavita, 10–11.

90. Lew-Williams, *Chinese Must Go*, 55.

91. Lew-Williams, 56.

92. Lew-Williams, 70.

93. Torrie Hester, "'Protection, Not Punishment': Legislative and Judicial Formation of U.S. Deportation Policy," *Journal of American Ethnic History* 30, no. 1 (2010): 13.

94. Erika Lee, "Enforcing the Borders: Chinese Exclusion along the U.S. Borders with Canada and Mexico, 1882–1924," *Journal of American History* 89, no. 1 (2002): 56. Chinese laborers who had been in the United States when the act was passed were permitted to reenter, adding another layer of complication to determining who could legitimately cross the border.

95. Lew-Williams, *Chinese Must Go*, 70–72.

96. Lee, "Enforcing the Borders," 63.

97. Calavita, "Paradoxes of Race, Class, Identity, and 'Passing,'" 17.

98. Calavita, "Collisions at the Intersection of Gender, Race, and Class," 261–262.

Chapter 3. The Legal Battle over Exclusion

1. Erika Lee, *At America's Gates: Chinese Immigration during the Exclusion Era, 1882–1943* (Chapel Hill: University of North Carolina Press, 2003), 138–140.

2. Lee, 139.

3. Robert Barde, "An Alleged Wife: One Immigrant in the Chinese Exclusion Era," *Prologue* 36, no. 1 (Spring 2004), http://www.archives.gov/publications /prologue/2004/spring/alleged-wife-1.html.

4. Lucy Salyer, "*Chew Heong v. United States*: Chinese Exclusion and the Federal Courts," 2006, prepared for inclusion in the project Federal Trials and Great Debates in United States History, https://www.fjc.gov/history/famous -federal-trials/chew-heong-v-us-chinese-exclusion-and-federal-courts.

5. Lucy Salyer, *Laws Harsh as Tigers: Chinese Immigrants and the Shaping of Modern Immigration Law* (Chapel Hill: University of North Carolina Press, 1995), 40; Erika Lee, "Defying Exclusion: Chinese Immigrants and Their Strategies during the Exclusion Era," in *Chinese American Transnationalism: The Flow of People, Resources, and Ideas between China and America during the Exclusion Era*, ed. Sucheng Chan (Philadelphia: Temple University Press, 2006), 17–18.

6. Lee, *At America's Gates*, 139.

7. Lee, 139.

8. US Treasury Department, Report of Special Agent O. L. Spaulding, 49th Cong., 1st Sess. 1885–1886, Sen. Exec. Doc. No. 103 (S.N. 2340), as reported in Hudson N. Janisch, "The Chinese, the Courts, and the Constitution: A Study of the Legal Issues Raised by Chinese Immigration to the United States, 1850–1902" (JD thesis, University of Chicago, 1971), 2:678. Erika Lee uses Spaulding's figure as well. This fee would be approximately $2,445 in 2017 dollars (http://www.in2013dollars.com/1885-dollars-in-2017?amount=100).

9. Janisch, "The Chinese, the Courts, and the Constitution," 2:680. Four hundred thousand dollars in 1888 dollars is the equivalent of $10 million in 2014. We used http://www.davemanuel.com/inflation-calculator.php. That figure is pretty close to this site's 2013 figure; http://www.in2013dollars.com /1888-dollars-in-2014?amount=100.

10. Daniel R. Ernst, *Tocqueville's Nightmare: The Administrative State Emerges in America, 1900–1940* (Oxford: Oxford University Press, 2014), 5. Ernst seems

to be writing from a perspective closer to 1940 than 1900, since the court's embrace of civil liberties can hardly be said to be dominant in the earliest years of the nineteenth century. On the federal courts' interpretation of treaties to limit administrative discretion in the 1800s, see Christian Fritz, "A Nineteenth Century 'Habeas Corpus Mill': The Chinese before the Federal Courts of California," *Journal of American History* 32, no. 4 (1988): 365.

11. Ellen D. Katz, "The Six Companies and the Geary Act: A Case Study in Nineteenth-Century Civil Disobedience and Civil Rights Litigation," *Western Legal History* 8, no. 2 (1995): 246.

12. Katz, 246.

13. Katz, 246.

14. Lee, *At America's Gates*, 139.

15. "Thomas D. Riordan Is Dead from Heart Failure," *San Francisco Call*, June 18, 1905.

16. Special Treasury agent Spaulding, report to Congress, quoted in Janisch, "The Chinese, the Courts, and the Constitution," 2:678.

17. Quotes from Janisch, 2:680.

18. The original source cited by Janisch is "Landing Chinese," *San Francisco Chronicle*, April 13, 1887; Janisch, "The Chinese, the Courts, and the Constitution," 2:680–681; quote at 681.

19. The Chinese contested the filing fees, managed to get them reduced, and recovered more than $16,000 in excess fees paid during 1887. *In re Moy Chee Kee* 33 F. 377 (C.C.N.D. Cal. 1887). Janisch, "The Chinese, the Courts, and the Constitution," 681, cites "Habeas Corpus Costs," *Alta California* December 28, 1887; "Restriction Act," *Alta California*, January 25, 1888.

20. Janisch, "The Chinese, The Courts, and the Constitution," 2:681.

21. Janisch, 2:681, citing "The Mongul Influx," *Alta California*, July 31, 1885.

22. Fritz, "Nineteenth Century 'Habeas Corpus Mill,'" 348. Cases filed on behalf of Chinese detained at ports came under the federal courts' admiralty docket. Fritz notes that between 1882 and 1890, Hoffman's general admiralty docket had 398 cases, but Chinese litigants filed 7,080 habeas petitions.

23. Fritz, 349.

24. Fritz, 371–372. Sawyer spent more than twenty years on the US Circuit Court for the Ninth Circuit and was reassigned to the US Court of Appeals in 1891, the year he died.

25. David C. Frederick, *Rugged Justice: The Ninth Circuit Court of Appeals and the American West, 1891–1941* (Berkeley: University of California Press, 1994), 75.

26. Frederick, 75.

27. Fritz, "Nineteenth Century 'Habeas Corpus Mill,'" 354.

28. Fritz, 355.

29. Fritz, 357.

30. Fritz, 357–358.

31. Fritz, 359.

32. Fritz, 362–363.

33. Fritz, 363.

34. Salyer, "*Chew Heong v. United States*," 5.

35. Fritz, "Nineteenth Century 'Habeas Corpus Mill,'" 364.

36. Fritz, 364.

37. Paul Kens, *Justice Stephen Field: Shaping Liberty from the Gold Rush to the Gilded Age* (Lawrence: University Press of Kansas, 1997), 212.

38. Kens, 212–213.

39. Fritz, "Nineteenth Century 'Habeas Corpus Mill,'" 366.

40. Andrew Urban, *Brokering Servitude: Migration and the Politics of Domestic Labor during the Long Nineteenth Century* (New York: New York University Press, 2017), 211–212.

41. Fritz, "Nineteenth Century 'Habeas Corpus Mill,'" 369.

42. Fritz, 369.

43. Garrett Epps, "The Ghost of Chae Chan Ping," *Atlantic*, January 20, 2018, https://www.theatlantic.com/politics/archive/2018/01/ghost-haunting-immigration/551015/.

44. Epps; Gabriel J. Chin, "*Chae Chan Ping* and *Fong Yue Ting*: The Origins of Plenary Power," in *Immigration Stories*, ed. David Martin and Peter Schuck (New York: Foundation Press, 2005), 11.

45. Chin, "Chae Chan Ping and Fong Yue Ting," 11.

46. Chin, 12.

47. Salyer, "*Chew Heong v. United States*," 33.

48. Chin, "Chae Chan Ping and Fong Yue Ting," 13.

49. *Chae Chan Ping v. United States*, 130 U.S. 581 (1889).

50. Chin, "Chae Chan Ping and Fong Yue Ting," 13–14.

51. *Chae Chan Ping v. United States*, 130 U.S. at 592.

52. *Chae Chan Ping v. United States*, 130 U.S. at 595–596.

53. *Chae Chan Ping v. United States*, 130 U.S. at 595.

54. *Chae Chan Ping v. United States*, 130 U.S. at 595.

55. *Chae Chan Ping v. United States*, 130 U.S. at 595.

56. *Chae Chan Ping v. United States*, 130 U.S. at 596–597.

57. *Chae Chan Ping v. United States*, 130 U.S. at 603.

58. *Chae Chan Ping v. United States*, 130 U.S. at 606.

59. *Chae Chan Ping v. United States*, 130 U.S. at 609.

60. Chin, "Chae Chan Ping and Fong Yue Ting," 16.

61. Richard Cole and Gabriel Chin, "Emerging from the Margins of Historical Consciousness: Chinese Immigrants and the History of American Law," *Law and History Review* 17, no. 2 (1999): 329.

62. Katz, "The Six Companies and the Geary Act," 227.

63. Katz, 228.

64. Chin, "Chae Chan Ping and Fong Yue Ting," 16.

65. Katz, "The Six Companies and the Geary Act," 227–228.

66. Chin, "Chae Chan Ping and Fong Yue Ting," 17.

67. Katz, "The Six Companies and the Geary Act," 228.

68. Katz, 246.

69. Katz, 252.

70. Katz, 256.

71. Katz, 257.

72. Katz, 257.

73. "Waiting for a Decision: Text of the Order Suspending the Geary Act," *Los Angeles Times*, May 5, 1893, 1; from Attorney General Olney to United States Attorney, May 4, 1893, in *The Executive Documents of the House of Representatives for the First Session of the Fifty-Third Congress/In One Volume/1893* (Washington, DC: Government Printing Office, 1893).

74. Katz, "The Six Companies and the Geary Act," 260–261.

75. Katz, 260. Justice Harlan did not participate in the case. Gabriel Chin, "The First Justice Harlan by the Numbers: Just How Great Was 'The Great Dissenter'?," *Akron Law Review* 32, no. 3 (1999): 643–644.

76. *Fong Yue Ting v. United States*, 149 U.S. 698 (1893), at 705.

77. *Fong Yue Ting v. United States*, 149 U.S. at 713.

78. *Fong Yue Ting v. United States*, 149 U.S. at 716.

79. *Fong Yue Ting v. United States*, 149 U.S. at 717.

80. *Fong Yue Ting v. United States*, 149 U.S. at 724.

81. *Fong Yue Ting v. United States*, 149 U.S. at 728.

82. Chin, "Chae Chan Ping and Fong Yue Ting," 19–20.

83. Katz, "The Six Companies and the Geary Act," 263–265.

84. Associated Press, "Ny Look: An Aged Celestial Applies for a Certificate in New York," *Los Angeles Times*, May 25, 1893, 1.

85. "Ny Look Ordered Deported, at the Same Time Set at Liberty by Judge Lacombe," *New York Times*, May 25, 1893, 1.

86. Joseph Hodges Choate, https://law.jrank.org/pages/5208/Choate-Joseph-Hodges.html. In 1887, Choate had lost in the Kansas liquor prohibition case *Mugler v. Kansas*, and he would be successful in challenging the 1894 income tax act in *Pollack v. Farmers' Loan and Trust* (1895).

87. Maxwell Evarts, https://www.findagrave.com/memorial/156668790/maxwell-evarts; see also https://en.wikipedia.org/wiki/Maxwell_Evarts.

88. "Judge Lacombe's Opinion," *Washington Post*, May 26, 1893, 1.

89. *In re Ny Look*, 56 F. 81 (C.C. S.D.N.Y. 1893), at 82.

90. "No Means for Deportation: Judge Lacombe Reiterates His Views in the Ny Look Case," *New York Times*, May 27, 1893, 12.

91. *In re Ny Look*, 56 F. at 83.

92. *In re Ny Look*, 56 F. at 83.

93. "Ny Look Ordered Deported," 1.

94. "Judge Lacombe's Opinion."

95. "The 'Ny Look' Case," *Washington Post*, May 28, 1893, 4.

96. Katz, "The Six Companies and the Geary Act," 263.

97. Katz, 264.

98. Katz, 265.

99. Katz, 266.

100. Katz, 268.

101. *Lem Moon Sing v. United States*, 158 U.S. 538 (1895), at 540.

102. *Lem Moon Sing v. United States*, 158 U.S. at 540–541.

103. *Lem Moon Sing v. United States*, 158 U.S. at 550.

104. Gerald L. Neuman, "*Wong Wing v. United States*: The Bill of Rights Protects Illegal Aliens," in *Immigration Stories*, ed. David Martin and Peter Schuck (New York: Foundation Press, 2005), 32.

105. Neuman, 35.

106. Neuman, 36. Neuman reports that the Chinese men were permitted to post bail and their deportations were postponed.

107. *Wong Wing v. United States*, 163 U.S. 228 (1896), at 232.

108. *Wong Wing v. United States*, 163 U.S. at 238.

109. See Mae M. Ngai, *Impossible Subjects: Illegal Aliens and the Making of Modern America* (Princeton, NJ: Princeton University Press, 2004), on the construction of the category of the illegal alien.

110. Beth Lew-Williams, *The Chinese Must Go: Violence, Exclusion, and the Making of the Alien in America* (Cambridge, MA: Harvard University Press, 2018), 227.

111. Peggy Pascoe, "Gender Systems in Conflict: The Marriages of Mission-Educated Chinese American Women, 1874–1939," *Journal of Social History* 22, no. 4 (1989): 635. As Pascoe notes, some of these women had been enticed into sham marriages and presented themselves as wives, others were purchased from desperate parents, and some were kidnapped and smuggled in.

112. Lew-Williams, *Chinese Must Go*, 227–228.

113. Pascoe, "Gender Systems in Conflict," 639.

114. Paul Yin, "The Narratives of Chinese-American Litigation during the Chinese Exclusion Era," *Asian American Law Journal* 19, no. 1 (2012): 158.

115. US Congress, Joint Special Committee to Investigate Chinese Immigration, "Report of the Joint Special Committee to Investigate Chinese Immigration," February 27, 1877 (Washington, DC: Government Printing Office, 1877), 10. Brooks represented the Chinese Six Companies in 1877; see Yucheng Qin, "A Century-Old 'Puzzle': The Six Companies' Role in Chinese Labor Importation in the Nineteenth Century," *Journal of American–East Asian Relations* 12, no. 3/4 (2003): 246.

116. *In re Ah Yup*, 1 F. Cas. 223 (C.C.D. Cal. 1878), at 223.

117. *In re Ah Yup*, 1 F. Cas. at 223.

118. *In re Ah Yup*, 1 F. Cas. at 224.

119. *In re Ah Yup*, 1 F. Cas. at 225.

120. Yin, "Narratives of Chinese-American Litigation," 159–160.

121. *State v. Ah Chew*, 16 Nev. 50 (1881), at 58.

122. *In re Look Tin Sing*, 21 F. 905 (C.C.D. Cal. 1884), at 905–906.

123. Editors, "The Question of Citizenship of American-Born Chinese Sweeping," *San Francisco Call*, November 13, 1895.

124. Yin, "Narratives of Chinese-American Litigation," 160.

125. *In re Look Tin Sing*, 21 F. at 906.

126. *In re Look Tin Sing*, 21 F. at 907.

127. *In re Look Tin Sing*, 21 F. at 909.

128. *In re Look Tin Sing*, 21 F. at 909.

129. *In re Look Tin Sing*, 21 F. at 910.

130. *In re Look Tin Sing*, 21 F. at 910–911.

131. *Ex parte Chin King*, 35 F. 354 (C.C.D. Ore. 1888), at 355.

132. *Ex parte Chin King*, 35 F. at 355.

133. David Alan Johnson, Quintard Taylor, and Marsha Weisiger, "Report on the History of Matthew P. Deady and Frederick S. Dunn," 9, http://media .oregonlive.com/education_impact/other/deady_dunn_final_report_08-05 -16.pdf.

134. Johnson, Taylor, and Weisiger, 11.

135. Johnson, Taylor, and Weisiger, 12.

136. *Ex parte Chin King*, 35 F. at 355.

137. *Ex parte Chin King*, 35 F. at 356.

138. *In re Yung Sing Hee*, 38 F. 437 (C.C.D. Ore. 1888).

139. *In re Wy Shing*, 36 F. 553 (C.C.N.D. Cal. 1888), at 553.

140. *In re Wy Shing*, 36 F. at 553.

141. *Gee Fook Sing v. United States*, 49 F. 146 (9th Cir. 1892), at 147.

142. *Gee Fook Sing v. United States*, 49 F. at 148.

143. *In re MacFarlane*, 11 Haw. 166 (1897).

144. *In re MacFarlane*, 11 Haw. at 172.

145. *In re MacFarlane*, 11 Haw. at 173–174.

Chapter 4. Who Was Wong Kim Ark?

1. For the 1871 date, see testimony on behalf of his eldest son on December 6, 1910, National Archives and Records Division, San Bruno, California, the first page of which is shown at https://commons.wikipedia.org/wiki/File :Wong_Kim_Ark_testimony_at_Wong_Yoke_Fun_hearing_1910_page_1.png. In testimony for the admission of his third son on March 20, 1925, Wong Kim Ark says he is fifty-six years old; see https://commons.wikipedia.org/wiki/File :Wong_Kim_Ark_testimony_at_Wong_Yook_Thue_hearing_1925_page_1. png. Beatrice McKenzie placed his birth as early as 1870 in "To Know a Citizen: Birthright Citizenship Documents Regimes in U.S. History," in *Citizenship in Question: Evidentiary Birthright and Statelessness*, ed. Benjamin N. Lawrance and Jacqueline Stevens (Durham, NC: Duke University Press, 2007), 119. Bethany Berger writes that he was born in either 1873 or 1871; see "Birthright Citizenship on Trial: *Elk v. Wilkins* and *United States v. Wong Kim Ark*," *Cardozo Law Review* 37 (2016): 1226. The facts agreed to by both parties in *United States v. Wong Kim Ark*, 169 U.S. 649 at 651 use the 1873 date, as do secondary sources such as William Wong, *Yellow Journalist: Dispatches from Asian America* (Philadelphia: Temple University Press, 2001), 52; Lucy E. Salyer, "*Wong Kim Ark*: The Contest over Birthright Citizenship," in *Immigration Stories*, ed. David A. Martin and Peter H. Schuck (New York: Foundation Press, 2005), 66; and Erika Lee, "Birthright Citizenship, Immigration, and the U.S. Constitution: The Story of *United States v. Wong Kim Ark*," in *Race Law Stories*, ed. Rachel Moran and Devon Carbado (New York: Foundation Press, 2008), 91.

2. See, e.g., Lee, "Birthright Citizenship, Immigration, and the U.S. Constitution," 91.

3. Langley's San Francisco Directory for the Year Commencing 1880 (D. M. Bishop & Co.), http://www.ebooksread.com/authors-eng/dm-bishop–co/lang leys-san-francisco-directory-for-the-year-commencing–volume-1880-fna/page -281-langleys-san-francisco-directory-for-the-year-commencing–volume-1880 -fna.shtml. Also see Francis Valentine and Co., Locate Organizations and Busi-nesses in San Francisco, 1861–1923 (except 1866, 1870, 1872, 1906), 933, Fold3 .com by Ancestry, 1879.

4. Chinatown lay between what is now the Financial District and Knob Hill.

5. Agreement by both parties as to the facts in *United States v. Wong Kim Ark*, 169 U.S. 649 at 651.

6. McKenzie, "To Know a Citizen," 121.

7. For the existence of at least one older brother, see McKenzie, 124.

8. McKenzie, 121, finds evidence in the NARA file from his return from the 1894–1895 trip that his three years of schooling in China constituted his only education.

9. Kelley Wallace, "Forgotten Los Angeles History: The Chinese Massacre of 1871," *Los Angeles Public Library Blog*, May 19, 2017, https://www.lapl.org /collections-resources/blogs/lapl/chinese-massacre-1871.

10. See Selig Perlman, "The Anti-Chinese Agitation in California," in *History of Labour in the United States*, ed. John Rogers Commons et al. (New York: Macmillan, 1918), vol. 2, chap. 5; Katie Dowd, "140 Years ago, San Francisco Was Set Ablaze during the City's Deadliest Race Riot," SFGate, July 23, 2017, https://www.sfgate.com/bayarea/article/1877-san-francisco-anti-chinese-race -riots-11302710.php.

11. Phil Dougherty, "Mobs Forcibly Expel Most of Seattle's Chinese Resi-dents Beginning on February 7, 1886," HistoryLink.org, November 17, 2013, accessed September 24, 2019, https://www.historylink.org/File/2745. A ship with many Chinse on board departed to San Francisco.

12. Liping Zhu, *The Road to Chinese Exclusion: The Denver Riot, 1880 Election, and Rise of the West* (Lawrence: University Press of Kansas, 2013), chap. 4; Mark R. Ellis, "Denver's Anti-Chinese Riot," in *Encyclopedia of the Great Plains*, http:// plainshumanities.unl.edu/encyclopedia/doc/egp.asam.011.

13. Ellis, "Denver's Anti-Chinese Riot."

14. Beth Lew-Williams, *The Chinese Must Go: Violence, Exclusion, and the Mak-ing of the Alien in America* (Cambridge, MA: Harvard University Press, 2018), 3. On violence against the Chinese on the West Coast, see also Jean Pfaelzer, *Driven Out: The Forgotten War against Chinese Americans* (Berkeley: University of California Press, 2008).

15. Oregon Constitution of 1857 (effective 1859), transcribed, Article XV §8, https://sos.oregon.gov/archives/exhibits/constitution/Documents/tran scribed-1857-oregon-constitution.pdf.

16. California Constitution of 1879, original, Article XIX, https://www.cpp .edu/~jlkorey/calcon1879.pdf.

17. California Constitution of 1879, Article I, Section 17.

18. See Carol Nackenoff and Julie Novkov, "Building the Administrative State: Courts and the Admission of Chinese Persons to the United States, 1870s–1920s," in *Stating the Family: New Directions in the Study of American Politics*,

ed. Julie Novkov and Carol Nackenoff (Lawrence: University Press of Kansas, 2020), 197–239; Julie Novkov and Carol Nackenoff, "Civic Membership, Family Status, and the Chinese in America, 1870s–1920s," *Polity* 41, no. 2 (2016): 170.

19. Sucheng Chan, "The Exclusion of Chinese Women, 1870–1943," in *Entry Denied: Exclusion and the Chinese Community in America, 1882–1943*, ed. Sucheng Chan (Philadelphia: Temple University Press, 1991), 94.

20. L. P. Patil, "Anti-Miscegenation in California," Foundations of Law and Society, 2016, https://foundationsoflawandsociety.wordpress.com/2016/12/09/anti-miscegenation-in-california/.

21. Judge Lorenzo Sawyer to historian, publisher, and writer Hubert Howe Bancroft, September 22, 1886, quoted in Catherine Lee, *Fictive Kinship: Family Reunification and the Meaning of Race and Nation in American Immigration* (New York: Russell Sage Foundation, 2013), 58.

22. See note 1. Beatrice McKenzie, who reviewed Wong Kim Ark's file at the National Archives and Record Administration, San Bruno, California, says he was nineteen when he departed for China to marry. The discrepancy on year of birth means he may have been eleven when he returned in 1881. McKenzie, "To Know a Citizen," 119.

23. One of Wong Kim Ark's witnesses for his 1890 departure document attested that he had known the family for more than twenty years (they had lived at the 751 Sacramento Street address for at least five or six years prior to 1875). McKenzie, 120; Berger, "Birthright Citizenship on Trial," 1226.

24. Michael Williams, *Returning Home with Glory: Chinese Villagers around the Pacific, 1849 to 1949* (Hong Kong: Hong Kong University Press, 2018), 4–7.

25. McKenzie, "To Know a Citizen," 119.

26. A congressional act, entitled the Fifteen Passenger Bill, passed in 1879 and stipulating that no sea vessel could bring more than fifteen Chinese passengers to the United States, had been vetoed by President Rutherford Hayes as a violation of the Burlingame Treaty.

27. See Williams, *Returning Home with Glory*.

28. Chinese Exclusion Act of 1882, U.S. Statutes at Large 22 (1882), Section 6.

29. Nackenoff and Novkov, "Building the Administrative State."

30. Chinese Exclusion Act of 1882, U.S. Statutes at Large 22 (1882), 58, section 4.

31. Chinese Exclusion Act of 1884, U.S. Statutes at Large 23 (1884), 115, section 4.

32. Scott Act of 1888, https://immigrationhistory.org/item/scott-act/. See also *Chae Chan Ping v. United States*, 130 U.S. 581 (1889).

33. McKenzie, "To Know a Citizen," 118.

34. McKenzie, 119.

35. McKenzie, 119.

36. *United States v. Wong Kim Ark*, 169 U.S. 649 at 651.

37. Chan, "Exclusion of Chinese Women," 96–97.

38. See Candice Lewis Bredbenner, *A Nationality of Her Own: Women, Marriage and the Law of Citizenship* (Berkeley: University of California Press, 1998).

39. Chan, "Exclusion of Chinese Women," 122.

40. See especially Lucy E. Salyer, *Laws Harsh as Tigers: Chinese Immigrants and the Shaping of Modern Immigration Law* (Chapel Hill: University of North Carolina Press, 1995).

41. Wong Kim Ark testimony at Wong Yook Jim hearing, 1926, National Archives and Records, San Francisco, https://commons.wikimedia.org/wiki/File:Wong_Kim_Ark_testimony_at_Wong_Yook_Jim_hearing_1926_page_1.png.

42. Wong, *Yellow Journalist*, 54.

43. See https://www.google.com/maps/@22.8011093,108.9913713,6z; https://en.wikipedia.org/wiki/Taishan,_Guangdong.

44. David Pierson, "Taishan's U.S. Well Runs Dry," *Los Angeles Times*, May 21, 2007, https://www.latimes.com/archives/la-xpm-2007-may-21-fg-taishan21-story.html; see also https://en.wikipedia.org/wiki/Taishan,_Guangdong.

45. Pierson, "Taishan's U.S. Well Runs Dry."

46. Ronald Skeldon, "Migration from China," *Journal of International Affairs* 49, no. 2 (1996): 436–437.

47. Skeldon, 435.

48. Pierson, "Taishan's U.S. Well Runs Dry."

49. McKenzie, "To Know a Citizen," 124.

50. McKenzie, 120.

51. McKenzie, 119–121.

52. Carol Ann Benedict, *Bubonic Plague in Nineteenth-Century China* (Palo Alto, CA: Stanford University Press, 1996), 134.

53. "The Plague in China," *Evening Bulletin* (Maysville, KY), June 19, 1894, 1.

54. Benedict, *Bubonic Plague*, 142.

55. Carol Benedict, "Bubonic Plague in Nineteenth-Century China: The Third Pandemic of Bubonic Plague." *Modern China* 14, no. 2 (1988): 132.

56. Benedict, 136.

57. "China: The Bubonic Plague in Canton," *Public Health Reports* (1896–1970) 11, no. 25 (June 19, 1896): 567.

58. The affidavit states that he departed on the *Belcio*, but it seems that the steamer was the *Belgic*, since we have found no evidence of the existence of a Pacific steamship named the *Belcio* around 1894.

59. Berger, "Birthright Citizenship on Trial," 1229.

60. Berger, 1228 and 1254, citing Testimony of Wong Kim Ark, In re Wong Yok Jim, Case No. 25141/5–6, at 2 (July 26, 1926) (on file at Box 3061, Loc. 3279 H, RG 85, NARA, San Bruno). There is some discrepancy about birth order of the second and third sons, but in immigration hearings in 1925 for Wong Yook Thue, his father states that Wong Yook Sue, his third son, was there with him as a witness, making Yook Thue the second son. In other testimony, he made clear that Yook Thue was second and Yook Sue was third in birth order. https://commons.wikimedia.org/wiki/File:Wong_Kim_Ark_testimony_at_Wong_Yook_Thue_hearing_1925_page_1.png.

61. McKenzie, "To Know a Citizen," 121.

62. Tsai Chutung, "The Chinese Nationality Law, 1909," *American Journal of International Law* 4, no. 2 (1910): 404.

63. These residents were linked with polygamy, sodomy, and opium; they

were called "coolies" or unfree labor (despite the fact this was frequently inaccurate), and thus perpetuating slavery, of which the nation had just rid itself.

64. McKenzie, "To Know a Citizen," 121. The official was Henry Foote.

65. Salyer, "Wong Kim Ark," 65–66.

66. The text of the Geary Act can be found at http://www.sanfrancisco chinatown.com/history/1892gearyact.html.

67. Dan Kanstroom, *Deportation Nation: Outsiders in American History* (Cambridge, MA: Harvard University Press, 2007).

68. Kelly Lytle Hernández, *City of Inmates* (Chapel Hill: University of North Carolina Press, 2017), 82–86.

69. Craig Robertson, *The Passport in America: The History of a Document* (New York: Oxford University Press, 2010), 15. On the movement of whites, see John C. Torpey, *The Invention of the Passport: Surveillance, Citizenship and the State* (New York: Cambridge University Press, 2018), 15, 113.

70. Nathan Perl-Rosenthal, *Citizen Sailors: Becoming American in the Age of Revolution* (Cambridge, MA: Belknap Press of Harvard University Press, 2015). Roughly one hundred thousand such certificates were issued between 1796 and 1803.

71. Mark B. Salter, *Rights of Passage: The Passport in International Relations* (Boulder, CO: Lynne Rienner, 2003), 22.

72. The phrase "passport regime" comes from Salter, 81. One scholar who looks to the aftermath of World War I is Robertson, *Passport in America.*

73. Salter, *Rights of Passage*, 78.

74. Named for Norwegian Fridtjof Nansen, high commissioner for repatriation of prisoners of war under the League of Nations, and subsequently named by that body to become high commissioner for Russian refugees when, in 1921, Lenin revoked citizenship for about eight hundred thousand Russian expatriates who fled during the Bolshevik Revolution and instantly became stateless. See Cara Giaimo, "The Little-Known Passport That Protected 450,000 Refugees," Atlas Obscura, February 7, 2017, https://www.atlasobscura.com/articles/nansen-passport-refugees.

75. Isabel Kaprielan-Churchill, "Rejecting 'Misfits': Canada and the Nansen Passport," *International Migration Review* 28, no. 2 (1994): 281–306.

76. Salter, *Rights of Passage*, 77. Exclusion was also a factor in Canada according to Kaprielan-Churchill, "Rejecting 'Misfits,'" 285.

77. Robertson, *Passport in America*, 16.

78. H. L. Brumberg, D. Dozor, and S. G. Golombek, "History of the Birth Certificate: From Inception to the Future of Electronic Data," *Journal of Perinatology* 32 (2012): 407–411. Until the mid-nineteenth century, churches, rather than government officials, tended to record births; see Magdalena Krajewska, *Documenting Americans: A Political History of National ID Card Proposals in the United States* (Cambridge: Cambridge University Press, 2017), 42.

79. Annette R. Appell, "Certifying Identity," *Capital University Law Review* 42 (2014): 372.

80. Appell, 373.

81. Appell, 373.

82. Erin Blakemore, "The History of Birth Certificates Is Shorter Than You Might Think," History.com, last updated August 22, 2018, https://www.history.com/news/the-history-of-birth-certificates-is-shorter-than-you-might-think.

83. Krajewska, *Documenting Americans*, 42.

84. Berger, "Birthright Citizenship on Trial," 1230.

85. Newspapers.com was the repository that yielded this count made by CJN on June 13, 2019.

86. "Chinese as Citizens," *San Francisco Call*, January 4, 1896, 5, https://img2.newspapers.com/clip/22263739/1896_look_tin_sing/.

87. "Chinese Born Here Are Citizens," *New York Times*, March 29, 1898.

88. This count includes only papers archived in newspapers.com from the date of decision (March 28) until the end of 1898. Papers generally republished one of two articles.

89. "20,000 New Voters," *Topeka State Journal*, June 29, 1898, https://newscomwc.newspapers.com/image/323082932/?terms=wong%2Bkim%2Bark&pqsid=IcnGqi8ZNDaCgSSFz1IjSA:145000:1561812162.

90. Lauren L. Basson, "Fit for Annexation but Unfit to Vote? Debating Hawaiian Suffrage Qualifications at the Turn of the Twentieth Century," *Social Science History* 29, no. 4 (2005): 576.

91. Alfred S. Hartwell, "The Organization of a Territorial Government for Hawaii," *Yale Law Journal* 9, no. 3 (1899): 112, quoting from the Cullom bill.

92. Basson, "Fit for Annexation but Unfit to Vote?," 576, 582.

93. Bartholomew H. Sparrow, *The Insular Cases and the Emergence of American Empire* (Lawrence: University Press of Kansas, 2006), 160.

94. Gabriel J. Chin, "'A Chinaman's Chance' in Court: Asian Pacific Americans and Racial Rules of Evidence," *University of California Irvine Law Review* 3 (2013): 973.

95. Erika Lee and Judy Yung, *Angel Island: Immigrant Gateway to America* (New York: Oxford University Press, 2012), 88 in the e-book. The 1931 form bore a slightly different title: "Application of Alleged American Citizen of the Chinese Race for Preinvestigation of Status."

96. Lee and Yung, 84.

97. Erika Lee, "Defying Exclusion: Chinese Immigrants and Their Strategies during the Exclusion Era," in *Chinese American Transnationalism: The Flow of People, Resources, and Ideas between China and America during the Exclusion Era*, ed. Sucheng Chan (Philadelphia: Temple University Press, 2006), 20.

98. Lee and Yung, *Angel Island*, 83.

99. Charles J. McClain, *In Search of Equality: The Chinese Struggle against Discrimination in Nineteenth-Century America* (Berkeley: University of California Press, 1996), 346n18.

100. Lee and Yung, *Angel Island*, 91.

101. Erika Lee, *At America's Gates: Chinese Immigration during the Exclusion Era, 1882–1943* (Chapel Hill: University of North Carolina Press, 2003), 140. Lee (140) quotes Charlie D. O'Connor's advertisement in *Chung Sai Yat Po* (February 27, 1906), promising "fast, convenient, and cheap" service and stating he had worked for the Bureau of Immigration for more than ten years.

102. "Two Attorneys Disbarred Following the Expose of Chinese Smuggling Ring," *San Francisco Bee*, August 22, 1917.

103. Wong Kim Ark testimony on behalf of his fourth son, Wong Yook Jim, July 23, 1926, https://commons.wikimedia.org/wiki/File:Wong_Kim_Ark _testimony_at_Wong_Yook_Jim_hearing_1926_page_1.png; Berger, "Birthright Citizenship on Trial," 1185, 1227–1228.

104. Wong, *Yellow Journalist*, 54. Berger raises the possibility of paper sons in footnotes to "Birthright Citizenship on Trial."

105. McKenzie, "To Know a Citizen," 124. She compared ages of relatives in Ong Sing Village.

106. Mae M. Ngai, *Impossible Subjects: Illegal Aliens and the Making of Modern America* (Princeton, NJ: Princeton University Press, 2004), 204–205.

107. On paper sons, see especially Estelle T. Lau, *Paper Families* (Durham, NC: Duke University Press, 2006); Madeline Y. Hsu, "Gold Mountain Dreams and Paper Son Schemes: Chinese Immigration under Exclusion," in *Chinese America: History and Perspectives* 11 (San Francisco: Chinese Historical Society of America, 1997), 46–60; Lee, *At America's Gates*, chaps. 5–6; "Paper Sons," Virtual Museum of the City of San Francisco, http://www.sfmuseum.org/hist11 /papersons.html.

108. See Nackenoff and Novkov, "Building the Administrative State."

109. Lee, *Fictive Kinship*, 71.

110. Ngai, *Impossible Subjects*, 205.

111. The evidence in this paragraph is from McKenzie, "To Know a Citizen," 123–124. One of the reasons steamship companies hired good lawyers for the Chinese was so they would not have to pay return fare for those barred from entry.

112. Note alternate spellings of Yook, Yok, and Yuk for the sons.

113. McKenzie, "To Know a Citizen," 124. McKenzie identifies Yook Thue as the third son, but he was fairly clearly the second, though the third to try to land. See NARA testimony discussed in Berger, "Birthright Citizenship on Trial," 1228, 1254. See also Wong Kim Ark testimony for the admission of his fourth son, Wong Yook Jim, July 23, 1926. https://commons.wikimedia.org /wiki/File:Wong_Kim_Ark_testimony_at_Wong_Yook_Jim_hearing_1926 _page_1.png.

114. Berger, 1254.

115. McKenzie, "To Know a Citizen," 124.

116. Wong, *Yellow Journalist*, 54. The author is working with a statement from the son; though the son claimed Wong Kim Ark left China when he was two, this is improbable since Wong Kim Ark departed from San Francisco in October 1913 and was back applying for a certificate of identity in November 1914.

117. Wong, 54.

118. According to his 1913 departure statement, Wong Kim Ark resided at 766 Clay Street.

119. The 1931 application of alleged American citizen of the Chinese race for preinvestigation of status (as the 1931 form was called) was the only one

that listed Wong Kim Ark's height and that mentioned the scar. See images of the 1913 and 1931 applications at https://catalog.archives.gov/OpaAPI /media/18556183/content/san-francisco/gallery/12017_42223-010.pdf.

120. Wong, *Yellow Journalist*, 55.

121. Wong, 55.

122. Wong, 53–55.

Chapter 5. Wong Kim Ark v. United States

1. *In re Wong Kim Ark*, 71 F. 382 (N.D. Cal. 1896), at 383.

2. Erika Lee, "Birthright Citizenship, Immigration, and the U.S. Constitution: The Story of *United States v. Wong Kim Ark*," in *Race Law Stories*, ed. Rachel Moran and Devon Carbado (New York: Foundation Press, 2008), 96.

3. Lee, 96.

4. *In re Wong Kim Ark*, 71 F. at 383; Bethany Berger, "Birthright Citizenship on Trial: *Elk v. Wilkins* and *United States v. Wong Kim Ark*," *Cardozo Law Review* 37 (2016): 1230.

5. Erika Lee, "*Wong Kim Ark v. United States*," 90.

6. Berger, "Birthright Citizenship on Trial," 1230.

7. V. F. Dewey, "Editorial Notes," *Hanford Semi-Weekly Journal* (Hanford, CA), October 15, 1895, 4.

8. "Social and Personal," *Sacramento Record-Union* (Sacramento, CA), June 26, 1889, 2.

9. "John Will Stay Yet Awhile," *San Francisco Call*, September 12, 1893, 2.

10. "John Will Stay Yet Awhile."

11. "Serious Charge: Lawyer Riordan Accused of Bribery," *San Francisco Call*, November 9, 1894, 5.

12. "Serious Charge."

13. "Caminetti Angry and Disappointed," *San Francisco Call*, February 16, 1895, 2.

14. Berger, "Birthright Citizenship on Trial," 1246; Lucy E. Salyer, "*Wong Kim Ark*: The Contest over Birthright Citizenship," in *Immigration Stories*, ed. David A. Martin and Peter H. Schuck (New York: Foundation Press, 2005), 65.

15. "Attorney Collins' Part," *San Francisco Call*, November 14, 1895, 11.

16. Salyer, "*Wong Kim Ark*," 65.

17. Salyer, 65–66.

18. *In re Wong Kim Ark*, 71 F. at 384.

19. "All Asiatics Affected," *San Francisco Call*, November 13, 1895, 9.

20. "All Asiatics Affected."

21. "All Asiatics Affected."

22. "All Asiatics Affected."

23. *In re Wong Kim Ark*, 71 F. at 384.

24. *In re Wong Kim Ark*, 71 F. at 385.

25. *In re Wong Kim Ark*, 71 F. at 383.

26. *In re Wong Kim Ark*, 71 F. at 384.

27. Lee, "*Wong Kim Ark v. United States*," 99.

28. *In re Wong Kim Ark*, 71 F. at 386.

29. *In re Wong Kim Ark*, 71 F. at 386–387.

30. *In re Wong Kim Ark*, 71 F. at 387–389.

31. *In re Wong Kim Ark*, 71 F. at 390–391.

32. *In re Wong Kim Ark*, 71 F. at 391.

33. *In re Wong Kim Ark*, 71 F. at 392.

34. *In re Wong Kim Ark*, 71 F. at 392.

35. Berger, "Birthright Citizenship on Trial," 1230.

36. Judiciary Act of 1891, 26 Stat. 826, 51st Cong., 2nd Sess., Ch. 517, March 3, 1891.

37. Berger, "Birthright Citizenship on Trial," 1246–1248.

38. Holmes Conrad and George Collins, "Brief on the Behalf of the Appellant: *United States v. Wong Kim Ark*," in *Landmark Briefs and Arguments of the Supreme Court of the United States*, vol. 14, ed. Philip Kurland and Gerhard Casper (Arlington, VA: University Publications of America, 1975), 3.

39. Conrad and Collins, 9–10.

40. Conrad and Collins, 19.

41. Conrad and Collins, 26.

42. Conrad and Collins, 37.

43. Holmes Conrad, "Brief for the United States: *United States v. Wong Kim Ark*," in *Landmark Briefs and Arguments of the Supreme Court of the United States*, vol. 14, ed. Philip Kurland and Gerhard Casper (Arlington, VA: University Publications of America, 1975), 59–60.

44. Conrad, 62–65.

45. Conrad, 67–68.

46. Conrad, 76–79.

47. Conrad, 88.

48. Conrad, 89–90.

49. Conrad, 91.

50. Conrad, 93.

51. Berger, "Birthright Citizenship on Trial," 1247.

52. Thomas Riordan, "Brief for Respondent: *United States v. Wong Kim Ark*," in *Landmark Briefs and Arguments of the Supreme Court of the United States*, vol. 14, ed. Philip Kurland and Gerhard Casper (Arlington, VA: University Publications of America, 1975), 47.

53. Riordan, 47–48.

54. Riordan, 49. By this time, the Fuller Court had embraced a narrow view of the core rights that attached to citizenship, and robust protection for voting was not among them. See Pamela Brandwein, *Rethinking the Judicial Settlement of Reconstruction* (New York: Cambridge University Press, 2011).

55. Conrad, "Brief for the United States," 80–84.

56. Berger, "Birthright Citizenship on Trial," 1248.

57. Maxwell Evarts, "Brief for the Appellee on Reargument: *United States v. Wong Kim Ark*," in *Landmark Briefs and Arguments of the Supreme Court of the United*

States, vol. 14, ed. Philip Kurland and Gerhard Casper (Arlington, VA: University Publications of America, 1975), 107.

58. Evarts, 107–108.
59. Evarts, 109.
60. Evarts, 112.
61. Evarts, 113–116.
62. Evarts, 119.
63. Evarts, 126.
64. Evarts, 132–134.
65. Evarts, 161.
66. Evarts, 162–168.
67. J. Hubley Ashton, "Brief for the Appellee on Reargument: *United States v. Wong Kim Ark*," in *Landmark Briefs and Arguments of the Supreme Court of the United States*, vol. 14, ed. Philip Kurland and Gerhard Casper (Arlington, VA: University Publications of America, 1975), 190.
68. Ashton, 193–195.
69. Ashton, 207.
70. Ashton, 214.
71. Ashton, 221.
72. Ashton, 232.
73. Ashton, 240.
74. Ashton, 240–241.
75. Ashton, 247–248.
76. Ashton, 261.
77. Ashton, 271.
78. Holmes Conrad, "Reply Brief for the United States: *United States v. Wong Kim Ark*," in *Landmark Briefs and Arguments of the Supreme Court of the United States*, vol. 14, ed. Philip Kurland and Gerhard Casper (Arlington, VA: University Publications of America, 1975), 277–278.
79. Conrad, 281–282.
80. Conrad, 287–288.
81. Conrad, 299. Ashton responded to this reply, supplying more evidence that the British alienage rules were as he and Evarts had portrayed them in their original briefs. J. Hubley Ashton, "Note in Answer," in *Landmark Briefs and Arguments of the Supreme Court of the United States*, vol. 14, ed. Philip Kurland and Gerhard Casper (Arlington, VA: University Publications of America, 1975), 301–304.
82. Elbridge Davis and Harold Davis, "Mr. Justice Horace Gray: Some Aspects of His Judicial Career," *American Bar Association Journal* 41 (1955): 424, 468.
83. *United States v. Wong Kim Ark*, 169 U.S. 649 (1898), at 652.
84. *United States v. Wong Kim Ark*, 169 U.S. at 653–654.
85. *United States v. Wong Kim Ark*, 169 U.S. at 654.
86. *United States v. Wong Kim Ark*, 169 U.S. at 655–656.
87. *United States v. Wong Kim Ark*, 169 U.S. at 658.
88. *United States v. Wong Kim Ark*, 169 U.S. at 658.
89. *United States v. Wong Kim Ark*, 169 U.S. at 659.

90. *United States v. Wong Kim Ark*, 169 U.S. at 659–660.

91. *United States v. Wong Kim Ark*, 169 U.S. at 661.

92. *United States v. Wong Kim Ark*, 169 U.S. at 663–664.

93. *United States v. Wong Kim Ark*, 169 U.S. at 665–666.

94. *United States v. Wong Kim Ark*, 169 U.S. at 667.

95. *United States v. Wong Kim Ark*, 169 U.S. at 668.

96. *United States v. Wong Kim Ark*, 169 U.S. at 672–673.

97. *United States v. Wong Kim Ark*, 169 U.S. at 674.

98. *United States v. Wong Kim Ark*, 169 U.S. at 675.

99. *United States v. Wong Kim Ark*, 169 U.S. at 675.

100. *United States v. Wong Kim Ark*, 169 U.S. at 676.

101. *United States v. Wong Kim Ark*, 169 U.S. at 678.

102. *United States v. Wong Kim Ark*, 169 U.S. at 679–680.

103. *United States v. Wong Kim Ark*, 169 U.S. at 684.

104. *United States v. Wong Kim Ark*, 169 U.S. at 685–686.

105. *United States v. Wong Kim Ark*, 169 U.S. at 688.

106. *United States v. Wong Kim Ark*, 169 U.S. at 689.

107. *United States v. Wong Kim Ark*, 169 U.S. at 694.

108. *United States v. Wong Kim Ark*, 169 U.S. at 696.

109. *United States v. Wong Kim Ark*, 169 U.S. at 697.

110. *United States v. Wong Kim Ark*, 169 U.S. at 700–701.

111. *United States v. Wong Kim Ark*, 169 U.S. at 702–703.

112. *United States v. Wong Kim Ark*, 169 U.S. at 704.

113. Brandwein, *Rethinking the Judicial Settlement of Reconstruction.*

114. *United States v. Wong Kim Ark*, 169 U.S. at 706.

115. *United States v. Wong Kim Ark*, 169 U.S. at 708–709.

116. *United States v. Wong Kim Ark*, 169 U.S. at 711–712.

117. *United States v. Wong Kim Ark*, 169 U.S. at 718.

118. Thomas Bayard, "Mr. Bayard to Mr. Winchester," in Martin B. Gold, *Forbidden Citizens: Chinese Exclusion and the U.S. Congress: A Legislative History* (Washington, DC: Capitol Net, 2011), 238–239. Bayard would go on to negotiate the Bayard-Zhang Treaty, which would have eliminated almost all Chinese migration to the United States, but China rejected the treaty in 1888.

119. *United States v. Wong Kim Ark*, 169 U.S. at 719–720.

120. *United States v. Wong Kim Ark*, 169 U.S. at 721–722.

121. *United States v. Wong Kim Ark*, 169 U.S. at 726.

122. *United States v. Wong Kim Ark*, 169 U.S. at 726.

123. *United States v. Wong Kim Ark*, 169 U.S. at 729.

124. *United States v. Wong Kim Ark*, 169 U.S. at 730–731.

125. *United States v. Wong Kim Ark*, 169 U.S. at 731.

126. *United States v. Wong Kim Ark*, 169 U.S. at 732.

127. *Plessy v. Ferguson*, 163 U.S. 537 (1896), at 559.

128. Gabriel J. Chin, "The Plessy Myth: Justice Harlan and the Chinese Cases," *Iowa Law Review* 82 (October 1996): 159–160.

129. In *Chew Heong v. United States* (112 U.S. 536 (1884)), Justice Harlan wrote the Court's opinion that a US resident who was outside the United States

when the 1884 amendments to the Chinese Exclusion Act required those departing to carry return certificates went into effect could not be required to produce what it would have been impossible for him to produce, and that the requirement contravened the Angell Treaty of 1880. Justice Harlan also joined a unanimous Supreme Court in *Wong Wing v. United States* (163 U.S. 228 (1896)), holding that the Constitution required indictment and a jury trial before a deportable Chinese person could be criminally punished for being in the United States; this invalidated a section of the 1892 Geary Act stipulating a year of hard labor prior to deportation for a Chinese person found without the required certificate of residence. Chin finds Harlan "a faithful opponent of the constitutional rights of Chinese for much of his career on the Court" (Chin, "Plessy Myth," 156).

130. Eric Schepard, "The Great Dissenter's Greatest Dissents: The First Justice Harlan, the 'Color-Blind' Constitution and the Meaning of His Dissents in the *Insular Cases* for the War on Terror," *American Journal of Legal History* 48 (April 2006): 120.

131. Schepard, 129.

132. Schepard, 137–138.

133. "An Important Decision," *New York Sun*, March 29, 1898, 9.

134. "Citizenship of Chinese," *Vermont Sun* (Saint Albans, VT), April 22, 1898, 2.

135. "Chinese Who Are Citizens: Mongols Born in This Country Have All the Privileges of Natives," *San Francisco Examiner*, March 29, 1898, 16.

136. "Citizen Wong Kim Ark," *Los Angeles Herald*, July 24, 1898, 17.

137. "Comment," *Yale Law Journal* 7 (1898): 366–367.

138. Marshall Woodworth, "Who Are Citizens of the United States?—Wong Kim Ark Case—Interpretation of the Fourteenth Amendment," *American Law Review* 32 (1898): 554.

139. Woodworth, 555. In 1905, he would participate in the test case *United States v. Ju Toy*, in which the Court ruled that even individuals claiming birthright citizenship were not entitled to a judicial consideration of their pleas to enter absent any evidence of problematic behavior in the administrative determination phase. A few years later, he joined a law firm that was busily filing petitions seeking judicial review of administrative decisions on the ground that they were improperly handled. See Lucy Salyer, "*Chew Heong v. United States*: Chinese Exclusion and the Federal Courts," prepared for inclusion in the project Federal Trials and Great Debates in United States History, 2006, https://www.fjc.gov/history/famous-federal-trials/chew-heong-v-us-chinese-exclusion-and-federal-courts.

140. Woodworth, "Who Are Citizens of the United States?," 560–561.

141. William Guthrie, *Lectures on the Fourteenth Article of Amendment to the Constitution of the United States* (Minneapolis: University of Minnesota Press, 1898), 20–21.

142. Guthrie, 21.

143. Guthrie, 38.

144. Guthrie, 53.

145. Guthrie, 57.

146. Guthrie, 57.

147. Guthrie, 57. Guthrie read in the gender requirement, which was not expressed explicitly in the Constitution.

148. Thomas Cooley, *The General Principles of Constitutional Law in the United States* (New York: Little, Brown, 1898), 268.

149. Cooley, 270.

150. Cooley, 270.

151. Lee, "*Wong Kim Ark v. United States*," 103–104.

152. Lee, 92.

153. Lee, 106.

Chapter 6. Citizenship and Immigration: The Next Battles

1. Rachel E. Rosenbloom, "Policing the Borders of Birthright Citizenship: Some Thoughts on the New (and Old) Restrictionism," *Washburn Law Journal* 51, no. 2 (2012): 314.

2. Alexander Keyssar, *The Right to Vote* (New York: Basic Books, 2000), 252–255.

3. Elizabeth F. Cohen, *Semi-citizenship in Democratic Politics* (New York: Cambridge University Press, 2010), 4–5.

4. "Who Was Shut Out? Immigration Quotas, 1925–1927," http://historymatters.gmu.edu/.

5. Rosenbloom, "Policing the Borders of Birthright Citizenship," 315.

6. Quoted in Rosenbloom, 316–317.

7. Quoted in Rosenbloom, 317.

8. "Westerners Unite to Curb Japanese," *New York Times,* April 21, 1921, https://timesmachine.nytimes.com/timesmachine/1921/04/21/107014075.html?pageNumber=15.

9. Robin Dale Jacobson, Daniel Tichenor, and T. Elizabeth Durden, "The Southwest's Uneven Welcome: Immigrant Inclusion and Exclusion in Arizona and New Mexico," *Journal of American Ethnic History* 37, no. 3 (2018): 19.

10. "Westerners Unite to Curb Japanese"; Rosenbloom, "Policing the Borders of Birthright Citizenship," 318.

11. Jacobson, Tichenor, and Durden, "Southwest's Uneven Welcome," 25–26.

12. Rosenbloom, "Policing the Borders of Birthright Citizenship," 319; Greg Robinson, "*Regan v. King*," https://encyclopedia.densho.org/Regan_v._King/; *Regan v. King*, 49 F. Supp. 222 (N.D. Cal. 1942).

13. Robinson, "*Regan v. King*."

14. Robinson; *Regan v. King*, 49 F. Supp. 222.

15. *Morrison v. California*, 291 U.S. 82 (1934), at 85.

16. *Perkins v. Elg*, 307 U.S. 325 (1939), at 329.

17. *Regan v. King*, 134 F. 2d 413 (9th Cir. 1943); Robinson, "*Regan v. King*"; Greg Robinson, "When Birthright Citizenship Was Last 'Reconsidered': REGAN

v. KING and Asian Americans, Part V," The Faculty Lounge, August 10, 2010, https://www.thefacultylounge.org/2010/08/when-birthright-citizenship-was -last-reconsidered-regan-v-king-and-asian-americans-part-v.html.

18. See Rosenbloom, "Policing the Borders of Birthright Citizenship," 319.

19. "Hawaii," https://history.house.gov/Exhibitions-and-Publications/APA /Historical-Essays/Exclusion-and-Empire/Hawaii/.

20. Thomas J. Osborne, "The Main Reason for Hawaiian Annexation in July, 1898," *Oregon Historical Quarterly* 71 (June 1970): 161, 167, 176.

21. Osborne, 173–175.

22. Hawaiian Organic Act, Persons Born in Hawaii, 8 U.S. Code § 1405, https://www.law.cornell.edu/uscode/text/8/1405.

23. Lauren L. Basson, "Fit for Annexation but Unfit to Vote? Debating Hawaiian Suffrage Qualifications at the Turn of the Twentieth Century," *Social Science History* 29, no. 4 (2005): 582.

24. Vanessa Romo, "American Samoans' Citizenship Status Still in Limbo after Judge Issues Stay," NPR, December 13, 2019, https://www.npr.org/2019 /12/13/787978353/american-samoans-citizenship-status-still-in-limbo -after-judge-issues-stay.

25. Treaty of Peace between the United States and Spain, December 10, 1898, Article IX, https://avalon.law.yale.edu/19th_century/sp1898.asp.

26. Charles R. Venator-Santiago, "The Jones Act Made Puerto Ricans Citizens, Yet Not Fully American," *Baltimore Sun*, March 15, 2018, https://www .baltimoresun.com/opinion/op-ed/bs-ed-op-0316-puerto-rico-20180314-story .html. See also Charles R. Venator-Santiago, "The Law That Made Puerto Ricans U.S. Citizens, Yet Not Fully American," *Zocalo Public Square*, March 6, 2018, https://www.zocalopublicsquare.org/2018/03/06/law-made-puerto-ricans-u-s -citizens-yet-not-fully-american/ideas/essay/; Bartholomew H. Sparrow, *The* Insular Cases *and the Emergence of American Empire* (Lawrence: University Press of Kansas, 2006), 68. The authoritative legislative history of this period in US–Puerto Rican relations is José A. Cabranes, "Citizenship and the American Empire: Notes on the Legislative History of the United States Citizenship of Puerto Ricans," *University of Pennsylvania Law Review* 127, no. 2 (1978): 391–492.

27. "The Philippines, 1898–1946," https://history.house.gov/Exhibitions -and-Publications/APA/Historical-Essays/Exclusion-and-Empire/The-Philip pines/.

28. Paul A. Kramer, *The Blood of Government: Race, Empire, the United States, and the Philippines* (Chapel Hill: University of North Carolina Press, 2006).

29. Sparrow, *The* Insular Cases, 4–5.

30. Sam Erman, *Almost Citizens: Puerto Rico, the U.S. Constitution, and Empire* (Cambridge: Cambridge University Press, 2019), 142.

31. *Downes v. Bidwell,* 182 U.S. 244 (1901) at 287.

32. *Downes v. Bidwell,* 182 U.S. at 279.

33. *Downes v. Bidwell,* 182 U.S. at 283. The Chinese exclusion cases cited were *Yick Wo v. Hopkins,* 118 U.S. 356 (1886); *Fong Yue Ting v. United States,* 149 U.S. 698 (1893); *Lem Moon Sing v. United States,* 158 U.S. 538 (1895), at 547; and *Wong Wing v. United States,* 163 U.S. 228 (1896). See chapter 3.

34. Sparrow, *The* Insular Cases, 90–93.

35. White, J. concurring in *Downes v. Bidwell*, 182 U.S. at 341–342.

36. See Sparrow, *The* Insular Cases, 5–7.

37. Christina Duffy Burnett [Ponsa], "Untied States: American Expansion and Territorial Deannexation," *University of Chicago Law Review* 72 (Summer 2005): 798.

38. Sparrow, *The* Insular Cases, 7.

39. Sparrow, 197; *Balzac v. People of Porto Rico*, 258 U.S. 298 (1922).

40. Erman, *Almost Citizens*, 74–76.

41. Erman, 78–79.

42. Erman, 80–81.

43. Erman, 83–84.

44. Erman, 86–87.

45. Cabranes, "Citizenship and the American Empire," 395–396.

46. Venator-Santiago, "The Law That Made Puerto Ricans U.S. Citizens." See also Puerto Rico: Citizenship Archives Project, University of Connecticut, http://scholarscollaborative.org/PuertoRico/exhibits/show/historical/individual.

47. Erman, *Almost Citizens*, 142. Individuals could choose to opt out within a year.

48. Erman, 133.

49. Erman, 141–142.

50. Erman, 133.

51. Cabranes, "Citizenship and the American Empire," 487.

52. Senator Foraker quoted in Cabranes, 397.

53. Cabranes, 416, 487.

54. Sparrow, *The* Insular Cases, 202.

55. Sparrow, 204.

56. Erman, *Almost Citizens*, 131–132.

57. Venator-Santiago, "The Law That Made Puerto Ricans U.S. Citizens."

58. Charles Venator-Santiago, "Puerto Rican Citizenship Timeline," in "U.S. Citizenship in Puerto Rico: One Hundred Years after the Jones Act," special issue, *CENTRO: Journal of the Center for Puerto Rican Studies* 29, no. 1 (2017): 6–10.

59. Venator-Santiago, "The Law That Made Puerto Ricans U.S. Citizens."

60. Nationality Act of 1940, 54 Stat. 1137, 76th Cong., 3d Sess., Ch. 876, Title II, Sec. 201 (1940). Native American citizenship will be discussed later, but the 1940 Nationality Act also contained a clause that stated: "A person born in the United States to a member of an Indian, Eskimo, Aleutian, or other aboriginal tribe: Provided, That the granting of citizenship under this subsection shall not in any manner impair or otherwise affect the right of such person to tribal or other property."

61. Venator-Santiago, "The Law That Made Puerto Ricans U.S. Citizens."

62. Mae M. Ngai, "Birthright Citizenship and the Alien Citizen," *Fordham Law Review* 175, no. 5 (2007): 2527.

63. *Fitisemanu v. United States*, 426 F. Supp. 3d 1155 (D. Utah 2019). The other "unincorporated territories" are the Northern Marianas, Guam, US Virgin Islands, and Puerto Rico. See Sparrow, *The* Insular Cases, 7.

64. *Fitisemanu v. United States*, 426 F. Supp. 3d at 1179–1192. See Carol Nackenoff and Julie Novkov, "Who Is Born a US Citizen?," *The Conversation*, January 15, 2020, https://theconversation.com/who-is-born-a-us-citizen-127403.

65. *In re Rodriguez*, 81 F. 337, 349 (D. Tex. 1897).

66. *In re Rodriguez*, 81 F. at 353.

67. Natalia Molina, "'In a Race All Their Own': The Quest to Make Mexicans Ineligible for U.S. Citizenship," *Pacific Historical Review* 79, no. 2 (2010): 170–173. The Naturalization Act of 1870 was codified as Sec. 2169 of U.S. Revised Statutes (16 Stat. 254), July 14, 1870.

68. Molina, "'In a Race All Their Own,'" 170.

69. Molina, 170.

70. Robert A. Pastor, "U.S. Immigration Policy and Latin America: In Search of the 'Special Relationship,'" *Latin American Research Review* 19, no. 3 (1984): 38–41.

71. Erika Lee, "Enforcing the Borders: Chinese Exclusion along the U.S. Borders with Canada and Mexico, 1882–1924," *Journal of American History* 89, no. 1 (2002): 54–86.

72. Mae M. Ngai, *Impossible Subjects: Illegal Aliens and the Making of Modern America* (Princeton, NJ: Princeton University Press, 2004), 64–67; see also Pastor, "U.S. Immigration Policy and Latin America," 50.

73. Don M. Coerver, Suzanne B. Pasztor, and Robert M. Buffington, *Mexico: An Encyclopedia of Contemporary Culture and History* (Santa Barbara, CA: ABC-CLIO, 2004), 224.

74. Pastor, "U.S. Immigration Policy and Latin America," 50.

75. Schomberg Center for Research in Black Culture, "Caribbean Immigration: Coming to the United States," http://www.inmotionaame.org/migrations/topic.cfm?migration=10&topic=5.

76. Pastor, "U.S. Immigration Policy and Latin America," 39.

77. Schomberg Center for Research in Black Culture, "Caribbean Immigration: Shutting the Door," http://www.inmotionaame.org/migrations/topic.cfm?migration=10&topic=6.

78. Ngai, *Impossible Subjects*, 67, 294n41.

79. Ngai, 64–67.

80. Molina, "'In a Race All Their Own,'" 180–181, 167. The decisions were *Ozawa v. United States* and *United States v. Thind*. These individuals were now either "incorporated" with the United States or "unincorporated," with only the former having the full protections of the Constitution. The court reasoned that Puerto Rico and the other new territories were "inhabited by alien races," so governing them "according to Anglo-Saxon principles may for a time be impossible." These islands were "foreign in a domestic sense"—a phrase borrowed from the White concurrence in *Downes* (1901); *Ozawa v. United States*, 260 U.S. 178 (1922) and *United States v. Bhagat Singh Thind*, 261 U.S. 204 (1923). See later in this chapter for further discussion of these cases.

81. Pastor, "U.S. Immigration Policy and Latin America," 42.

82. Ngai, *Impossible Subjects*, 68.

83. Ngai, "Birthright Citizenship and the Alien Citizen," 2522.

84. Pastor, "U.S. Immigration Policy and Latin America," 41–42.

85. Pastor, 42.

86. Ngai, "Birthright Citizenship and the Alien Citizen," 2523, 2529.

87. Ngai, 2522.

88. Torrie Hester, *Deportation: The Origins of U.S. Policy* (Philadelphia: University of Pennsylvania Press, 2017), 172.

89. Abraham Hoffman, *Unwanted Mexican Americans in the Great Depression: Repatriation Pressures 1929–1939* (Tucson: University of Arizona Press, 1974), 38.

90. Hoffman, 83.

91. Hester, *Deportation*, 152; Brian Gratton and Emily Merchant, "Immigration, Repatriation, and Deportation: The Mexican-Origin Population in the United States, 1920–1950," *International Migration Review* 47, no. 4 (2013): 944–975.

92. Hoffman, *Unwanted Mexican Americans in the Great Depression*; Ngai, "Birthright Citizenship and the Alien Citizen," 2522.

93. Would-be immigrants were warned, in a National Council of Jewish Women leaflet distributed in Russia and European ports of departure, that if they sent a child under fourteen to work or failed to send a child to school they could be deported; see Faith Rogow, *Gone to Another Meeting: The National Council of Jewish Women, 1893–1993*, foreword by Joan Bronk (Tuscaloosa: University of Alabama Press, 1993), 138–139.

94. Hester, *Deportation*, 61–67.

95. Grace Abbott and the Immigrants' Protective League took up their cause. See Carol Nackenoff, "The Private Roots of American Political Development: The Immigrants' Protective League's 'Friendly and Sympathetic Touch,' 1908–1924," *Studies in American Political Development* 28, no. 2 (2014): 147 and notes 153–154.

96. Jacobson, Tichenor, and Durden, "Southwest's Uneven Welcome," 16.

97. Robert K. Murray, *Red Scare: A Study in National Hysteria* (Minneapolis: University of Minnesota Press, 1955), 211–213.

98. Murray, 196, 211–212.

99. Murray, 213.

100. Adam Hochschild, "When America Tried to Deport Its Radicals," *New Yorker*, November 11, 2019), https://www.newyorker.com/magazine/2019/11/11/when-america-tried-to-deport-its-radicals.

101. Hester, *Deportation*, 132.

102. Hester, 72–74.

103. Hester, 74–76.

104. Hester, 77–78.

105. Paul Spickard, *Almost All Aliens: Immigration, Race, and Colonialism in American History and Identity* (New York: Routledge, 2007), 302–303.

106. Pastor, "U.S. Immigration Policy and Latin America," 42–43. Nevertheless, he noted, Caribbean immigration almost quadrupled between 1953 and 1965 compared with the previous decade, led by Cuba and later joined by the Dominican Republic; spouses and children of US citizens were not included in the quota.

107. Pastor, 45.

108. Pastor, 47.

109. Pastor, 47.

110. Pastor, 48.

111. Candice Lewis Bredbenner, *A Nationality of Her Own: Women, Marriage and the Law of Citizenship* (Berkeley: University of California Press, 1999), 15–17, quoting Immigration Act of February 5, 1917, 39 Stat. 874 at 889.

112. Bredbenner, 15–16.

113. Nancy F. Cott, "Marriage and Women's Citizenship in the United States 1830–1934," *American Historical Review* 103 (December 1998): 1462.

114. Bredbenner, *A Nationality of Her Own*, 16.

115. Cott, "Marriage and Women's Citizenship," 1464.

116. Bredbenner, *A Nationality of Her Own*, 100.

117. Bredbenner, 98–99.

118. Lester B. Orfield, "The Citizenship Act of 1934," *University of Chicago Law Review* 2, no. 1 (1934): 101.

119. Orfield, 101.

120. Orfield, 102.

121. "Immigration to the United States, 1933–1941," *Holocaust Encyclopedia*, US Holocaust Museum, https://encyclopedia.ushmm.org/content/en/article/immigration-to-the-united-states-1933–41.

122. Daniel A. Gross, "The U.S. Government Turned Away Thousands of Jewish Refugees, Fearing That They Were Nazi Spies," *Smithsonian Magazine*, November 18, 2015, https://www.smithsonianmag.com/history/us-government-turned-away-thousands-jewish-refugees-fearing-they-were-nazi-spies-180957324/.

123. "Immigration to the United States, 1933–1941"; Dara Lind, "How America's Rejection of Jews Fleeing Nazi Germany Haunts Our Refugee Policy Today," *Vox*, January 27, 2017, https://www.vox.com/policy-and-politics/2017/1/27/14412082/refugees-history-holocaust.

124. A December 1945 Gallup Poll indicated only 5 percent of those Americans surveyed were willing to admit more European immigrants than were accepted before the war, according to "Immigration to the United States, 1933–1941."

125. "Immigration to the United States, 1933–1941." The statement and directive can be found at https://www.presidency.ucsb.edu/documents/statement-and-directive-the-president-immigration-the-united-states-certain-displaced.

126. Ngai, "Birthright Citizenship and the Alien Citizen," 2522.

127. *Ex parte Endo*, 323 U.S. 283 (1944); *Korematsu v. United States*, 323 U.S. 214 (1944).

128. Immigration Act of 1952, https://encyclopedia.densho.org/Immigration_Act_of_1952/. In 1952, the Japanese quota was higher than that for most other Asians (185).

129. Jia Lynn Yang, *One Mighty and Irresistible Tide: The Epic Struggle over American Immigration, 1924–1965* (New York: W. W. Norton, 2020); see also Jia Lynn Yang, "How Family Ties Changed Us," *New York Times*, June 14, 2020, SR 6.

NOTES TO PAGES 147–151 | 231

130. Maddalena Marinari, "'Americans Must Show Justice in Immigration Policies Too': The Passage of the 1965 Immigration Act," *Journal of Policy History* 26, no. 2 (2014): 221.

131. Marinari, 238–239.

132. 39 Stat. 874.

133. Constitution of the Immigrant Restriction League, 1894, https://iiif.lib .harvard.edu/manifests/view/drs:5233215$1i. Some immigrants, such as wives and relatives over a certain age, were exempted from the literacy test.

134. 1 Stat. 103 Ch. III, March 26, 1790, allowed a "free white person . . . of good character" to naturalize; the language in 1 Stat. 414, Ch. XX, January 29, 1795, spoke of a "free white person . . . of a good moral character."

135. David M. Reimers, *Unwelcome Strangers: American Identity and the Turn against Immigration* (New York: Columbia University Press, 1998), 13–14.

136. In exchange, the federal government persuaded San Francisco to rescind a 1906 policy segregating Asians in public schools. Koreans began migrating to Hawaii around 1903 to work on sugar and pineapple plantations.

137. Tae-Ung Baik and Duk Hee Lee Murabayashi, "The Historical Development of Early Korean Immigration to Hawaii and Its Legal Structure," *Journal of Korean Law* 11 (December 2011): 77, 78, 90.

138. *Ozawa v. United States*, 260 U.S. 178 at 189.

139. An Act to Establish a Bureau of Immigration and Naturalization and to Provide for a Uniform Rule for the Naturalization of Aliens throughout the United States, 59th Cong., 1st Sess., Ch. 3592, 1906, https://www.loc.gov/law /help/statutes-at-large/59th-congress/session-1/c59s1ch3592.pdf.

140. *Ozawa v. United States*, http://encyclopedia.densho.org/Ozawa_v._United _States/.

141. *Ozawa v. United States*, http://encyclopedia.densho.org/Ozawa_v._United _States/.

142. *Ozawa v. United States*, 1922 U.S. LEXIS 2357, 10.

143. *Ozawa v. United States*, 260 U.S. 178 (1922), Mr. George W. Wickersham, Counsel, with Mr. David L. Withington.

144. Counsel for Ozawa, *Ozawa v. United States*.

145. *Ozawa v. United States*.

146. Brief of Mr. Solicitor General Beck and Mr. Alfred A. Wheat, Special Assistant to the Attorney General, *Ozawa v. United States*.

147. *Ozawa v. United States*, 260 U.S. at 197.

148. *Ozawa v. United States*, 260 U.S. at 197; see *In re Ah Yup*, 1 F. Cas. 223 (C.C.D. Cal. 1878).

149. *Ozawa v. United States*, 260 U.S. at 198.

150. *Ozawa v. United States*, 260 U.S. at 194–195; quote at 195.

151. *Ozawa v. United States*, 260 U.S. at 192–193.

152. *Ozawa v. United States*, 260 U.S. at 194.

153. *Ozawa v. United States*, 260 U.S. at 190–192; quote at 192.

154. *Ozawa v. United States*, 260 U.S. at 193–194.

155. *United States v. Bhagat Singh Thind* 261 U.S. 204 (1923), at 207.

156. *United States v. Thind*, 261 U.S. at 207, quoting *Ozawa*.

157. *United States v. Thind*, 261 U.S. at 213, both quotes.

158. *United States v. Thind*, 261 U.S. at 211. For this proposition, Sutherland relied on A. H. Keane, a linguist, ethnologist, and journalist, citing his book *The World's Peoples*. A. H. Keane, *The World's Peoples: A Popular Account of Their Bodily and Mental Characters, Beliefs, Traditions, Political and Social Institutions* (London: Hutchinson & Co., 1908).

159. *United States v. Thind*, 261 U.S. at 212. Various authorities are noted.

160. *United States v. Thind*, 261 U.S. at 208.

161. *United States v. Thind*, 261 U.S. at 208, quote at 209, citing *Maillard v. Lawrence*, 16 Howard 251, 261 (1854).

162. *United States v. Thind*, 261 U.S. at 209.

163. *United States v. Thind*, 261 U.S. at 215; Immigration Act of February 5, 1917.

164. *United States v. Thind*, 261 U.S. at 215.

165. *Toyota v. United States*, 268 U.S. 402, 406–407 (1925).

166. *Toyota v. United States*, 268 U.S. at 408–409, referring to the seventh subdivision of Section 4 of the Act of June 29, 1906, as amended May 9, 1918, 34 Stat. 601, 40 Stat. 542; Act of July 19, 1919, 41 Stat. 222.

167. *Toyota v. United States*, 268 U.S. at 410.

168. *Toyota v. United States*, 268 U.S. at 412.

169. *Cherokee Nation v. Georgia*, 30 U.S. 1 (1831), at 17.

170. *Cherokee Nation v. Georgia*, 30 U.S. at 17.

171. Act to Establish a Uniform Rule of Naturalization (March 26, 1790), 1 Stat. 103.

172. Taney, C.J., opinion of the Court in *Dred Scott v. Sandford*, 60 U.S. 393 (1857), at 404.

173. Brad Tennant, "'Excluding Indians Not Taxed': *Dred Scott, Standing Bear, Elk* and the Legal Status of Native Americans in the Latter Half of the Nineteenth Century," *International Social Science Review* 86, no. 1–2 (2011): 25.

174. Quoted in Scott Bomboy, "The 14th Amendment's Tortuous Relationship with American Indians," *Constitution Daily* (blog), National Constitution Center, March 12, 2014, https://constitutioncenter.org/blog/the-14th-amendments-tortuous-relationship-with-american-indians1.

175. *Elk v. Wilkins*, 112 U.S. 94 (1884); see chapter 3.

176. See Carol Nackenoff, "Constitutionalizing Terms of Inclusion: Friends of the Indian and Citizenship for Native Americans, 1880s–1930s," in *The Supreme Court and American Political Development*, ed. Ronald Kahn and Ken I. Kersch (Lawrence: University Press of Kansas, 2006): 366–413; Michael T. Smith, "The History of Indian Citizenship," *Great Plains Journal* 10 (Fall 1970): 26–29.

177. *Matter of Heff*, 197 U.S. 488 (1905).

178. *United States v. Nice*, 241 U.S. 591 (1916), at 598.

179. *Winton v. Amos*, 255 U.S. 373 (1921), at 392. See John T. McMinn and Carol Nackenoff. "Native Americans: Citizenship," in *American Governance*, vol. 3, ed. Stephen Schechter et al. (Farmington Hills, MI: Macmillan Reference USA, 2016), 306–308.

180. Kevin Bruyneel, *Third Space of Sovereignty: The Postcolonial Politics of U.S.-Indigenous Relations* (Minneapolis: University of Minnesota Press, 2007),

99. Chapter 4 examines complex reactions to US citizenship and some of the complexities of now-simultaneous US and tribal citizenship.

181. Tennant, "'Excluding Indians Not Taxed,'" 24.

182. 8 U.S.C. Section 1401; Bruyneel. *Third Space of Sovereignty*, chap. 4.

183. See, for example, *Santa Clara Pueblo v. Martinez*, 436 U.S. 49 (1978).

184. See Bruyneel, *Third Space of Sovereignty*, 101–102, 107–108.

185. See Bruyneel, 114–116.

186. Rosenbloom, "Policing the Borders of Birthright Citizenship," 326.

187. Quote from Muzaffar Chishti, Doris Meissner, and Claire Bergeron, "At Its 25th Anniversary, IRCA's Legacy Lives On," Migration Policy Institute, November 16, 2011, https://www.migrationpolicy.org/article/its-25th-anniversary-ircas-legacy-lives; see Rosenbloom, "Policing the Borders of Birthright Citizenship," 326.

188. Peter Schuck and Rogers M. Smith, *Citizenship without Consent: Illegal Aliens in the American Polity* (New Haven, CT: Yale University Press, 1985).

Chapter 7. Revisiting Jus Soli: Contemporary Developments

Marit Vike graduated with high honors from Swarthmore College in 2019 with a bachelor of arts in political science and history. She is currently working as an antitrust paralegal at Cohen Milstein Sellers & Toll PLLC, a firm specializing in complex plaintiff-side litigation in Washington, DC.

1. Sandra Wong, great-granddaughter of Wong Kim Ark, interviewed by Robert Siegel, NPR, October 2, 2015, https://www.npr.org/2015/10/02/445346769/he-famously-fought-for-his-u-s-citizenship-where-are-his-descendants-now.

2. Creation of record of lawful permanent resident status for person born under diplomatic status in the United States, Code of Federal Regulations, Title 8, Ch. 1, Subchapter B, Part 101.3, https://www.ecfr.gov/cgi-bin/text-idx?&node=se8.1.101_13. See also US Department of Homeland Security, US Citizenship and Immigration Services, Policy Manual, chap. 3, accessed June 25, 2019, https://www.uscis.gov/policy-manual/volume-7-part-o-chapter-3.

3. Donald J. Trump, interview with Jonathan Swan, *Axios on HBO*, October 30, 2018.

4. Zolan Kanno-Youngs and Maggie Haberman, "'A Constant Game of Musical Chairs' amid Another Homeland Security Shake-Up," *New York Times*, June 25, 2019, https://www.nytimes.com/2019/06/25/us/politics/mark-morgan-ice-cbp.html.

5. Laura Powers, "Trump's Acting Immigration Director Claims Ending Birthright Citizenship Would Not Require Constitutional Amendment," *Newsweek*, October 20, 2019, https://www.newsweek.com/trumps-acting-immigration-director-claims-ending-birthright-citizenship-would-not-require-1465728.

6. Iseult Honohan, "The Theory and Politics of Ius Soli," June 2010, 2, EUDO Citizenship Observatory, http://cadmus.eui.eu/bitstream/handle/1814/19574/Honohan_IusSoli_2010.pdf?sequence=1&isAllowed=y.

7. Discussed in Honohan, 1.

8. Sarah Buhler, "Babies as Bargaining Chips? In Defence of Birthright Citizenship in Canada," *Journal of Law and Social Policy* 17 (2002): 100; quoted in Amanda Colvin, "Birthright Citizenship in the United States: Realities of de Facto Deportation and International Comparisons toward Proposing a Solution," *St. Louis University Law Journal* 53, no. 1 (2008): 233.

9. Elizabeth Schumacher, "Revoking Citizenship: How It Works across the EU," May 3, 2019, https://www.dw.com/en/revoking-citizenship-how-it-works-across-the-eu/a-47773802.

10. Honohan, "Theory and Politics of Ius Soli," 3.

11. Honohan, 5–6.

12. Honohan, 7.

13. Emma Lazarus, "The New Colossus," *Statue of Liberty*, 1883.

14. Devan Cole and Caroline Kelly, "Cuccinelli Rewrites Statue of Liberty Poem to Make Case for Limiting Immigration," *CNN Politics* August 13, 2019. https://www.cnn.com/2019/08/13/politics/ken-cuccinelli-statue-of-liberty/index.html.

15. Polly Price, "Jus Soli and Statelessness: A Comparative Perspective from the Americas," in *Citizenship in Question: Evidentiary Birthright and Statelessness*, ed. Benjamin Lawrance and Jacqueline Stevens (Durham, NC: Duke University Press, 2017), 27.

16. Price, 29–32.

17. Scott Bomboy, "What Do Other Countries' Constitutions Say about Birthright Citizenship?," National Constitution Center, accessed June 11, 2019, https://constitutioncenter.org/blog/what-do-other-countries-constitutions-say-about-birthright-citizenship/.

18. The Law Library of Congress, "Birthright Citizenship around the World," November 2018, https://www.loc.gov/law/help/birthright-citizenship/birthright-citizenship-around-the-world.pdf.

19. World Population Review, "Countries with Birthright Citizenship 2020," counts 35 nations; The Law Library of Congress counts 33, and other counts indicate at least 30. See http://worldpopulationreview.com/countries/countries-with-birthright-citizenship/, accessed November 29, 2020; Law Library of Congress, "Birthright Citizenship around the World," November 2018, https://www.loc.gov/law/help/birthright-citizenship/birthright-citizenship-around-the-world.pdf.

20. Law Library of Congress, "Birthright Citizenship around the World.

21. Bomboy, "What Do Other Countries' Constitutions Say about Birthright Citizenship?"

22. Law Library of Congress, "Citizenship Based on Birth in Country," May 2012, compiled by Constance A. Johnson, http://www.loc.gov/law/help/citizenship-birth-country/citizenship-birth-country.pdf. The study included France, Germany, Spain, Portugal, Italy, Greece, and the United Kingdom. There are a few other circumstances under which birthright citizenship may apply, depending on country, such as foundlings and stateless persons.

23. Charlotte Alfred, Elise Foley, and Roque Planas, "These Countries Show Why Losing Birthright Citizenship Could Be a Disaster," *Huffington Post*, Au-

gust 27, 2015, https://www.huffpost.com/entry/birthright-citizenship-other
-countries_n_55df2a82e4b08dc0948699f3.

24. Evelyn Nakano Glenn, "Settler Colonialism as Structure: A Framework
for Comparative Studies of U.S. Race and Gender Formation," *Sociology of Race
and Ethnicity* 1, no. 1 (2015): 54–74. On settler colonialism, see Edward Cavanagh and Lorenzo Veracini, eds., *Routledge Handbook of the History of Settler
Colonialism* (Abingdon: Routledge, 2017); Lorenzo Veracini, *Settler Colonialism:
A Theoretical Overview* (New York: Palgrave Macmillan, 2010); Walter L. Hixson,
American Settler Colonialism: A History (New York: Palgrave Macmillan, 2013).

25. On Native American citizenship complexities and confusion under
the Dawes Act, see Carol Nackenoff, "Constitutionalizing Terms of Inclusion:
Friends of the Indian and Citizenship for Native Americans 1880s–1930s," in
The Supreme Court and American Political Development, ed. Ronald Kahn and Ken
I. Kersch (Lawrence: University Press of Kansas, 2006), 366–413.

26. See Alexander Keyssar, *The Right to Vote* (New York: Basic Books, 2000).

27. See Alastair Davidson, *From Subject to Citizen: Australian Citizenship in the
Twentieth Century* (Cambridge: Cambridge University Press, 1997); John Chesterman and Brian Galligan, *Citizens without Rights: Aborigines and Australian Citizenship* (Cambridge: Cambridge University Press, 1997).

28. *Report of the Royal Commission on Aboriginal Peoples*, vol. 1, "Looking Forward, Looking Back," 1996, http://data2.archives.ca/e/e448/e011188230-01
.pdf. See also Harold Cardinal, *The Unjust Society*, 2nd ed. (Vancouver: Douglas
& McIntyre, 1999).

29. Law Library of Congress, "Birthright Citizenship around the World."

30. The 2004 referendum to remove unconditional jus soli from the constitution "to preserve the 'integrity' of Irish citizenship" passed by an overwhelming majority; Bernard Ryan, "The Celtic Cubs: The Controversy over Birthright
Citizenship in Ireland," *European Journal of Migration and Law* 6 (2004): 187–
190; cited in Colvin, "Birthright Citizenship in the United States," 240.

31. Honohan, "Theory and Politics of Ius Soli," 18; Joanne M. Mancini and
Graham Finlay, "'Citizenship Matters': Lessons from the Irish Citizenship Referendum," *American Quarterly* 60, no. 3 (2008): 575.

32. Mancini and Finlay, "'Citizenship Matters,'" 575.

33. Mancini and Finlay, 582.

34. Mancini and Finlay, 583.

35. Annie Menzel, "Birthright Citizenship and the Racial Contract: The
United States' Jus Soli Rule against the Global Regime of Citizenship," *Du Bois
Review: Social Science Research on Race* 10, no. 1 (2013): 30.

36. Menzel, 30.

37. Colvin, "Birthright Citizenship in the United States," 240.

38. Ed O'Loughlin, "In Ireland, Bid to Restore Birthright Citizenship Gains
Ground," *New York Times*, November 24, 2018; Manpreet K. Gill, "Irish Government Opposes Restoring Right to Birthright Citizenship, Despite Popular
Support," *Jackson Lewis Immigration Blog*, November 30, 2018, https://www
.globalimmigrationblog.com/2018/11/irish-government-opposes-restoring
-right-to-birthright-citizenship-despite-popular-support/.

39. Ediberto Román and Ernesto Sagas, "Birthright Citizenship under Attack: How Dominican Nationality Laws May Be the Future of US Exclusion," *American University Law Review* 66 (2016): 1389.

40. Román and Sagas, 1390. Even the insinuation that a political candidate might have some Haitian descendancy was enough to sink his political prospects.

41. Jonathan M. Katz, "What Happened When a Nation Erased Birthright Citizenship," *Atlantic*, November 12, 2018.

42. Katz.

43. See Ricardo Rojas, "Dominican Court Ruling Renders Hundreds of Thousands Stateless," Reuters, October 12, 2013, https://www.reuters.com /article/us-dominicanrepublic-citizenship/dominican-court-ruling-renders -hundreds-of-thousands-stateless-idUSBRE99B01Z20131012.

44. Price, "Jus Soli and Statelessness," 31.

45. Katz, "What Happened When a Nation Erased Birthright Citizenship."

46. Katz.

47. Price, "Jus Soli and Statelessness," 31–32.

48. Price, 32–34.

49. Colvin, "Birthright Citizenship in the United States," 232.

50. Elke Winter and Adina Madularea, "Quo Vadis Canada? Tracing the Contours of Citizenship in a Multicultural Country," in *Immigration, Racial, and Ethnic Studies in 150 Years of Canada: Retrospects and Prospects*, ed. Shibao Guo and Lloyd Wong (Leiden: Brill, 2018), 191–208.

51. The Canadian Standing Committee on Citizenship and Immigration recommended the abandonment of jus soli in favor of a policy granting citizenship only to children with at least one Canadian citizen parent; no tangible legislation materialized. See Colvin, "Birthright Citizenship in the United States," 233.

52. Buhler, "Babies as Bargaining Chips?," quoted in Colvin, "Birthright Citizenship in the United States," 233.

53. Philip E. Wolgin, "Family Reunification Is the Bedrock of U.S. Immigration Policy," Center for American Progress, February 12, 2018, https://www .americanprogress.org/issues/immigration/news/2018/02/12/446402/family -reunification-bedrock-u-s-immigration-policy/.

54. Almost all Chinese were already denied entry, Japan limited Japanese immigration under the Gentlemen's Agreement of 1907, and Filipinos were allowed entry since the Philippines was a US colony.

55. Gabe Ignatow and Alexander T. Williams, "New Media and the 'Anchor Baby' Boom," *Journal of Computer-Mediated Communication* 17, no. 1 (2011): 60.

56. Ignatow and Williams, 60.

57. Pamela Chan, "The History and Stereotypes behind the Term 'Anchor Babies,'" Generation Progress, September 17, 2015, https://genprogress.org /the-history-and-stereotypes-behind-the-term-anchor-babies/.

58. Joon K. Kim, Ernesto Sagás, and Karina Cespedes, "Genderacing Immigrant Subjects: 'Anchor Babies' and the Politics of Birthright Citizenship," *Social Identities* 24, no. 3 (2017): 312–326.

59. David Thronson, "Entering the Mainstream: Making Children Matter in Immigration Law," *Fordham Urban Law Journal* 38, no. 1 (2010): 404.

60. Thronson, 405.

61. Colvin, "Birthright Citizenship in the United States," 220, 227, 230. The US attorney general and courts have at times been sensitive to arguments against deportation based on extreme hardship.

62. President Donald J. Trump, State of the Union Address, January 30, 2018, https://www.whitehouse.gov/briefings-statements/president-donald-j-trumps-state-union-address/. In fact, US citizens can sponsor a wider range of relatives than can legal residents.

63. Trump, State of the Union Address.

64. Unmarried children of a US citizen over twenty-one years of age; married children of a US citizen, spouses, and minor children; and siblings of a US citizen, their spouses, and minor children all fall under the quota system.

65. US Department of State, Bureau of Consular Affairs, Family Immigration, https://travel.state.gov/content/travel/en/us-visas/immigrate/family-immigration/family-based-immigrant-visas.html.

66. US Department of State, Bureau of Consular Affairs, Visa Bulletin for August 2019, https://travel.state.gov/content/travel/en/legal/visa-law0/visa-bulletin/2019/visa-bulletin-for-august-2019.htm.

67. US Department of Homeland Security Rule, Inadmissibility on Public Charge Grounds, *Federal Register* 41292, August 14, 2019, https://www.federalregister.gov/documents/2019/08/14/2019-17142/inadmissibility-on-public-charge-grounds.

68. Kaiser Family Foundation, "Changes to 'Public Charge' Inadmissibility Rule: Implications for Health and Health Coverage," August 12, 2019, https://www.kff.org/disparities-policy/fact-sheet/proposed-changes-to-public-charge-policies-for-immigrants-implications-for-health-coverage/.

69. Patricia Manson, "Challenge to 'Public Charge' Rule Gets OK," *Chicago Daily Law Bulletin*, May 21, 2020, https://www.chicagolawbulletin.com/challenge-to-public-charge-rule-gets-ok-20200521.

70. Julia Gelatt, "Dramatic Change to Family Immigration, Less So for the Employment-Based System," Migration Policy Institute, Commentaries, August 2017, https://www.migrationpolicy.org/news/raise-act-dramatic-change-family-immigration-less-so-employment-based-system.

71. See Kim, Sagás, and Cespedes, "Genderacing Immigrant Subjects."

72. Jennifer Pak, "Why Chinese Parents Come to America to Give Birth," Marketplace, March 6, 2019, https://www.marketplace.org/2019/03/06/why-chinese-parents-come-america-give-birth/. The lower figure is from the Center for Immigration Studies, a conservative think tank. Steven A. Camarota, "There Are Possibly 36,000 Birth Tourists Annually," Center for Immigration Studies, April 28, 2015, https://cis.org/Camarota/There-Are-Possibly-36000-Birth-Tourists-Annually. See also Laura Santhanam and Gretchen Frazee, "What the Data Says about Birthright Citizenship," Public Broadcasting Service, October 30, 2018, https://www.pbs.org/newshour/politics/what-the-data-says-about-birthright-citizenship.

73. Roxana Kopetman and Scott Schwebke, "Federal Agents Charge 19 for Birth Tourism in Southern California," *The O.C. Register*, January 31,

2019, https://www.ocregister.com/2019/01/31/20-charged-in-birth-tourism
-scheme-that-helped-chinese-mothers-have-babies-in-southern-california/.

74. Miriam Jordan, "3 Arrested in Crackdown on Multimillion-Dollar 'Birth Tourism' Businesses," *New York Times*, January 31, 2019, https://www.nytimes .com/2019/01/31/us/anchor-baby-birth-tourism.html.

75. Kylie Atwood, Geneva Sands, and Jennifer Hansler, "US Issues New Rules Restricting Travel by Pregnant Foreigners, Fearing the Use of 'Birth Tourism,'" CNN, January 24, 2020, https://edition.cnn.com/2020/01/23/politics/us -new-rules-restricting-travel-fearing-birth-tourism/index.html.

76. Yuming Fang, "Inside the World of Birth Tourism—Featured Stories," *Medium*, December 9, 2018, https://medium.com/s/story/inside-the-world-of -birth-tourism-4d6e382346b0. See also Brandon J. Folse, "Aspirational Migration: The Case of Chinese Birth Tourism in the U.S." (master's thesis, University of Oregon, 2017), https://scholarsbank.uoregon.edu/xmlui/handle/1794/22749.

77. Daniel Horowitz. "Fixing the Birthright Citizenship Loophole: Myth vs. Fact." *Conservative Review*, August 18, 2015, https://www.conservativereview.com /news/fixing-the-birthright-citizenship-loophole-myth-vs-fact/.

78. In early March 2020, a federal judge held that Cuccinelli was unlawfully appointed to his USCIS position, rendering some of his policies (e.g., about asylum) void. Any nomination to the directorship requires approval by Congress. Cuccinelli also serves as acting deputy secretary of DHS.

79. Donald Trump, Twitter, October 31, 2018, 6:25 a.m., reproduced by Felicia Sonmez and John Wagner in the *Washington Post* later that day at https:// www.washingtonpost.com/politics/trump-presses-on-with-case-to-end-birth right-citizenship-one-way-or-the-other/2018/10/31/bcd69dc2-dd12-11e8 -85df-7a6b4d25cfbb_story.html.

80. Donica Phifer, "Donald Trump Wants to Remove 'Ridiculous' Birthright Citizenship, but Can He Do It without Congress?," *Newsweek*, August 21, 2019, https://www.newsweek.com/birthright-citizenship-trump-executive-order -congress-1455582.

81. Peter H. Schuck and Rogers M. Smith, "The Question of Birthright Citizenship," *National Affairs*, Summer 2018, https://www.nationalaffairs.com /publications/detail/the-question-of-birthright-citizenship. Schuck and Smith cite a National Academies of Sciences, Engineering and Medicine report from 2016 that finds that legal and illegal immigrants contribute less in annual taxes than other Americans, though they make other contributions to the GDP.

82. Schuck and Smith, "The Question of Birthright Citizenship."

83. "Ryan Says 'Obviously' Trump Can't End Birthright Citizenship," MPR, October 31, 2018, https://www.mprnews.org/story/2018/10/30/paul-ryan -obviously-trump-cant-end-birthright-citizenship.

84. Michael Anton, "Citizenship Shouldn't Be a Birthright," *Washington Post*, July 19, 2018, A19. There was quite a bit of reaction to Anton's op-ed, including claims that he inserted a word into his quote from 1866 congressional deliberations that altered the meaning. See John Eastman, "Birthright Citizenship Is Not Actually in the Constitution," *New York Times*, December 22, 2015, for this reading of "subject to the jurisdiction thereof."

85. Anton, "Citizenship Shouldn't Be a Birthright."

86. Anton.

87. Hans A. von Spakovsky, "Why Trump Can End Birthright Citizenship by Executive Order," Heritage Foundation, November 5, 2018, https://www.heritage.org/immigration/commentary/why-trump-can-end-birthright-citizenship-executive-order.

88. Richard Gonzales, "America No Longer a 'Nation of Immigrants,' USCIS Says," NPR, February 22, 2018, https://www.npr.org/sections/thetwo-way/2018/02/22/588097749/america-no-longer-a-nation-of-immigrants-uscis-says. See USCIS website, accessed October 30, 2019, https://www.uscis.gov/aboutus.

89. Brian Tashman, "Trump Picks Family Separation Advocate Kevin McAleenan to Be Acting Secretary of Homeland Security," American Civil Liberties Union, April 10, 2019, https://www.aclu.org/blog/immigrants-rights/trump-picks-family-separation-advocate-kevin-mcaleenan-be-acting-secretary.

90. Dara Lind, "Homeland Security Secretary Kirstjen Nielsen's Resignation, Explained," *Vox*, April 7, 2019.

91. Brett Samuels, "Trump Administration Revives Talk of Action on Birthright Citizenship," *The Hill*, November 20, 2020, https://thehill.com/homenews/administration/526950-trump-administration-revives-talk-of-action-on-birthright-citizenship.

92. 7 Fam 1100 Appendix D, Acquisition of U.S. Citizenship at Birth—Assisted Reproductive Technology, accessed June 23, 2019, https://web.archive.org/web/20160806231603/; https://fam.state.gov/fam/07fam/07fam1100apD.html. One provision states: "A child born abroad to a surrogate, whose genetic parents are a U.S. citizen father and anonymous egg donor, is considered for citizenship purposes to be a person born out of wedlock of a U.S. citizen father, with a citizenship claim adjudicated under INA 309(a). This is the case regardless of whether the man is married and regardless of whether his spouse is the legal parent of the child at the time of birth." See Scott Bixby, "State Department to LGBT Couples: Your 'Out of Wedlock' Kids Aren't Citizens," *Daily Beast*, May 17, 2019, https://www.thedailybeast.com/state-department-to-lgbt-married-couples-your-out-of-wedlock-kids-arent-citizens; Tim Fitzsimons, "U.S. Appeals Ruling That Granted Gay Couple's Son Citizenship," NBC News, May 7, 2019, https://www.nbcnews.com/feature/nbc-out/u-s-appeals-ruling-granted-gay-couple-s-son-citizenship-n1002916.

93. Amanda Frost, "The Fragility of American Citizenship," *Atlantic*, October 9, 2019, https://www.theatlantic.com/ideas/archive/2019/10/fourteenth-amendment-protects-citizenship-politics/599554/.

94. US Department of Justice, Office of Public Affairs, "Justice Department Secures First Denaturalization as a Result of Operation Janus" (Washington, DC: Department of Justice, January 2018).

95. US Department of Justice, *Justice News*, February 26, 2020, https://www.justice.gov/opa/pr/department-justice-creates-section-dedicated-denaturalization-cases; Katie Benner, "Justice Department Establishes Office to Denaturalize Immigrants," *New York Times*, February 26, 2020, updated April 29, 2020,

https://www.nytimes.com/2020/02/26/us/politics/denaturalization-immi grants-justice-department.html.

96. Frost, "Fragility of American Citizenship."

97. Andrew C. McCarthy, "Can Trump End Birthright Citizenship by Executive Order?," *National Review*, October 30, 2018.

98. von Spakovsky, "Why Trump Can End Birthright Citizenship by Executive Order."

99. Garrett Epps, "The Citizenship Clause Means What It Says," *Atlantic*, October 30, 2018, https://www.theatlantic.com/ideas/archive/2018/10/birth right-citizenship-constitution/574381/.

100. Garrett Epps, "The Citizenship Clause: A 'Legislative History,'" *American University Law Review* 60, no. 2 (2010): 341.

101. Section 301 of the Immigration and Nationality Act of 1952 amends the Immigration and Nationality Act of 1940, substituting language of "physical presence" in the United States for language about residency. See https://fam .state.gov/FAM/08FAM/08FAM030107.html.

102. *Oforji v. Ashcroft*, 354 F. 3d 609, 620 (7th Cir. 2003), Posner, J. concurring.

103. *Oforji v. Ashcroft*, 354 F. 3d 609 at 621.

104. *Oforji v. Ashcroft*, 354 F. 3d 609 at 621.

105. Rachel E. Rosenbloom, "Policing the Borders of Birthright Citizenship: Some Thoughts on the New (and Old) Restrictionism," *Washburn Law Journal* 51, no. 2 (2012): 311–330.

106. Peter H. Schuck and Rogers M. Smith, *Citizenship without Consent: Illegal Aliens in the American Polity* (New Haven, CT: Yale University Press, 1985), 90 (quote), 96.

107. Schuck and Smith, "Question of Birthright Citizenship"; Schuck and Smith, *Citizenship without Consent*.

108. Schuck and Smith, "Question of Birthright Citizenship."

109. *Elk v. Wilkins*, 112 U.S. 94 (1884) at 103.

110. Schuck and Smith, "Question of Birthright Citizenship."

111. Schuck and Smith.

112. Dan Stein and John Bauer, "Interpreting the Fourteenth Amendment: Automatic Citizenship for Children of Illegal Immigrants?," *Stanford Law and Policy Review* 7 (1996): 127–130.

113. Stein and Bauer, 129.

114. Stein and Bauer, 129–130.

115. Stein and Bauer, 128.

116. See Lino A. Graglia, "Birthright Citizenship for Children of Illegal Immigrants: An Irrational Public Policy," *Texas Review of Law and Politics* 14 (2009): 10–11.

117. *Plyler v. Doe*, 457 U.S. 202 (1982) at 211n10; Graglia, "Birthright Citizenship for Children of Illegal Immigrants," 11.

118. Graglia, "Birthright Citizenship for Children of Illegal Immigrants," 11–12.

119. Edward J. Erler, "Trump's Critics Are Wrong about the 14th Amend-

ment and Birthright Citizenship," *National Review*, August 19, 2015, https://www.nationalreview.com/2015/08/birthright-citizenship-not-mandated-by-constitution/.

120. Erler.

121. *Texas v. Johnson*, 491 U.S. 397 (1989). When the federal Flag Protection Act was signed into law, the Supreme Court invalidated it as well in *United States v. Eichman*, 496 U.S. 310 (1990).

122. Jon Feere, "Flashback: Sen. Reid on Birthright Citizenship," Center for Immigration Studies, January 4, 2011, https://cis.org/Feere/Flashback-Sen-Reid-Birthright-Citizenship.

123. Feere.

124. Feere.

125. Michael Brice-Saddler, "Harry Reid Once Said 'No Sane Country' Would Allow Birthright Citizenship. He Regrets It Again," *Washington Post*, October 31, 2018, https://www.washingtonpost.com/politics/2018/10/31/harry-reid-once-said-no-sane-country-would-allow-birthright-citizenship-he-regrets-it-again/?utm_term=.1227b80eef4e.

126. Brice-Saddler.

127. Lucas Pleva, "Reid Bashes Republicans for a Position on Immigration That He Once Pushed," *Politifact*, August 25, 2010, https://www.politifact.com/factchecks/2010/aug/25/harry-reid/reid-bashes-republicans-position-immigration-he-on.

128. Pleva, citing the *Las Vegas Review-Journal* from December 13, 1999.

129. Members' forum on immigration: Hearing Before the Subcommittee on Immigration and Claims of the Committee on the Judiciary, House of Representatives, 104th Cong., 1st Sess., May 24, 1995. See also https://www.congress.gov/bill/104th-congress/house-bill/1363; https://www.congress.gov/bill/104th-congress/house-joint-resolution/93.

130. See Colvin, "Birthright Citizenship in the United States," 226.

131. US House of Representatives, Hearing before the Subcommittee on Immigration and Border Security of the House Judiciary Committee, Serial number 114-21: "Birthright Citizenship: Is It the Right Policy for America?," 114th Cong., 1st Sess., April 29, 2015, https://www.hsdl.org/?view&did=791855.

132. US Senate, S. 723, Birthright Citizenship Act of 2011, https://www.congress.gov/bill/112th-congress/senate-bill/723.

133. US House of Representatives, H.R. 140, Birthright Citizenship Act of 2019, https://www.congress.gov/bill/116th-congress/house-bill/140/text.

134. Congressman Steve King, Representing the Fourth District of Iowa, accessed July 25, 2019, https://steveking.house.gov/issues/immigration.

135. Patrick Murray, "What Americans Really Think of Birthright Citizenship," Monkey Cage, *Washington Post*, November 2, 2018, https://www.washingtonpost.com/news/monkey-cage/wp/2018/11/02/what-americans-really-think-about-birthright-citizenship/. The polls he reports are from 2015.

136. American Barometer, Harris X and Hill TV Poll, *The Hill*, November 9, 2018, https://thehill.com/hilltv/what-americas-thinking/415941-57-percent-say-a-child-born-to-parent-with-a-temporary-visa-in. See also Emily Elkins,

"What Americans Think about Birthright Citizenship," Cato Institute, November 14, 2018, https://www.cato.org/blog/what-americans-think-about-birth right-citizenship.

137. David Drucker, "Marco Rubio Sticks by Support for Birthright Citizenship," *Washington Monthly*, August 23, 2015, https://www.washingtonexaminer .com/marco-rubio-sticks-by-support-for-birthright-citizenship; for a video clip of his later remark, see https://www.theepochtimes.com/rubio-speaks-on-trumps -interpretation-of-birth-citizenship_2706496.html. See also Eric Bradner, "Jeb Bush Opposes Donald Trump on Birthright Citizenship," CNN, August 18, 2015, https://www.cnn.com/2015/08/18/politics/jeb-bush-donald-trump -birthright-citizenship-2016/index.html.

138. John Yoo, "Settled Law: Birthright Citizenship and the 14th Amendment," *American Mind*, updated March 18, 2019, https://americanmind.org /features/the-case-against-birthright-citizenship/settled-law-birthright-citizen ship-and-the-14th-amendment/?fbclid=IwAR1MdMMSdGgvXLEmJFRfox 1Lps4ASSo3eVzBqB1H1ETWgvo2dZPTNojLpo4.

139. Deanna Paul, "Trump Wants to End Birthright Citizenship. A Judge He Appointed Says He Can't," *Washington Post*, October 30, 2018.

140. John C. Eastman and Linda Chavez, "Birthright Citizenship: A Discussion," *Claremont Review of Books*, February 10, 2016, https://claremontreviewof books.com/digital/birthright-citizenship/.

141. See, for example, *Shelby County v. Holder*, 570 U.S. 529 (2013), on equal protection; *Boerne v. Flores*, 521 U.S. 507 (1997), on the application of the Religious Freedom Restoration Act to the states; the Fourteenth Amendment aspect of *U.S. v. Morrison*, 529 U.S. 598 (2000).

142. A provision of the law that was in effect at the time Morales-Santana was born, but that was subsequently changed to require of an unmarried citizen father only five years of residency in the United States, two of which were after age fourteen.

143. See Amy Howe, "Opinion Analysis: Court Rejects Gender-Based Distinctions in Citizenship Laws," *Scotusblog*, June 12, 2017, on *Sessions v. Morales-Santana*, 582 U.S. __ (2017). As a result of the decision, which invalidated a lower court opinion granting Morales-Santana (who had been a legal resident of the United States since 1975) citizenship, and in light of criminal convictions, a deportation order against Morales-Santana was likely to be carried out.

144. Ian Millhiser, "The Supreme Court Just Made Our Ugly, Messed-Up Immigration Law Even Uglier," *ThinkProgress*, June 12, 2017, https://think progress.org/scotus-immigration-gender-bf65cebccf9d/.

Bibliography

Primary Sources

CASES

Adamson v. California, 332 U.S. 46 (1947)
Balzac v. People of Porto Rico, 258 U.S. 298 (1922)
Blight's Lessee v. Rochester, 20 U.S. 535 (1822)
Boerne v. Flores, 521 U.S. 507 (1997)
Bradwell v. Illinois, 83 U.S. 130 (1873)
Calvin's Case, 7 Coke Report 377 (1608)
Chae Chan Ping v. United States, 130 U.S. 581 (1889)
Cherokee Nation v. Georgia, 30 U.S. 1 (1831)
Chew Heong v. United States, 112 U.S. 536 (1884)
Chy Lung v. Freeman, 92 U.S. 275 (1876)
Corfield v. Coryell, 6 Fed. Cas. 546 at 551 (C.C. E.D. Pa. 1823)
Downes v. Bidwell, 182 U.S. 244 (1901)
Dred Scott v. Sandford, 60 U.S. 393 (1857)
Elk v. Wilkins, 112 U.S. 94 (1884)
Ex parte Chin King, 35 F. 354 (C.C.D. Ore. 1888)
Ex parte Endo, 323 U.S. 283 (1944)
Fitisemanu v. United States, 426 F. Supp. 3d 1155 (D. Utah 2019)
Fong Yue Ting v. United States, 149 U.S. 698 (1893)
Gee Fook Sing v. United States, F. 49 146 (9th Cir. 1892)
Hirabayashi v. United States, 320 U.S. 81 (1943)
Inglis v. Trustees of Sailor's Snug Harbor, 28 U.S. 99 (1830)
In re Ah Fong, 1 F. Cas. 213 (D. Cal. 1874)
In re Ah Yup, 1 F. Cas. 223 (C.C.D. Cal. 1878)
In re Look Tin Sing, 21 F. 905 (C.C.D. Cal. 1884)
In re MacFarlane, 11 Haw. 166 (1897)
In re Moy Chee Kee, 33 F. 377 (C.C.N.D. Cal. 1887)
In re Ny Look, 56 F. 81 (C.C. S.D.N.Y. 1893)
In re Rodriguez, 81 F. 337 (W.D. Tex. 1897)
In re Wong Kim Ark, 71 F. 382 (N.D. Cal. 1896)
In re Wy Shing, 36 F. 553 (C.C.N.D. Cal. 1888)
In re Yung Sing Hee, 38 F. 437 (C.C.D. Ore. 1888)
Korematsu v. United States, 323 U.S. 214 (1944)
Lem Moon Sing v. United States, 158 U.S. 538 (1895)
Lynch v. Clarke & Lynch, 3 N.Y. Leg. Obs. 236 (1844)

Matter of Heff, 197 U.S. 488 (1905)
McIlvaine v. Coxe's Lessee, 8 U.S. 209 (1808)
Minor v. Happersett, 88 U.S. 162 (1875)
Morrison v. California, 291 U.S. 82 (1934)
Murray v. The Charming Betsey, 6 U.S. (2 Cranch) 64 (1804)
Oforji v. Ashcroft, 354 F.3d 609 (7th Cir. 2003)
Ozawa v. United States, 260 U.S. 178 (1922)
Perkins v. Elg, 307 U.S. 325 (1939)
Plessy v. Ferguson, 163 U.S. 537 (1896)
Plyler v. Doe, 457 U.S. 202 (1982)
Regan v. King, 49 F. Supp. 222 (N.D. Cal. 1942)
Regan v. King, 134 F.2d 413 (9th Cir. 1943)
Santa Clara Pueblo v. Martinez, 436 U.S. 49 (1978)
Sessions v. Morales-Santana, 582 U.S. __ (2017)
Shelby County v. Holder, 570 U.S. 529 (2013)
Slaughter-House Cases, 83 U.S. 36 (1873)
State v. Ah Chew, 16 Nev. 50 (1881)
Texas v. Johnson, 491 U.S. 397 (1989)
Toyota v. United States, 268 U.S. 402 (1925)
United States v. Bhagat Singh Thind, 261 U.S. 204 (1923)
United States v. Eichman, 496 U.S. 310 (1990)
United States v. Morrison, 529 U.S. 598 (2000)
United States v. Nice, 241 U.S. 591 (1916)
United States v. Wong Kim Ark, 169 U.S. 649 (1898)
Winton v. Amos, 255 U.S. 373 (1921)
Wong Wing v. United States, 163 U.S. 228 (1896)
Yick Wo v. Hopkins, 118 U.S. 356 (1886)

BRIEFS

Ashton, J. Hubley. "Brief for the Appellee on Reargument: *United States v. Wong Kim Ark*." In *Landmark Briefs and Arguments of the Supreme Court of the United States*, vol. 14, edited by Philip Kurland and Gerhard Casper, 171–274. Arlington, VA: University Publications of America, 1975.
———. "Note in Answer." In *Landmark Briefs and Arguments of the Supreme Court of the United States*, vol. 14, edited by Philip Kurland and Gerhard Casper, 301–304. Arlington, VA: University Publications of America, 1975.
Conrad, Holmes. "Brief for the United States: *United States v. Wong Kim Ark*." In *Landmark Briefs and Arguments of the Supreme Court of the United States*, vol. 14, edited by Philip Kurland and Gerhard Casper, 51–102. Arlington, VA: University Publications of America, 1975.
———. "Reply Brief for the United States: *United States v. Wong Kim Ark*." In *Landmark Briefs and Arguments of the Supreme Court of the United States*, vol. 14, edited by Philip Kurland and Gerhard Casper, 275–300. Arlington, VA: University Publications of America, 1975.

Conrad, Holmes, and George Collins. "Brief on the Behalf of the Appellant: *United States v. Wong Kim Ark.*" In *Landmark Briefs and Arguments of the Supreme Court of the United States*, vol. 14, edited by Philip Kurland and Gerhard Casper, 3–42. Arlington, VA: University Publications of America, 1975.

Evarts, Maxwell. "Brief for the Appellee on Reargument: *United States v. Wong Kim Ark.*" In *Landmark Briefs and Arguments of the Supreme Court of the United States*, vol. 14, edited by Philip Kurland and Gerhard Casper, 103–170. Arlington, VA: University Publications of America, 1975.

Riordan, Thomas. "Brief for Respondent: *United States v. Wong Kim Ark.*" In *Landmark Briefs and Arguments of the Supreme Court of the United States*, vol. 14, edited by Philip Kurland and Gerhard Casper, 43–50. Arlington, VA: University Publications of America, 1975.

STATUTES, TREATIES, AND OTHER LEGAL DOCUMENTS

An Act to Establish a Bureau of Immigration and Naturalization and to Provide for a Uniform Rule for the Naturalization of Aliens throughout the United States. 59th Cong., 1st Sess., Ch. 3592, 1906. https://www.loc.gov/law/help/statutes-at-large/59th-congress/session-1/c59s1ch3592.pdf.

Act to Establish a Uniform Rule of Naturalization. March 26, 1790. 1 Stat. 103.

Angell Treaty of 1880. 22 Stat. 826. Treaty Series 49. Entered into force July 19, 1881. https://www.loc.gov/law/help/us-treaties/bevans/b-cn-ustoooo 06-0685.pdf.

Burlingame Treaty of 1868. 16 Stat. 739. Treaty Series 48. Entered into force November 23, 1869. https://www.loc.gov/law/help/us-treaties/bevans/b-cn -ustoooo06-0680.pdf.

California Constitution of 1879. Original. https://www.cpp.edu/~jlkorey/cal con1879.pdf.

Chinese Exclusion Act of 1882. US Statutes at Large 22 (1882).

Chinese Exclusion Act of 1884. US Statutes at Large 23 (1884).

Civil Rights Act of 1866. 14 Stat. 27, 39th Cong., 1st Sess., Ch. 31, April 9, 1866.

Code of Federal Regulations. Title 8, Ch. 1, Subchapter B, Part 101.3. https://www.ecfr.gov/cgi-bin/text-idx?node=se8.1.101_13.

Geary Act of 1892. http://www.sanfranciscochinatown.com/history/1892geary act.html.

Gentlemen's Agreement of 1907. http://encyclopedia.densho.org/Gentlemen %27s_Agreement/.

Hawaiian Organic Act, Persons Born in Hawaii. 8 U.S. Code § 1405. https:// www.law.cornell.edu/uscode/text/8/1405.

Immigration Act of February 5, 1917. 39 Stat. 874. https://www.loc.gov/law /help/statutes-at-large/64th-congress/session-2/c64s2ch29.pdf.

Immigration and Nationality Act of 1952. 66 Stat. 163. https://encyclopedia .densho.org/Immigration_Act_of_1952/.

Indian Citizenship Act of 1924. 8 U.S.C. Section 140. http://d1vmz9r13e2j4x .cloudfront.net/nebstudies/0707_0801citizen.pdf.

Judiciary Act of 1891. 26 Stat. 826, 51st Cong., 2nd Sess., Ch. 517, March 3, 1891. https://www.loc.gov/law/help/statutes-at-large/51st-congress/session-2/c51s2ch517.pdf.

Nationality Act of 1940. 54 Stat. 1137, 76th Cong., 3d Sess., Ch. 876, Title II, Sec. 201 (1940).

Naturalization Act of 1795. 1 Stat. 414, Ch. XX, January 29, 1795.

Naturalization Act of 1870. Sec. 2169 U.S. Revised Statutes (16 Stat. 254), July 14, 1870.

Oregon Constitution of 1857 (effective 1859). Transcribed. Article XV §8. https://sos.oregon.gov/archives/exhibits/constitution/Documents/transcribed-1857-oregon-constitution.pdf.

Reforming American Immigration for Strong Employment Act (RAISE). 115th Cong. (2017–2018). https://www.congress.gov/bill/115th-congress/senate-bill/354.

Scott Act of 1888. https://immigrationhistory.org/item/scott-act/.

Treaty of Peace between the United States and Spain, December 10, 1898, Article IX. https://avalon.law.yale.edu/19th_century/sp1898.asp.

US Department of Homeland Security, US Citizenship and Immigration Services. Policy Manual, Ch. 3. Accessed June 25, 2019. https://www.uscis.gov/policy-manual/volume-7-part-o-chapter-3.

US Department of Homeland Security Rule, Inadmissibility on Public Charge Grounds. *Federal Register* 41292, August 14, 2019. https://www.federalregister.gov/documents/2019/08/14/2019-17142/inadmissibility-on-public-charge-grounds.

US Department of State. Foreign Affairs Manual, 8 FAM 301.4–1(D), Acquisition by Birth Abroad to U.S. Citizen Parent(s) and Evolution of Key Statutes (11–07–2018). https://fam.state.gov/FAM/08FAM/08FAM030104.html#M301_4_1_D_1.

US Department of State, Bureau of Consular Affairs. Family Immigration. https://travel.state.gov/content/travel/en/us-visas/immigrate/family-immigration/family-based-immigrant-visas.html.

US Department of State, Bureau of Consular Affairs. Visa Bulletin for August 2019. https://travel.state.gov/content/travel/en/legal/visa-lawo/visa-bulletin/2019/visa-bulletin-for-august-2019.html.

US House of Representatives. Hearing before the Subcommittee on Immigration and Border Security of the House Judiciary Committee. Serial number 114–21: "Birthright Citizenship: Is It the Right Policy for America?" 114th Cong., 1st Sess. April 29, 2015. https://www.hsdl.org/?view&did=791855.

———. H.R. 140, Birthright Citizenship Act of 2019. https://www.congress.gov/bill/116th-congress/house-bill/140/text.

Wong Kim Ark. "Application of Alleged American Citizen of the Chinese Race for Preinvestigation of Status." 1931. National Archives and Records Division, San Francisco, California. https://catalog.archives.gov/OpaAPI/media/18556183/content/san-francisco/gallery/12017_42223-010.pdf.

———. "Application of Alleged U.S. Citizen for Reentry into the United States." 1913, 1931. National Archives and Records Division, San Francisco, Califor-

nia. https://catalog.archives.gov/OpaAPI/media/18556183/content/san
-francisco/gallery/12017_42223–010.pdf.

———. In testimony for the admission of his third son on March 20, 1925.
https://commons.wikipedia.org/wiki/File:Wong_Kim_Ark_testimony_at
_Wong_Yook_Thue_hearing_1925_page_1.png.

———. Testimony for the admission of his fourth son, Wong Yook Jim, July
23, 1926. https://commons.wikimedia.org/wiki/File:Wong_Kim_Ark
_testimony_at_Wong_Yook_Jim_hearing_1926_page_1.png.

———. Testimony on behalf of his eldest son on December 6, 1910. National
Archives and Records Division, San Bruno, California. https://commons
.wikipedia.org/wiki/File:Wong_Kim_Ark_testimony_at_Wong_Yoke_Fun
_hearing_1910_page_1.png.

NEWSPAPERS, CONTEMPORARY COMMENTARY,
AND OTHER ARCHIVAL SOURCES

"All Asiatics Affected." *San Francisco Call*, November 13, 1895, 9.
Associated Press. "Ny Look: An Aged Celestial Applies for a Certificate in New
York." *Los Angeles Times*, May 25, 1893, 1.
"Attorney Collins' Part." *San Francisco Call*, November 14, 1895, 11.
Bayard, Thomas. "Mr. Bayard to Mr. Winchester." In Martin B. Gold, *Forbidden
Citizens: Chinese Exclusion and the U.S. Congress: A Legislative History*, 238–239.
Washington, DC: Capitol Net, 2011.
"Caminetti Angry and Disappointed." *San Francisco Call*, February 16, 1895, 2.
"China: The Bubonic Plague in Canton." *Public Health Reports* (1896–1970) 11,
no. 25 (June 19, 1896): 567.
"Chinese as Citizens." *San Francisco Call*, January 4, 1896, 5. https://img2.news
papers.com/clip/22263739/1896_look_tin_sing/.
"Chinese Born Here Are Citizens." *New York Times*, March 29, 1898.
"Chinese Who Are Citizens: Mongols Born in This Country Have All the Privi-
leges of Natives." *San Francisco Examiner*, March 29, 1898, 16.
"Citizenship of Chinese." *Vermont Sun* (Saint Albans, VT), April 22, 1898, 2.
"Citizen Wong Kim Ark." *Los Angeles Herald*, July 24, 1898, 17.
"Comment." *Yale Law Journal* 7 (1898): 365–368.
Constitution of the Immigrant Restriction League. 1894. https://iiif.lib.harvard
.edu/manifests/view/drs:5233215$1i.
Cooley, Thomas. *The General Principles of Constitutional Law in the United States.*
New York: Little, Brown, 1898.
Dewey, V. F. "Editorial Notes." *Hanford Semi-Weekly Journal* (Hanford, CA), Oc-
tober 15, 1895, 4.
Editors. "The Question of Citizenship of American-Born Chinese Sweeping."
San Francisco Call, November 13, 1895.
Francis Valentine and Co., Locate Organizations and Businesses in San Fran-
cisco, 1861–1923 (except 1866, 1870, 1872, 1906). Fold3.com by Ances-
try.

Guthrie, William. *Lectures on the Fourteenth Article of Amendment to the Constitution of the United States.* Minneapolis: University of Minnesota Press, 1898.

"An Important Decision." *New York Sun,* March 29, 1898, 9.

Johnson, Andrew. "Message to the Senate." *Journal of the Senate of the United States of America, 1789–1873,* June 22, 1866. Online by Gerhard Peters and John T. Woolley, The American Presidency Project. https://www.presidency.ucsb .edu/node/202310.

"John Will Stay Yet Awhile." *San Francisco Call,* September 12, 1893, 2.

"Judge Lacombe's Opinion." *Washington Post,* May 26, 1893, 1.

Kent, Chancellor James. *Commentaries on American Law.* Vol. 2. New York: Chancellor James Kent, 1836.

Langley's San Francisco Directory for the Year Commencing 1880. D. M. Bishop & Co. http://www.ebooksread.com/authors-eng/dm-bishop–co /langleys-san-francisco-directory-for-the-year-commencing–volume-1880 -fna/page-281-langleys-san-francisco-directory-for-the-year-commencing –volume-1880-fna.shtml.

Lazarus, Emma. "The New Colossus." *Statue of Liberty,* 1883.

"No Means for Deportation: Judge Lacombe Reiterates His Views in the Ny Look Case." *New York Times,* May 27, 1893, 12.

"The 'Ny Look' Case." *Washington Post,* May 28, 1893, 4.

"Ny Look Ordered Deported, at the Same Time Set at Liberty by Judge Lacombe." *New York Times,* May 25, 1893, 1.

"Paper Sons." Virtual Museum of the City of San Francisco. http://www.sf museum.org/hist11/papersons.html.

"The Plague in China," *Evening Bulletin* (Maysville, KY), June 19, 1894, 1.

Puerto Rico: Citizenship Archives Project, University of Connecticut. http:// scholarscollaborative.org/PuertoRico/exhibits/show/historical/individual.

Report of the Royal Commission on Aboriginal Peoples, vol. 1, "Looking Forward, Looking Back." 1996. http://data2.archives.ca/e/e448/e011188230-01.pdf.

"Serious Charge: Lawyer Riordan Accused of Bribery." *San Francisco Call,* November 9, 1894, 5.

"Social and Personal." *Sacramento Record-Union* (Sacramento, CA), June 26, 1889, 2.

Story, Joseph. *Commentaries on the Conflict of Laws.* Boston: Hilliard, Gray, and Company, 1834.

"Thomas D. Riordan Is Dead from Heart Failure." *San Francisco Call,* June 18, 1905.

Trump, Donald J. Interview with Jonathan Swan. *Axios on HBO,* October 30, 2018.

———. State of the Union Address. January 30, 2018. https://www.whitehouse .gov/briefings-statements/president-donald-j-trumps-state-union-address/.

"20,000 New Voters." *Topeka State Journal,* June 29, 1898. https://newscomwc .newspapers.com/image/323082932/?terms=wong%2Bkim%2 Bark&pqsid=IcnGqi8ZNDaCgSSFz1IjSA:145000:1561812162.

"Two Attorneys Disbarred Following the Expose of Chinese Smuggling Ring." *Sacramento Bee,* August 22, 1917, p. 10. Newspapers.com.

US Central Intelligence Agency. *The World Factbook 2020*. Washington, DC: Central Intelligence Agency, 2020. https://www.cia.gov/library/publications/the-world-factbook/fields/310.html.

US Congress, Joint Special Committee to Investigate Chinese Immigration. "Report of the Joint Special Committee to Investigate Chinese Immigration." February 27, 1877. Washington, DC: Government Printing Office, 1877.

US Department of Homeland Security, US Citizenship and Immigration Services. About Us. Accessed October 30, 2019. https://www.uscis.gov/about-us.

US Department of Justice. *Justice News*, February 26, 2020.

US Department of Justice, Office of Public Affairs. "Justice Department Secures First Denaturalization as a Result of Operation Janus." Washington, DC: Department of Justice, January 2018.

"Waiting for a Decision: Text of the Order Suspending the Geary Act." *Los Angeles Times*, May 5, 1893, 1. From Attorney General Olney to United States Attorney, May 4, 1893. In *The Executive Documents of the House of Representatives for the First Session of the Fifty-Third Congress/In One Volume/1893*. Washington, DC: Government Printing Office, 1893.

"Westerners Unite to Curb Japanese." *New York Times*, April 21, 1921. https://timesmachine.nytimes.com/timesmachine/1921/04/21/107014075.html?pageNumber=15.

Wong, Sandra (great granddaughter of Wong Kim Ark). Interviewed by Robert Siegel, NPR, October 2, 2015. https://www.npr.org/2015/10/02/445346769/he-famously-fought-for-his-u-s-citizenship-where-are-his-descendants-now.

Woodworth, Marshall. "Who Are Citizens of the United States?—Wong Kim Ark Case—Interpretation of the Fourteenth Amendment." *American Law Review* 32 (1898): 554–563.

Secondary Sources

Abrams, Kerry, "Polygamy, Prostitution, and the Federalization of Immigration Law." *Columbia Law Review* 105, no. 3 (2005): 641–716.

Alfred, Charlotte, Elise Foley, and Roque Planas. "These Countries Show Why Losing Birthright Citizenship Could Be a Disaster." *Huffington Post*, August 27, 2015. https://www.huffpost.com/entry/birthright-citizenship-other-countries_n_55df2a82e4b08dc0948699f3.

American Barometer. Harris X and Hill TV Poll. *The Hill*, November 9, 2018. https://thehill.com/hilltv/what-americas-thinking/415941-57-percent-say-a-child-born-to-parent-with-a-temporary-visa-in.

Anderson, David. "The Diplomacy of Discrimination: Chinese Exclusion, 1876–1882." *California History* 57, no. 1 (1978): 32.

Anton, Michael. "Citizenship Shouldn't Be a Birthright." *Washington Post*, July 19, 2018, A19.

Appell, Annette R. "Certifying Identity." *Capital University Law Review* 42 (2014): 361–405.

Atwood, Kylie, Geneva Sands, and Jennifer Hansler. "US Issues New Rules Restricting Travel by Pregnant Foreigners, Fearing the Use of 'Birth Tourism.'" CNN, January 24, 2020. https://edition.cnn.com/2020/01/23/politics/us-new-rules-restricting-travel-fearing-birth-tourism/index.html.

Baik, Tae-Ung, and Duk Hee Lee Murabayashi. "The Historical Development of Early Korean Immigration to Hawaii and Its Legal Structure." *Journal of Korean Law* 11 (December 2011): 77–99.

Barde, Robert. "An Alleged Wife: One Immigrant in the Chinese Exclusion Era." *Prologue* 36, no. 1 (2004). http://www.archives.gov/publications/prologue/2004/spring/alleged-wife-1.html.

Barnett, Randy E. *Restoring the Lost Constitution.* Updated edition. Princeton, NJ: Princeton University Press, 2013.

Barnett, Randy E., and Evan D. Bernick. "The Privileges or Immunities Clause Abridged: A Critique of Kurt Lash on the Fourteenth Amendment." *Notre Dame Law Review* 95, no. 2 (2020): 499–589.

Basson, Lauren L. "Fit for Annexation but Unfit to Vote? Debating Hawaiian Suffrage Qualifications at the Turn of the Twentieth Century." *Social Science History* 29, no. 4 (2005): 575–598.

Benedict, Carol Ann. *Bubonic Plague in Nineteenth-Century China.* Palo Alto, CA: Stanford University Press, 1996.

———. "Bubonic Plague in Nineteenth-Century China: The Third Pandemic of Bubonic Plague." *Modern China* 14, no. 2 (1988): 107–155.

Benner, Katie. "Justice Department Establishes Office to Denaturalize Immigrants." *New York Times*, February 26, 2020, updated April 29, 2020. https://www.nytimes.com/2020/02/26/us/politics/denaturalization-immigrants-justice-department.html.

Berger, Bethany. "Birthright Citizenship on Trial: *Elk v. Wilkins* and *United States v. Wong Kim Ark.*" *Cardozo Law Review* 37 (2016): 1185–1258.

Bixby, Scott. "State Department to LGBT Couples: Your 'Out of Wedlock' Kids Aren't Citizens." *Daily Beast*, May 17, 2019. https://www.thedailybeast.com/state-department-to-lgbt-married-couples-your-out-of-wedlock-kids-arent-citizens.

Blakemore, Erin. "The History of Birth Certificates Is Shorter Than You Might Think." History.com, last updated August 22, 2018. https://www.history.com/news/the-history-of-birth-certificates-is-shorter-than-you-might-think.

Bomboy, Scott. "The 14th Amendment's Tortuous Relationship with American Indians." *Constitution Daily* (blog), National Constitution Center, March 12, 2014. https://constitutioncenter.org/blog/the-14th-amendments-tortuous-relationship-with-american-indians1.

———. "What Do Other Countries' Constitutions Say about Birthright Citizenship?" National Constitution Center. Accessed June 11, 2019. https://constitutioncenter.org/blog/what-do-other-countries-constitutions-say-about-birthright-citizenship/.

Bradner, Eric. "Jeb Bush Opposes Donald Trump on Birthright Citizenship." CNN, August 18, 2015. https://www.cnn.com/2015/08/18/politics/jeb -bush-donald-trump-birthright-citizenship-2016/index.html.

Brandwein, Pamela. *Rethinking the Judicial Settlement of Reconstruction.* New York: Cambridge University Press, 2011.

Bredbenner, Candice Lewis. *A Nationality of Her Own: Women, Marriage and the Law of Citizenship.* Berkeley: University of California Press, 1998.

Brice-Saddler, Michael. "Harry Reid Once Said 'No Sane Country' Would Allow Birthright Citizenship. He Regrets It Again." *Washington Post,* October 31, 2018. https://www.washingtonpost.com/politics/2018/10/31/harry-reid -once-said-no-sane-country-would-allow-birthright-citizenship-he-regrets-it -again/?utm_term=.1227b80eef4e.

Brumberg, H. L., D. Dozor, and S. G. Golombek. "History of the Birth Certificate: From Inception to the Future of Electronic Data." *Journal of Perinatology* 32 (2012): 407–411.

Bruyneel, Kevin. *Third Space of Sovereignty: The Postcolonial Politics of U.S.-Indigenous Relations.* Minneapolis: University of Minnesota Press, 2007.

Burnett [Ponsa], Christina Duffy. "Untied States: American Expansion and Territorial Deannexation." *University of Chicago Law Review* 72 (Summer 2005): 797–880.

Cabranes, José A. "Citizenship and the American Empire: Notes on the Legislative History of the United States Citizenship of Puerto Ricans." *University of Pennsylvania Law Review* 127, no. 2 (1978): 391–492.

Calavita, Kitty. "Collisions at the Intersection of Gender, Race, and Class: Enforcing the Chinese Exclusion Laws," *Law and Society Review* 40, no. 2 (2006): 249–282.

———. "The Paradoxes of Race, Class, Identity, and 'Passing': Enforcing the Chinese Exclusion Acts, 1882–1910." *Law and Social Inquiry* 25, no. 1 (2000): 1–40.

Camarota, Steven A. "There Are Possibly 36,000 Birth Tourists Annually." Center for Immigration Studies. April 28, 2015. https://cis.org/Camarota /There-Are-Possibly-36000-Birth-Tourists-Annually.

Cardinal, Harold. *The Unjust Society.* 2nd ed. Vancouver: Douglas & McIntyre, 1999.

Carson, Scott Alan. "Chinese Sojourn Labor and the American Transcontinental Railroad." *Journal of Institutional and Theoretical Economics* 161, no. 1 (2005): 80–102.

Cavanagh, Edward, and Lorenzo Veracini, eds. *Routledge Handbook of the History of Settler Colonialism.* Abingdon: Routledge, 2017.

Chan, Pamela. "The History and Stereotypes behind the Term 'Anchor Babies.'" Generation Progress, September 17, 2015. https://genprogress.org /the-history-and-stereotypes-behind-the-term-anchor-babies/.

Chan, Sucheng. "The Exclusion of Chinese Women, 1870–1943." In *Entry Denied: Exclusion and the Chinese Community in America, 1882–1943,* edited by Sucheng Chan, 91–146. Philadelphia: Temple University Press, 1991.

Chen, Yong. "The Internal Origins of Chinese Emigration to California Reconsidered." *Western Historical Quarterly* 28 (1997): 520–546.

Chesterman, John, and Brian Galligan. *Citizens without Rights: Aborigines and Australian Citizenship.* Cambridge: Cambridge University Press, 1997.

Chin, Gabriel J. "*Chae Chan Ping* and *Fong Yue Ting*: The Origins of Plenary Power." In *Immigration Stories,* edited by David Martin and Peter Schuck, 7–30. New York: Foundation Press, 2005.

———. "'A Chinaman's Chance' in Court: Asian Pacific Americans and Racial Rules of Evidence." *University of California Irvine Law Review* 3 (2013): 965–990.

———. "The First Justice Harlan by the Numbers: Just How Great Was 'The Great Dissenter'?" *Akron Law Review* 32, no. 3 (1999): 629–655.

———. "The Plessy Myth: Justice Harlan and the Chinese Cases." *Iowa Law Review* 82 (October 1996): 151–182.

Chishti, Muzaffar, Doris Meissner, and Claire Bergeron. "At Its 25th Anniversary, IRCA's Legacy Lives On." Migration Policy Institute, November 16, 2011. https://www.migrationpolicy.org/article/its-25th-anniversary-ircas -legacy-lives.

Choate, Joseph Hodges. https://law.jrank.org/pages/5208/Choate-Joseph -Hodges.html.

Chutung, Tsai. "The Chinese Nationality Law, 1909." *American Journal of International Law* 4, no. 2 (1910): 404–411.

Coerver, Don M., Suzanne B. Pasztor, and Robert M. Buffington. *Mexico: An Encyclopedia of Contemporary Culture and History.* Santa Barbara, CA: ABC-CLIO, 2004.

Cohen, Elizabeth F. *Semi-citizenship in Democratic Politics.* New York: Cambridge University Press, 2010.

Cole, Devan, and Caroline Kelly. "Cuccinelli Rewrites Statue of Liberty Poem to Make Case for Limiting Immigration." *CNN Politics,* August 13, 2019. https://www.cnn.com/2019/08/13/politics/ken-cuccinelli-statue-of -liberty/index.html.

Cole, Richard, and Gabriel Chin. "Emerging from the Margins of Historical Consciousness: Chinese Immigrants and the History of American Law." *Law and History Review* 17, no. 2 (1999): 325–364.

Colvin, Amanda. "Birthright Citizenship in the United States: Realities of De Facto Deportation and International Comparisons toward Proposing a Solution." *St. Louis University Law Journal* 53, no. 1 (2008): 219–246.

Cott, Nancy F. "Marriage and Women's Citizenship in the United States 1830–1934." *American Historical Review* 103 (December 1998): 1440–1474.

Davidson, Alastair. *From Subject to Citizen: Australian Citizenship in the Twentieth Century.* Cambridge: Cambridge University Press, 1997.

Davis, Elbridge, and Harold Davis. "Mr. Justice Horace Gray: Some Aspects of His Judicial Career." *American Bar Association Journal* 41 (1955): 421–424, 468–471.

Dougherty, Phil. "Mobs Forcibly Expel Most of Seattle's Chinese Residents beginning on February 7, 1886." HistoryLink.org. November 17, 2013. Accessed September 24, 2019. https://www.historylink.org/File/2745.

Dowd, Katie. "140 Years Ago, San Francisco Was Set Ablaze during the City's Deadliest Race Riot." SFGate, July 23, 2017. https://www.sfgate.com/bay area/article/1877-san-francisco-anti-chinese-race-riots-11302710.php.

Drucker, David. "Marco Rubio Sticks by Support for Birthright Citizenship." *Washington Monthly*, August 23, 2015. https://www.washingtonexaminer.com/marco-rubio-sticks-by-support-for-birthright-citizenship.

Eastman, John. "Birthright Citizenship Is Not Actually in the Constitution." *New York Times*, December 22, 2015. https://www.nytimes.com/roomfor debate/2015/08/24/should-birthright-citizenship-be-abolished/birth right-citizenship-is-not-actually-in-the-constitution.

Eastman, John C., and Linda Chavez, "Birthright Citizenship: A Discussion." *Claremont Review of Books*, February 10, 2016. https://claremontreviewof books.com/digital/birthright-citizenship/.

Elkins, Emily. "What Americans Think about Birthright Citizenship." Cato Institute, November 14, 2018. https://www.cato.org/blog/what-americans -think-about-birthright-citizenship.

Ellis, Mark R. "Denver's Anti-Chinese Riot." In *Encyclopedia of the Great Plains*. http://plainshumanities.unl.edu/encyclopedia/doc/egp.asam.011.

Epps, Garrett. "The Citizenship Clause: A 'Legislative History.'" *American University Law Review* 60, no. 2 (2010): 331–388.

———. "The Citizenship Clause Means What It Says." *Atlantic*, October 30, 2018; https://www.theatlantic.com/ideas/archive/2018/10/birthright -citizenship-constitution/574381/.

———. *Democracy Reborn: The Fourteenth Amendment and the Fight for Equal Rights in Post–Civil War America.* New York: Henry Holt, 2006.

———. "The Ghost of Chae Chan Ping." *Atlantic*, January 20, 2018. https://www .theatlantic.com/politics/archive/2018/01/ghost-haunting-immigration /551015/.

———. "Interpreting the Fourteenth Amendment: Two Don'ts and Three Dos." *William and Mary Bill of Rights Journal* 16, no. 2 (2007): 433–463.

Erler, Edward J. "Trump's Critics Are Wrong about the 14th Amendment and Birthright Citizenship." *National Review*, August 19, 2015. https://www .nationalreview.com/2015/08/birthright-citizenship-not-mandated-by -constitution/.

Erman, Sam. *Almost Citizens: Puerto Rico, the U.S. Constitution, and Empire.* Cambridge: Cambridge University Press, 2019.

Ernst, Daniel R. *Tocqueville's Nightmare: The Administrative State Emerges in America, 1900–1940.* Oxford: Oxford University Press, 2014.

Evarts, Maxwell. https://www.findagrave.com/memorial/156668790/maxwell -evarts.

Fang, Yuming. "Inside the World of Birth Tourism—Featured Stories." *Medium*, December 9, 2018. https://medium.com/s/story/inside-the-world-of -birth-tourism-4d6e382346b0.

Feere, Jon. "Flashback: Sen. Reid on Birthright Citizenship." Center for Immigration Studies. January 4, 2011. https://cis.org/Feere/Flashback-Sen -Reid-Birthright-Citizenship.

Fitzsimons, Tim. "U.S. Appeals Ruling That Granted Gay Couple's Son Citizenship." NBC News, May 7, 2019. https://www.nbcnews.com/feature /nbc-out/u-s-appeals-ruling-granted-gay-couple-s-son-citizenship -n1002916.

Folse, Brandon J. "Aspirational Migration: The Case of Chinese Birth Tourism in the U.S." Master's thesis, University of Oregon, 2017. https://scholars bank.uoregon.edu/xmlui/handle/1794/22749.

Frederick, David C. *Rugged Justice: The Ninth Circuit Court of Appeals and the American West, 1891–1941*. Berkeley: University of California Press, 1994.

Fritz, Christian. "A Nineteenth Century 'Habeas Corpus Mill': The Chinese before the Federal Courts of California." *Journal of American History* 32, no. 4 (1988): 347–372.

Frost, Amanda. "The Fragility of American Citizenship." *Atlantic*, October 9, 2019. https://www.theatlantic.com/ideas/archive/2019/10/fourteenth -amendment-protects-citizenship-politics/599554/.

Gelatt, Julia. "Dramatic Change to Family Immigration, Less So for the Employment-Based System." Migration Policy Institute, Commentaries, August, 2017. https://www.migrationpolicy.org/news/raise-act-dramatic -change-family-immigration-less-so-employment-based-system.

Giaimo, Cara. "The Little-Known Passport That Protected 450,000 Refugees." Atlas Obscura, February 7, 2017. https://www.atlasobscura.com/articles /nansen-passport-refugees.

Gill, Manpreet K. "Irish Government Opposes Restoring Right to Birthright Citizenship, Despite Popular Support." *Jackson Lewis Immigration Blog*, November 30, 2018. https://www.globalimmigrationblog.com/2018/11 /irish-government-opposes-restoring-right-to-birthright-citizenship-despite -popular-support/.

Glenn, Evelyn Nakano. "Settler Colonialism as Structure: A Framework for Comparative Studies of U.S. Race and Gender Formation." *Sociology of Race and Ethnicity* 1, no. 1 (2015): 54–74.

Gonzales, Richard. "America No Longer a 'Nation of Immigrants,' USCIS Says." NPR, February 22, 2018. https://www.npr.org/sections/thetwo-way /2018/02/22/588097749/america-no-longer-a-nation-of-immigrants-us cis-says.

Graber, Mark. *Dred Scott and the Problem of Constitutional Evil.* New York: Cambridge University Press, 2006.

Graglia, Lino A. "Birthright Citizenship for Children of Illegal Immigrants: An Irrational Public Policy." *Texas Review of Law and Politics* 14 (2009): 1–14.

Gratton, Brian, and Emily Merchant, "Immigration, Repatriation, and Deportation: The Mexican-Origin Population in the United States, 1920–1950." *International Migration Review* 47, no. 4 (2013): 944–975.

Gray, Horace, and John Lowell. *A Legal Review of the Case of Dred Scott: As Decided the Supreme Court of the United States.* Boston: Crosby, Nichols, and Co., 1857.

Gross, Daniel A. "The U.S. Government Turned Away Thousands of Jewish Refugees, Fearing That They Were Nazi Spies." *Smithsonian Magazine*, November 18, 2015. https://www.smithsonianmag.com/history/us-government

-turned-away-thousands-jewish-refugees-fearing-they-were-nazi-spies
-180957324/.

Hartwell, Alfred S. "The Organization of a Territorial Government for Hawaii."
Yale Law Journal 9, no. 3 (1899): 107–113.

"Hawaii." https://history.house.gov/Exhibitions-and-Publications/APA/His
torical-Essays/Exclusion-and-Empire/Hawaii/.

Hernández, Kelly Lytle. *City of Inmates.* Chapel Hill: University of North Carolina Press, 2017.

Hester, Torrie. *Deportation: The Origins of U.S. Policy.* Philadelphia: University of
Pennsylvania Press, 2017.

———. "'Protection, Not Punishment': Legislative and Judicial Formation of
U.S. Deportation Policy." *Journal of American Ethnic History* 30, no. 1 (2010):
11–36.

Hixson, Walter L. *American Settler Colonialism: A History.* New York: Palgrave Macmillan, 2013.

Hochschild, Adam. "When America Tried to Deport Its Radicals." *New Yorker,*
November 11, 2019. https://www.newyorker.com/magazine/2019/11/11
/when-america-tried-to-deport-its-radicals.

Hoffman, Abraham. *Unwanted Mexican Americans in the Great Depression: Repatriation Pressures 1929–1939.* Tucson: University of Arizona Press, 1974.

Honohan, Iseult. "The Theory and Politics of Ius Soli." EUDO Citizenship
Observatory. June 2010. http://cadmus.eui.eu/bitstream/handle/1814
/19574/Honohan_IusSoli_2010.pdf?sequence=1&isAllowed=y.

Horowitz, Daniel. "Fixing the Birthright Citizenship Loophole: Myth vs. Fact."
Conservative Review, August 18, 2015. https://www.conservativereview.com
/news/fixing-the-birthright-citizenship-loophole-myth-vs-fact/.

Howe, Amy. "Opinion Analysis: Court Rejects Gender-Based Distinctions in Citizenship Laws" (on *Sessions v. Morales Santana*). *Scotusblog,* June 12, 2017.

Hsu, Madeline Y. "Gold Mountain Dreams and Paper Son Schemes: Chinese
Immigration under Exclusion." In *Chinese America: History and Perspectives,*
11, pp. 46–60. San Francisco: Chinese Historical Society of America, 1997).

Ignatow, Gabe, and Alexander T. Williams. "New Media and the 'Anchor Baby'
Boom." *Journal of Computer-Mediated Communication* 17, no. 1 (2011): 60–76.

"Immigration to the United States, 1933–1941." *Holocaust Encyclopedia.* US Holocaust Museum. https://encyclopedia.ushmm.org/content/en/article
/immigration-to-the-united-states-1933–41.

Jacobson, Robin Dale, Daniel Tichenor, and T. Elizabeth Durden. "The Southwest's Uneven Welcome: Immigrant Inclusion and Exclusion in Arizona
and New Mexico." *Journal of American Ethnic History* 37, no. 3 (2018): 5–36.

Janisch, Hudson N. "The Chinese, the Courts, and the Constitution: A Study
of the Legal Issues Raised by Chinese Immigration to the United States,
1850–1902." 3 vols. JD thesis, University of Chicago, 1971.

Johnson, David Alan, Quintard Taylor, and Marsha Weisiger. "Report on the
History of Matthew P. Deady and Frederick S. Dunn." http://media.oregon
live.com/education_impact/other/deady_dunn_final_report_08-05-16
.pdf.

Jones, Martha S. *Birthright Citizens: A History of Race and Rights in Antebellum America.* New York: Cambridge University Press, 2018.

Jordan, Miriam. "3 Arrested in Crackdown on Multimillion-Dollar 'Birth Tourism' Businesses." *New York Times,* January 31, 2019. https://www.nytimes.com/2019/01/31/us/anchor-baby-birth-tourism.html.

Kaiser Family Foundation. "Changes to 'Public Charge' Inadmissibility Rule: Implications for Health and Health Coverage." August 12, 2019. https://www.kff.org/disparities-policy/fact-sheet/proposed-changes-to-public-charge-policies-for-immigrants-implications-for-health-coverage/.

Kanazawa, Mark. "Immigration, Exclusion, and Taxation: Anti-Chinese Legislation in Gold Rush California." *Journal of Economic History* 65, no. 3 (2005): 779–805.

Kanno-youngs, Zolan, and Maggie Haberman. "'A Constant Game of Musical Chairs' amid Another Homeland Security Shake-Up." *New York Times,* June 25, 2019. https://www.nytimes.com/2019/06/25/us/politics/mark-morgan-ice-cbp.html.

Kanstroom, Dan. *Deportation Nation: Outsiders in American History.* Cambridge, MA: Harvard University Press, 2007.

Kaprielan-Churchill, Isabel. "Rejecting 'Misfits': Canada and the Nansen Passport." *International Migration Review* 28, no. 2 (1994): 281–306.

Katz, Ellen. "The Six Companies and the Geary Act: A Case Study in Nineteenth-Century Civil Disobedience and Civil Rights Litigation." *Western Legal History* 8, no. 2 (1995): 227–272.

Katz, Jonathan M. "What Happened When a Nation Erased Birthright Citizenship." *Atlantic,* November 12, 2018.

Kens, Paul. *Justice Stephen Field: Shaping Liberty from the Gold Rush to the Gilded Age.* Lawrence: University Press of Kansas, 1997.

Keyssar, Alexander. *The Right to Vote.* New York: Basic Books, 2000.

Kim, Joon K., Ernesto Sagás, and Karina Cespedes. "Genderacing Immigrant Subjects: 'Anchor Babies' and the Politics of Birthright Citizenship." *Social Identities* 24, no. 3 (2017): 312–326.

King, Congressman Steve. Representing the 4th District of Iowa. Accessed July 25, 2019. https://steveking.house.gov/issues/immigration.

Kopetman, Roxana, and Scott Schwebke. "Federal Agents Charge 19 for Birth Tourism in Southern California." *The O.C. Register,* January 31, 2019. https://www.ocregister.com/2019/01/31/20-charged-in-birth-tourism-scheme-that-helped-chinese-mothers-have-babies-in-southern-california/.

Krajewska, Magdalena. *Documenting Americans: A Political History of National ID Card Proposals in the United States.* Cambridge: Cambridge University Press, 2017.

Kramer, Paul. *The Blood of Government: Race, Empire, the United States, and the Philippines.* Chapel Hill: University of North Carolina Press, 2006.

Lau, Estelle T. *Paper Families.* Durham, NC: Duke University Press, 2006.

Law, Anna O. "Lunatics, Idiots, Paupers, and Negro Seamen—Immigration Federalism and the Early American State." *Studies in American Political Development* 28 (2014): 107–128.

Law Library of Congress. "Birthright Citizenship around the World." November 2018. https://loc.gov/law/help/birthright-citizenship/birthright-citizen ship-around-the-world.pdf.

———. "Citizenship Based on Birth in Country." Compiled by Constance A. Johnson. May 2012. http://www.loc.gov/law/help/citizenship-birth-country /citizenship-birth-country.pdf.

Lee, Catherine. *Fictive Kinship: Family Reunification and the Meaning of Race and Nation in American Immigration.* New York: Russell Sage Foundation, 2013.

Lee, Erika. *At America's Gates: Chinese Immigration during the Exclusion Era, 1882–1943.* Chapel Hill: University of North Carolina Press, 2003.

———. "Birthright Citizenship, Immigration, and the U.S. Constitution: The Story of *United States v. Wong Kim Ark.*" In *Race Law Stories,* edited by Rachel Moran and Devon Carbado, 89–109. New York: Foundation Press, 2008.

———. "Defying Exclusion: Chinese Immigrants and Their Strategies during the Exclusion Era." In *Chinese American Transnationalism: The Flow of People, Resources, and Ideas between China and America during the Exclusion Era,* edited by Sucheng Chan, 1–21. Philadelphia: Temple University Press, 2006.

———. "Enforcing the Borders: Chinese Exclusion along the U.S. Borders with Canada and Mexico, 1882–1924." *Journal of American History* 89, no. 1 (2002): 54–86.

Lee, Erika, and Judy Yung. *Angel Island: Immigrant Gateway to America.* New York: Oxford University Press, 2012.

Lessard, Hester, Rebecca Johnson, and Jeremy Webber, eds. *Storied Communities: Narratives of Contact and Arrival in Constituting Political Community.* Vancouver: University of British Columbia Press, 2011.

Lew-Williams, Beth. *The Chinese Must Go: Violence, Exclusion, and the Making of the Alien in America.* Cambridge, MA: Harvard University Press, 2018.

Lind, Dara. "Homeland Security Secretary Kirstjen Nielsen's Resignation, Explained." *Vox,* April 7, 2019.

———. "How America's Rejection of Jews Fleeing Nazi Germany Haunts Our Refugee Policy Today." *Vox,* January 27, 2017. https://www.vox.com/policy -and-politics/2017/1/27/14412082/refugees-history-holocaust.

Mancini, Joanne M., and Graham Finlay. "'Citizenship Matters': Lessons from the Irish Citizenship Referendum." *American Quarterly* 60, no. 3 (2008): 575–599.

Manson, Patricia. "Challenge to 'Public Charge' Rule Gets OK." *Chicago Daily Law Bulletin,* May 21, 2020. https://www.chicagolawbulletin.com/challenge -to-public-charge-rule-gets-ok-20200521.

Marinari, Maddalena. "'Americans Must Show Justice in Immigration Policies Too': The Passage of the 1965 Immigration Act." *Journal of Policy History* 26, no. 2 (2014): 219–245.

McCarthy, Andrew C. "Can Trump End Birthright Citizenship by Executive Order?" *National Review,* October 30, 2018.

McClain, Charles J. *In Search of Equality: The Chinese Struggle against Discrimination in Nineteenth-Century America.* Berkeley: University of California Press, 1996.

McKenzie, Beatrice. "To Know a Citizen: Birthright Citizenship Documents Regimes in U.S. History." In *Citizenship in Question: Evidentiary Birthright and*

Statelessness, edited by Benjamin N. Lawrance and Jacqueline Stevens, 117–131. Durham, NC: Duke University Press, 2007.

McMinn, John T., and Carol Nackenoff. "Native Americans: Citizenship." In *American Governance*, vol. 3, edited by Stephen Schechter et al., 306–308. Farmington Hills, MI: Macmillan Reference USA, 2016.

Mei, June. "Socioeconomic Origins of Emigration: Guangdong to California, 1850–1882." *Modern China* 5, no. 4 (1979): 463–501.

Menzel, Annie. "Birthright Citizenship and the Racial Contract: The United States' Jus Soli Rule against the Global Regime of Citizenship." *Du Bois Review: Social Science Research on Race* 10, no. 1 (2013): 29–58.

Millhiser, Ian. "The Supreme Court Just Made Our Ugly, Messed-Up Immigration Law Even Uglier." *ThinkProgress*, June 12, 2017. https://thinkprogress.org/scotus-immigration-gender-bf65cebccf9d/.

Molina, Natalia. "'In a Race All Their Own': The Quest to Make Mexicans Ineligible for U.S. Citizenship." *Pacific Historical Review* 79, no. 2 (2010): 167–201.

Murray, Patrick. "What Americans Really Think about Birthright Citizenship." Monkey Cage, *Washington Post*, November 2, 2018. https://www.washingtonpost.com/news/monkey-cage/wp/2018/11/02/what-americans-really-think-about-birthright-citizenship/.

Murray, Robert K. *Red Scare: A Study in National Hysteria*. Minneapolis: University of Minnesota Press, 1955.

Nackenoff, Carol. "Constitutionalizing Terms of Inclusion: Friends of the Indian and Citizenship for Native Americans 1880s–1930s." In *The Supreme Court and American Political Development*, edited by Ronald Kahn and Ken I. Kersch, 366–413. Lawrence: University Press of Kansas, 2006.

———. "The Private Roots of American Political Development: The Immigrants' Protective League's 'Friendly and Sympathetic Touch,' 1908–1924." *Studies in American Political Development* 28, no. 2 (2014): 129–160.

Nackenoff, Carol, with Allison Hrabar. "Quaker Roles in Making and Implementing Federal Indian Policy: From Grant's Peace Policy through the Early Dawes Act Era (1869–1900)." In *Quakers and Native Americans*, edited by Geoffrey Plank and Ignacio Gallup-Diaz, 171–292. Leiden: Koninklijke Brill, 2019.

Nackenoff, Carol, and Julie Novkov. "Building the Administrative State: Courts and the Admission of Chinese Persons to the United States, 1870s–1920s." In *Stating the Family: New Directions in the Study of American Politics*, edited by Julie Novkov and Carol Nackenoff, 197–239. Lawrence: University Press of Kansas, 2020.

———. "Who Is Born a US Citizen?" *The Conversation*, January 15, 2020. https://theconversation.com/who-is-born-a-us-citizen-127403.

Nash, Gerald. "A Veritable Revolution: The Global Economic Significance of the California Gold Rush." *California History* 77, no. 4 (1998/1999): 276–292.

Neuman, Gerald L. "*Wong Wing v. United States*: The Bill of Rights Protects Illegal Aliens." In *Immigration Stories*, edited by David A. Martin and Peter H. Schuck, 31–50. New York: Foundation Press, 2005.

Ngai, Mae M. "Birthright Citizenship and the Alien Citizen." *Fordham Law Review* 175, no. 5 (2007): 2521–2530.

———. *Impossible Subjects: Illegal Aliens and the Making of Modern America*. Princeton, NJ: Princeton University Press, 2004.

———. "The Strange Career of the Illegal Alien: Immigration Restriction and Deportation Policy in the United States, 1921–1965." *Law and History Review* 21, no. 1 (2003): 69–107.

Novkov, Julie. *Racial Union: Law, Intimacy, and the White State in Alabama, 1865–1964*. Ann Arbor: University of Michigan Press, 2008.

Novkov, Julie, and Carol Nackenoff. "Civic Membership, Family Status, and the Chinese in America, 1870s–1920s." *Polity* 48, no. 2 (2016): 165–185.

O'Loughlin, Ed. "In Ireland, Bid to Restore Birthright Citizenship Gains Ground." *New York Times*, November 24, 2018.

Orfield, Lester B. "The Citizenship Act of 1934." *University of Chicago Law Review* 2, no. 1 (1934): 99–118.

Osborne, Thomas J. "The Main Reason for Hawaiian Annexation in July, 1898." *Oregon Historical Quarterly* 71 (June 1970): 161–178.

Ozawa v. United States. http://encyclopedia.densho.org/Ozawa_v._United_States/.

Pak, Jennifer. "Why Chinese Parents Come to America to Give Birth." Marketplace, March 6, 2019. https://www.marketplace.org/2019/03/06/why-chinese-parents-come-america-give-birth/.

Parker, Kunal M. *Making Foreigners: Immigration and Citizenship Law in America, 1600–2000*. Cambridge: Cambridge University Press, 2015.

Pascoe, Peggy. "Gender Systems in Conflict: The Marriages of Mission-Educated Chinese American Women, 1874–1939." *Journal of Social History* 22, no. 4 (1989): 631–652.

———. *What Comes Naturally: Miscegenation Law and the Making of Race in America*. New York: Oxford University Press, 2009.

Pastor, Robert A. "U.S. Immigration Policy and Latin America: In Search of the 'Special Relationship.'" *Latin American Research Review* 19, no. 3 (1984): 35–56.

Patil, L. P. "Anti-Miscegenation in California." Foundations of Law and Society, 2016. https://foundationsoflawandsociety.wordpress.com/2016/12/09/anti-miscegenation-in-california/.

Paul, Deanna. "Trump Wants to End Birthright Citizenship. A Judge He Appointed Says He Can't." *Washington Post*, October 30, 2018.

Peffer, George Anthony. "Forbidden Families: Emigration Experiences of Chinese Women under the Page Law, 1875–1882." *Journal of American Ethnic History* 6, no. 1 (1986): 28–46.

Perlman, Selig. "The Anti-Chinese Agitation in California." In *History of Labour in the United States*, edited by John Rogers Commons et al., 2:252–268. New York: Macmillan, 1918.

Perl-Rosenthal, Nathan. *Citizen Sailors: Becoming American in the Age of Revolution*. Cambridge, MA: Belknap Press of Harvard University Press, 2015.

Pfaelzer, Jean. *Driven Out: The Forgotten War against Chinese Americans*. Berkeley: University of California Press, 2008.

Phifer, Donica. "Donald Trump Wants to Remove 'Ridiculous' Birthright Citizenship, but Can He Do It without Congress?" *Newsweek*, August 21, 2019. https://www.newsweek.com/birthright-citizenship-trump-executive-order -congress-1455582.

"The Philippines, 1898–1946." https://history.house.gov/Exhibitions-and-Pub lications/APA/Historical-Essays/Exclusion-and-Empire/The-Philippines/.

Pierson, David. "Taishan's U.S. Well Runs Dry." *Los Angeles Times*, May 21, 2007. https://www.latimes.com/archives/la-xpm-2007-may-21-fg-taishan21-story .html.

Pleva, Lucas. "Reid Bashes Republicans for a Position on Immigration That He Once Pushed." *Politifact*, August 25, 2010. https://www.politifact.com/fact checks/2010/aug/25/harry-reid/reid-bashes-republicans-position-immi gration-he-on/.

Powers, Laura. "Trump's Acting Immigration Director Claims Ending Birthright Citizenship Would Not Require Constitutional Amendment." *Newsweek*, October 20, 2019. https://www.newsweek.com/trumps-acting-immigration -director-claims-ending-birthright-citizenship-would-not-require-1465728.

Price, Polly. "Jus Soli and Statelessness: A Comparative Perspective from the Americas." In *Citizenship in Question: Evidentiary Birthright and Statelessness*, edited by Benjamin Lawrance and Jacqueline Stevens, 27–42. Durham, NC: Duke University Press, 2017.

———. "Natural Law and Birthright Citizenship in Calvin's Case (1608)." *Yale Journal of Law and the Humanities* 9 (1997): 73–145.

Qin, Yucheng. "A Century-Old 'Puzzle': The Six Companies' Role in Chinese Labor Importation in the Nineteenth Century." *Journal of American–East Asian Relations* 12, no. 3/4 (2003): 225–254.

Reimers, David M. *Unwelcome Strangers: American Identity and the Turn against Immigration*. New York: Columbia University Press, 1998.

Robertson, Craig. *The Passport in America: The History of a Document*. New York: Oxford University Press, 2010.

Robinson, Greg. "*Regan v. King*." https://encyclopedia.densho.org/Regan_v ._King/.

———. "When Birthright Citizenship Was Last 'Reconsidered': REGAN v. KING and Asian Americans, Part V." The Faculty Lounge, August 10, 2010. https://www.thefacultylounge.org/2010/08/when-birthright-citizenship -was-last-reconsidered-regan-v-king-and-asian-americans-part-v.html.

Rogow, Faith. *Gone to Another Meeting: The National Council of Jewish Women, 1893–1993*. Foreword by Joan Bronk. Tuscaloosa: University of Alabama Press, 1993.

Rojas, Ricardo. "Dominican Court Ruling Renders Hundreds of Thousands Stateless." Reuters, October 12, 2013. https://www.reuters.com/article/us -dominicanrepublic-citizenship/dominican-court-ruling-renders-hundreds -of-thousands-stateless-idUSBRE99B01Z20131012.

Román, Ediberto, and Ernesto Sagas. "Birthright Citizenship under Attack: How Dominican Nationality Laws May Be the Future of US Exclusion." *American University Law Review* 66 (2016): 1383–1431.

Romo, Vanessa. "American Samoans' Citizenship Status Still in Limbo after Judge Issues Stay." NPR, December 13, 2019. https://www.npr.org/2019/12/13/787978353/american-samoans-citizenship-status-still-in-limbo-after-judge-issues-stay.

Rosenbloom, Rachel E. "Policing the Borders of Birthright Citizenship: Some Thoughts on the New (and Old) Restrictionism." *Washburn Law Journal* 51, no. 2 (2012): 311–330.

"Ryan Says 'Obviously' Trump Can't End Birthright Citizenship." MPR, October 31, 2018. https://www.mprnews.org/story/2018/10/30/paul-ryan-obviously-trump-cant-end-birthright-citizenship.

Salter, Mark B. *Rights of Passage: The Passport in International Relations.* Boulder, CO: Lynne Rienner, 2003.

Salyer, Lucy. "*Chew Heong v. United States*: Chinese Exclusion and the Federal Courts." Prepared for inclusion in the project Federal Trials and Great Debates in United States History. 2006. https://www.fjc.gov/history/famous-federal-trials/chew-heong-v-us-chinese-exclusion-and-federal-courts.

———. *Laws Harsh as Tigers: Chinese Immigrants and the Shaping of Modern Immigration Law.* Chapel Hill: University of North Carolina Press, 1995.

———. "*Wong Kim Ark*: The Contest over Birthright Citizenship." In *Immigration Stories*, edited by David A. Martin and Peter H. Schuck, 51–85. New York: Foundation Press, 2005.

Samuels, Brett. "Trump Administration Revives Talk of Action on Birthright Citizenship." *The Hill*, November 20, 2020, https://thehill.com/homenews/administration/526950-trump-administration-revives-talk-of-action-on-birthright-citizenship.

Santhanam, Laura, and Gretchen Frazee. "What the Data Says about Birthright Citizenship." Public Broadcasting Service. October 30, 2018. https://www.pbs.org/newshour/politics/what-the-data-says-about-birthright-citizenship.

Schepard, Eric. "The Great Dissenter's Greatest Dissents: The First Justice Harlan, the 'Color-Blind' Constitution and the Meaning of His Dissents in the *Insular Cases* for the War on Terror." *American Journal of Legal History* 48 (April 2006): 119–146.

Schomberg Center for Research in Black Culture. "Caribbean Immigration: Coming to the United States." http://www.inmotionaame.org/migrations/topic.cfm?migration=10&topic=5.

———. "Caribbean Immigration: Shutting the Door." http://www.inmotionaame.org/migrations/topic.cfm?migration=10&topic=6.

Schrecker, John. "'For the Equality of Men—For the Equality of Nations': Anson Burlingame and China's First Embassy to the United States, 1868." *Journal of American–East Asian Relations* 17 (2010): 9–34.

Schuck, Peter, and Rogers M. Smith, *Citizenship without Consent: Illegal Aliens in the American Polity.* New Haven, CT: Yale University Press, 1985.

———. "The Question of Birthright Citizenship" *National Affairs*, Summer 2018. https://www.nationalaffairs.com/publications/detail/the-question-of-birthright-citizenship.

Schumacher, Elizabeth. "Revoking Citizenship: How It Works across the EU." May 3, 2013. https://www.dw.com/en/revoking-citizenship-how-it-works -across-the-eu/a-47773802.

Seo, Jungkun. "Wedge-Issue Dynamics and Party Position Shifts: Chinese Exclusion Debates in the Post-Reconstruction US Congress, 1879–1882." *Party Politics* 17, no. 6 (2010): 823–847.

Sinn, Elizabeth. "Beyond 'Tianxia': The 'Zhongwai Xinwen Qiribao' (Hong Kong 1871–1872) and the Construction of a Transnational Chinese Community." *China Review* 4 (Spring 2004): 89–122.

Skeldon, Ronald. "Migration from China." *Journal of International Affairs* 49, no. 2 (1996): 434–455.

Smith, Michael T. "The History of Indian Citizenship." *Great Plains Journal* 10 (Fall 1970): 26–29.

Sparrow, Bartholomew H. *The* Insular Cases *and the Emergence of American Empire.* Lawrence: University Press of Kansas, 2006.

Spickard, Paul. *Almost All Aliens: Immigration, Race, and Colonialism in American History and Identity.* New York: Taylor and Francis, 2007.

Stein, Dan, and John Bauer. "Interpreting the Fourteenth Amendment: Automatic Citizenship for Children of Illegal Immigrants?" *Stanford Law and Policy Review* 7 (1996): 127–130.

Tashman, Brian. "Trump Picks Family Separation Advocate Kevin McAleenan to Be Acting Secretary of Homeland Security." American Civil Liberties Union. April 10, 2019. https://www.aclu.org/blog/immigrants-rights/trump -picks-family-separation-advocate-kevin-mcaleenan-be-acting-secretary.

Teng, Emma Jinhua. *Eurasian: Mixed Identities in the United States, China, and Hong Kong, 1842–1943.* Berkeley: University of California Press, 2013.

Tennant, Brad. "'Excluding Indians Not Taxed': *Dred Scott, Standing Bear, Elk* and the Legal Status of Native Americans in the Latter Half of the Nineteenth Century." *International Social Science Review* 86, no. 1–2 (2011): 24–43.

Thronson, David. "Entering the Mainstream: Making Children Matter in Immigration Law." *Fordham Urban Law Journal* 38, no. 1 (2010): 393–413.

Torpey, John C. *The Invention of the Passport: Surveillance, Citizenship and the State.* New York: Cambridge University Press, 2018.

Urban, Andrew. *Brokering Servitude: Migration and the Politics of Domestic Labor during the Long Nineteenth Century.* New York: New York University Press, 2017.

Venator-Santiago, Charles R. "The Jones Act Made Puerto Ricans Citizens, Yet Not Fully American." *Baltimore Sun*, March 15, 2018; https://www .baltimoresun.com/opinion/op-ed/bs-ed-op-0316-puerto-rico-20180314 -story.html.

———. "The Law That Made Puerto Ricans U.S. Citizens, Yet Not Fully American." *Zocalo Public Square*, March 6, 2018. https://www.zocalopublicsquare .org/2018/03/06/law-made-puerto-ricans-u-s-citizens-yet-not-fully -american/ideas/essay/.

———. "Puerto Rican Citizenship Timeline." In "U.S. Citizenship in Puerto Rico: One Hundred Years after the Jones Act." Special issue, *CENTRO: Journal of the Center for Puerto Rican Studies* 29, no. 1 (2017): 6–10.

Veracini, Lorenzo. *Settler Colonialism: A Theoretical Overview*. New York: Palgrave Macmillan, 2010.

von Spakovsky, Hans A. "Why Trump Can End Birthright Citizenship by Executive Order." Heritage Foundation, November 5, 2018. https://www.heritage .org/immigration/commentary/why-trump-can-end-birthright-citizenship -executive-order.

Wallace, Kelley. "Forgotten Los Angeles History: The Chinese Massacre of 1871." *Los Angeles Public Library Blog*, May 19, 2017. https://www.lapl.org /collections-resources/blogs/lapl/chinese-massacre-1871.

Wheeler, Harvey. "Calvin's Case (1608) and the McIlwain-Schuyler Debate." *American Historical Review* 61, no. 3 (1956): 587–597.

"Who Was Shut Out? Immigration Quotas, 1925–1927." http://historymatters .gmu.edu/.

Williams, Michael. *Returning Home with Glory: Chinese Villages around the Pacific, 1849 to 1949*. Hong Kong: Hong Kong University Press, 2018.

Winter, Elke, and Adina Madularea. "Quo Vadis Canada? Tracing the Contours of Citizenship in a Multicultural Country." In *Immigration, Racial, and Ethnic Studies in 150 Years of Canada: Retrospects and Prospects*, edited by Shibao Guo and Lloyd Wong, 191–208. Leiden: Brill, 2018.

Wolgin, Philip E. "Family Reunification Is the Bedrock of U.S. Immigration Policy." Center for American Progress. February 12, 2018. https://www .americanprogress.org/issues/immigration/news/2018/02/12/446402 /family-reunification-bedrock-u-s-immigration-policy/.

Wong, William. *Yellow Journalist: Dispatches from Asian America*. Philadelphia: Temple University Press, 2001.

World Population Review. "Countries with Birthright Citizenship 2020." Accessed November 29, 2020. http://worldpopulationreview.com/countries /countries-with-birthright-citizenship/.

Yang, Jia Lynn. "How Family Ties Changed Us." *New York Times*, June 14, 2020, SR6.

———. *One Mighty and Irresistible Tide: The Epic Struggle over American Immigration, 1924–1965*. New York: W. W. Norton, 2020.

Yin, Paul. "The Narratives of Chinese-American Litigation during the Chinese Exclusion Era." *Asian American Law Journal* 19, no. 1 (2012): 145–169.

Yoo, John. "Settled Law: Birthright Citizenship and the 14th Amendment." *American Mind*, updated March 18, 2019. https://americanmind.org /features/the-case-against-birthright-citizenship/settled-law-birthright -citizenship-and-the-14th-amendment/?fbclid=IwAR1MdMMSdGgvXLEm JFRfox1Lps4ASSo3eVzBqB1H1ETWgvo2dZPTNojLpo4.

Zhu, Liping. *The Road to Chinese Exclusion: The Denver Riot, 1880 Election, and Rise of the West*. Lawrence: University Press of Kansas, 2013.

Zietlow, Rebecca. "Exploring the History, Evolution, and Future of the Fourteenth Amendment: Juriscentrism and the Original Meaning of Section Five." *Temple Political and Civil Rights Law Review* 13 (2004): 485–513.

Index